PEOPLE OF THE UCAYALI
The Shipibo and Conibo of Peru

INTERNATIONAL MUSEUM OF CULTURES
Publication 12

William R. Merrifield
Series Editor

Desmond C. Derbyshire
General Editor
Academic Publications Coordinator

PEOPLE OF THE UCAYALI
The Shipibo and Conibo of Peru

Lucille Eakin
Erwin Lauriault
Harry Boonstra

International Museum of Cultures
Dallas, Texas
1986

© 1986 by the Summer Institute of Linguistics, Inc.

Library of Congress Catalog Card No. 86-082643
ISBN: 0-88312-163-8
ISSN: 0197-3746

This title is available at

THE INTERNATIONAL MUSEUM OF CULTURES
7500 W. Camp Wisdom Road
Dallas, TX   75236

CONTENTS

ILLUSTRATIONS

PREFACE

This work was prepared in order to provide a holistic introduction to an indigenous people of the Peruvian jungle whom many know only by their magnificent ceramics, weaving, and other artistic achievements.

It has been more than thirty years since Erwin Lauriault wrote down his observations concerning the Shipibo culture, compiled over many years of missionary service among them. Additional observations were made by Lucille Eakin of the Summer Institute of Linguistics between 1968 and 1973, during which time she served as consultant to bilingual school teachers in many Shipibo villages. Shipibo speakers aided in her research, among them: Guillermo Ramírez Guimarais, born in Paococha in 1925 and now living in Maputay; Wilfredo Ramírez Cairuna, son of Guillermo Ramírez; and Pablo Gonzáles Valles, a young man of Callería.

Harry Boonstra, a short-term member of SIL during 1973-74, organized the data of Lauriault and Eakin and wrote the original manuscript in 1974, with the exception of the description of the kinship terminology which was written by Mary Ruth Wise and revised for this slightly updated English edition by William R. Merrifield. (See Eakin, Lauriault and Boonstra 1980 for the Spanish edition.) We wish to express our gratitude to Dean Arnold for his assistance to Eakin during the gathering of the data and to David Coombs, Paul Powlison, Nancy Beasley, Elinor Abbot, and others who reviewed the manuscript and gave helpful suggestions.

Unfortunately, it is not possible to present an exhaustive description of all the rich folklore and culture of the Shipibos in these few pages; nevertheless, we hope that this study will be useful for evaluating and understanding these people and their ways.

The authors

1 INTRODUCTION

This study is primarily a description of the Shipibo people of eastern Peru, but also subsumes at least two other closely related groups, the Shetebo and the Conibo.

The Shetebo, who were once located north of the Shipibo, have been greatly reduced through epidemics and warfare in the past two hundred years; a remnant has been integrated with the Shipibo through conquest and intermarriage.

The Conibo can be distinguished only with difficulty from the Shipibo. The town of Pucallpa is still somewhat of a dividing line, with Shipibo to the north and Conibo to the south (see figure 2), but the division is only marginally tenable. Apparently the languages were never very different, and today the distinction is largely a matter of pronunciation and some lexical items. Cultural differences are minimal; moreover, extensive intermarriage has nearly erased any separation between the two groups.

Thus, although we will continue to speak of the Shipibo, the study, in effect, includes the Shetebo and Conibo as well. The reader should note, too, that the dialect spoken on the Pisqui River is also a variant and the Pisquibo are sometimes referred to as though they were a separate group.

Contemporary (1974) Shipibos inhabit the valley of the Ucayali River from about 6° to 10° south. There are approximately 12,000 living in ninety to one hundred villages along the Ucayali proper and along some of the tributaries, such as the Cushabatay, Pisqui, Aguaytía, and the lower Pachitea on the left bank, and the Maquía, Cashiboya, Roaboíllo, Tamaya, Sheshea, and Callería on the right bank. This territory is a flood plain about two hundred meters above sea level. To the east lies the Contamana Range; to the west are the highlands stemming from the peaks of the Azul and Ventanilla Mountains and further south are the foothills of the Andes.

The Shipibo speak a language of the Panoan family. McQuown (1955) lists about eighty Panoan languages, but Loos believes that number to be somewhat inflated due to inaccurate name reduplica-

1

tion. The number of Panoan languages today is certainly much less; Loos (1969:3) estimates about twenty in Peru and Brazil, scattered between the Amazon and northern Bolivia.

Neighboring Panoan groups include the Capanahua and Amahuaca to the east and the Cashibo to the west. Also to the west and south are the Arawakan Amuesha, Campa Ashéninca, Campa Asháninca, Machiguenga, and Piro. North of the Shipibo are the Cocama of the Tupí-Guaraní family.

Tessmann and others use the designation Chama for the Panoan groups along the Ucayali, but the Shipibo consider the term derogatory. It is used as a term of insult by both the Shipibo and other ethnic groups of the area.

History

Written histories concerning the Shipibo and other Amazonian peoples are fragmentary and unreliable. Early histories are mainly drawn from the accounts of missionaries, soldiers, adventurers, and travelers. Often contacts were ephemeral and communication was superficial. The jungle's geography was relatively unknown, hence difficult to map; moreover, the mobility of the inhabitants made identification uncertain. Expectedly then, anthropological and linguistic data were sketchy. The following historical sketch is based primarily on Steward and Métraux (1948), which in turn is a compilation of data from Izaguirre (1922) and other sources.

The recorded history of the Shipibo is largely a record of their relations with other tribes and of their contacts with white men who entered the area. The first known displacement of the Shipibo occurred in the early seventeenth century, when the Campa forced the Cashibo to move to the Upper Aguaytía River, thus pushing the Shipibo to the mouth of the river, displacing the Conibo. After this the Shipibo settled at various places along the Ucayali, often contesting with other groups for territory.

The Shipibo, Conibo, and Shetebo, dominant in the Ucayali area, frequently engaged in raids and warfare with smaller groups, such as the Cashibo and Amahuaca. It is reported that in the seventeenth century the Conibo sold captives as slaves to the Cocama in exchange for iron tools. They continued their slave raids into the nineteenth century "among all tribes from the Mayoruna near the Amazon to the Amahuaca of the upper Ucayali" (Steward and Métraux 1948:563). The Shipibo battled the weakened Shetebo in the eighteenth century until the latter were driven to accept the protection of local missions. The earlier dominance of the Shipibo and Conibo can still be seen in current settlement patterns: they are located mainly along the Ucayali, while smaller groups, e.g., Capanahua, Cashibo, and Amahuaca, are located along lesser rivers.

The Shipibo had their initial contact with whites in the mid-1600s, when both missionaries and soldiers penetrated the area. The outcome of this first contact foreshadowed the subsequent tension between the Shipibo and the invaders: the Shipibo killed the missionaries in 1657. In 1660 the Shipibo joined the Cocama in a raid against the Huallaga River mission. Another attack, ten years later, probably also involved the Shipibo. A combined group of Shetebo and Calliseca, often identified as Shipibo, attacked the Panatahua mission in 1670.

Conibo contacts with whites were very similar. In the 1680s, Franciscans and Jesuits competed for the first Conibo mission, with the Jesuits gaining the field. They established several mission stations, succeeding partly because their supply of iron tools was valued by the Conibo. But in 1695 the Conibo revolted against this religious domination and, partly in protest against the enforced conscription of Conibo for a Spanish expedition against the Jivaro, massacred the Spanish. Then in 1698, the Conibo joined forces with the Shipibo and Shetebo to repel a Spanish punitive force.

Mission activity ceased for some time after these attacks, but stations were reported in operation again by the 1740s--only to be destroyed in the uprising of 1767. This uprising was a widespread revolt led by Rungato who united Shipibo, Conibo and Shetebo in a massacre of the missionaries, again interrupting mission activity. It was resumed in 1790. Since then it has continued intermittently, and generally more peacefully, until today.

Protestant missions were first established in the 1930s.

Acculturation

Although the Shipibo have had contact with white civilization for about three centuries, only in the last seventy-five years has it been very extensive. Travelers on the Ucayali, government controls, conscription into the army, schools, missions--all these have brought the Shipibo face to face with non-Indian culture. The growth of the town of Pucallpa in the middle of Shipibo territory has further intensified outside influences.

One might, therefore, expect a strong impact of Western civilization and the consequent erosion of tribal traditions. Certainly the evidences of outside influence are many. In the use of implements, for example, one encounters the ubiquitous machete, metal and plastic kitchen utensils, treadle sewing machines, and many other items. Some of the men work for Spanish-speaking employers, fitting into the normal working hours of the nation. Also, because of their contact with the outside world, the men have mostly abandoned the cushma for shirt and trousers. Many other changes could be mentioned.

Although both the Cocama and the Shipibo have had similar exposure to the outside world, a comparison shows that Shipibo culture is surprisingly viable. While young adults do not speak Cocama and have become acculturated to a great degree, the Shipibo have maintained much of their traditional life-style. One cause, apparently, is the bilingual school system which, for more than thirty years, has given prestige to the language. As of 1983, the Shipibo had daily broadcasts in their own language over a commercial radio station in Pucallpa and an indigenous newspaper. Although most of the people speak some Spanish, the Shipibo language continues to be the language of the home and of virtually all intragroup communication. Moreover, life in most of the settlements is similar in many ways to what it has been for the past several hundred years.

In the following description there will often be attempts to determine what constitutes indigenous ways and what are importations and changes. However, it is extremely difficult to ascertain if a particular pattern is indigenous or if it has been adopted at some point in the past three hundred years. In religious matters, for example, often one cannot readily separate Christian from indigenous features. In the use of implements, it is difficult to know what is Western and what is indigenous. Even though the machete was imported, its use is so pervasive that one may well consider it an integral part of the material culture.

This description does not limit itself to a fixed ethnographic present. Lauriault's data reflects his residence among the Shipibo from 1938 to 1975; Eakin's was gathered during travel to Shipibo villages from 1968 to 1973. Both also elicited material from Shipibo of different villages and of varying ages; the older ones especially had excellent recall of former traditions.

2 SUBSISTENCE

During the past fifty years many Shipibo men have begun to work as day laborers, either for a local patrón or for an outside entrepreneur. Many families, however, continue to be largely self-sufficient, obtaining by their own efforts food, building materials, and some clothing from the immediate environment. Food supply and preparation will be discussed here; acquisition and manufacture of other material goods is dealt with in the section on Economy.

(For a detailed account of Shipibo subsistence, see Bergman (1974), which became available to the authors after this ethnographic sketch was in draft.)

Hunting and Fishing

Hunting and fishing constitute major means of Shipibo subsistence. The blowgun was traditionally used for hunting, and continued to be used sporadically as recently as the 1950s; today its use has died out. One reason for its discontinuance is that the Shipibo did not normally make their own, but bought them, along with poison for their darts, from the Yagua. The blowgun was used mainly for birds and small animals, especially monkeys. The 30-35 cm. darts were made from slivers of the trunk of the shapaja palm (Scheelea) or from the frond ribs of various palm leaves.

Shipibo bows generally measure about 1.5 m. Chonta (Bactris) palm wood is commonly used, but comosehue is preferred, when available. Hunting bows are plain, but ceremonial bows are adorned by wrapping colored threads around the grip and ends, with small feathers inserted under the thread. This wrapping is then painted with geometric designs. The ceremonial bow is seldom used today, but is manufactured for the tourist trade. The fibrous bark of the shiari, a tree similar to the cetico, is twisted for bowstrings; some, however, use bark fibers of balsa, a silk-cotton tree (Ceiba pentandra).

5

Arrow shafts are made from the flowering stalks of the caña brava (Gynerium sagittatum) which are gathered in quantity and dried for subsequent use. Before adding the point and feathers, the shaft of about 1.2 m. is straightened, sometimes by heating and bending. Fishing arrows are not feathered, since they are shot at a short distance. Feathers for other arrows are obtained from duck, crane, or other birds. The feathers are fastened to form a spiral, which causes the arrow to turn in flight, ensuring greater accuracy.

Arrows are fitted with one of seven different heads, depending on the kind of animal to be hunted. The simplest arrowhead is a pencil-shaped spike of pona (Iriartea exorrhiza) or chonta (Bactris) palm. It is a rod about 40 cms. long, inserted into the pithy center of the shaft with about 12 cms. protruding. A specially designed arrowhead for bird hunting ends in a knob with a small projecting point; the knob prevents the head from piercing the bird and ruining its feathers. Harpoon arrows with detachable heads are used for large fish. A metal point is set into a wooden rod and inserted into the long arrow shaft. The detachable head is fastened to the arrow with chambira (Astrocaryum) cord.

The Shipibo prefer to hunt singly or in pairs, and only occasionally in parties. Although they hunt throughout the year, the rainy season is the most favorable time along the Ucayali, since flooding drives the game out of the lowlands. Larger game is usually hunted with the shotgun, although bow and arrow are sometimes used, having the dual advantages of silence and economy. Today more than half of the Shipibo men possess a 16-gauge shotgun. Occasionally one still sees a muzzle-loading shotgun.

Larger animals are tracked down, often with the help of dogs, and shot from cover. At other times animals are either trapped or killed with a shotgun set across the path and triggered by the animal as it approaches. Deer and tapir (Tapir americanus) are hunted for meat; jaguar (Felis onca) was hunted for its skin until recent law prohibited hunting or capturing it. The whitelipped peccary (Dycotiles labiatus), which can weigh as much as sixty kilograms, travel in herds of fifty to one hundred fifty. When bow and arrow are used, hunters are usually able to shoot several, but at the first shotgun blast, the herd takes flight. The smaller, collared peccary (Dycotiles torcuatus) sleep in holes and burrows, and hunters trap them there. Peccary meat is edible, and the hides were formerly sold for a good profit. The largest rodents are the capybara (Hidrochoerus capybara) which weigh up to seventy kilograms and travel in groups of four or five. They are hunted both on land and in the water; the meat is eaten, and the skin sold for manufacturing gloves. Two kinds of armadillos live along the Ucayali and are hunted by the Shipibo. The smaller is the yahuish (Dasypus); the larger is the yancontoro (Prionodontes) which can be up to 90 cms. long. Hunters try to trap the animals in their burrows. Monkey is also a staple item in the Shipibo diet, including spider monkey (Paniscus longimembrus), woolly monkey (Lagothrix), howler monkey (Alouatta senisulcus), and several others. The young are often captured and kept as pets.

Birds are shot, snared, or caught by spreading the glue-like juice of the breadfruit tree (Artocarpus) on the branches of a tree. The meat is eaten and the feathers are used for ornaments. Leg bones of wading birds serve as pipe stems. The catalog of birds on the Amazon basin is large, and many species are hunted by the Shipibo, including doves, parrots, macaws, toucans, and numerous others.

The largest aquatic animal that the Shipibo hunt in the Ucayali is the manatee (Trechichus inunquis), which is used both for its blubber and its meat. The animal is first harpooned, then killed by driving wooden pegs into its nostrils. As late as 1940 there was an abundance of cayman in the Ucayali. In the last decades, however, these large alligators have been systematically hunted by commercial hunters to obtain hides, and the number has been drastically reduced. Although the Shipibo have never hunted alligators for food, they hunted them for other uses until the recent prohibition. The method they employed was to hunt at night, using a flashlight to locate and mesmerize the cayman until it could be speared. Other aquatic fauna hunted include turtles, otters, crabs, and snails. Small dolphin (Innia geofrensis and Delphinus fuviatilis) are abundant in the Ucayali and its tributaries, but the Shipibo fear the spirits of the dolphin and never hunt them.

Since the Shipibo live along the Ucayali and its tributaries, fish supply much of their protein needs. The Shipibo fish in whatever way produces the best yield. Some fish are caught by hand, especially those which dig into the river bank, like eel and lungfish. The largest number of fish, however, are caught by hook and line from a canoe. These include sardines (Chalcinus elongatus), various kinds of catfish (Trychomicteros), sunfish, and piranhas (Serragalmus piraya). When the fish run in schools, or when they swim near the surface, the Shipibo use bow and arrow, the hollow arrow shafts being sufficiently buoyant to permit retrieval from the water. Harpoons are used on the larger fish, including the gamitana (Serrasalmus rumbus), paco (Procnilodus), dorado (Ilisha deauratus), and other large catfish such as the saltón, and the stingray (Raya nasuta). When a fish or manatee becomes visible in the water, its movements are traced through the water, and it is speared at the first opportunity. The lance shaft drops from its socket and is retained by the line; the float of balsa wood retards the speed of the fish, and the fish is eventually captured. Net fishing is sometimes done simply by dropping a basket over the side of a canoe and scooping up the fish. Shrimp are caught at the shore in the same manner. Casting nets made of commercial cordage or of twine from the chambira palm (Astrocaryum) are used very effectively. Finally, before it became illegal, the Shipibo used various kinds of vegetable poisons to obtain fish. The most common is barbasco (which may be either Tephrosia toxicaria or Lonchocarpus). The long fibrous roots are pounded between two stones and the resulting pulpy mass thrown into the water. The poison kills all the fish within the area of its diffusion, and the larger ones are gathered for food. Other poisons used by the Shipibo kill or stun only small fish.

Agriculture

Small-scale agriculture occupies an important place among the Shipibo since they grow most of their staple foods in small fields cut out of the jungle. Their fields may be located very close to their homes or at some distance in the jungle. Land high enough not to flood during the rainy season is preferred. Like other jungle peoples, the Shipibo practice slash-and-burn agriculture which enables them to extract a crop from the jungle with simple tools. At the beginning of a dry season the plot is prepared for cultivation. The underbrush is cut, the trees are felled and, after drying, the field is burned. Extremely thick tree trunks rarely burn fully and these are usually left to decay while smaller ones are eventually cut up for firewood. Stumps are left in the ground.

The first crop planted is usually rice or corn. Seeds are randomly planted with a dibble stick because stumps, debris, and uneven ground prevent row planting. Weeding is done by cutting all extraneous growth at ground level with a machete. Both corn and rice are grown as cash crops and are also used for home consumption; corn provides chicken feed as well.

The second main crop from a field is usually cassava (Manihot) or plantain (Musa paradisiaca). Cassava is extremely valuable to the Shipibo and to other Amazonian peoples because of its easy growth and varied consumption. Plants are spaced several feet apart, and tubers radiate from the base of the stalk. Different types of cassava have maturation times ranging from four to eighteen months.

The plantain is a variety of banana which is usually cooked and eaten while still green. Among the Shipibo the plantain is perhaps even more important than cassava as a staple. Plantain shoots are planted at ten-foot intervals and produce a crop in about eight months. After the harvest, the stalk is cut down, cut into pieces, and placed between and around the young stalks that have grown out of its base, thus serving as fertilizer. Each young stalk will grow to maturity, and in turn produce its crop and shoots. Thus, the plantain clump will thicken through the multiplication of stalks until in time it becomes necessary to thin the plants.

In addition to these standard crops, the Shipibo plant small plots of various other produce such as sweet potatoes, beans, peanuts, squash, and melons. A small cane patch is often planted near the house to provide sweets and cane juice. Hot peppers are grown for seasoning food, and sometimes the hollow branches of the plant are used for making pipes for the tourist trade. Sometimes one also finds annatto (Bixa orellana) whose seeds produce red paint, **huito** (Genipa americana) for black paint, a nettle (genus Urtica) used for curing purposes, and tobacco which is smoked in pipes by both men and women. They customarily plant fruit trees near their houses: cashews, mangos, oranges, lemons, and others.

Animal Husbandry

Animal husbandry is seldom practiced on a large scale, but nearly all Shipibo families have several dogs, both for hunting and as pets. They are fed scraps from meals or leftovers from the hunt, but are largely left to fend for themselves. Other pets include monkeys, cats (largely for rat control), and a wide assortment of birds such as parrots, macaws, and herons.

Other animals are raised principally for food or cash. Many families have chickens, ducks, and turkeys for eggs and meat, either for home consumption or for trading. Other animals raised for meat, especially for festival consumption, are deer, peccary, tapir, turtle, paca (Coelogenys fulvus or Coelogenys paca), and capybara. (The capybara doubles as a watch animal, since it raises an alarm when strangers approach at night.)

Food Preparation and Consumption

Cassava is an important staple, and is prepared in various ways. It can be boiled or roasted after it is peeled and often serves as a main dish. It is also grated and the juice pressed out, leaving the pulp to be roasted later for several hours. The resulting farina can be used either as flour to bake bread, or eaten in meat or fish broth.

Much Shipibo food is prepared by boiling, including meats, fish, eggs, and vegetables. For example, stews of tapir, deer, peccary or large fish, mixed with cassava and flavored with onions or hot peppers, are very common. Hard corn may be soaked and boiled, or made into hominy by use of ashes. Tamales are made of fresh corn, crushed, mixed with lard and salt, wrapped in corn-husks, and boiled. Squash, palm heart, and breadfruit seeds are also boiled. Fish, meat, and plantains may also be roasted on a grill of iron, wire, or on one made of green stakes. Eggs, corn-in-the-husk, and green bananas are frequently roasted in coals.

Some foods are smoked. If men are on extended hunting trips, for example, they smoke the meat in the jungle. If salted and covered after reaching home, it will keep for a month. Fish are also frequently smoked.

A cooking fire usually consists of three, four, or more logs with several smaller sticks between them, all placed together at their ends and extending radially. The fire is lit at the central point, and the various firesticks are pushed in as they burn.

In addition to river water, various prepared drinks are consumed. The most popular is chapo, made by boiling ripe plantains and mashing them to a paste. This paste is stored in pottery jars, taken out as needed, and mixed with water in a drinking bowl. Chicha and masato are also widely drunk. Chicha is made by grinding maize and cooking it in water with cane juice, or sugar, if available. The watery gruel is left in a jar to ferment for a few days. Masato is prepared from peeled cassava, boiled in a huge pot. When cool enough, it is mashed, and some of it is chewed by the women; after being well mixed with saliva, it is spit back into the pot to speed up fermentation. Mashed boiled sweet potatoes or cane juice are sometimes added. The mixture is left in the masato jar for a week to ferment, and like chapo is mixed with water in the drinking bowl. A number of unfermented drinks other than chapo are also made as the ingredients become available in their season. These consist of fruit juices or pulp, either raw or cooked, mixed with water and sweetened if possible. Cooked varieties are made from squash and the fruit of the aguaje palm (Mauritia flexuosa). Uncooked drinks are produced from watermelon, pineapple, papaya, and tumbo (Passiflora). Cane juice is drunk either fresh or fermented.

Cooking and eating implements are sometimes purchased, sometimes homemade. (The grill, metal cooking pots, and spoons are bought if the family can afford them.) Clay pots made by Shipibo women include a large cooking pot (**quentí**), a bowl (**quencha**) used as a plate, a gourd-shaped drinking bowl (**quempo**), and a jar (**chomo**) for liquids.

Mealtimes vary from family to family and are often determined by the amount of food available or by the work schedule. Most families, however, adhere to a pattern of three meals a day if circumstances permit. Breakfast, between 7:30 and 9:30 a.m., usually consists of chapo, supplemented by cassava, plantains, fish or meat. The noon meal consists of broth, plantains, and perhaps maize pudding; and the evening meal of broth, plantains, cassava, and fish. It is served around 5:30 p.m.

The Shipibo do not eat at tables, but sit on mats or squat on the ground near the cooking pot. Relatives from other homes are often invited to share the food. Men eat in one group, women and children in another. Some families eat from the cooking pot; others use dishes.

A woman serves the drinking bowl to her husband. If other men are present, the host will pass the bowl around the circle. Hands are washed after the meal.

3 ECONOMIC ORGANIZATION AND MANUFACTURE

External Economic Relations

Until forty or fifty years ago when contact with white people began to increase, the Shipibo engaged in barter with the outside world for a small number of goods. Prices were not fixed, but were determined largely by the Shipibo's relative need for the object. Iron tools, especially machetes and axes, have always been greatly desired and needed, and these have been procured from the white man ever since initial contact. The Shipibo paid with lumber, agricultural products, fish, skins, and canoes, or in personal services.

Today, although there is still occasional barter, most trading is on a cash basis. Goods that are purchased include shotguns and ammunition, boat motors, metal items such as machetes, cooking pots, and spoons, and some Western-style clothes and beads.

Shipibos also relate economically to the outside world by working for hire. One form is to work for a large company which exploits the jungle and hires local people on a temporary basis. Lumber has been obtained from the jungle by outside entrepreneurs for a number of years, and many Shipibo today are involved in cutting and transporting lumber. Although some still work for large concerns, an increasing number of Shipibo are engaged in cutting and selling lumber independently, dealing directly with sawmills in Pucallpa. The rubber boom of the early part of the century did not have as devastating consequences for the Shipibo as for other groups, but the Shipibo did work for rubber barons, and the culture was probably deeply affected.

If an employer establishes a more permanent business, and if a Shipibo works for him over an extended period of time, the familiar patrón system may develop. Although one cannot generalize about all patrones (some treat their workers well), it remains true that the system tends to exploit the jungle peoples. Wages are frequently minimal and the work demanding. Moreover, the patrón frequently assumes a prominent role in the community, not only as employer but also as policeman, judge, advocate, representative, and storekeeper. The latter function, especially, tends to place the Shipibo and other jungle people in economic bondage. The flow of outside supplies is completely controlled by the patrón and, since credit is readily extended, the situation usually encourages an interminable relationship of economic subservience. Both the government and concerned private groups have sought to curb the power of the patrón; consequently the Shipibo, at least, have been largely successful in gaining independence from this traditional system.

Property

The internal economic system among the Shipibo is relatively nondiversified: each family is still largely self-sufficient, and there is little specialization of labor. Trade is necessary, however, to obtain a number of items not manufactured by the family.

Isolated aspects of material culture have been alluded to several times, but it may be well to summarize the extent of a Shipibo family's property. Of course there are differences between families, but the following list constitutes a rather general inventory of a typical family's possessions:

> house
> cook house
> pottery-making shed
> benches
> various kinds of storage and drying racks
> cooking pots and stirring paddles
> plates and spoons
> sleeping mats
> blankets (usually fewer than one per person)
> mosquito nets
> clothing (in most cases two or three changes
>   of clothes per person)
> canoes (one large, one small)
> boat motor (fewer than one-tenth of the families)
> bows and arrows
> shotgun
> machetes (two or three per family)
> other tools, such as a hammer and an axe

The house is generally considered joint property: in case of polygamy each wife has her own house. The man's tools and hunting gear are his own, while the pottery belongs to the woman. Inheritance procedures are simple, both because the property is usually minimal and because many of a person's possessions are destroyed at his death.

Until recently the house was burned when a man died. His widow would move in with another member of the family, usually her older brother. Other possessions such as bow and arrows, canoe, and clothing are still burned or thrown into the river. Purchased tools are not disposed of, however, since these are too valuable and are not identified with the dead person in the same way as items he himself made. These items are normally inherited by the oldest son.

A similar procedure is followed when a woman dies. Her purchased cookware is distributed among her daughters, but pottery made by her is broken; her clothes, pieces of cloth she wove, and even her weaving equipment are thrown out or burned. The large canoe which her husband made for her is sold or given away.

Manufacture

Shipibo houses are usually built completely from materials available in the jungle: trees for the frame, jungle vine (Carludovica) to hold the frame together, and palm leaves for the roof. The frame of the house consists largely of hardwood poles. First, upright posts are set in the ground for the sides of the house. There are three to five of these on each side, depending on the length of the house. These posts are spanned at the top by one long beam, or two if necessary, to run the length of the house. The two sides are then connected with crossbeams which extend about 1 m. beyond each post. Rafters are erected from the long side beams to form a double-pitched roof. The builders tie cane poles between the rafters to construct a network which will support the palm (Phytelephas, Scheelea cephalotes, or Scheelea bassleriana) thatch. Gable ends are also filled in with a cane pole and thatch. Most homes do not have walls, but many have a raised floor of palm (Iriartea) bark. Long pieces of palm bark are flattened out until they can form a planklike floor. A few families have aluminum roofs and sawed lumber for floor and siding. Nails are used in such constructions.

Many household items have traditionally been made by the Shipibo themselves. Furniture, as such, is limited. The Shipibo formerly did not have tables, but now they often make or purchase them. These are not generally used for meals, since the Shipibo typically squat around a common pot for eating as mentioned previously. Outdoor benches are made from the bottom and sides of old canoes.

Food utensils include long stirring paddles made of balsa or other wood. Mortar and pestle for mashing maize and hulling rice are made of quinilla, one of the jungle hardwoods. The mortar bowl is shaped by burning and scraping out a log, which may be 1 m. high. The pestle usually has two rounded ends with a handle in between. The cassava grater used in the production of farina is a paddle-shaped piece of wood into which small wires have been inserted. A food or clay sifter is made by stretching thin strips of the cortex of the bombonaje (Carludovica palmata) leaf stem crosswise over a frame.

A simple press for extracting sugar-cane juice is found in most villages. The press consists of a hardwood post set into the ground. A slot is cut into the post and a lever passed through the slot. A heart-shaped projection with canals at each side is formed under the slot to drain off the juice. A stalk of cane is placed lengthwise over the projection and the lever is pushed down to crush the cane at that point and squeeze out the juice.

Homes were lighted traditionally by means of cotton and grease wicks wrapped around a stick. The cotton was soaked in tapir or paiche (Vastres gigas, Arapaima gigas or Sudas pirarucu) lard. Today the Shipibo use small lamps consisting of a cotton wick soaked in kerosene in a metal container, such as an instant coffee tin.

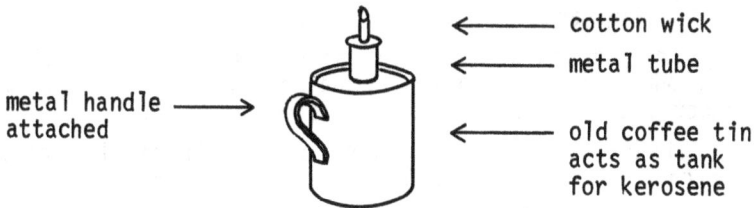

cotton wick

metal tube

metal handle attached

old coffee tin acts as tank for kerosene

Figure 1. Kerosene lamp

Fire was started at one time by wood-on-wood friction or by striking flint on steel, but today matches are a common household item. By always keeping a log burning, fire is preserved.

Sleeping and sitting mats are made very simply from materials at hand. The most common sleeping mat, the **pishin,** is made of a single leaf of either the shebón or shapaja palm. When leaves are cut for thatching, unopened central leaves are reserved for the mats. Fronds are bent backward to the other side of the stem, where they are plaited with the ends tucked in to form a smooth edge. Two of these placed together side by side, rib sides outwards, make a comfortable sleeping mat. The **cahuin** sleeping mat is made of narrow strips of the aguaje palm leaf stem cortex, held together by diagonally woven strips of a jungle vine (**nishi**) also used for thatching. Such mats are used by many ethnic groups for sleeping mats as well as for sunshades and temporary inner walls. The pithy center of the aguaje leaf stem is also converted into a sleeping mat by interweaving strips of vine. These mats are thick and pliable, so that they produce a mattresslike effect. Finally,

a durable sleeping mat is sometimes made of the inner bark of the
llanchama tree (Manicaria saccifera). The bark is taken off in
large pieces, after which the fine outer surface is beaten off.
This leaves a piece of bark cloth of flexible, interlaced fibers
about .5 cm. thick. Since the llanchama tree is now scarce, aguaje
bark is sometimes substituted.

The Shipibo make various kinds of baskets. Carrying baskets are
woven of split jungle vine in a diagonally locked, open checker
weave, and are about 60 cms. in diameter, and 35 cms. deep. The
weaving is tight enough to permit beans to be carried. Lightweight
baskets (**caquit**) are made of strips of shebón palm fronds, about 5
cms. wide. These baskets, about 30 cm. deep and 45 cms. in
diameter, are used for carrying cotton and other light materials.
The **sintan** basket is about 30 cms. in diameter, with 10-cm.-high
sloping sides. The weave is herringbone, from the fronds of the
yahuaranqui palm. It is used for keeping cotton and small
articles. A small workbasket, also called **sintan** is about 25 cms.
square and 15 cms. deep. It is made from panisama (Astrocaryum
huicungo) palm and serves to hold a woman's spinning or sewing
equipment, toilet articles, beads, and similar items.

Pottery making constitutes a major part of Shipibo manufacture
and art production. The pottery, made solely by the women, is for
both domestic use and sale to the outside world.

Some Shipibo must travel as much as a full day by canoe to
obtain proper clay, though other villages have deposits nearby.
Dark clay is used for cookware, and a white or red mixture for
other vessels.

Clay is dug up and taken home in balls. It is subsequently
pulverized in a wooden mashing trough, sifted through a handmade
screen and mixed with water and apacharama bark. This 1.5-cm.-
thick bark is from a large hardwood tree, and after being charred,
the ashes from it are ground to powder and mixed with the clay to
serve as a temper.

The pot is fashioned by the coil method. A small quantity of
clay is rolled into a rope which is coiled into a circle, and the
pot is built up by successive layers. The pot is then set aside
for partial drying before being smoothed by scraping with a piece
of calabash shell. It is finished by polishing with a smooth
stone.

Cooking pots are black and unpainted. Other vessels, however,
are painted either with colored clay or with the juice of the
genipa. First a background wash is painted on and allowed to dry.
Then geometric designs are added freehand in another color, using
thin slivers of reed. The usual color schemes are black and red on
white, or white on red. Some pot interiors are painted black with
genipa.

The vessel is fired when the paint has dried. Firewood is placed on end around the pots, the fire is lit, and the pots become red hot within minutes, although the firing process takes about a half hour. While still hot, the pots are glazed inside and out to make them waterproof with resins, either copal or lacre, applied to the inside with the curved rib of a tapir.

Cookware and other vessels come in various shapes and sizes. The cooking pot is normally about 45 cms. in diameter at its widest point, and 30 cms. high, with an opening of about 40 cms. Although cooking pots are not usually painted, they are decorated around the upper edge with, for example, fingernail incisions. The cassava cooking pot for preparing masato is larger than others and shaped like a top. Other pottery includes the food bowl (**quencha**), the drinking bowl (**quempo**), and the water jar (**chomo**). Water jars are often about 35 cms. at the widest circumference, with an opening and base of about 15 cms. and a height of 25 cms. Chicha jars are even larger.

Shipibo women are entirely responsible for the production of fabric, from the cultivation of cotton plants to the making of decorative designs. Cotton bolls are harvested, stored in bundles, securely wrapped in large leaves and hung from the rafters. In lieu of carding, the cotton is picked apart and laid on a mat to be beaten with a stalk of wild cane. The fluffed cotton is then rolled around a stick to form a cylinder, from one end of which the spinning is begun. As the woman rotates the spindle, drawing the roll of cotton away, the strand emerges and is twisted into thread. The thread is wound into balls, and accumulated for weaving.

The Shipibo weave much of their own cloth, generally on a horizontal belt loom. A number of sticks are first put into the ground at desired intervals, and the weaving process is begun by walking around the sticks, stringing the thread until the warp reaches the desired height. This warp is then kept on two sticks, one of which is attached to a house post. The woman holds the other stick in front of her by means of a strap behind her back. (Deerhide was formerly used for the strap.) She sits on a mat and, by leaning back, tightens the threads sufficiently for the weaving of the woof. The shed is produced by placing a piece of wood between the two layers. The shuttle is made of pona (hard palm wood).

Several smaller looms are also used. The Ucayali loom, for example, for weaving narrow strips such as ankle bands and handles for woven bags, consists of a small oval frame. The warp is produced first by passing the threads across the frame, keeping them in place with sticks. These sticks are replaced by the woof strands.

Bark dyes of brown, red, or yellow are frequently used to paint designs on cloth with a sliver of reed. Lines or areas which need

to be black are smeared with wet clay, which combines with the dye
to produce the black color. Other areas are filled in with
annatto. Women also frequently decorate their skirts with embroidery and appliqué.

As with pottery, the distinctive and typical geometric design
is employed with variations according to the artistic ability and
whim of the individual making the item.

Transportation

The canoe is certainly the most common means of conveyance
among the Shipibo, ranging from the 3 m. fishing-and-hunting canoe
to the 12 m. transport canoe. They are preferably made of cedar,
which will last as long as ten years. Canoes are usually shaped
inside and out using an adze and ax rather than by partial burning, although the Shipibo do seal the outside by charring. The
finished canoe is about one inch thick at the upper edge, increasing to about three inches at the bottom. The prow is pointed, the
stern usually squared, and some canoes have a small keel. Often
there are no seats; passengers may sit on a small board and place
cargo on boards or poles if there is water in the canoe. The
paddler normally sits on the back, although he may sit in the prow
if the canoe has a keel.

The montería is a variation of the canoe. It has a dugout bottom, usually widened by heating and stretching, and sides built up
with planking. These larger boats sometimes have a covering of
palm leaves for protection from sun and rain on long trips.

The transportation of large, heavy cargoes has been made easier
with the increasing availability of motorized boats; therefore the
raft is not used as much as it once was, although rafts made of
balsa logs lashed together with vines are still seen on the
Ucayali River. Large oars, blades up to about 50 cms. across, are
attached to steer the raft. If the cargo has to be transported a
great distance, travelers may construct a small platform and/or
roof for cooking and sleeping. The raft survives most commonly
today as the log rafts that are floated to sawmills. Logs are
lashed together with vines, ropes or steel cables, and temporary
shelters are erected for the duration of the trip.

Various motors are in use, but the most common by far is the
peque-peque, a Briggs-Stratton 9 hp. air-cooled engine without
muffler.

4 ARTS, DRESS, AND RECREATION

Various modes of artistic expression are unified by a common Shipibo design with idiosyncratic variations. This design typically consists of a number of interlocking geometric motifs, with a dominant right-angle step. The resultant pattern is a profusion of lines, squares, rectangles, and especially crosses. Triangles are less common; curves appear in Conibo designs but not in Shipibo.

The application of the design to pottery and fabrics was discussed in chapter 3; it also appears on other artifacts, tools, in body-painting motifs, and formerly on canoes and paddles. A more recent application of the design is found in villages that cater to the tourist trade. Tourist artifacts, such as minature canoes, paddles, bows, and letter openers are usually decorated with the traditional motif.

Attire

The Shipibo have adopted western-style clothing to the extent that men now wear shirts and trousers bought from the traveling merchant or in the market or retail stores of Pucallpa and other nearby towns. Some men still wear the traditional cushma (a long, full tunic) in the evening for extra warmth, for protection against mosquitos, or on festive occasions. The cushma is usually hand woven. A design is woven into the edges of the cloth, and then the cloth is elaborately decorated with painted geometric designs.

Women's garb consists of a tubular skirt, a blouse, and sometimes a shawl of cotton cloth. A colorful silk scarf for dressy occasions is popular today. The skirt is wide enough so that after it is pulled to one side to make it snug, it can be doubled (or lapped) over to form a pleat in front. The top front section is then rolled out and down to hold the skirt up. The skirt is always decorated with geometric designs, either painted on, or in a combination of embroidery and appliqué. The blouse is made of

several different brightly colored pieces of purchased cloth. It
is rather straight, short in the front, and with a ruffle in the
back and tight sleeves, reaching almost to the wrist. The shawl, a
strip of cloth about 1.5 ms. long, is worn to ward off the chill
or mosquitoes, and may double as a baby sling. It is sometimes
worn over the shoulders in place of a blouse.

Beadwork is the most prevalent form of ornament among the
Shipibo. Tiny, purchased beads are strung in intricate, colorful
designs to make bracelets of various widths. The women, and less
frequently, the men, may wear one or several wrist bands, each
about 3 cms. wide. Occasionally, a woman still wears a narrow band
with a string passed through the pierced earlobe. For festivals
men may wear beaded collars about 4 cms. wide, chestpieces 15 by
20 cms., headbands, and crowns. Except for the crowns, these are
made of beads, woven in multicolored patterns. Women also wear
multiple strings of small, white beads as belts. The number of
strings a woman wears partially indicates her economic status in
the community. Women are also fond of six or seven strands of
larger, purchased, glass or plastic beads for necklaces. They do
not wear the seed and bead necklaces they make to see to non-
Shipibos.

Various kinds of metal adornments are also worn. Although not
as commonly as before, the women still wear elaborate necklaces of
large and sometimes very old coins or other metal disks, possibly
as many as fifty disks. The men sometimes have metal disks
suspended from their chestpieces. Men, women, and children
traditionally wore a metal nosepiece, frequently shaped from a
silver coin, suspended with a thin metal wire from the pierced
septum. So, with the lip ornament: a wooden peg might be inserted
in the lower lip, but the usual labret, seldom seen today, was a
metal strip suspended from a tanglike projection. Some women also
wear rings on several fingers. These are either purchased or made
from scrap metal pipes.

Other ornamentation includes body painting, especially for
festivities. Both men and women paint their faces with the same
geometric designs; the women paint their own or each other's faces
as well as those of the men. Men used to paint their torsos and
arms; today they paint only their arms. Women paint both arms and
legs. The paint is sometimes the red annatto, but is usually the
black genipa.

Women cut their hair in bangs, long on the sides, and longer in
back. Men sometimes still wear bangs, but more often have conventional western-style haircuts. Men sometimes make tweezers of two
shells tied together to pull out their sparse facial hair.

Until very recently, the Shipibo practiced cranial reshaping on
babies for beautification. Soon after birth, a board and pad were
applied to the baby's forehead with a wide strap around the back

of the head. The board remained in place for about three months
and was tightened periodically, producing a rounded face and
slanted forehead. Missionaries discouraged the practice for years
with little result. A more potent deterrent has been ridicule from
the outside world. In mestizo culture a Shipibo with a slanted
forehead, especially a young army recruit whose short haircut
exposes his forehead, is often ridiculed. Consequently, the custom
is dying out.

Music and Dance

Shipibo make a number of musical instruments. The flute (**rehue**)
is a popular instrument. It is made of cane (**huai-huanti**) about 2
cms. in diameter and 45 cms. long. It usually has one hole on the
underside and from four to six on the upper side.

The vertical flute (**paca ati**) is made of a hollowed-out section
of cane (**paca tocoro**) about 6 cms. in diameter and between 50 cms.
and 1 m. long. There is a small hole at the bottom end of the
cylinder; air is blown across the open end. The sound is similar
to that produced by blowing across the mouth of a bottle, and
since the **paca** produces only one tone, several people usually play
together, each with a different length **paca** producing different
tones. The **paca** is played only at ceremonial feasts, such as the
girls' haircutting feast. **Paca** players are selected according to
custom and appointed well in advance of the occasion.

The panpipe (**yupana**) consists of 8-12 tubes of carrizo (**sinco**)
bamboo varying from 8 to 20 cms. held together by two sticks and
thread. The player blows on each separate tube to produce a tune.

Drums are made of cedar logs, 20-30 cms. in diameter and about
60 cms. high, hollowed by scraping and burning. The preferred
drumhead is made from a cayman esophagus; but skins of ocelot,
peccary, or other animals are also used, stretched over both ends
of the drum.

The most important of the dances done at the girls' haircutting
festival is the **mashai icai**. A very similar dance was apparently
also performed during the traditional subincision rite, discussed
under Puberty. The dance usually involves between ten and twenty
participants, many of whom also have another function at the
ceremony, such as the cutting of the girl's hair or the killing of
the ceremonial animal. The girl, fully painted with body paint and
wearing only a skirt, is one of the participants in the dance and
is always flanked by two to four women. The participants hold
hands or link arms and form an elongated circle, facing inward,
while the girl faces out. Some of the men carry war clubs or
arrows over the left shoulder. The group, led by the girl, moves
either in a circular fashion, or in a forward and backward walk
--sometimes slow, sometimes almost at a run. The dance is accom-

panied by a drum and several vertical flutes, while the dancers sing ceremonial songs, including a song about the animal that is going to be killed that day.

Less important dances at any fiesta may include the Jumping Dance (**nahuarinca**), a strenuous one in which both men and women participate. The Singing Dance (**behua**) focuses on men's songs, sung without instrumental accompaniment while men and women dance in parallel columns. In the **ishori icai** dance, women sing about the ceremonial bird or animal to be killed. Still remembered but no longer performed is the **yopatáti**, a warrior dance, in celebration of escape or victory.

Celebrations

Initiation rites and the postmourning haircutting ceremony are described below in sections on puberty and death. Besides these, the Shipibo have several other feasts related to work and economic activities. One is the Feast to Break the Peccary Tooth. A white-lipped peccary is domesticated, and the owner allows its tusks to grow until the animal becomes dangerous. A day is then set aside to break the tusks. All the men of the village are invited for generous amounts of **masato** and hilarity. After some time, the animal is tied up and one of the men tries to break the tusks by hitting them with a stone; if he is not successful, he files the tusks and breaks them off.

A related feast involves the slaughter of a domesticated animal, usually a white-lipped or a collared peccary or, at times, a chicken. This event also occurs as part of the festivities of the girls' haircutting ceremony in which case the girl or her family may have raised the animal. The killing is preceded by dancing, **masato** drinking, and singing a song about the animal, relating its actions and imitating its sounds. The celebration may last for several days before the actual slaughter. The animal is tied to a cross and shot with arrows. The men are sufficiently drunk and their aim poor enough that all participants are afforded a chance to take a turn.

Other communal parties are held during harvest. The people help each other with the harvesting of some crop; payment consists of food, drink, and later reciprocal help when needed.

Today, the importance of indigenous feasts is declining as borrowed feast days, either Christian or national, supplant them. Christmas and Easter, for example, are celebrated, as are Peruvian Independence Day on July 28, and St. John's Day on June 24.

5 POLITICAL AND SOCIAL ORGANIZATION

Authority Structure

Men are the acknowledged heads of the Shipibo household, but women nevertheless play very significant roles. Their judgment and voice in family decisions are clearly recognized. A projected family move or the choosing of a mate for a child, for example, is usually discussed between husband and wife. Women actively participate in discussions but do not always vote at village meetings, where they usually sit on the floor at one side or at the back. Official authority, however, rests with men who are the heads of both the nuclear and extended families. Men represent the family in all community affairs, vote in community decisions, and are eligible to hold public office.

Authority in the village is exercised by a chief or headman. The office of chief is fluid and informal. Today it is in a period of transition. In the tradition of the past two or three generations, circumstances and personality were the deciding factors in obtaining leadership. If there was a power vacuum, one of the men assumed a leadership role; if his suggestions were accepted, the people recognized his authority. A headman could readily abandon his role, however, if he became dissatisfied or tired of the job. Also the villagers could simply refuse to recognize his authority when they no longer had confidence in him or desired a change for some other reason.

In recent years the people have looked for a leader over thirty-five years of age, a hard worker, a good family man, and one who exhibits sound judgment. His performance is measured partly by his success in attracting help for the community, such as the establishment of a school, or the securing of an aluminum roof for the school house. He may also serve as recruiter for laborers for village cleanup projects or for outside employment. One of the leader's duties is calling people together for village meetings, over which he presides. Community issues are always discussed thoroughly, and the headman cannot impose an unpopular decision by force.

23

Today the role of the leader is changing in several ways. One shift involves his age; another, his ability to speak Spanish. Traditional headmen, who still play a prominent role in many villages, are in their forties or fifties and may not understand or speak Spanish well. They are, consequently, hampered in their contacts with the national life of Peru, which is making an increasing impact upon Shipibo life. There is, therefore, a tendency to choose younger men who have attended school and are proficient in Spanish.

This change is coupled with a greater integration into the Peruvian system through the use of popular elections. Leaders chosen in this fashion, moreover, are designated by the Peruvian government as officials. The **agente municipal** for example, is responsible for public work projects, while the **teniente goberna-dor** carries out political functions. These men work as a team conducting meetings, discussions, and community affairs.

Offences and Sanctions

The number of punishable offences in the Shipibo community is small, and the enforcing of sanctions rather unstructured. Since they live primarily among relatives where material possessions are few and readily identifiable, theft is infrequent. If something is stolen, the victim's only recourse is to try to reclaim the stolen property. If unsuccessful, he may seek the intervention of the headman, but will more often simply drop the issue.

Homicide is rare among the Shipibo. If it occurs, it usually takes place during a drinking party rather than as a premeditated act. In times past the family was expected to revenge the death of a family member, but this has not been customary for many generations. Today, a homicide case is turned over to local authorities and the accused is judged by Peruvian law.

The most common form of intragroup justice concerned adultery. If a husband discovered that his wife had had sexual relations with another man, he had the right to punish the offender.

The traditional weapon of revenge is a curved adultery knife (**hueshati**), 10-15 cms. in length, made by each man himself. The knife is fashioned from a piece of machete blade, ground labori-ousely on a wet sandstone. Some men practice ceremonial fasting while making the knife to give it greater potency. The handle is incised with geometrical designs, and occasionally the tooth of a poisonous snake is implanted, again to secure greater power. When finished, the knife is hung from a woven loop around the man's neck and carried on his back.

The encounter may take different forms. The most frequent was during the girls' puberty rites. All the men drank masato preceding the fighting. The knifing sometimes followed a fight with clubs, so the aggrieved husband cut his opponent after knocking him senseless. At other times the guilty party willingly submitted to the cutting. Karsten (1955) describes a highly ceremonious attack in which each man cuts the head of the person who happens to dance in front of him. He discounts the adultery motive on the basis of Indian psychology and suggests that the Shipibo consider the fight a struggle with evil spirits. Some other author thought they did it to have their blood flowing in sympathy with the girl who was being operated on. These interpretations have not been corroborated by any of our informants, who always stressed the adultery motive. Legend and song further confirm this motive.

The actual knifing consisted of a horizontal cut on the lower back of the head. The wound was subsequently washed with **piripiri** solution. Sand was sometimes rubbed into the cut to promote healing. After two to three weeks, a permanent and prominent scar remained. The wound might be deep, but revenge was kept within bounds. The cut was not intended to, and rarely did, produce permanent maiming or death. Neither was there lasting animosity between the parties, since the knifing was recognized as due punishment and an opportunity to satisfy the demands of revenge. No social stigma was attached either to the fighting or to the resulting scar.

Adultery knifing still takes place today, but much less frequently than it once did. As revenge killings for murder have been supplanted by the national system of justice, similarly, customary punishment for adultery is apparently also disappearing. But in this case there is almost no judicial substitute.

Social and Residential Structure

Lathrap (1970:181) wrote that "The degree to which the large Shipibo-Conibo communities were broken down under the stress of missionization and the rubber boom, and reassembled under various strong Western influences, makes it difficult to assess the structure of the prehistoric community." It appears, however, that the extended, matrilocal family is a continuing tradition, with the family either living in one house or in very close proximity, and having extensive contact and interaction. For the past several generations, the extended family, in effect, constituted the community, with two to five houses in a grouping. These small communities were seminomadic, since they frequently abandoned their homes and relocated elsewhere, usually to find new land for their gardens. Such small communities are still found, but the trend is toward larger communities. Even the isolated family unit is often only a satellite of a larger village.

The establishment of schools has been a principal factor in the growth of communities. The Shipibo value education highly and are willing to move into larger communities in order to make schooling available to their children. The size of villages now ranges from about five homes in smaller villages to about seventy-five in larger ones, with most villages in the fifteen to twentyfive range. The population of a village varies from approximately thirty people to over five hundred. Larger villages generally continue the extended-family pattern as fostered by matrilocal residence. Married daughters and their families share a house with the wife's parents or live nearby.

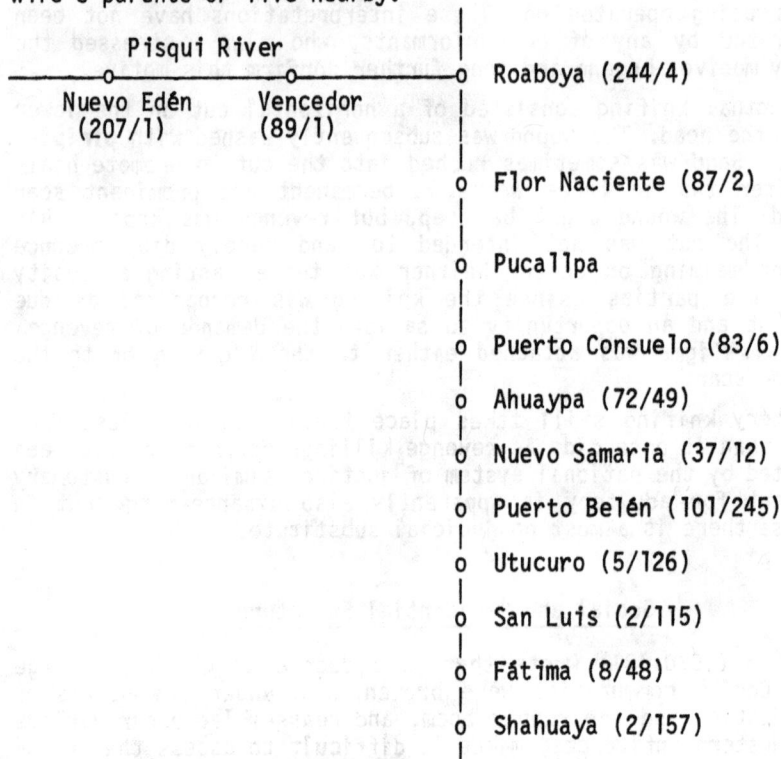

```
       Pisqui River                     |
──────────o──────────o──────────────────o  Roaboya (244/4)
      Nuevo Edén      Vencedor          |
       (207/1)        (89/1)            |
                                        o  Flor Naciente (87/2)
                                        |
                                        o  Pucallpa
                                        |
                                        o  Puerto Consuelo (83/6)
                                        |
                                        o  Ahuaypa (72/49)
                                        |
                                        o  Nuevo Samaria (37/12)
                                        |
                                        o  Puerto Belén (101/245)
                                        |
                                        o  Utucuro (5/126)
                                        |
                                        o  San Luis (2/115)
                                        |
                                        o  Fátima (8/48)
                                        |
                                        o  Shahuaya (2/157)
                                        |
```

Figure 2. Shipibo/Conibo population ratios

Even the seminomadic tradition has not been completely abandoned, since many families continue to move frequently. The most common reason for moving is still the search for better land. After the floods of 1973 and 1974, for example, many families and sometimes whole communities relocated. Family reasons may also be a significant factor; the move of certain relatives to a new location may soon prompt others to move. At other times, community quarrels are cited for large-scale relocations.

During 1973-1974, Eakin, with the help of bilingual schoolteachers, took a census of twenty villages. Of these, twelve had returns which especially lent themselves to tabulation and comparison. The following figures are based on data concerning 1703 individuals from these twelve communities. Figure 2 is a schematic representation of the twelve villages located along the Ucayali and Pisqui Rivers and indicates the ratio of Shipibo to Conibo inhabitants. These data show the two traditional concentrations of Shipibo to the north and Conibo to the south, with the dividing line somewhat to the south of Pucallpa. They also show increasing numbers of immigrants from each of the two areas as the village in focus lies farther from the dividing line. It also appears that more Shipibos have moved south than Conibos have moved north. These migrations are the result of intermarriage and of the relocation of families or even entire villages.

Age in years					Total population
over 70		1	1		2
61-70		11	5		16
51-60	862 MEN	37	28	841 WOMEN	65
41-50		58	52		110
31-40		105	111		216
26-30		71	71		142
21-25		69	87		156
16-20		80	86		166
11-15		123	75		198
6-10		112	140		252
0-5	195			185	380

Figure 3. Population of 12 villages by age and sex

Shipibo descent is generally described as matrilineal (Karsten 1955:155; Girard 1958:245; Tschopik 1958:937). Census data suggest, however, that matrilineal descent does not necessarily extend to larger group affiliation. When asked for identity in terms of parentage, the vast majority of the respondents selected the paternal line. Furthermore, when two fathers try to determine if a proposed marriage between their children is suitable, they ask each other first, "Who was your father?" and then, "Who was your mother?" In case of the death or divorce of the parents of a small child, Shipibos say that either the father's or the mother's family may raise the child. In practice, however, it appears more often to be a member of the father's family. Finally, males insist that descent is through the father: "The mother is just the container for the fetus."

Figure 3 is a population pyramid showing the distribution by age and sex of the inhabitants of the twelve communities. Although there are perhaps more older people among the Shipibo than among some other jungle tribes, the number is small. The statistical sample is perhaps too small to be determinative, but the male-female ratio seems to bear out the informal observation that there are fewer older women than men, perhaps due to deaths in childbirth.

Movement patterns can be discerned from figure 4. The data for Vencedor and Nuevo Edén suggest that these villages on the Pisqui are residentially more stable than those on the Ucayali. The degree of movement can be further seen from the Puerto Belén census where the 238 immigrants came from 62 different villages.

Village	Native-Born	Emigrants
Nuevo Edén	175	33
Vencedor	70	20
Roaboya	119	129
Flor Naciente	9	80
Puerto Consuelo	18	71
Ahuaypa	59	62
Nuevo Samaria	3	46
Puerto Belén	123	223
Utucuro	63	68
San Luis	101	16
Fátima	25	31
Shahuaya	122	37
Total	887	816

Figure 4. Change of residence in 12 communities

Kinship Terminology

A fairly elaborate inventory of referent kinship terms distinguish Shipibo consanguineal and affinal kinsmen. Some of these are also used in direct address, with several special vocative terms also occurring, and with ranges of reference shifting in a few cases between vocative and referential use of terms. Ranges of reference of terms are indicated below by the use of the abbreviations presented in figure 5.

P	parent
C	child
S	spouse
m	male
f	female
a ... a	ego and alter, same sex
a ... b	ego and alter, opposite sex
e	alter is older than ego
y	alter is younger than ego
=	parallel kinsmen only
x	cross kinsmen only
G	collateral extension within primary generation
=G	Collateral extention within primary generation to parallel kinsmen only
1	extension both (1) lineally and (2) collaterally through primary generation and generations further removed from ego
2	extension both (1) lineally and (2) collaterally through the generation one degree closer to ego than the primary generation and through generations further removed from ego
S-	affinal extension to spouse's corresponding kinsman
fS-	affinal extension to spouse's corresponding kinsmen for female ego only (where avoidance rules out application for male ego)
-S	affinal extension to corresponding kinsman's spouse
V	reciprocal (of affinal relationship)

Figure 5. Kinship terms and abbreviations

Consanguineal kinsmen are identified generically as **rarebo** 'kinsmen'. Terms of reference for **rarebo** are presented in figure 6, organized into subgroups on the basis of a number of other generic terms.

Grandkinsmen are either **yosibo** 'kinsmen of the second or third ascending generation' or **bababo** 'kinsmen of the second descending generation'. Beyond the third ascending generation, ancestors are **non moabo** 'our ancient ones'. The Shipibos admit to no generic terms for descendants beyond the second descending generation since "they have not yet been seen."

Yosibo	PP(1) (Plural)	Grandparents
1. **jochi yosi**	PPPm(G,S-,-S)	great-grandfather
2. **chipi yoshan**	PPPf(G,S-,-S)	great-grandmother
3. **papa yosi**	PPm(G,S-,-S)	grandfather
4. **tita yoshan**	PPf(G,S-,-S)	grandmother

Bababo	CC(G) (Plural)	Grandchildren
5. **baba**	CC(G,S-,-S)	grandchild

Papabo	Pm(G) (Plural)	Fathers
6. **papa**	Pm, (SPm(G,-S))	father
7. **epa**	=PPCm(G),(PSm)G,S-))	father's brother
8. **coca**	xPPCm(G)	mother's brother

Titabo	Pf(G) (Plural)	Mothers
9. **tita**	Pf,(SPf(G,V,S))	mother
10. **huata**	=PPCf(G),(SPPCf(G,V,S))	mother's sister
11. **nachi**	xmPPCf(G)	man's father's sister
12. **yaya**	xfPPCf(G)	woman's father's sister

Baquebo	C(Plural)	Children
13. **baque**	C	child
14. **nosha**	=mPCC(G),(mSC(=G))	man's brother's child
15. **pia**	xmPCC(G),(xmSPCC(G))	man's sister's child
16. **coco**	=fPCCm(G)	woman's sister's child
17. **ini**	=fPCCf(G)	woman's sister's daughter
18. **chio, chio baque**	xfPCC(G)	woman's brother's child

Huetsabo	aPCa(G) (Plural)	Same-sex siblings
19. **huetsa**	aPCa(G)	same-sex sibling

Poibo	aPCb(G) (Plural)	Opposite-sex siblings
20. **poi**	aPCb(G)	opposite-sex sibling
21. **jochi**	ePCm(G)	elder brother
22. **chipi**	ePCf(G)	elder sister
23. **yosi**	yPCm	younger brother
24. **yoshan**	yPCf(vocative)	younger sister
25. **chio**	yPC	younger sibling

Figure 6. Shipibo consanguineal terms of reference

Extension of terms beyond these primary ranges are indicated in figure 6 in parentheses using rules of extension defined by Merrifield (1981). All grandkinsman terms extend collaterally to all known kinsmen of each respective generation by Rule G, and, as mentioned, **yosibo** extends to the third ascending generation as well as through the second by Rule 1. These terms are also optionally extended to corresponding affinal kinsmen even though affinal terms may also be used for them. Specifically, they may extend to kinsman of spouse (Rule S-), spouse of kinsman (Rule -S), applied separately or even to coaffinals--spouse of kinsman of spouse, applying both together.

The suffix **-bo** which marks plural generic terms may also occur with grandfather or grandmother terms to designate kinsmen of the second ascending generation only:

papa yosibo	PPm(G)(plural)	grandfathers
tita yoshanbo	PPf(G)(plural)	grandmothers

Note that generic terms do not extend to corresponding affinal kinsmen. While more specific terms do extend to affinals, they are used out of respect only. These terms refer basically to **rarebo** and sanctions against marriage between **rarebo** do not apply to affines to whom these terms may extend by courtesy. A particular affinal kinsman might be referred to by any of several consanguineal terms. A woman might refer to the husband of her husband's parental aunt, for example, either as **papa** 'father' or as **epa** 'father's brother'.

In the first ascending and descending generations, the sex of ego, alter, and of linking kinsman is important for classifying kinsmen. Three terms classify male kinsmen of the first ascending generation and four classify females, in a bifurcate collateral pattern. Six terms classify kinsmen of the first descending generation, with the sex of ego being marked more often than the sex of alter. Bifurcation is apparently of the Seneca type (Merrifield 1983), in which parallel and cross categories are determined by comparing the sex of the senior member of the ego-alter dyad with that of the junior member's parent who links ego with alter.

The generic term **baquebo** is uncharacteristic of other generic terms in that it does not extend collaterally to the children of siblings or cousins, but is limited in reference to ego's own children. The specific term **baque** does occur, however, in compound with **chio** as an alternative means of referring to a woman's brother's child.

In ego's generation, siblings, parallel cousins, and cross cousins are distinguished by just two terms which mark relative sex of ego and alter. Ego may further explain the relationship. "He's the child of my **coca**," or, "... my **epa**." If ego wishes to emphasize the sibling relationship, he might say something like,

"We have the same father," or he might postpose **quiquin** 'the real one' to the sibling term.

Tschopik (1958) lists most of the basic referential terms and their denotata, the specific kinsmen to which they refer, for consanguineal and affinal kin. Our data include a few additional terms, further denotata, terms of address, and terms for relative age. Tschopik did not find elder and younger siblings to be distinguished, but our observation is that terms for elder and younger siblings are used rather frequently in conversations. All of these terms appear elsewhere in the list of kinship terms; the first four in phrases referring to grandparents, the last as the short form for a woman's brother's child. It will be seen below that these terms have wide-ranging use as vocative terms as well. **yoshan** is included in figure 6 to fill out the pattern but is apparently only used alone in a vocative sense and never in reference.

Shipibo consanguineal terms of address are listed in figure 7. A number of terms of reference are also used in direct address, but several terms are used only vocatively. These latter terms appear in boldface in figure 7 to facilitate their identification by the reader. Also in boldface are those PC strings which denote enlarged ranges of reference in comparison with corresponding terms of reference.

1. **jochi papa**	PPm(G,S-,-S)	great-grandfather
2. **chipi tita**	PPPf(G,S-,-S)	great-grandmother
3. **papa yosi**	PPm(G,S-,-S)	grandfather
4. **tita yoshan**	PPf(G,S-,-S)	grandmother
5. **baba**	CC(G,S-,-S)	grandchild
6. **papa**	Pm(G,fS-,-S)	father
7. **epa**	=PPCm(G), (PSm(G,S-))	father's brother
8. **coca**	xPPCm(G)	mother's brother
9. **tita**	Pf, (SPf(G,V,-S))	mother
10. [NAME] + **tita**	PPCf(G,S-,-S)	parent's sister
11. [NAME]	C	child
12. **nosha**	=mPCC(G), (mSC(=G))	man's brother's child
13. **pia, piaca**	xmPCC(G), (xmSPCC(G))	man's sister's child
14. **jomo**	=fPCCm(G), mPCCm	woman's sister's son
15. **chimin**	=fPCCf(G), mPCCf	woman's sister's daughter
16. **chore**	xfPCC(G), mPCC	woman's brother's child
17. **huetsa, jochi,** [NAME]	aPCa(G)	same-sex sibling
18. **poi jochi**	aPCb(G)	opposite-sex sibling
19. **yosi**	yPCm(1,S-,-S)	younger brother
20. **yoshan**	yPCf(1,S-,-S)	younger sister

Figure 7. Shipibo consanguineal terms of address.

Vocative terms for great-grandparents employ parent terms as endings rather than the grandparent endings used in reference. Both parent terms may extend in direct address to collateral kinsmen of the first ascending generation, although regular terms of reference are also used for uncles while a personal name followed by the mother term may be used for aunts. Vocative terms which correspond to those used in reference for nephews and nieces by female ego are also used by male ego in direct address, as alternates to the regular male terms and without reference to bifurcate categories. The initial element of the great-grandfather term appears in vocative terms for siblings, while the final elements in grandparent terms name younger siblings or collaterals of the first descending generation, presumably when younger than ego.

Affinal terms of reference and address are presented in figures 8 and 9, respectively. A single term designates reciprocally the relationship between a man and his wife's parents, but a corresponding vocative term is never used since such kinsmen never speak directly to one another. A joking relationship exists, on the other hand, between a man and his wife's grandparents, to whom consanguineal terms apply.

1. **bene**	Sm	husband
2. **ahuin**	Sf	wife
3. **rayos**	mSP(R,G)	man's parent-in-law, son-in-law
4. **benen papa**	fSPm(=G,-S)	woman's father-in-law
5. **benen tita**	fSPf(=G,S)	woman's mother-in-law
6. **baban ehua**	CSf(=G)	daughter-in-law
	fSPfP(2)	husband's maternal kinsman
7. **chai**	mSPCm(V,G)	man's brother-in-law
8. **ahuin huetsa**	mSPCf(V,G)	man's sister-in-law
9. **bene itsa**	fSPCm(V,)	woman's brother-in-law
10. **tsabe**	fSPCf(V,)	woman's sister-in-law
11. **isho**	fSPCSf	woman's cosister-in-law

Figure 8. Shipibo Affinal Terms of Reference

Women who marry brothers (**isho**) traditionally do not get along well since each is a potential mate for the other's husband should her own die. There is often rivalry as to which is the better worker, insults may be traded, sometimes eventuating in hair-pulling quarrels.

No terms exist for other co-sibling-in-law relationships, between males or between persons of the opposite sex.

1.	*	Sm	husband
2.	*	Sf	wife
3.	*	MSP(F,G)	man's parent-in-law, son-in-law
4.	papa	fSPm(=G,-S)	woman's father-in-law
5.	tita	fSPf(=G,-S)	woman's mother-in-law
6.	yosi	fCSm	woman's son-in-law
7.	yoshan	CSf	daughter-in-law
8.	chai	mSPCm(V,G)	man's brother-in-law
9.	[NAME]	aSPCb(V,G)	opposite-sex sibling-in-law
10.	*	fSPCf(V,G)	woman's sister-in-law
11.	*	fSPCSf	woman's cosister-in-law

* Direct address prohibited.

Figure 9. Shipibo Affinal Terms of Address

Most kinship terms are shared by both Shipibo and Conibo speakers, but a few uniquely Conibo uses are presented in figure 10.

1.	jochi papa	PPPm(G,S-,-S)	great-grandfather
2.	chicho yoshan	PPPf(G,S-,-S)	great-grandmother
3.	papashoco	PPm(G,S-,-S)	grandfather
4.	titashoco	PPF(G,S-,-S)	grandmother
5.	bene huetsa	FSPCm(V)	woman's brother-in-law

Figure 10. Uniquely Conibo Terms of Reference

Marriage

In arranging marriages, the principal consideration of the two fathers is to ascertain that the prospective bride and groom are not too closely related. Descent is thoroughly discussed to determine whether a relationship can be traced. If a relationship can be traced to a common ancestor within five ascending generations, marriage is prohibited. If one of the pair is from the fifth descending generation and the other the sixth, marriage is frowned upon and the couple would generally have to move to another community. The couple would be compared to dogs or howler monkeys

because of lack of discrimination in choosing a mate. In the sixth
descending generation marriages were formerly prohibited but may
be contracted at present. Again, the couple are called dogs or
howler monkeys. If relationship can be traced back to the seventh
generation, reluctant approval is granted, and with each succeeding generation there is less censure.

To illustrate how relationships extend through many generations
and how descent is traced to ascertain the acceptability of two
potential marriage partners, one Shipibo cited the following case.

A met J outside the language area, and without parental consul-
tation, they decided to get married. They lived together for about
a year. While J was pregnant with their child, it was learned that
she was, according to Shipibo reckoning, A's niece (**nošha**). A
begged his father's pardon, the couple separated, and J returned
to her home village. A's father stated that although this marriage
could not continue, he was willing to raise their child and is
presently doing so.

Clans

There is some evidence that formerly there were five patri-
lineally determined clans: lightning, tiger, macaw, bird, and
snake. At present, most Shipibo do not know to which clan they
belong. An older Shipibo reported that each clan had a song and
that the girl's clan song was sung at her haircutting ceremony.

According to legend, particular clans originated in the following way. A father saw a bird, for example, and said, "What a
pretty bird! If he were a man I would give my daughter to him."

In a little while a man appeared claiming the daughter for his
wife. "But I was talking about a bird," said the father.

"It was I," the man replied.

So the father gave his daughter to the man, and from their
sons, who were human, the clan originated.

6 MAN AND THE SUPERNATURAL

Myth

Shipibo myths concerning supernatural beings and creation do not form a unified cycle. Stories are often fragmentary or conflicting, and may differ from one village to another. Moreover, indigenous and Christian elements have often been fused. The following summaries are only a brief sampling of many extant myths.

The Shipibo generally hold that the sky, to which the shaman has access, is the abode of God and spirits. At one time, before the Shipibo had fire, the sky was much lower than it is today, and the sun served for cooking. Later, the sky moved further away from earth, with continued contact between heaven and earth by means of a staircase. The following story tells how this staircase came into being.

A set of twin boys spent most of their time making and shooting arrows. One day they told their grandmother they were going to shoot at the sky. They shot their arrows into the air, but they all fell back down. The next day they tried again, and shot a great number of arrows. These all disappeared. But then they saw one arrow seemingly fixed in the sky. It then became clear that all the arrows that had been shot were attached end to end, reaching from the earth to the sky. The next day the twins saw that the arrows had turned into a stairway, each one piercing the lower end of the one before it. Many animals and people began to mount the stairs carrying food with them. Then either God or the person whose food they were taking became angry and cut the stairs loose. All the people fell back to earth. Many died; others were changed into armadillos.

In one version, the twins became angry upon seeing so many animals and people going up the stairs. They therefore damaged the stairs, causing many to fall to their death. The women who were carrying food in baskets were changed into armadillos when they

36

fell to earth. In still another version the stairs still exist, and spirits and shamans can use them.

Creation accounts sometimes credit God with the creation of all creatures; other stories make the sun the creator of animals. Although the sun is not always presented as creator, it is always given human characteristics. It is frequently portrayed as a person canoeing on a river in the sky, and is said to be accompanied by two buzzards who serve as oarsmen. When the sun sets, he continues to travel a river under the earth all night. He is conceived of as being dressed in a sacklike garment, with a fire inside the garment.

The moon is also thought of in human terms. One tale relates how he came to be placed in the sky. A young man entered a girl's mosquito net one night uninvited. She had no idea who he was. The next night, she was ready for him should he return. When he came again, she slapped black **huito** juice on one side of his face so that he could be identified the next day. The young man fled, and when the **huito** would not come off, he was apparently embarrassed and moved to the sky to become the moon. He is still there and the **huito** still has not worn off. Every "dark moon" the black side of his face is seen.

Another legend tells of the origin of stars. An alligator had turned himself into a canoe to transport a group of men across a river. When the men disembarked, the alligator-canoe said, "Don't step on the prow." The last person to get off defied the warning and stepped on it. The alligator promptly bit his leg off. The men drained the lake and killed the alligator to recover the leg. At the end of the story the men and the alligator are turned into stars.

The origin of the Shipibo themselves is vague, but they do have this tale about the neighboring Cashibo, whom they traditionally held in contempt. The great Inca king who lived in Santa Rosa planned to give a fiesta. He told everyone that first he wanted to go get a plant whose sap could be used for bathing, and instructed them to wait for his return. However, the men did not wait. They began to drink, and in the ensuing drunken brawl one of the young men was killed. When the Inca returned, he was very angry and told the people, "You are not dependable, and you don't follow instructions. You are worse than animals, since an animal kills another creature only when he is hungry and needs food. Now you have to cook the dead man, and eat him." The people complied, and in another drunken spree, ate the dead man. Then the Inca said, "You have eaten your brother. You are not really men, but bats, since only bats eat people. You are going to be Bat People (cashibo). As punishment you have to move to the headwaters of the Aguaytía River, where you have to live without clothes, or axes, or machetes." These were the first Cashibo.

The relation between earth and sky is often seen as a stairlike
connection. When under the influence of **ayahuasca** (Banisterium),
the shaman is able to ascend these stairs to heaven. The stairs
veer off in different directions at various points because of prevailing winds. There are several villages along the stairs, some
identified and described by the Shipibo, others merely numbered or
named, without further identification. The bottom step of this
stairway is about 2 m. from the ground and the shaman must leap up
in order to begin his journey.

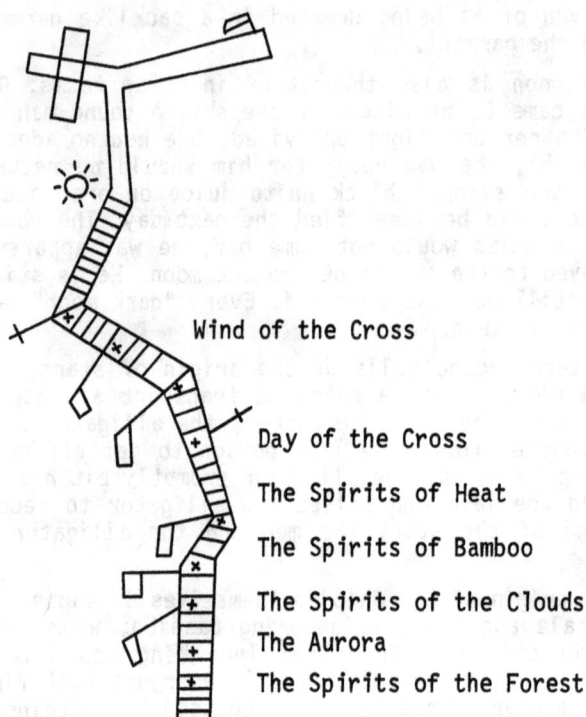

Wind of the Cross

Day of the Cross

The Spirits of Heat

The Spirits of Bamboo

The Spirits of the Clouds

The Aurora

The Spirits of the Forest

Figure 11. The Spirit Villages

The accompanying map drawn by Elas Sánchez (figure 11) lists
the various villages located along the stairs. The first is the
village of the jungle spirits. There are many such spirits since
every tree is represented by a separate spirit. The spirits of the
second village are not clearly distinguished from those of the
first. They also are jungle spirits, but are especially responsible for the coming of the dawn. The third is the village of
cloud spirits. After the third village the shaman's journey becomes dangerous. He must wear disguises in order to pass safely.
The village of bamboo spirits is apparently assigned a place of

prominence because bamboo was the principal source for knives prior to the introduction of metal. Some Shipibo believe that bamboo spirits cause hail. The spirits of heat are not identified with the sun, but they are responsible for creating heat on earth. The sun is located near the top of the stairs making this a dangerous place to pass. At the summit, which is sometimes identified as the place of God, one finds a cross and a flag. The shaman attempts to climb this far.

The Spirit World

In 1948 (Steward and Métraux), it was already difficult to separate Christian from indigenous ideas in the religion of the modern Shipibo. This is even more true today, more than a generation later. Girard (1958:249), for example, discusses the Shipibo **Ibo** 'owner,' a supreme being who created earth and heaven and now lives in the sky. It is very probable that this concept is now heavily influenced by Christian teaching.

Indigenous animistic beliefs, however, are still common. Central to Shipibo religion is the belief that both animate and inanimate objects have spirits that initiate and govern most natural phenomena. Some of the myths cited above indicate this relation between natural and supernatural, as does their concept of spirit villages along the stairs to the sky.

The Shipibo typically interpret meteorological phenomena in animate terms. An eclipse is thought to be caused by the sun closing his eyes, or putting on a black garment. The people then appeal to the sun to change back to his normal appearance. They interpret the occurrence of clouds appearing to be stationary or an unusual color as the design of an evil spirit intending to harm them. A whirlwind is a huge dancing demon who will attempt to snatch away the soul of a child. Thunder is interpreted as conversation between the souls of the dead. In one song, a dead man sings to his orphaned sister, telling her he is making thunder with his heels.

Likewise, each plant or tree is or has a spirit. A tree spirit, moreover, often has a human likeness. The **tsais ati** trees are said to resemble the Cashibo people, and the tree's crown is its hat. The mangrove tree consists of a number of small people or spirits, each wearing a robe. The spirit of the majestic **lupuna** tree (Ceiba) is the most powerful; when the spirits of the **catahua** (Erythroxylum or Hura crepitans) challenged those of the **lupuna**, they were defeated and imprisoned inside the **lupuna**. The **lupuna** spirit is said to have wings and in more contemporary versions rides a bicycle with wings. This spirit can be dangerous to man. Some believe that if touched by people, it becomes angry and causes rain. If the tree is struck and its seeds fall, the guilty person will

die. The **lupuna** spirit may also carry away the souls of children,
or bewitch grown men.

Among the most feared animal spirits are poisonous snakes, the
dolphin, and the water boa. These are regarded either as incarnations of a shaman or as his emissaries sent to attack people.
Snakebite, for example, is regarded as an indication of witch-
craft. The dolphin is especially dangerous to a menstruating woman
since the dolphin will attempt either to have relations with her
or to kill her.

Man's Spirit

Contemporary Shipibo beliefs about man's soul or spirit are not
easily summarized. It is difficult to derive a composite picture
from individuals who differ by age, village, Christian influence,
and so forth. To do justice to contemporary Shipibo beliefs, one
must acknowledge discrepancies in the data.

Various individuals list from one to four different spirits.
Most Shipibo today speak of man's soul (**caya**) as being in his
heart during life and as going to God (or the gods) upon death.
This belief seems to be of Christian origin, even though the term
for soul is Shipibo. Another noncorporeal entity is man's shadow
(**bei**), a spirit which accompanies man until death. After death
this spirit, now also called the death-spirit (**mahua yoshin**),
assumes a wandering existence. It may appear as a skeleton or in
the outward appearance of the deceased. It haunts the village or
home of relatives, or those against whom he held a grudge. After
several days or weeks it leaves to assume an existence of rather
indefinite wanderings. The Shipibo also recognize one or two spirits which reside in the eye (**bero-yoshin**). These also apparently
leave the body upon death. The further existence of these spirits
is usually not specified, although some Shipibo say that eye-
spirits go to the Incas.

Magical Plants

There are a number of magical plants, including a wide variety
of marsh plants of the sedge family (Cyperaceae) called **piripiri**.
The Shipibo do not always make a distinction between plants which
are curative and those which are magical, but **piripiri** plants are
given a special designation: they have potential beyond that of
other herbs, more like a magical charm, although some of their
uses are medicinal. A small but representative listing of **piripiri**
plants and their uses is presented in figure 12. For all these
uses, the tubers of the plants are first grated and then used in
the various ways described.

KIND	PURPOSE	USE
Dove	attract mate	sprinkle on body
Back-turn	repulse man or woman	mix with juice of diarrhea herb, paint on body
Oppossum	promote conception	mix with water, drink
Capybara	reduce birth pains	mix with water, drink on five successive afternoons a month before confinement
Snake hawk	avoid snakebite	rub gratings on body, carry some in bag or pocket
Bamboo	heal knife wound	sprinkle in wound
Rubbing	pacify enemy	rub on body
Hair	grow hair	mix with **huito,** drink daily for one week
Fat	get fat	mix with water, drink two portions

Figure 12. **Piripiri** plants and their uses.

7 MEDICINE

Medical Conditions

Among the Shipibo today, modern medicine is used frequently, while native treatments continue to be practiced widely as well. The mixture of the Western and indigenous traditions is seen, for example, when a Shipibo speaks of microbes which have been implanted by evil spirits, or when a patient alternates visits to a medical clinic with visits to the shaman. Western medicine and medicinal herbs are also frequently taken together. In the following description, the focus will be on indigenous medical practices. This emphasis, however, must not obscure the fact that most Shipibo are well aware of the benefits of modern medicine. Failure to make use of Western medicine is often due to lack of availability and finances rather than to mistrust.

Gastrointestinal diseases are the most common form of illness among the Shipibo, as they are for many other jungle peoples. The lack of sanitation, proper nutrition, and the drinking of unboiled water account for many intestinal ailments. Worms, amoebas, and other parasites have a general debilitating effect, and are also the cause for numerous complaints of abdominal pain. Diarrhea and vomiting are especially devastating for small children, who tend to become dehydrated in one or two days and often die as a result. Vomiting and diarrhea are very common during the rainy season, due to flooding and consequent deterioration of sanitary conditions.

A number of other ailments are also serious. Anemia is common, especially among women who have borne a large number of children and are lacking in adequate nutrition. Respiratory ailments range from the common cold and pneumonia to tuberculosis, which is prevalent. Tuberculosis is difficult to deal with because of the need for prolonged treatment and also because of a lack of understanding of the necessity of isolation. Skin diseases are most common during floods when people must wade through contaminated water, and tend to have closer contact with others. Eye infections are prevalent, but blindness is rare. Other physical

42

handicaps are also found. The Shipibo sometimes used to kill handicapped or deformed children at birth, but today they are kept and generally well cared for.

The people are afraid of some diseases, especially those which tend to be epidemic. If a case of whooping cough or measles is diagnosed, the people will often evacuate a village and live in temporary shelters in the jungle until the danger has passed.

Ethnomedicine

The Shipibo use a combination of dietary restrictions, medicinal herbs, and the practice of the shaman to combat disease. The entire family is very solicitous of a patient, attending to his needs, giving massages and preparing special foods during his confinement to his mosquito net.

Because Shipibo perceive a close relationship between food and illness, various food restrictions are enforced during sickness, either at the suggestion of the herb doctor or shaman, or as dictated by general tribal lore, including sympathetic magic. The patient observes a diet, but family members may also restrict their eating, since failure to do so might aggravate the illness. In one example of perceived transference, a woman attempted to send a message to her husband who was away from home, asking what he had eaten, because their small infant was having breathing difficulties.

Common prohibitions are sweet foods (such as sugar cane), salt, fat, and citrus fruits. The latter are forbidden because they are considered to have spines which are held responsible for many illnesses. (This fear of spines used to extend to fear of the hypodermic needle.) The general result of food restrictions is debilitating, since a patient often weakens further, because of insufficient nutrition.

A large number of curative herbs are used in illness. Some of these are cultivated, others grow wild in the jungle. At times, herbs are specifically prepared by an herb doctor, while many others are brewed at home and administered according to tribal medical lore. A representative selection of medicinal herbs is presented in figure 13.

Other homemade potions are also used, such as one concocted of cowhorn shavings. The horn shavings are boiled in water and administered to a vomiting child as a drink. For abdominal distress (gas), the treatment is more elaborate. Shavings are mixed with sealing wax and copal, and the mixture is wrapped in cotton. The cotton is then used to rub the child's body. The cotton is afterwards rolled up like a ball, and bounced on the floor. If bouncing produces a "pom pom" sound, it is an indication that the gas has left the child and is now in the ball.

ILLNESS	SHIPIBO NAME	SPANISH NAME	BOTANICAL NAME	PART OF PLANT USED	PREPARATION AND USE
malaria	**sananco**	sanango	Tabernaemontana sanango	root	grated, mixed with water, drunk; emetic
kidney, uri- nary tract	**boaí**	sacha ajo	Allium sativum		pounded; poultice
measles	**yoná rao**	lancetilla	Peperomia		emetic
stomach ache		chirisanango	Rauwolfia		emetic
		chahua			
	rosasisa	rosa-sisa	Tagetes erecta, Dahlia variabilis		crushed, drunk in **chapo**; purge
	paíco	paíco	Chenopodium		crushed, drunk in **chapo**; purge
		ajo sacha	Allium sativum		crushed, drunk in **chapo**; purge
vomiting		amasisa	Erythrina	sap	purge
intestinal parasites	**shomi**				
dysentery	**yoshin-jihui**	palo de sangre	Peltogyne		scrapings mixed with water, drunk; purge
fever	**yoná rao**	lancetilla	Peperomia	leaves	
headache	**hinintani nishi**	bejuco			shampoo
mange		limón	Citrus limon	juice	roast, mix with salt and apply to affected skin

Ailment	Name	Scientific name	Part	Preparation
sore eyes	caimito	Lucuma caimito	leaf	sap applied to eye
	guava	Inga edulis	bark	mixed with water, applied to eye
boils	**chaupi**			
	bejuco			poultice
	huito	Genipa americana		paint affected parts
	pan de árbol	Artocarpus communis Artocarpus incisa	sap	applied
	chuchu huasha	Heisteria pallida	bark	
skin irritations	verbena	Verbena		grated, baked, poultice
sprains	pan de árbol	Artocarpus communis, Artocarpus incisa	sap	
rheumatism	copaiba	Copaifera		
	kapeten raonishi bejuco			
		Sanchezia	stem, leaves	boiled; patient takes steambath and bathes in mixture
snake bite	piripiri	Cyperaceae	juice	drink
grippe	limón	Citrus limon	juice	drink
	llantén	Plantago major	leaves	pounded, juice mixed in **chapo**; drunk
sexual impotence	huayusa	Ilex guayusa	leaves	boiled and drunk

Figure 14. Medicinal Plants Used by the Shipibo

Nettles are also used for curing purposes; when a person has body pain, the nettles are passed over the affected part (but never the head) several times.

The role of the shaman is not as significant as it once was, but there are still a relatively large number of Shipibo shamans. The work of the shaman, whose power is spiritual, is often distinguished from that of the herb doctor, who relies on herbs. In some cases, however, the two roles merge and the same healer may use herbs and seek help from the spirit world via the hallucinogenic **ayahuasca.** There are also sorcerers, or evil shamans, who have supernatural power, but always use it to cause illness or death.

If a patient's illness defies the medical knowledge of his family, they may take him to a shaman. The shaman will attempt a healing unless he discovers that the illness is caused by another shaman who has much greater power, or if the patient is suffering from a white man's disease.

An important aspect of the shaman's healing is his use of **ayahuasca.** The **ayahuasca** vine is chopped into small pieces and boiled for an entire day, resulting in an orange-black brew. The shaman drinks one or two cups to induce a trance, which begins in about one hour. He may continue to drink during the healing session, thus prolonging the trance for hours. In his trance he sees animals, people, and spirits, in distorted, grotesque forms. When the spirits ask the shaman what he wants, he responds with a request about the nature of the illness.

The shaman usually begins the healing session by cracking his knuckles, rubbing his hands and blowing smoke over them. Later he blows smoke over the patient, or swishes him with nettles in order to drive out the illness. The treatment is accompanied by a sing-song commentary in which the shaman explains the treatment, such as, "A big wind is coming to take away your fever." The treatment usually ends with the shaman sucking on the affected part of the body. When it is believed that another shaman may have caused the illness by sending "darts" or other objects, such as pebbles or pieces of glass, the cure is sought by sucking out these objects. At other times the treatment is conceived in terms of a struggle for the patient's soul. A sorcerer has taken away the patient's soul, evidenced by the patient's lassitude, and then the healer attempts to wrest the soul from the evil shaman.

Western Medicine

The National Department of Health, the Hospital Amazónico in Puerto Callao, and the medical department of the Summer Institute of Linguistics in Peru have been supplying medical care to the Shipibo people for a number of years.

Mass inoculations are an imporant part of the health program. Most Shipibo villages have had inoculations against smallpox, DPT, and measles; there have been more limited vaccination programs against yellow fever and tuberculosis.

Another area of the health program has been the training of native health workers. The health workers seek to improve sanitary conditions and to teach nutritional principles, thus fostering preventive health care. They are also trained to diagnose and treat many common illnesses and to administer vaccinations.

8 LIFE CYCLE

Pregnancy and Childbirth

The Shipibo recognize the relation between sexual intercourse and conception. One individual interpreted the reproductive process as follows: The woman has a series of eggs which are waiting for the man. Menstruation has no relation to the eggs; each egg waits its turn until it is fertilized, and then the next egg in the series is ready. At menopause all the eggs are used; so the woman cannot bear more children. A couple does not engage in intercourse during menstruation, the last three months of pregnancy, or the first three months after childbirth.

The cessation of menses is recognized as an indication of pregnancy. During pregnancy the woman is excused from heavy work in the field, but continues all other activities.

Various food taboos are observed during pregnancy. Many of these are restrictions against eating large animals, including tapir and deer, but not peccary, lest the fetus become too large. Monkeys are taboo, except for the spider monkey. **Paiche** (Arapaima gigas) and large land turtles, such as the **charapa** (Podocnemis expansa) are also forbidden. The man is often prohibited from hunting or fishing these animals.

There are also nonmeat taboos. Eating pineapple is believed to cause excessive bleeding during labor. Older taboos included cassava, taro (Colocasia), yam (Dioscorea), and avocado (Persea), all of which were believed to cause birth complications.

The most common method of birth control is through the use of a variety of plants (see magical plants), one of which has been identified by Nicole Maxwell (private communication) as Cyperur corymbosis. The sedge root is grated and mixed with water; a woman takes a cupful at intervals of two or three days for about three weeks. While taking the **piripiri**, she cannot tolerate turtle or fatty foods which cause diarrhea and vomiting. Others use boiled lemon: some of the juice is drunk, and some is absorbed into

48

cotton which is pushed into the vaginal tract. Married women do not often seek to induce abortion, but an unmarried girl may attempt abortion by asking another woman to squeeze her abdomen. **Piripiri** and other birth control methods do not appear to be very effective, however, since most women bear more children than they wish. Those who have more contact with the outside world are eager to discover western birth control methods.

If a woman has taken **piripiri** and does seem to be sterile, but then wishes to become fertile again, she has recourse to a number of remedies. One involves eating ground oppossum tooth mixed with honey.

Childbirth formerly took place away from the house in the jungle, sometimes in a hastily constructed shelter, often in the open. Today most women give birth at home, in or very near to the house. Several women usually assist with the birth, including the woman's mother and other relatives. Occasionally the husband is present as well. A woman gives birth in a slightly elevated sitting position, sometimes on a few boards. She grasps a rope or something overhead while one woman presses on her abdomen as labor progresses and pains increase in intensity.

Upon birth the umbilical cord is tied with cotton thread. The cord was traditionally cut with a bamboo knife, but today it is cut with whatever cutting tool is available, such as a pair of scissors or a razor blade. The cord and placenta are usually buried, although some Shipibo throw them out, since they fear that burial might forecast the imminent burial of the baby. The baby is washed with lukewarm water.

At one time the Shipibo blackened their babies with **huito** soon after birth; by the time the **huito** had worn off, the baby's skin would seem new and clean. The custom of painting black spots and bands on various parts of the baby's body, apparently for beautification, still survives.

Both parents observe food taboos for several months after a baby's birth. Most of these are to prevent the effects of sympathetic magic on the baby's health. Tapir, large fish, beef, and pork are avoided because the eating of them would cause the baby to have diarrhea. Similarly, eating armadillo is thought to cause whooping cough; white monkey, anemia; noodles, worms; pineapple, skin infections; papaya, eye infections. Likewise, the father abstains from hunting; killing tiger, otter (Lutra felina), or the poisonous fer-de-lance (Bothrops atrox) causes the child to have diarrhea.

Other restrictions are also observed. A mother is normally excused from all her chores for a week after the birth, and from heavy work for some time after that. A father limits his activities from two weeks. He does not hunt, engage in heavy labor, or use heavy tools, and restricts his fishing to the use of hook and line. A contemporary taboo forbids the father to play soccer during these weeks, since it is believed the baby's abdomen might swell up like a ball.

Often a baby is given a temporary name immediately after birth. The Shipibo fear that if a name is not given at once, the devil will name the child. The devil will then have control over the child, call his name, and perhaps cause the baby to die. Another name is sometimes chosen in about a week, since it is felt that the child now has a reasonable chance for survival. Both names are often the names of relatives or godparents. The child is not called by his name, rather he is called **chaqui** (little child).

Infanticide is apparently still practiced occasionally by the Shipibo, but is done more surreptitiously than it once was. Traditionally, malformed children and one or both of a set of twins might be buried alive immediately after birth, since twins were considered to be children of the devil. Illegitimate children were also frequently disposed of, and that practice is still occasionally found today.

Childhood

Children are nursed for about eighteen months. If the mother must for some reason be temporarily absent, another nursing relative will suckle the child. In order to wean a child, the mother absents herself for one or two days. If a child continues to insist on nursing, she may put hot pepper on her nipples to discourage him. Ripe bananas are sometimes added to the diet when a child is one month old, and as he gets older, he begins to eat portions of adult food.

A child spends much time with his mother until he can walk. He sleeps with her at night, and during the day is often carried in a sling on her hip. But when a mother's activities prevent her from attending to her child, a grandmother or one of the older siblings watches him or carries him around. It is not unusual to see a seven- or eight-year-old expertly carry an infant in a sling. At nap times a child will be in a small hammock which the mother swings from a distance by means of an attached rope. Bars are sometimes placed horizontally in the house to aid a child in learning to walk and to confine him within a certain area.

At two or three years of age, a child is allowed to roam in the area around the house, although both parents and older siblings continue to watch him closely. Tools and open fires are a constant danger, but there are relatively few mishaps, since the child soon learns to avoid these dangers. A child's crying is often ignored, as are his temper tantrums. Disciplining does not seem to follow any established pattern. Since a child's restrictions are relatively few, there is little occasion for punishment. If a child is disobedient, he may be struck with nettles; or if a parent becomes very angry, the child may receive a sound switching with nettles.

At one time informal instruction formed an important part of a child's life. Boys especially were given careful instruction by their father or grandfather in various practical skills. They learned how to fell a tree and shape a canoe, how to make bows and arrows, how to construct a house. Today, when many of the children spend a large part of the day in school, and many men work away from home, this instruction is much less common. Much learning, however, continues to be by informal observation and imitation. Girls learn how to string beads and make pottery by working alongside their mothers. As they grow older, they are given more responsibility in cooking and working in the garden. Boys spend endless hours fishing, either from the shore or from a canoe, and helping with men's chores. They begin to accompany the men on hunting trips at about age ten.

Children's games are often imitations of typical adult activities. Girls cook on small fires or play with homemade dolls; boys hunt lizards with bow and arrow. Hide-and-seek is popular, as are a number of games and toys introduced from western culture, including stilts and tops.

Formal Education

In addition to traditional ways of educating children, the Shipibo have also had access to formal education for many years. Catholic missions have often had schools, conducted in Spanish, as did some Protestant missions; and patrones have occasionally hired teachers as well.

The largest school system today among the Shipibo-Conibo, however, is the Bilingual School Program of the Ministry of Education. In 1984, there were approximately 69 schools and 72 teachers. Six years of primary education are provided in most schools, usually by a single teacher. The Shipibo are interested in formal education for their children, and many more communities have made application for a school. In years past, some communities erected a school building in advance, waiting for a teacher. School buildings are typically constructed by the people in the same manner as their homes, from materials available in the jungle.

A fundamental aspect of these bilingual schools is implied in the name: most instruction is given in Shipibo in the first years, with progressively more Spanish each year until by the last year of primary school the child receives instruction primarily in Spanish. Since many reading experts now agree that it is virtually impossible to learn to read for the first time with understanding in a language which one neither understands or speaks, the child is taught to read in Shipibo first. At the same time, the child is taught Spanish as a second language, and as he becomes more proficient, he is able to read Spanish and receive instruction in other subjects as well in his second language.

The same principle of proceeding from the known to the unknown is applied to other aspects of the school. Social studies and science texts begin with a description of the jungle environment, and then the student is introduced to the larger world. Arithmetic is first taught through counting exercises and mathematical problems based on village situations.

The role of the teacher in the bilingual school is significant. He too is a Shipibo and understands the student's home and community situation, as well as his language. A student does not have to deny or be ashamed of his culture.

The teacher is also trained in Spanish, and he has received education that has brought him into contact with the national culture and the outside world in general. For several years he spends his annual vacation in government courses for bilingual teachers at the Ministry of Education Training Center in Yarinacocha. The teacher is, therefore, a link between old and new, and the school becomes a bridge between Shipibo life and the national culture.

Puberty

Puberty rites for boys are not practiced among the Shipibo. Their teen years were apparently never marked by any dramatic changes. They gained skills gradually and assumed more and more responsibility until they were considered old enough to be married.

Puberty rites for girls, however, were conducted soon after the first menstruation, as preparation for marriage. After the girl had been tired out from dancing and stupefied with drink, she was subjected to a genital subincision, which involved the penetration of the hymen and in many cases included a clitorectomy or labioectomy. The operation was performed by one of the older women, using a bamboo knife. Excessive bleeding and infection were counteracted by applying a piripiri solution. The girl was subsequently isolated in a little hut until her wound had healed.

The girl's hair-cutting ceremony is still carried on today, though becoming less common. It is not clear whether it was earlier performed in association with subincision, or if it supplanted that rite. Prior to the haircutting ceremony, a girl does not cut her bangs for up to two years, permitting her hair to become long all over. During the ceremony, one of the older women cuts the girl's bangs in the manner described under Attire.

The rites were accompanied by a public celebration for which preparations were made months in advance. Festive clothes were prepared as well as a plentiful supply of food and **masato**. A peccary or other animal was raised to be killed at the feast. The festival lasted several days and often included **hueshati** knife fights described under Offenses and Sanctions.

Marriage Preparations

Marriage patterns among the Shipibo are not completely uniform. Customs vary from village to village and from family to family, but the following description is typical for many families.

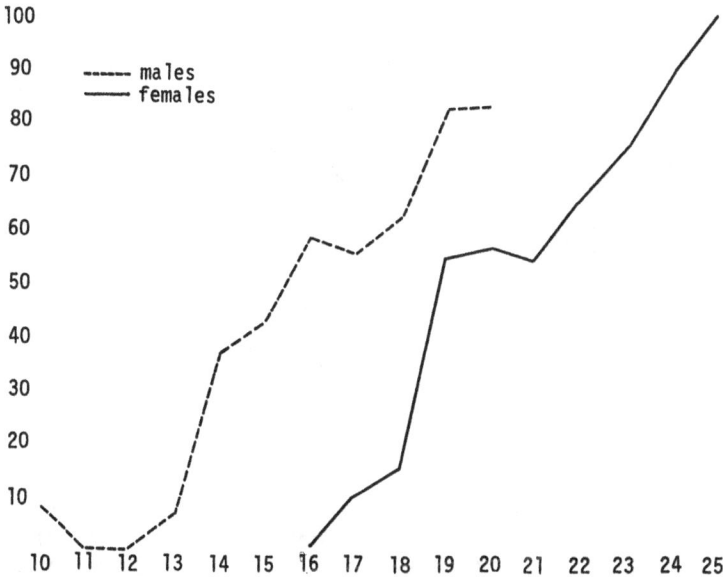

Figure 14. Percentage of Population Already
Married at Time of Survey

Formerly, a girl two or three years of age might be promised for marriage and might be made to live with her husband as early as age seven or eight. Today, child marriages are rare, and most girls marry between the ages of fourteen and sixteen, although a few marry as early as eleven or twelve. The marriage age for young men covers a wider spread, and may be anywhere from seventeen to thirty with the nineteen to twenty-five bracket as the most common. Figure 15 charts a survey of 349 people showing the ages and percentages of 163 males and 186 females already married. The percentage of various age groups already married of the population surveyed is also recorded in figure 14.

Some marriages are arranged without consulting the wishes of the young people, but more often their preferences are considered. Although an older man may approach a girl's father directly to propose marriage, it is customary for the two fathers to discuss any potential marriage, partly because they are more fully aware of kinship relations.

The discussions which take place at the young man's home and last two or three evenings, cover the suitability of the couple, but the meeting is also a ritual performance. The boy's father engages in a formalized apology for his son's lack of ability.

"My son doesn't know how to hunt, or build a house, or plant a garden."

The girl's father may reciprocate with a catalog of his daughter's failings. At a certain point in the discussion the girl's father says:

"I'm like your son. We're all alike, and I'm going to give my daughter to him."

On a succeeding night, however, the father praises his son and suggests to the girl's father that he look elsewhere for a husband. At the conclusion of the talks, usually at the third meeting, the fathers reach an agreement about the proposed marriage. The young man is called in and he modestly expresses his own unworthiness, until his father says, "He at least can help you to close the chicken coop at night," or some similar minor task. At this they all laugh and conclude the proceedings by eating and drinking together.

The girl's mother participates in the marriage preparations by making two special earthenware dishes: a **quencha** for serving cooked bananas and fish, and a **quempo** for the **chapo** drink. There is no elaborate wedding ceremony as such. The girl puts on her new clothes and takes the food to the young man at his home. If her friends are near, they eat the food with him. The girl, who has been watching from a distance, then gathers up the dishes and carries them back to her home. Later, the girl's mother fetches the young man's mosquito net to the girl's home. This is the last step before the young man sleeps with the girl and becomes part of her household. In some villages, a wedding celebration is held. A young man will often sleep with his new wife, but continue to spend most of the day away from her house, since he does not as yet feel at home there.

Soon after the marriage the couple exchange gifts. The husband may make a bronze ring or a spindle; the wife, a wide bead bracelet or a woven belt and a flowered handkerchief. The parents may also offer gifts. The young man often receives hunting weapons from his father-in-law, and the girl, cooking utensils from her parents-in-law. Sometimes the sets of parents exchange food gifts as well.

Married Life

A couple continues in matrilocal residence for an indefinite period. Some couples build their own home in a matter of months, while others may continue to live with the woman's parents for a number of years depending upon available space, number of children in the house, and domestic tranquility or the lack of it. When a couple moves into their own house, it is usually near that of the wife's parents.

Since the young man is considered part of his parents-in-law's household, he must contribute to it by his work. He hunts with his father-in-law and works in the family garden. This service continues even after the couple has moved into their own home. They also continue to eat their meals with the family.

The conduct of the son-in-law is further circumscribed by an avoidance code. He may not address his parents-in-law directly, nor may they speak directly to him. All such communication is conducted through his wife or another intermediary. If there is need for conversation when no one else is present, the son-in-law speaks as though his wife were present, directing his remarks to her, and the parent-in-law responds in the same manner. The wife has no such restrictions with her husband's parents.

Polygamy used to be more widespread than it is today, but apparently it was never universal. It has virtually disappeared among the Shipibo along the Ucayali, but is more common in villages like those on the Pisqui and Aguaytía rivers which have less contact with the outside. Even there, multiple marriage is usually limited to two wives; very rarely does one encounter a man with three. Polygamy is nearly always sororal, and co-wives tend to live in separate but neighboring houses. In other cases, they may occupy the same sleeping house but have separate cooking houses.

Termination of Marriage

A marriage is terminated without ceremony. If a man decides to end his marriage, he simply moves out, usually to take up residence with another woman. A wife can take the initiative by forcing her husband to move out, by moving in with one of her relatives, or by running off with another man. If the woman is young, her parents may take her back into the parental home, or, if the couple still lives with the parents, they may force the husband to leave.

A Shipibo man may separate from his wife if she refuses to prepare food for him or wash his clothes, or if she generally neglects her wifely duties. Continual ill temper and quarrelsomeness are also sufficient cause. Adultery may sometimes occasion separation, but more often the husband will take revenge on the woman's lover (as discussed under Offences and Sanctions). Another reason for separation is the failure to bear girls, since a husband does not relish the thought of old age without the support of sons-in-law. A husband may also be lured away by a more attractive or personable woman.

A Shipibo woman claims the right to separation if her husband mistreats her physically or if he fails to perform his work. Adultery is again a potential reason, but the wife too may prefer vengeance on the other woman, usually in a hair-pulling fight, especially if the husband is a good provider and if the adultery is incidental.

Death

The Shipibo recognize both natural and supernatural causes of death. Natural causes are old age, injury, or disease, especially when contagious. Death, however, is more often ascribed to the spirit world or the power of a shaman.

The approach of death is recognized when a person refuses food or if his physical functions become greatly impaired. Or a patient may dream that he loses all his hair, and this dream is considered an indication of impending death. Death omens include the call of a certain bird, the gurgling sound of a fox's stomach, or a dog burying sticks in the ground. When death seems imminent, family members may enter the mosquito net, both to give relief to the patient by massaging and to cry and wail.

Relatives are called to the house when it seems certain their kinsman will die. Both men and women cry loudly just before and after a family member dies. A mother or wife especially expresses her grief in loud wailing, continuing throughout most of a day.

A widow observes one year of mourning when her husband dies. Another widow cuts her hair to about one-half inch in length, and bathes during the night. The couple's mosquito net is cut in half. The deceased is wrapped for burial in one half, and the other half is used by the bereaved woman to make a skirt and blouse to wear during her year of mourning. A widower may follow a similar pattern in having his hair cut and being bathed during the night by an elderly widow.

The Shipibo may have buried their dead in urns at one time, since such urns have been excavated along the Ucayali; but apparently this has not been practiced in the past century. Graves are now used for burial.

The body of a deceased person is dressed in his or her finest clothing and wrapped in a mosquito net as indicated above. The face is sometimes painted with the customary geometric designs (figure 16). The body is placed either in a coffin or in an old canoe supplied with a covering.

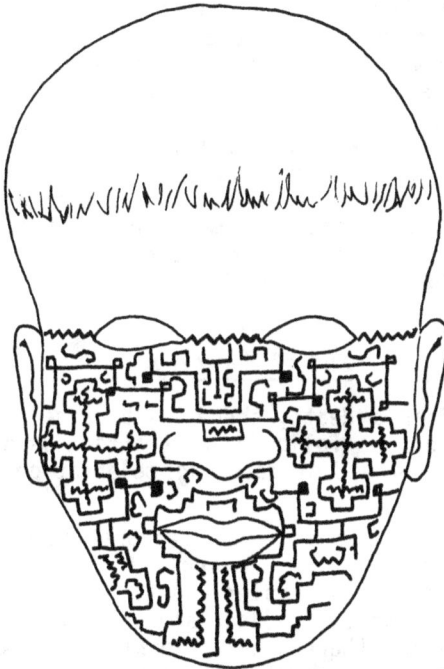

Figure 15. Face Painting of the Deceased

Colors used for designs:
——   black
ᵐᵐᵐ   red
□   blue, red, and green

Burial takes place on the day of death or, more often, the next day. Male family members other than the father carry the body of a small child to the cemetery. There the coffin is lowered into the grave and a number of personal belongings may be added before it is covered with dirt by all present. Ashes are strewn over the grave so that any trace of footprints will be evident should the spirit of the deceased walk there. A cross is now often placed at the head of a grave. The family sometimes erects a roof of palm leaves to protect the grave from rain. This roof is repaired or replaced later, usually during a subsequent funeral.

As mentioned before, survivors dispose of most of a person's belongings either by burial with the body, burning, discarding, or by selling expensive items. Traditionally, the house was burned when a man died; but since building materials have become very scarce, some families now continue to occupy the house.

Beliefs about spirits and souls have already been discussed. It should be repeated, however, that although there is a belief that man's soul enters a nonearthly afterlife, the death spirit may haunt the grave or village areas for some time. Footprints in the ashes spread over a grave indicate that the spirit is near, and men will sometimes stand guard to shoot at it. The spirit may return to the house where the family is staying and pull on someone's mosquito net or throw mud balls at the house. If the spirit persists in haunting a house, the help of a shaman will be secured or the people themselves may sing an incantation in the night. Even the spirit of a loved one changes at death to something evil and bothersome to the living.

End of Mourning

About a year after a death, there may be a celebration to mark the end of mourning. The following description is based on Lauriault's notes about an end-of-mourning celebration on January 1, 1950:

"We were invited to come to the celebration of Lucila's end-of-mourning at seven a.m. When we arrived, the house was already full of relatives and other invited guests. More were arriving and the chief went out into the village street to await new arrivals. In front of the house there were several grass mats upon which guests piled their gifts--drinking bowls, a white painted skirt with a jungle seed fringe, a painted shawl, coin necklaces, monkey-teeth bracelets, a **cushma**, and many other items. Bowls of **masato** were passed around, and everyone drank freely. Soon the chief arrived with about twenty more guests, and now there were well over seventy-five people present. The men stood around in clusters, while the women, much more solemn, sat down together.

"Juana, who was to perform the ceremony, put on an old shawl over her clothes and sat down on one of the mats. Then Lucila came out, dressed in old clothes, and sat down in front of Juana.

"Juana began the ornamentation process by putting newly-woven ankle bands on Lucila, followed by several bracelets on each wrist, two beaded and one consisting of four rows of monkey teeth. A silver nosepiece was hung from her septum, and bead-and-seed ear pendants were hung from each ear. Last of all, a multiple necklace of large beads and several rows of silver coins was added.

"Then Juana combed Lucila's hair. Parting it across the head, with the hair hanging in long strands over the face, Juana carefully cut Lucila's bangs from ear to ear. When Juana began to comb the hair, a chorus of four women set up a plaintive chant which they continued until the conclusion of the ceremony.

"Next, Juana painted geometric designs on Lucila's lower legs with annatto, while another woman painted Lucila's face and inserted a silver ornament in her lower lip.

"Now the women helped Lucila to take off her old clothes and put on new ones. She received a new blouse, a skirt, and a white shawl.

ucila, who had sat through the whole ceremony with downcast eyes, smiling slightly from time to time, now became more animated. Then the general solemnity began to give way to lively conversation, and all the onlookers again helped themselves to **masato.**

"When the chief decided the celebration had lasted long enough, he spoke a brief word. The **masato** bowls were returned and divided among the women who had in some way participated in the celebration. The people dispersed, and Lucila arose and went into the house."

Remarriage

A widow or widower waits a year before remarriage because an earlier marriage would endanger the life of the new spouse. By this time a widow's hair has grown out; she is allowed to wear regular clothes and jewelry, and is eligible to remarry.

Remarriage does not normally involve the deliberation of fathers, although a relative is usually asked to serve as intermediary. In the case of an older widow, the intermediary may even be her grown son. If a new husband is willing to keep the children from an earlier marriage, they may stay with their mother; more often, however, these children are raised by grandparents, another family, or by a childless couple of the village.

REFERENCES

Bergman, Roland Wallace. 1974. Shipibo subsistence in the upper Amazon rainforest. Ph.D. dissertation, Univ. of Wisconsin.

Bradfield, R.B. and J. Lauriault (Loriot). 1961. Diet and food beliefs of Peruvian jungle tribes. Journal of the American Dietetic Association 9:126-28.

Carrasco, Francisco. 1901. Principales palabras del idioma de las cuatro tribus infieles: antis, piros, conibos y shipibos. Boletín de la Sociedad Geográfica de Lima 11:205-11.

Chirif Tirado, Alberto, Carlos Mora Bernasconi, and Roque Moscoso Miranda. 1977. Los Shipibo-Conibo del Ucayali: Diagnóstico Socio-económico. Unidad de Apoyo a las Comunidades Nativas, SINAMOS.

Eakin, Lucille, Erwin Lauriault and Harry Boonstra. 1980. Bosquejo etnográfico de los shipibo-conibo del Ucayali. Lima: Prado Pastor.

Faust, Norma. 1973. Lecciones para el aprendizaje del idioma shipibo-conibo. (Documento de Trabajo No. 1) Lima: Instituto Lingüístico de Verano.

Farrier, Robert L. 1970. The Inca Tupu and the Shipibo Indians. Bulletin de la Société des Américanistes. 450-58.

Girard, Rafael. 1958. Los shipibo. In Indios selváticos de la Amazonía Peruana. Mexico: Libro Mex. Pp. 231-62.

Hoffman, Hans. 1964. Money, ecology, and acculturation among the Shipibos of Peru. In Explorations in cultural anthropology, ed. by W.H. Goodenough. New York: McGraw-hill. Pp. 259-76.

Izaguirre, Bernardino. 1922. Historia de las misiones franciscanas y narración de los progresos de la geografía en el oriente del Perú 1619-1921. (14 volumes)

Karsten, Raphael. 1955. Los indios shipibo del río Ucayali. Revista del Museo Nacional 24:154-73.

Lathrap, Donald W. 1970. The upper Amazon. In Ancient peoples and places. Vol. 70. Thames and Hudson.

Lauriault, James. 1948. Alternate-mora timing in Shipibo. International Journal of American Linguistics 14:22-24.

———.1954. ¿Solamente una cueva o un hallazgo arqueolóogico en el río Ucayali? Perú Indígena 5.13:179-80.

——— and Barbara Hollenbach. 1970. Shipibo paragraph structure. Foundations of Language 6:43-66.

Loos, Eugene E. 1969. The phonology of Capanahua and its grammatical basis. (SIL Publications in Linguistics and Related Fields 20). Norman: Summer Institute of Linguistics of the Univ. of Oklahoma.

McQuown, Norman A. 1955. Indigenous languages of Latin America. American Anthropologist 57:501-70.

Merrifield, William R. 1981. Proto Otomanguean Kinship. (IMC Publication 11) Dallas: International Museum of Cultures.

———. 1983. On the formal analysis of kinship terminologies. In Essays in Honor of Charles F. Hockett, ed. by Frederick B. Agard and others. Leiden: Brill. Pp. 371-405.

Murdock, George Peter. 1970. Kin terms, patterns, and their distribution. Ethnology 9:165-207.

Myers, Thomas P. 1972. Sarayacu: Archaeological investigations at a 19th century Franciscan mission in the Peruvian montaña. Actas y Memorias del XXXIX Congreso Internacional de Americanistas 4:25-37.

Steward, Julian H. and Alfred Métraux. 1948. Tribes of the Peruvian and Ecuadorian montaña. Handbook of South American Indians, ed. by Julian H. Steward. Bulletin of the Bureau of American Ethnology 143.3:535-656.

Tessmann, Gunter. 1928. Menschen ohne Gott: Ein Besuch bei den Indianern des Ucayali. Stuttgart: Strecker und Schroder.

Trujillo Ferrari, Alfonso. 1955. Desorganización tribal de los pano del medio Ucayali. XXXI Congreso Internacional de Americanistas 63-72.

Tschopik, Harry, Jr. 1958. Shipibo kinship terms. American Anthropologist 60:937-39.

Villarejo, P. Avencio. 1959. La selva y el hombre. Lima: Editorial Ausonia.

REGENERATING
the FEMININE

PSYCHE, CULTURE, and NATURE

APRIL C. HEASLIP

FOREWORD BY

DENNIS PATRICK SLATTERY

UNIVERSITY PRESS OF MISSISSIPPI / JACKSON

The University Press of Mississippi is the scholarly publishing agency of the Mississippi Institutions of Higher Learning: Alcorn State University, Delta State University, Jackson State University, Mississippi State University, Mississippi University for Women, Mississippi Valley State University, University of Mississippi, and University of Southern Mississippi.

Odilon Redon's *Envocation of Butterflies* image courtesy of incamerastock / Alamy Stock Photo

www.upress.state.ms.us

The University Press of Mississippi is a member of the Association of University Presses.

Publisher: University Press of Mississippi, Jackson, USA
Authorised GPSR Safety Representative: Easy Access System Europe - Mustamäe tee 50, 10621 Tallinn, Estonia, *gpsr.requests@easproject.com*

Library of Congress Control Number: 2025015496

Hardback ISBN 9781496856951 | Paperback ISBN 9781496856968
Epub single ISBN 9781496856975 | Epub institutional ISBN 9781496856982
PDF single ISBN 9781496856999 | PDF institutional ISBN 9781496857002

British Library Cataloging-in-Publication Data available

For those who swooped in
with perfect timing,

especially
my circle of women
&
the remarkable healers of the 11th Floor
of
Mass Eye & Ear.

Your generous, loving, regenerative
connective tissue
made all the difference.

In memory of
Walter Odajnyk & Deldon Anne McNeely,
mighty souls who have gone ahead.

CONTENTS

ACKNOWLEDGMENTS

Creative work is a group effort; though my name is on the cover, this book is infused with invaluable support of many folks over time. From shared resources to flourishing ideas and soul connections, this study emerges from complex, sustaining matrices. I hope to match the generosity I've received in gratitude.

The wonderful folks of University Press of Mississippi have created a mighty and intimate feminist press; it has made all the difference. Special thanks to director Craig Gill for his mythic call to adventure. I'm extremely grateful to my marvelous editor, Lisa McMurtray, whose capacity to hold the long view with me—spaciously, with emotional intelligence—has been invaluable. The entire team has been remarkably supportive, including Cassie Winship for the stunning cover and book design. I am especially grateful for the excellent work of Lisa Williams and Corley Longmire, who walked with me through the editing process, gracefully and vulnerably, embodying core teachings central to this study.

When I began this research on regeneration, I never imagined it would be such an embodied act, including surviving "terminal" throat cancer. I received support on all levels; I am writing the details in my forthcoming memoir. And this book would also not be here without many amazing humans—from lifelong friends to strangers who became dear companions.

The same disease caused the death of two scholars central to my journey—cherished professor Walter Odajnyk (who died suddenly during my final semester of doctoral studies) and our founding cultural mythologist, Joseph Campbell. Regaining my voice has also been an act of devotion on behalf of their love of myth and trust in the regenerative capacity of the quest.

My regenerative capacity was directly informed by the revitalizing practices I discuss here, giving me essential, somatic purchase. I was able to regenerate via the remarkably generous connective tissue offered by many folks in myriad ways. They arrived with impeccable timing and open and curious stances, tirelessly asking the priceless question, "How can I help?"

Though I don't discuss my health overtly in the book—both because it was so near completion at the time of my diagnosis and treatment and because it (curiously) wanted to retain its original shape—several sections poignantly signaled upcoming necessary healing. Three specific elements I'd written about erupted in my life—the bricolaged scars of cancer survivors, the loss of (my singing) voice, and how typing can be an embodied dialogue between brain hemispheres. My body is now a bricolaged wonder, with my new throat crafted from my leg tissue. Losing my voice box (and voice) meant my communication suddenly depends upon writing (and often typing for speed and sharing). Synchronicity was at play, foreshadowing.

An unfathomably powerful circle of support formed out of the ethers and offered relentless support. Enormous gratitude to the mighty women: Alexandra Dragin, Laurie Larsen, Ailie Ham, Susan McDormand, Jamie Nash, Jenny Wood, Kim Wheeter, Betsy Casey, Anne Comitta Ragusin, Kris Seraphine, Clara Oropeza, Julia Jean (Aditi Devi), Daniela Foltran Lagazzi, Mérys Gonzaga, Elenita Faria Lopes, Giselle Dalgé, Meara Baldwin, and Stephanie Goley (and the entire Goley family, including Christi Poore). Their generosity does not fit on any page or within any words.

My beloved family has been invaluable, including my nieces Guinevere Duli and Caitlin Millat, "brother-in-the-law" Nick Duli, and my most extraordinary sister and sometime twin—Sandy Heaslip Duli. I have an astonishing network of extended, chosen family, both in the US and in Brazil. The Comittas, Villelas, Slatterys, and Foltran-Lagazzis all live in my heart.

I've been fortunate to receive extraordinary professional and personal mentoring throughout my life. I wouldn't be here without my three phenomenal long-term mentors, Carolyn Comitta, Gail Morrison, and Dennis Slattery; these treasured teachers have become my constructed kin. What a joy to have such incredible elders in my life. Here I also bow deeply to Sid Reger, Donna Read, Del McNeely, and Patrick Mahaffey. May we acknowledge and pay our respect to our wise and loving elders—past, present, and emerging—who hold and honor memory, tradition, and culture.

Early support from the remarkable Tatyana Yassukovich and Lili Pierrepont proved invaluably sustaining and was foundational to the project, as well as my sanity. Many, many more folks stepped in and up with practical support, including Beth Girshman, Tim Menerey, Mark Brimhall-Vargas, Joe Kaufman, and Mark Kelly. I thank you all, deeply. Thank you to Sylvia Gilbertson and Camillo Castelnuevo for your timely, generous hospitality during these final steps.

So many healers helped in myriad ways! I want to remember them all and apologize for not knowing all their names; they all made a remarkable impact on me. Thanks to the invaluable Cape Wellness Collaborative, and Sarah Beals (a stellar woman), who magically massaged my body back together, somehow reoxygenating me cell by cell. Karen O'Brien and Patricia Vesey-McGrew generously jumped in. Massachusetts General Hospital and Mass Eye & Ear are staffed with extraordinary humans—nurses, staff, residents, physicians— patient healers all. I want to celebrate the women who washed my hair and held my hand. Jude Weinstein-Jones and Camille Mitjans lent me their voices. I'm especially glad for Lipi Marion's fine company; she has walked me through the endocrinology maze with such warm compassion and humor!

Finally, we come to Allen Feng—the dazzling surgeon who stepped up when I was suddenly dying and operating seemed impossible. How can I possibly do justice to the magnitude of how this man's skill and courage has supported my life? Allen's radiance comes from within; he gracefully walks with me through the tough questions, and the challenging times. May we all find such support through the dark.

I extend my gratitude out from the personal to *communitas* and our place in the natural world, as this book is grounded in these three interconnected realms. I have benefited greatly from ancestral support and indigenous wisdom across many lands and customs. This book was written over time and in many places, and I am grateful to the traditional peoples of the stunning landscapes where I have lived and traveled while writing, including Santa Barbara County, California; Southern Vermont; Southeastern Pennsylvania; São Paulo state and Rio Grande do Sul, Brazil; Black Mountain, North Carolina; Western Massachusetts; Cape Cod; and Lecco Province, Italy. I pay my respect to all First Nations peoples, traditional custodians of the land.

As the recipient of bounty from both culture and Nature, I note my special, indescribable debt to the many animal companions I've been fortunate to live with. We are deeply interconnected with the life-giving forces of this remarkable planet; as we move about and live our lives, wherever we are, may we honor Her and recognize our identity and responsibilities *within* Nature.

FOREWORD

DENNIS PATRICK SLATTERY

If a myth is organic and alive, then it is resilient enough to withstand revisions and renewals. April Heaslip's original and persuasive study of Mary Magdalene as she embodies the feminine is such an image that undergirds an entire mythology of nature, psyche, and culture currently enjoying a radical regeneration.

Her methodology or, better said, her mythology, is depth psychological, historical, multidisciplinary and creative. One of her favorite images is bricolage, the "craft of creating beautiful and functional art by piecing together what is at hand, constructed from shattered fragments of what came before." The result is a nuanced, mythopoetic reappraisal of a historical figure that has the power and valence to renew the feminine in each of us and to restore to the masculine what it has forgotten, discarded, or never considered. One of its most effective means of accomplishing this is interdisciplinary conversation.

The most current thinking and writing on ecofeminism is reinforced by April's courage to travel into uncertainty, where ideas, points of view, and new ways of thinking have space to unfurl, even as a sense of surprise can infiltrate the imagination to ward off cliched thinking and stale bromides. One of her unique claims fosters "regenerating wastelands" previously ignored.

The freshness of April's thought and her courage in risking ways of parsing ideas through the vibrant filters of imaginal inquiry give her study energy, stamina, and largesse. What she gives special attention to is who and what she meets along the way, unbidden presences that steer the subject matter into uncommon reserves, there to be seen anew.

While finding layers of value in Joseph Campbell's work on myth, she also wants to lean into accepted patterns of thought, to break them open to see what they may be harboring that requires new alliances in order to renew them. Empowerment is her watchword, and "bridal agency" one of her sustained angles of vision.

Throughout the entire study, however, what captivated me were the numerous stories that April presented from personal experience, novels, films, documentaries—the structures that cultures show themselves through. Such, it seems, is the mirroring power of mythic consciousness and the adhesive strength of forging community through story.

The ancient Greeks had a word for this phenomenon: *mimesis*. What is mimetic is the re-presentation of a narrative in its archetypal core that connects us universally with the deep patterns of psyche that activate and animate our lives within a world of meaning. Through the mythopoetic imagination, we become the other in force, energy, and identity; their story becomes, for a brief time, our narrative world of meaning. Magdalene, an archetypal bride, is the central figure for such mimetic action.

As our guide, April assists the reader through a series of charts and graphs as an economical way of ordering large numbers of patterns. Ancient myths continue to bump up against more recent historical accounts of similar plots. The result is a vital intimacy created between the present phenomena of culture and the ancient resonances of these same occurrences. The consequence is the creation of what anthropologist Victor Turner has called *communitas*, which links us as a species to our ancestry and to those who live next door to us. It also links us as readers to her project that underscores mutual transdisciplinary voices to be heard by others on a similar quest.

But perhaps equally powerful is our common heritage with the unconscious, both personal and collective, where the universal forms emerge in their particularity through the specific stories we read, create, imagine, and embody. For the world of human agency is incarnational as well as imaginal and historical. April keeps this tension alive throughout her study, which affords it a tensile strength that can empower the reader in her/his quest for meaning, coherence and compassion for self and others.

She does this often by pushing the meaning of words, perhaps inventing new ones, such as *phallacy*, to describe "a falsehood in service to outmoded and dangerous patriarchal values." Such rhetorical disturbances push us to pay attention to how things are called and for what ends. Words can fall asleep to their own presence and foster a dull and habitual mind-set toward gender, race, class, and culture in its largest orbit.

Old stories of the prince, the bride, the conquest, the masculine in charge are shallow readings of deeper archetypal realities that if deconstructed, as April suggests, can expose a more wholistic account of relationships that have been trivialized by the Disneyfied field of sentimentality. They need to be liberated, as April reveals repeatedly, so they can breathe afresh. Such is true most importantly, perhaps, with Magdalene herself, whose previous projections have incarcerated her in clichés while ignoring her deeper nature.

April's study, then, carries the intentions of reclamation, renewal, reinterpretation, and newly researched representations that have been overlooked or undervalued. She is, to my thinking, a bard of the soul, whose creative self is in a deepening communion with her own genius.

She is insistent, in concert with other thinkers she admires, that "the wounded masculine reciprocally heals and evolves as the once-abandoned Bride is reclaimed. The return of the Bride is not for her-Self alone" but a tendency toward partnership, "the sacred marriage at the root of Western traditions." Both energies are necessary for a true *coniunctio*; this belief, this vision, April keeps before her throughout her voyage to reclaim the divine feminine and the valued masculine. Such a task is epic in design, spiritual in intent, and essential for healing our current fractured culture.

DENNIS PATRICK SLATTERY is Distinguished Professor Emeritus in Mythological Studies at Pacifica Graduate Institute and author, most recently, of *The Way of Myth: Stories' Subtle Wisdom* and *The Fictions in Our Convictions: Essays on the Cultural Imagination*.

REGENERATING the FEMININE

QUESTING

WITH AND FOR THE FEMININE

Whenever feminists engage in energy-raising mythic/symbolic thought
and image-making, capable of reconceptualizing reality and changing
the world, this is what I call *psychic activism*.
—JANE CAPUTI, "ON PSYCHIC ACTIVISM: FEMINIST MYTHMAKING" (426)

This book is a quest to unravel the mystery of the undervalued, lost, and returning feminine principle. What exactly is the feminine and how do we know it/she was lost and is now returning? Discovering the meaning behind these qualities and expressions, inherent in all people and one-half of human potentiality can be an invitational deep dive into the three interconnected realms of psyche, culture, and Nature. Along with emerging science, data, and the arts from myriad fields, this is an exploration into the power of imaginal, creative, and mythic content.

Mystery loves a quest. According to Jungian psychology, myths develop from an intrinsically creative collective unconscious, gifting us with stories infused with potent messages from psyche, often threatening dominant paradigms. Within the fertile liminality between myth, history, and culture much information can be mined.

With this in mind, what a time to be investigating both the feminine and regeneration! Tracking these often-elusive, fluid, and ever-forming sequences has been a wild and revitalizing quest. I've always been attracted to the vitality and fecundity of new patterns. Long repressed, dishonored, and at times lost to us, the relational, creative feminine force in all people is returning.

This research began fourteen years ago, chronicling this rise of the feminine and evidence of cultural shifts. During this time the world has been in quite a season of swift and seismic social growth, collectively experiencing an unprecedented global pandemic, the #MeToo and Black Lives Matter (BLM) sociopolitical movements, and desperate backlash attempts to revert to old, worn-out ways, including the invasion of Ukraine, the Capitol insurrection, and genocide in Gaza.

The world—academically, interpersonally, and broadly—is rebalancing, reintegrating the lost and returning feminine. One expression of this is our collective metabolizing of inclusion and diversity, becoming more comfortable with and embracing interdisciplinary and transdisciplinary approaches, intersectionality, and our need for continual decolonization of institutions, including the academy, and our minds. These are regenerative acts.

We've witnessed the remarkable rise of women's presence and contributions in writing and publishing masterworks. Terse, truth-telling sociopolitical manifestos have emerged, including Isabel Wilkinson's *Caste*, Angela Saini's *The Patriarchs*, and Soraya Chamali's *Rage Becomes Her: The Power of Women's Anger*, normalizing women's lived experience and resiliency. These are signs and signals of the mainstreaming of ideas. Kimberlé Crenshaw's work on intersectionality emerged anew in *#SayHerName: Black Women's Stories of Police Violence and Public Silence*. Jodi Kantor and Megan Twohey, after changing the world through their work at *The New York Times* exposing Harvey Weinstein, penned *She Said: Breaking the Sexual Harassment Story That Helped Ignite a Movement*, now an acclaimed motion picture.

We are witnessing an unprecedented blossoming of feminist research across myriad creative forms. From Emily Wilson's veneer-stripping, recalibrating translation of the *Odyssey* to Linda Falcone and Jane Fortune's work reclaiming five hundred years of lost art by Florentine women to Elinor Claghorn's study of *Unwell Women: Misdiagnosis and Myth in a Man-Made World*, women are both excavating and reclaiming lost historical contributions and reconditioning our comprehension of women's lived experience while broadening our understanding of gender and humanity's potential writ large. Another benefit of these emerging creative models of transdisciplinary scholarship is the gaining of much-needed collective dialogue between the arts and sciences, somatics and the environment, expanding upon the tremendous impact of interdisciplinary studies by going even deeper toward decolonizing academia and our minds.[1] Arts-based research has been a huge component in supporting women's emerging voices, opening up expansive research vistas and scholarly opportunities. The personal and collective healing potential of arts-based methodologies shines in the work of *The Dancer's Voice: Performance and Womanhood in Transnational India* by Rumya Sree Putcha, and Megan Sweeney's *Mendings*. The fine and lively arts are not so far from scholarship anymore.

Cultural theorists have amplified the impact of feminism and women's experience. From the ongoing creative works of historian and mythographer Marina Werner, folklorist Maria Tatar, and ecofeminist Jane Caputi we find complex and lively analyses of what is developing from myriad perspectives—across historical, sociopolitical, and cultural levels.

Meanwhile, the deep, collective longing for the feminine in men is palpable. My heart breaks recalling how a male classmate in graduate school repeatedly begged to join our women's gatherings after classes. He wanted what we had built—connection, support, a space to process the vast amounts of psychoactive material we were studying. Unwilling to acknowledge our unique need for a healing container to discuss our lived experience, he was also unwilling to address his own trauma and resultant addictions. I address this type of (unconscious) necrotic, co-opting behavior in the final chapter, including movement required for regeneration. Recognizing when we are attempting to usurp something from the outside (psychic theft) rather than doing the seemingly arduous work of cultivating it from within supports the liberation of our agency. The longing for the feminine is palpable. Yet to (unconsciously) crave the feminine without recognizing the gravity of wounding suffered by women and the cost to us all keeps us stuck in addiction, reenacting traumatizing patterns.

Consider the immense popularity of (immature, *puer*) Ken from the *Barbie* movie; he gets to live in her pink world and individuate. Notice how Barbie's own trajectory is unclear, unfinished (we leave her at the gynecologist's, begging for a sequel). Yet Ken is now wearing pink, dancing and singing at the Oscars, even nominated for an Academy Award (via Ryan Gosling's performance). He has the attention of the collective. Ken's comic and energetic expression is a fascinating example of cinematic amplification. (Meanwhile, Barbie, in the form of Margo Robbie, was laughing offstage, still underground—quite a necessary regenerative stage.)

---

1. For a fruitful analysis of possible differences between interdisciplinary and transdisciplinary approaches, see Patricia Leavy's *Handbook of Arts-Based Research*.

REMYTHOLOGIZING: BUILDING CONNECTIVE TISSUE

New to the conversation is an exploration of how remythologizing the lost feminine has deepening psychological significance for contemporary consciousness, providing healing potentiality within intersecting psychic, cultural, and environmental landscapes. By exploring the feminine through a depth psychological and archaeomythological perspective, we can better activate its regenerative qualities and application within these imaginal and embodied realms. Additionally, tracking the surges of appearances of, devotion to, and function of the feminine through a mythological prism raises the question, Why now? Considering the magnitude of contemporary psychic and cultural stress, compounded by the danger of further ecological collapse, how might the lost and returning feminine offer tangible regeneration?

Part of my role seems to be chronicling the rise of the feminine in cultures, amplifying emerging patterns. Another is to make critical connections that make meaning. Once upon a time, I had an invaluable conversation with a mentor, Jungian analyst and theorist Deldon McNeely, where I was taking for granted what I understood and the connections I was making, dismissing it all with, "But doesn't everyone know this, isn't it obvious?" She was urging me to honor how unique my perspective was, and she took the time to discuss with me how common it (still) can be for women to undervalue their perspectives and contributions to the conversation.

TENDING THE IMPACT OF
CINEMATIC STORYTELLING, LANGUAGE, AND WRITING

Cinematic impact can now be broadly defined as moving images on large screens, with at-home streaming now providing home theater conditions within our private spaces—complete with ever-larger screens and surround sound—as the new viewing norm (as opposed to selectively moving into public spaces, attending a cinema for two hours). Similarly, there is now far less distinction between "film," television programing, online streaming, and the internet writ large. As such, the reporting of news and sports, as well as music videos and concerts, is now frequently dramatized, amplified, and glamorized on the level of film and must be included in any examination of the exponentially increasing magnitude of the impact of emerging archetypal moving images (i.e., storytelling via screens) of women and power.

Acclaimed storyteller Philip Pullman—creator of the tenacious, loquacious Lyra Silvertongue—answers readers' questions in *The Guardian*, including the inquiry "Do you think it's possible for a really good writer to come out of the internet age?" Pullman responds by tracking the historical evolution of storytelling:

> There have been maybe four or five great revolutions in storytelling in human history. The first was when we acquired language, with its tenses and its possibilities and we discovered we could say things that weren't actually true, but were enjoyable. The second was writing, making marks that preserve a story longer than the life of the person telling it. Then there was printing, which enabled stories such as the Bible and other things to be disseminated worldwide. Then in the 20th century there were the movies, another huge revolution. Now we've got the internet. Notice how these things are moving ever more quickly? Either that means we're coming to the end of the cycle or there's something new over the horizon we've not dreamed of yet, I don't know. But writers will continue to emerge because writing—telling stories and writing them down—is a very ancient thing. We've always done it, and as long as we're human beings we always will. (Pullman, "Philip Pullman")

Pullman's timeline reveals not only a logical—or logocentric—trajectory toward this accelerated state of storytelling but, in Jungian terms, an erotic one as well. By identifying these shifts as revolutions—disruption, significant growth—Pullman amplifies the radical impact these progressions make on culture and, in turn, the interconnected realms of psyche and Nature. The movement from language to writing to printing to film to the internet is also exponentially swift—a mathematical function describing the potential to gain dynamic momentum over time. Interestingly, such growth is predictable through the language of mathematics and potentially enormous in scope. (Grappling with comprehending the difference between one million and one billion, for instance, is an expression of this phenomenon.)

Considering Jung's transcendent—a term he credited to astronomer and analytical psychologist Rebekka Aleida Biegel (see Liz Greene's *Jung's Studies in Astrology* for more on how Jungian theory developed out of women's collective labor)—a study of the r/evolution of storytelling in our cinematic and internet age requires examining the functions of both Logos and Eros while holding the tension between them, anticipating the emergence of an exponentially potent elegant third form. For example, during our global pandemic, home streaming filled previously unimagined voids and needs, both conscious and unconscious. As theaters stood empty and actors, directors, and cinematographers were home with their smartphones turned toward new ways of creating content—some personal, some working toward social justice, and some industry specific—new creative forms and expressions emerged.

Revisiting the impact of language and writing on culture supports a reimagining and remythologizing of the consequences of these phenomenal leaps "forward" in relation to the regeneration of the feminine principle. In *The Alphabet Versus the Goddess: The Conflict Between Word and Image*, neurosurgeon Leonard Shlain theorizes that the linear nature of alphabets is logocentric, devoid of earlier image-based storytelling techniques found cross-culturally in the Neolithic era, a time marked by the worship of female deities. Shlain links the rise of alphabets—fundamentally linear in nature— and the "trading of an eye for an ear" with the appearance of patriarchal religions globally, which in turn repeatedly ban the use of images (as in Christianity's second commandment), while introducing war and mass suffering and "demonstrable madness." Results of this shift are evidenced in the erosion of women's rights, the disappearance of the goddess, and a loathing for images and imageable information. For Shlain, the movement away from "huge, imageless tomes written by esteemed white males" toward a historic resurgence of the image—most rapidly in the nineteenth century via photography, electromagnetism, then cinema and the internet—are clear expressions of the return of the feminine principle globally ("The Alphabet Versus the Goddess Lecture by Leonard Shlain").[2]

Furthermore, Shlain suggests that writing with only one (right) hand is also a logocentric activity. Arguing that the left hand has been demonized cross-culturally while right-handedness has been valued and cultivated, he posits that the keyboard serves to reunite the brain hemispheres through the integrated use of both hands—again, a practical application of Jung's transcendent function and the value of liaising.

Shlain also tracks how brains behave neurobiologically, emphasizing how the left hemisphere (which specializes in prioritizing linear, sequential,

---

2. Some of Shlain's ideas are problematic, most likely the result of incomplete scholarship in history and archaeomythology. As a self-identified feminist deconstructing patriarchal fallout after the loss of the feminine, he moves as an evolutionary biological essentialist and conflates gender and sex. Referring to Marija Gimbutas—as he attempts to refute her theories on the cost of patriarchal invasion—as a "woman archaeologist," he misdiagnoses pathologies in Greco-Roman creation myths and reproduces outdated heteronormative values. This is painfully evident as he concludes a *visual* presentation (which he argues is evidence of the feminine) saying, "I hope that this presentation has produced this response," while showing an "image of an audience of Victorian men applauding (see "The Alphabet Versus the Goddess," his Pepperdine lecture). Perhaps this was what he hoped for, to convince *men* to reconsider the value of the feminine. He missed Audre Lorde's rebuilding tutorial; the master's tools will never, ever be enough.

reductionist, and abstract behaviors) does not like or value the right hemisphere (holistic, simultaneous, synthesizing, nurturing behavior) and, if given more power, will act to put down its own other side. The implications of this deserve our attention, particularly in this era of regenerating our lost Eros in relation with our dominating Logos.

For example, scanning the brain's EEG brainwave patterns while reading shows the emission of beta waves, whereas viewing cinematic images produces alpha and theta waves, the same two waves resulting from meditation. As such, Shlain's research suggests that typing, image making, and—most significantly—viewing, all have the potential to become regenerative acts of integration between separated hemispheres.

In *Jungian Film Studies: The Essential Guide*, Helena Bassil-Morozow and Luke Hockley analyze cinematic images and the projective nature of film upon the unconscious. Bassil-Morozow writes:

Individuation and the archetypes—the core concepts of Jungian psychology—are none other than a flexible narrative framework and its changeable contents. In this sense, Jung's Analytical Psychology is more suitable for analysing narratives than any other psychotherapy theory. Unlike Lacan, Jung did not think that the unconscious is structured like a language. Its language is visual—it consists of images, of pictures, of archetypes. The unconscious is pre-civilised, pre-cultural and pre-linguistic. Only its "personal" layer is affected by culture, but its deepest layer and its collective one is shared by all, regardless of their backgrounds. Jungian psychology is also progressive and forward-looking as it is geared up for the creation of meaning in human narrative instead of being obsessed with the past roots of present problems. (27)

By identifying the visual nature of the unconscious, Bassil-Morozow highlights the potential impact of image-based storytelling, particularly as effective forms of active imagination—soul dialogue. She goes on to discuss how Jungian and post-Jungian psychology are uniquely situated to analyze this conversation between the unconscious and the world broadly Interestingly, she uses the prefix "pre-" to discuss the unconscious, which certainly relates to Shlain's historical motif, locating visual language before logocentric corruptions via linear alphabets. In light of her assertion of Jungian psychology's "progressive and forward-looking" commitment, perhaps more accurate prefixes might include "super-" or "trans-," indicating that while a goal of understanding the unconscious includes peeling off layers of (socialized, problematic, patriarchal) civilization, culture, and linguistics, it exists beyond these limited and limiting constructs.

As Pullman, Shlain, and Bassil-Morozow attest, moving images are making enormous impacts on psyche, culture, and Nature. Shlain amplifies how "film attendance surpassed church attendance within six years of its introduction" ("The Alphabet Versus the Goddess Lecture by Leonard Shlain"). We then moved from going (out) to the movies to (potentially traveling further within via) the home theater as cinematic temple.

At the dynamic convergence between film and the World Wide Web, we find Shlain's daughter, Tiffany Shlain, filmmaker, founder of the Webby Awards (celebrating excellence on the internet), and creatrix of the innovative television series *The Future Starts Here*. Taking visual storytelling to a creative, effective, and dizzying intensity, Tiffany Shlain—as a connectivity researcher and visual artist applying the moving image toward wellness, social justice, and environmental literacy—offers a healing example of a psychopomp for a s/heroic journey through this emerging and exponentially expanding cinematic realm.

A NOTE ON STRUCTURE, STYLE, AND LANGUAGE

I approach this scholarship from a range of disciplines and angles, a sustainable practice that reflects the permaculture principle that fecundity results from exchange at the borderlands. My academic training is in women's and gender studies, sustainability, social ecology, mythological studies, and depth psychology. Mythological studies sits within the humanities at the confluence of religious studies, literary and film theory, and depth psychology. Likewise, women's and gender studies are remarkably diverse and dynamic; my focus weaves between women's history, women and creativity, and ecofeminism. Social justice, diversity, and inclusion are essential. This is not easy material, and folks committed to a single discipline might want to run screaming; I invite you to stay instead, and to keep digging.

I use footnotes, many of them. Think of them as tent pegs, grounding vast swaths of connective tissue between disciplines and thinkers, writers, and artists, weaving and strengthening theory and practice. Since virtually all of my academic training has been in interdisciplinary fields and methodologies, this type of practice has always been central to creating the cross-fertilization and depth necessary for holistic study, meaning making, and problem solving. As an avid reader of footnotes, I dislike endnotes and the need to flip back and forth. (I am aware that Joseph Campbell critiqued the use of footnotes as a sign of uncertainty; I disagree.)

Language is alive and reflexive; Mary Daly and Jane Caputi effectively point this out in their wickedly humorous and diabolically intelligent *Websters' First New Intergalactic Wickedary of the English Language* (1994), a creative antidote to mindless adherence to a static notion of language and meaning making. I want to use words to convey as much meaning as possible. For example, "phallacy," to describe a falsehood in service to outmoded and dangerous patriarchal values.

Jungian terms can be complicated and convey more than a single meaning. Terms are interwoven throughout the book. For example, chapter 3 takes a deep dive into the archetype of the Bride, though I discuss it throughout the book, with the intention of layering meaning making.

CHAPTER SUMMARIES

Chapter 1, "Locating the Feminine: The Impoverishing Loss of the Bride and Quest to Find Her," tracks the centrality of the wound that is the loss of women's history, identity, and belonging, especially within the centrality of religion in the formation of Western cultures. Identifying and locating the archetypal Bride via the imaginal interplay between history and mythology in terms of voice, power, and agency, this chapter explores how historical understandings of Mary Magdalene have shifted, from early examples inspired by the resurfacing of the Gospel of Mary in 1955 to the post–*Da Vinci Code* eruption of scholarship and inquiry, to interdisciplinary responses within religious studies and related communities. Central to this is Magdalene's significance within Jungian individuation, from the so-called Mediterranean fertility cult lineage, the roots of Egyptian alchemy, sacred marriage.

Chapter 2, "Giving Away the Bride? Joseph Campbell, the S/Hero's Journey, and the Grail Quest," investigates our capacity for tending our inner masculine—an area of growth for women mostly ignored by modern culture and much of psychotherapy—is essential preparation for embodied sacred marriage. At the heart of the quest is the application of Campbell's grail lore toward understanding the archetypal Bride, utilizing grail clues to deconstruct Campbell's potential role as mythological father of the Bride by closely examining and revising his "hero's" journey model. Pioneering Jungians Marion Woodman and Deldon McNeely offer models for tracking the development of the Bride's inner masculine, while Jody Bower provides an insightful and revelatory counterpoint and guide to decoding women's literary and autobiographical journeys.

Chapter 3, "Bridal Agency: How Women's Literary Fiction and Memoir Crash the (Patriarchal) Wedding," discusses the significance of emerging, pervasive regenerative bridal consciousness—including new forms of agency—appearing in new literary fiction and film. Central to bridal power, awareness, and effective mobility are tools for interpreting the depth psychological value of literary fiction and memoir. I analyze several mapping projects provided by feminist authors, including Jane Austen, Elizabeth Gilbert, and Jody Bower, who have left critical clues for navigating bridal territories.

Chapter 4, "Exiled and Underground: The Lost Bride in European Fairy Tales," investigates Starbird's theory that four exceedingly popular European fairy tales—"Cinderella," "Snow White," "Sleeping Beauty," and "Rapunzel"—carry encoded accounts of the Magdalene heresy. A close examination of these stories and the mythemes of envy, confusion, and sovereignty creates a deeper understanding of the Bride's movement toward individuation and the relationship with the masculine. Connecting these to the mythology of Psyche further amplifies Magdalene's bridal pattern and significance.

Chapter 5, "Watching the Detectives: Regenerative Individuation via Tricky Sleuthing," revolves around how the archetypal Bride unexpectedly crashes her own wedding, disrupting outworn patriarchal patterns by asking new questions, searching for clues. The Bride shows up incognito as the tricky detective within both the Maisie Dobbs and Phryne Fisher literary mystery fiction series. Following clues via literary theory, ecofeminism, and depth psychology, this section tracks the revitalizing significance of these Magdalenian apparitions.

Chapter 6, "The Recessional: Regenerative Practices in Support of Bridal Questing," explores how regenerating the feminine carries and supports the curative powers of creativity, wonder, and synchronicity. Grounded in Jung's study of synchronicity, we come full circle with an analysis of how the creative art of bricolage—the practice of re/membering our fragmented, post-traumatic shards—acts as regenerative healing agent. Through cultural and literary expressions, from the evolution of Prince Harry to the novel *Broken for You*, the cumulative pool of bridal tools and analysis, the Bride's full comedic, regenerative cycle is revealed. The return of the Bride, bearing gifts for psyche, community, and Gaia, shifts the complex wasteland toward regeneration.

This quest for the feminine principle offers a complex, dynamic roadmap for regenerative potentialities worthy of our collective attention. Discovering how to navigate it and which tools to bring is the journey of this book, as is tracking the significance of her return. Perhaps the only true prerequisite for questing is a hearty open and curious stance.

CHAPTER 1

LOCATING THE FEMININE

THE IMPOVERISHING LOSS OF THE BRIDE AND QUEST TO FIND HER

> Denis de Rougemont suggests that when an important event is too
> dangerous to be discussed, it is formed as a myth and told as a story.
> This opinion, from his book *Love in the Western World* (first published in
> French in 1940), could be applied to the entire myth surrounding the
> lady with the alabaster jar.
> —MARGARET STARBIRD, *THE WOMAN WITH THE ALABASTER JAR* (46)

MIND THE GAP: HISTORY VS. MYTHOLOGY?

In his investigation into the power and effectiveness of parody, media professor Marwan Kraidy, who studies social media and TV in the Arab world, explores the gap between the original and a copy. In an interview with National Public Radio (NPR) in November of 2014 on the rise of parody of the "Islamic State" (IS), Kraidy describes the import of the rise of anti-ISIS satire:

> I think people are very afraid. And this is, I think, where parody is very important because if you listen to the interviews that the writer, the director, some of the actors in that specific show gave, all of them said we want our children to feel better. We want our children to be

less afraid. And in a way, this is how parody works, right? So you have the original. You have this very scary thing called ISIS. And what you do—you create a funny copy of it. And between the original and the copy, you have a gap, right? People see the two images. And within that gap, what you do is you explore the hypocrisies—the gap between what ISIS claims to be and what it is in fact or what people—the way people perceive it to be. ("ISIS, ISIL or Islamic State")[3]

The gap between the original and its copy describes a fecund region, teeming with uncertainty and potentiality. People often have difficulty distinguishing between the original and the copy, or even debate which is which. Sometimes, what might matter more is the relationship between the two and the potential to bridge the gap. This example also begs an investigation into the "accidental" conflation between a chthonic dark goddess—whose legacy can be tracked to the heart of Western cultures—and a terrorist organization enforced by political leadership and Western media.

One such gaping relationship exists between mythology and history. The modern discipline of "history" was the retelling of stories of what has come before without questioning who was telling the story or their access to personal and institutional power and privilege. Howard Zinn, in his landmark revisioning of the field, *A People's History of the United States: 1492–2001* (2003), describes this reporting of "history" as being from "the standpoint of the conquerors and leaders of Western civilization" in service to "the excuse of progress" (22). Traditionally penned by the victors—those colonialists, imperialists, and expansionists who generally benefited materially and financially by relating a story through their eyes and experiences—"history's" invisible privilege and unspoken, unexamined agendas have weighed in heavily. Asking who is telling the story and why begins to unpack these unconscious archives.

Women's studies, particularly since feminism's second wave in the 1960s, has been fertilizing a blooming of research, publication, and conversation that has infused the discipline of history—and indeed the entire academy—with new and expanding narratives, theory, and pedagogy. We now have thorough, extensive, emerging volumes of feminist scholarship chronicling, deconstructing, and reconstructing women's lost history from a range of perspectives. Critical tools emerging from the confluence of social justice movements at the heart of the civil rights movement and feminism include intersectionality (interlocking forms of oppression) and critical race theory (CRT)—crucial

---

3. For further discussion on the appropriateness and accuracy of the names ISIS, ISIL, or IS within Middle Eastern cultures see "ISIS, ISIL or Islamic State."

for expanding our research and understanding across layers of race, class, gender, gender identity, ableism, and other forms of hierarchal oppression.

Some of the most significant work in the reclamation of women's history lies within the interconnected realms of religious studies, art history, anthropology, and archaeomythology. For example, the identification and reclamation since 2006 of over two thousand pieces of Renaissance art created by women in Florence, Italy, has begun re/storing—and re/story-ing—these paintings and sculptures to their rightful place within existing canons of what we understand to be Florentine, Renaissance, and women's art. Once forgotten and moldering in church and museum storage basements and attics, these masterworks are now being identified, restored, and exhibited globally, thanks to the extraordinary efforts of Linda Falcone and philanthropist Jane Fortune. This re/storying of art history carries enormous impact. The European Renaissance holds a particularly weighty place within the collective Western psyche, as discussed by archetypal psychologist James Hillman in *Re-Visioning Psychology* (1997) and elsewhere; however, missing from the conversation are women's contributions.

How can we understand ourselves when we've lost half of our memory-text-history? Amnesia is a terrible risk. As women have gained agency and entrée to positions of power within the art world as curators, gallery owners, exhibited artists, and art historians, the industry has changed.[4] This single example in Florence amplifies the impact women have had on the reclamation of our lost collective history, especially considering the mastery required to achieve the refined artistic techniques of the times.

The Advancing Women Artists Foundation grew out of art detectives Fortune and Falcone's research, chronicled in their book *Invisible Women: Forgotten Artists of Florence* (2009). The organization's mission and incredible impact is tracked in the PBS documentary *Invisible Women* (2012).[5] A vast, collaborative, international network of women—including curators, art historians, conservator-restorers, and educators—emerged to conserve, fundraise, and educate the world about these lost masters. For fourteen years, the AWA restored and rebirthed over fifty works of art, creating multiple educational and community development opportunities. This emerging archive re/visions our understanding art history, women's history, curation, and material culture. Re/membering shifts and heals realms.

---

4. See Phoebe Hoban, "'We're Finally Infiltrating,'" *ARTnews*, 1 Feb. 2007, https://www.artnews.com/art-news/news/were-finally-infiltrating-158/.

5. See the now-mothballed AdvancingWomenArtists.org and this research's subsequent incarnation, CalliopeArts.org.

A similar transdisciplinary methodology can be found in archaeomythology. As a unique approach to cultural research and renewal, archaeomythology is inherently transdisciplinary as a decolonizing interweaving of fields and perspectives including, but not limited to, history, mythology, archaeology, art history, linguistics, ecology, genetics, epigenetics, and folklore—digging for truths across time and space.[6] With such diverse and polyvalent dialogue, what can result are reconstructed bridges of intricate and resilient lacework spanning chronological and spatial chasms.

One particularly precarious gap in our collective history of Western cultures involves the lack of women and female representation within Judeo-Christian mythologies. Considering how deeply steeped in religious beliefs and practices our cultures are, this gaping hole requires attention. Pioneering feminist research, such as Elisabeth Schüssler Fiorenza's groundbreaking revisionist text *In Memory of Her: A Feminist Theological Reconstruction of Christian Origins* (1995), reveal an early church historically and chronically steeped in the problems of patriarchal power. Addressing a plethora of remarkable fragments of women's history ready for excavation, Fiorenza's research tends several gaps as an evocative, mythopoetic suspension bridge between what has been and what could be.

Women's lost histories are being well tended recently via effective and vivid emerging documentary films—including those by British historians Bettany Hughes, Amanda Foreman, and Lucy Worsley—and have gained traction within the collective psyche. Hughes's evocative documentaries produced by the BBC, particularly the trilogy *Divine Women* (2012), examine archaeomythological evidence as quests for meaning making of our past. Part 2 of *Divine Women: Handmaids of God* looks at the roles of women within both Greco-Roman cultures and the early Christian church. Similarly, Amanda Foreman's extensive work in women's history spans her documentary series *The Ascent of Woman* (2015), exploring women's history over the past ten thousand years, as well as research on individual women's lives, such as her bestselling biography *Georgiana: Duchess of Devonshire*, which became the Academy Award–winning feature film *The Duchess* (2008). Prolific Lucy Worsley has researched British queens, the suffrage movement, and Agatha Christie as an author and BBC presenter. Thanks to these and myriad feminist historians globally, it is no longer outlandish to consider women's centrality to cultural and religious traditions and that their historical power and influence deserve

---

6. See Archaeomythology.org for a comprehensive introduction to the field and the living legacy of Marija Gimbutas. For necessary, revitalizing applications, see Joan Cichon's *Matriarchy in Bronze Age Crete*.

our attention. Moreover, their expertise has attained high visibility, shifting cultural norms about who historians are and how collective stories are re/membered and re/told.

One of the most significant cultural trends and contributions to women's history and religious studies has been the emergence of a collective fascination with goddess scholarship. Grounded in archaeological finds and the emergence of feminist analysis and integration within "traditional" male canons and ways of knowing, pioneering contributions from women such as Gertrude Bell, Marija Gimbutas, and Jeannine Davis-Kimball opened up more questions than answers about digs and artifacts previously analyzed by outworn and uncritical androcentric paradigms. Later scholars have been building extensive causeways between emerging feminist scholarship and the material evidence of public and private life, statuary initially diminished as "goddess figurines," and women's lived and recorded experience. Central to this surge is a quest to understand the centrality and impact of religious practices, from the Neolithic to the classical period. At the core of this grounded invocation is scholarly commitment to spaciousness, allowing lost and reclaimed voices to come through and for the centrality of curiosity rather than certainty.

One of the most fecund areas of this research is the layered greater Mediterranean borderlands between ancient histories and myths of Mesopotamia, Anatolia, and Egypt, later Greco-Roman cultural layerings, and Judeo-Christian practices and traditions. Tracking the feminine within these dialoguing mythological ladders and pathways provides much information about our lineages and legacies within Western cultures. From Inanna to the Shekinah, to Sophia and Lilith, feminine aspects of the divine are being excavated and reinterpreted across disciplines. We are in a time of great longing for what's been missing, lost, and repudiated.

One of the most searched-for and sought-after women within this global, interdependent surge in scholarship and art is Mary Magdalene. This chapter shows how deeply this cultural phenomenon reflects and informs the global quest for the feminine and our resultant psychological, cultural, and environmental regeneration. What has gone underground, also rises.

MISSING MARY MAGDALENE

Since the rediscovery of the Gospel of Mary and other Gnostic texts, there has been an eruption of curiosity, scholarship, and creative reimagining around the story and significance of Mary Magdalene, tapping into patterns that are archetypal—symbols and thoughts with structured and self-organizing meaning—and are appearing simultaneously through the creative arts, scholarship, and pilgrimage for Christians and non-Christians alike. From a depth psychological perspective, these seventy plus years of sifting and sorting have been a necessary process of meaning making.

Interdisciplinary scholarship has been questioning and documenting why and how elements of Mary Magdalene's identity and story were systematically suppressed, erased, and distorted within Christian Church doctrine and practice. My own study seeks to clarify Magdalene's embodied archetypal identity as, and antidote to, patriarchy's shadow—those disowned, dark components we have yet to accept consciously, including a disembodied fear of the feminine—and identify what her resurgence signifies. Unacknowledged shadows can attempt to colonize and devour. Instead, tending such polarities as shadow and light invites regenerative growth.

In this way history can be navigated and explored from fresh perspectives, inviting a renewal of open and curious scholarship while applying creative methodologies in service to crafting new paradigms and deeper understanding. The remythologizing of Mary Magdalene's story is a rich example of how the feminine has reclaimed territory that once denied her existence and power. Scholars in many fields have addressed facets of her resurgence, including her role as "apostle to the apostles," her relationship with Jesus, and the redemption of her character and sexuality. As a Middle Eastern woman embedded within a complex web of gendered religious history and mythology, Magdalene is a dynamic and enigmatic mystery. Rather than certainties, she offers potentialities and invites curiosity.

The emergence of Magdalenian apparitions and trends can be seen across scholarship and the arts, via literary fiction and cinematic expressions. By examining the phenomena of these erupting "appearances" and shifts, along with related gaps in literature and practice, it is possible to track the reformation of not only Mary Magdalene's history and mythology but women's history and cultural lived experience in general, into what I suggest is an embodied, feminist shift. This is a quest to understand the impact, meaning, and movement of the returning feminine within Western cultures and the human psyche as well as tracking evidence that her return heals wastelands—those bleak, barren, and neglected landscapes, both interior and exterior, personal and collective.

I suggest Magdalene returns bearing gifts for psyche. This chapter tracks how remythologizing Magdalene's story operates on various levels, rebalancing and revitalizing our relationship with psyche, Self, and Other. Why Magdalene in particular? Why now? How valuable is "accurate" "historical" analysis compared with making meaning via her stories and legends? Perhaps she has our collective attention because she was a spiritual teacher, perhaps the one who best understood original teachings on love at the core of emerging Christianity. Perhaps her return resonates with a cultural movement toward equality and partnership. Perhaps her identity as one who was lost, maligned, forgotten—as the negated and abandoned feminine aspect of life itself—aids reconnection with our own lost parts. Or perhaps it is because even if she were not any of these things, we now need her to be.

LOCATING THE FEMININE: FEMINIST POST-JUNGIAN PERSPECTIVES

C. G. Jung's visionary theory of psychological growth, individuation, is predicated upon developing and integrating a full range of human emotional skills. Heavily influenced by the late Romantic period and early modernity, emerging during the supposed "golden" era of colonialism and empire, depth psychology is deeply rooted in dysfunction while simultaneously reaching toward innovative healing. Originally delineated by binary gender roles strictly enforced within patriarchal society, women were seen as (inherently, "essentially") gifted at relationship and feeling—what Jung termed Eros—the erotic, internal, receptive principle of life—while men were "naturally" more skilled in Logos (logic and reason) as the complementary external, expansive life principle. Men's soul work was with their anima, the contrasexual component of their Self; women's was with their animus, though this model was originally derivative and disappointing.

Appreciating Elizabeth Nelson's straightforward, layered defining of Eros in *Knife* (2012), I borrow it here: "Though a simple translation of eros is love or desire, it is much more. Eros is what we long for, what we value, and what we create, the force that guides our fascinations and gives substance to our fears" (3). This reflexive summary of the erotic function evokes both the magnitude of its impact and the sweeping nature of its grip, including its shadowy relationship with fear (perhaps its inherent propulsion toward its enantiodromia, creating its own shadowy opposite).

Relevantly, Nelson's treatment of Psyche's missing knife is apropos when studying our missing (and returning) Magdalenian consciousness. When something is missing it can be extremely hard to track yet can hold so much information about a system/realm, especially its shadow. Considering how artists and scholars alike have not depicted/discussed or valued the lost knife discussed in the original myth, Nelson wonders about the reason for our collective amnesia; why do we desire to forget Psyche's knife (12)? She writes: "Imagining Psyche with her knife reminds us that she is not merely naïve, innocent, and obedient. Like any intriguing protagonist, Psyche makes a choice that irrevocably shapes her destiny. Many scholars fail to mention this at all, treat it in cursory fashion, or view Psyche's decision to confront Eros as a terrible mistake" (13). Studying what has been lost, we can learn about both its psychic content (asking: what is the symbolic significance of a knife, especially when wielded by a woman?) and the flavor of the incomplete responses (including asking: what are we afraid of knowing and why?). Her subsequent study investigates the knife on myriad levels pivoting around the centrality of Psyche's feminine agency and power.

When I was first studying Jungian theory, I was upset by the imbalance between gendered prescriptions for working with the inner "contrasexual" components of our psyches. Men seemed to be heading out for a nurturing yoga class, while the women were doomed to tax meetings with critical accountants. (It seemed to me that some men were rewarded for behaving badly and getting nurtured for their lack of nurturance.) Polarities are not inherently problematic; prioritizing one over the other is, as in Cartesian duality—reason valued over emotion, day over night, male over female, white over black, etc.

Jung saw our way toward healing via re/membering lost expressions of the feminine principle of consciousness, core embodiments of Eros, life-giving, vital energy. The erotic principle carries pranic properties fueling psychic growth and integration with the complementary logocentric masculine principle/consciousness, providing mental reason and thinking functionality. While Jung's original theories emerged during a time of relatively heteronormative, binary, and gendered understandings of psyche's capacity, post-Jungian feminist theory has evolved into more-inclusive, reflexive modalities committed to diversity and polyvocality. Evolving concepts of the inner masculine and inner feminine now more completely describe our capacity to explore how humans carry interior mirror images of our biological sex or, more creatively, how we are each able and encouraged to embody and live full lives predicated on experiencing the extraordinary range of human emotions and behaviors.

The terms *animus* and *anima* have complex and problematic histories. Having originated out of the aforementioned morass of sociopolitical misogyny, their definitions have evolved in a highly disordered and unregulated order, often reinforcing subsequent iterations of fear of the feminine. I find myself disagreeing with some current explanations of these terms and use them here simply to refer to internal components of psyche; even this language is problematic as theory grows in the twenty-first century.[7]

---

7. For further discussion on how the returning feminine displaces outworn definitions, see Deldon McNeely's treatment of the animus in *Animus Aeternus*.

Cultural and psychological conditioning, along with various psychological perspectives and transdisciplinary dialogues, have continuously seasoned and reshaped post-Jungian theory into a reflexive and lively postmodern model. This regenerative, practical quality of theory capable of growth is, I believe, at the heart of Jung's intention for his work and continuously informs depth psychology's reflectivity and efficacy. Rather than becoming concretized, it is a living tradition.

In this way early concepts of a woman's animus have developed into more open conversations on the masculine principle and creative support for women to tend their inner masculine. This might appear as agency, power, and extroversion. Men are encouraged on a complementary path toward developing their inner feminine, theoretically resulting in greater respect for the feminine principle—including women. For example, rather than attempted colonization by the wounded masculine, the healing masculine can learn to first relate to his own relationality and emotional needs.

Followers of Chinese Taoist teachings might recognize here the interconnected dynamics of yin and yang and complementarity, something Jung himself studied extensively. How marvelous it would be to discuss these issues in terms of such abstract and theoretical concepts! However, the trauma of patriarchy is written on the bodies of women, girls, boys, men, and the Earth. We need dialogues that address this embodied crisis, tending our trauma and grief.

Today, post-Jungian theory has developed various transdisciplinary branches with a range of approaches dedicated to finding healthy ways of understanding gendered patterns that move beyond limiting heteronormative beliefs about gender, gender identity, and sexual orientation, as well as race, class, ableism, and other interlocking forms of oppression. Rather than discuss gender as "opposites," gender theory now generally discusses gender in relation with each other, including experiences and skills within continuums. Rather than promotion of heteronormative language by reinforcing concepts of supposed "opposite" gender roles and experiences, my goal is to queer (trouble, question) these concepts by exploring expanded, empowering, and reflexive models for interpreting feminine and masculine principles in inclusive ways. Several rigorous studies have emerged that address these gendered legacies within depth psychology and in culture. Susan Rowland's *Jung: A Feminist Revision* (2002) provides a comprehensive introduction to Jungian theory and its evolution, including detailed discourse on contemporary post-Jungian developments; responses to Jung's misogyny, including postmodern Jungian feminisms and goddess scholarship; and a comprehensive survey of the evolution and defining of Jungian terms.

Locating Jungian theory within the context of the extensive and permeating influence of the women analysts and writers surrounding him, caring for him, and contributing to his evolution is essential to understanding women's vast contributions to the field of "Jungian" studies. Jung was a remarkable visionary, mystic, and theorist; he did not work alone and benefited greatly from the borrowed vitality of many brilliant and caring women. In *Sabina Spielrein: The Woman and the Myth*, Angela M. Sells offers an in-depth analysis of Jung's theoretical understanding of sex and gender, including a reclamation of pioneering psychoanalyst Spielrein's foundational theoretical contributions, detangling them from the co-opting by both Jung and Sigmund Freud. Sells's diligent research recasts our understanding of depth psychology's infancy, bridging the historical gap between amnestic exile and regeneration.

Finally, Lyn Cowan's unpublished yet highly referenced lecture "Dismantling the Animus" (1994) is a breath of fresh air in its critique of the term. Cowan writes, "I want to throw out the whole raggedy animus mantle. I don't like the style, the fabric is worn, the stitching is shabby, the buttons are missing, it doesn't fit. I want to throw it out even before I know what a new one will look like." Questioning heteronormative, moralistic, and patriarchal aspects of the framework, Cowan's critique is therapeutic, all the more powerful for her humor and expertise as a Jungian analyst.[8]

For Jung, the fullness of individuation via the maturation and integration of a developing soul becomes an embodied journey toward sacred marriage, the destination within alchemy, which Jung studied extensively. Alchemical divine union is attained via the transformation of psyche's lead to gold via the maturation of both the feminine and masculine aspects, qualities, or principles within a person. Like the composite symbol of yin and yang, the *taijitu*, the alchemical sacred marriage informed Jung's understanding of deep integration and the underlying nature of life and was centered around the potential of the sacred marriage to provide an understanding of wholeness.

This journey can be further extrapolated to understand the growth of groups and cultures. With this in mind, when the Bride (the individuating feminine, in this case broadly, culturally) is missing from her own marriage, we are in cultural crisis. This is why it might be crucial to identify and re/locate the lost and degraded archetypal Bride within our collective Western historic and mythological heritage, investigating what she is and does, her quest and her impact.

---

8. Lyn Cowan, "Dismantling the Animus." For a complementary exploration of Jung within the historical context of his contemporary emerging (male) theorists Freud and Alfred Adler, see Walter Odajnyk's illuminating *Archetype and Character*.

Within Jungian psychology archetypes animate the world, providing psyche/soul with facets of encoded insight and structure. Here I use the term "archetypes" to describe these self-organizing patterns of understanding that form and reform in relation to our personal unconscious and the greater collective unconscious, both inherited and fluidly creative. Archetypes can be culturally inflicted aspects of life expressing itself, containing cumulative spiritual legacy and mysterious potentiality. As such, Magdalene and the feminine principle embody potent transpersonal psychic energy bursting through life itself.

The Bride returns bearing gifts of integration and regeneration, reuniting Logos with the erotic, embodying the potentiality of re/union through transformative alchemical, sacred marriage. In the West our overreliance on a disembodied, "spiritual," "transcendent" masculine principle has resulted in global tragedy—personal, cultural, and ecological. We are all traumatized under patriarchy.

The reunion of the wounded masculine with a rising, neglected feminine suggests the necessity for complementary descent on his part. For example, the movement required evokes the image of the huge stone statue of Christ Redeemer above Rio de Janeiro lumbering down from Corcovado to meet his mysterious Other, Nossa Senhora Aparecida, Brazil's patron saint, who literally appeared, emerging dismembered from fecund and aqueous depths in 1717 after being lost in the Paraiba River; their meeting requires middle ground.[9] Another iteration of this movement in Christianity can be found in the reclamation of the feminine embodiment of spiritual wisdom, Sophia, as the erotic and mystical counterpart to Yahweh's exclusively Logos-centered form of creation; in order for them to partner, movement is required.

Many significant studies on the religious history of Mary Magdalene have emerged within recent decades, several of which also offer potential frameworks for psychological and cultural empowerment and understanding. The work of Susan Haskins, Jane Schaberg, Karen King, Cynthia Bourgeault, Mary Ann Beavis, and Anna Fedele provides copious amounts of thoughtfully excavated historical, religious, and—in the case of Fedele—anthropological data and perspectives on Mary Magdalene, her legacy, and her gravity in the twenty-first century. Applying post-Jungian theoretical frameworks to their findings can further clarify these studies.

---

9. I have written elsewhere about the potential for such honoring and integration of syncretic, dynamic, and living expressions of the divine feminine in Brazil. See "Securely Attached: Brazilians and Their Black Madonnas."

From this developing body of new scholarship, questions emerge regarding what is valuable and applicable to our lives today. Actively tending a multitude of questions—and cultivating curiosity in general—allows deep dialogue with ourselves, the unconscious, and our greater world. For what do we search? Jane Schaberg found herself again and again at the fence of the restricted archaeological site at Migdal, Israel, denied access yet aching to search through the rubble. What did she seek as a scholar, as a woman? What could a story about a long-dead woman offer a contemporary scholar? How could Mary Magdalene's life possibly inform our world today? How might what we call her—Mary Magdalen, Magdalene, *The* Magdalene, הירמ הנלדגמ, Madeleine, Magdalena, Μαγδαληνή, Magda—matter? And why might her status as disciple, apostle, leader, Bride, and/or equal partner make a tremendous difference in a postmodern techno/logical world supposedly seeking to liberate itself from religious dogma and patriarchy?

Magdalene's presence in the collective psyche has exploded in the past few decades. Numerous books have appeared recounting personal journeys and pilgrimages.[10] There have also appeared a large number of accounts purporting to "channel" or otherwise directly interpret Mary Magdalene. Though I never want to discount life's mysteries, or women's lived experience, accounts of "channeling" can be problematic when lacking scholarly research and psychological reflection (i.e., is this an egoic projection?).[11]

One notable hybrid contribution is Joanna Kujawa's entrée to an archetypal understanding of her journey, *The Other Goddess: Mary Magdalene and the Goddesses of Eros and Secret Knowledge* (2022). Kujawa, who describes herself as a "scholar and spiritual detective," begins an application of archetypal theory, including a rather shadowy perspective on Eros, informed by an abusive, necrotic relationship (253). Though part esoteric workbook investigating tantric and Sophia/sophic/wisdom Magdalenian expressions, Kujawa's research is certainly worth following.

Failing to deconstruct issues of power and other oppressive elements within frameworks (from "virginity" to tantra), while leaning heavily on esotericism, somewhat diminishes the potency of Kujawa's lived experience (including her refusal of anima projection). Her future scholarship is worth following, especially for her curiosity in Magdalene's sociohistoric

---

10. For an effective tracking and defining of this significant phenomenon from within religious studies, see James S. Mastaler's study "The Magdalene of Internet"; and anthropologist Anna Fedele's *Looking for Mary Magdalene*.

11. An interesting treatment of the complex topic of the effective role intuition can play in scholarship can be found in Roberta Bassett Corson's *Stepping out of the Shadows*.

experience and cultural reemergence, and for intuition's remarkable capacity to inform and deepen research.

My own inquiry into Magdalene is strongly rooted in an embodied eco-feminist practice of inquiry. I am neither Christian nor Jewish. My perspective is that of a North American woman who lived in South America for several years; I am a scholar benefiting from white privilege, though my grandmother did not. I am interested in what the multitude of Magdalenian stories now surfacing—"trending," if you will—have to tell us as humans striving for healing, sovereignty, connection, and a healthy ecosystem. Why her? Why now? How can we recognize her? What are the shadow sides of this reemergence? And, noticing that she does not simply reemerge unchanged, what defines her transformation, and how might we benefit from it? Like her exiled predecessors—including Inanna, Isis, and Ariadne—she returns after arduous journeys, renewed.

Primary to Jungian theory is the notion of the Self as sacred. Marion Woodman explains how Jung described the journey toward wholeness as "guided by the Self (the god-image within and regulating center of the personality)" (8). Clearly this definition is already problematic for women; as Mary Daly's famous blunt reasoning in *Beyond God the Father* (1973) points out, when God is male, the male is god. What about defining Self as the goddess-image within? How do we imagine that image when she's been missing for millennia?

Paramount to understanding our-Selves (collectively), historically and culturally, is acknowledging the global phenomena of the spreading influence and domination of Western cultures, at the roots of which are some concretized and incomplete ideological holdovers from both Judeo-Christian traditions and Greco-Roman mythology and philosophy. I use the plural term for Western cultures in this research to be more sensitive to the varieties, complexities, and multilayered diversities of what might once have been considered a singular "Western Culture." Rather, let us consider the tremendous flux of trade, language, and ideas, the liminality of borderlands, the resilience of tribal ways of being, and the rapid and fluid nature of emerging transnational communications as polyvalent, polyvocal expressions of overlapping territories and cultures, both geographic and psychic. This approach intends to add connective tissue between classes, races, genders, and other differences. To redefine *how* we talk about culture and cultivate inclusivity is an act of transgressive creative embodiment; as such, we more consciously craft the culture(s) we want to cocreate and inhabit.

Consider, for example, the surprising history of Haitian loa (or *lwa*) Erzulie as born out of a Polish tradition of Black Madonnas, introduced by

Polish mercenaries brought to the island of Haiti by Napoleon to put down the slave revolution in 1802. In "How the Polish Black Madonna Became Haitian Vodou Spirit Erzulie Dantor," Kate Kingsbury and Debra Neste write:

> Indeed, the Vodou religion played an integral role in inspiring the first and only successful mass slave rebellion, which resulted in the establishment of the world's first Black Republic and the birth of the second nation of the Americas in 1804. The Black Madonna became incorporated into the Vodou pantheon of Lwa.
>
> Upon encountering the image, Vodou practitioners identified with this powerful, dark-skinned Madonna merging her into their pantheon of Lwa, and meshing her with Erzulie Dantor. It should also be noted that at this time, it was considered most dangerous to worship images of African Lwa, whilst working on plantations those using Vodou iconography were subjected to violent punishments. Slaves, in order to conceal their activities, often utilised Catholic saint iconography but instead of typical Catholic devotion their praxis involved syncretic actions deriving from their African ancestry. (3)

Tracking these underworldly, bricolaged histories reminds us of the multiplicity of our heritage. Survival by going underground is a primal survival tool of the feminine. Syncretic fusion with archetypes approved by oppressors is another. We do not come from one source, but many. We are also born of those who survived, got tricky and courageous.

Returning to Daly, poet Audre Lorde publicly critiqued Daly's groundbreaking work in *Gyn/Ecology: The Metaethics of Radical Feminism* (1990) as missing vital contributions from women of color and their mythic heritage. Daly's response was that she was using only "those goddess myths and symbols that were direct sources of Christian myth."[12] Many argue that secondwave feminists were already doing much heavy lifting to define and expose patriarchal injustices, leaving for future generations the task of intersectionality—unpacking interlocking forms of oppression including race, gender, class, and sexual orientation.[13] Yet what if Daly had done more digging, as Lorde suggested? What if she had understood that mythological sources are anything but direct and had gotten curious as to who is missing from this

---

12. See Alexis de Veaux's *Warrior Poet.*
13. For a comprehensive study of intersectionality, see Patricia Hill Collins and Sirma Bilge, *Intersectionality.* For in-depth feminist analyses of power, see Starhawk, *Truth or Dare*; Mary Beard, *Women & Power*; and Jane Caputi, *Goddesses and Monsters.*

story? What if she had turned toward Erzulie and the Black Madonnas as sources and living traditions of the Christian myth?

THE PATRIARCH: WHEN PSYCHE IS OTHER

Depth psychology and mythological studies remind us to explore the impact of these stories about our history and mythology via their resultant cultural and psychic penetration. Rather than resigning our-Selves to the dominating aspects of Western cultures, perhaps the mystery of our history might lie in the reclamation of something older at the heart of Christian mythology: a divine couple in league with an older story, one which has been re-creating itself over time and across territories as evidenced in ancient material culture and archaeomythology. I believe this primal myth, alive and well, continues to morph and evolve with and through us regeneratively.

Patriarchy, with etymological roots in Greek literally meaning "rule of the father" or patriarch, is a social system prioritizing male access to personal and institutional power. The social sciences now recognize and track how insidiously patriarchal hierarchal oppression is extended exponentially via intersectionality as a matrix of domination. Perpetuating practices such as colonialism, capitalism, the modern industrial war complex, human trafficking, sexual exploitation, and agribusiness reinforce dominator paradigms that can then insidiously permeate private and public spheres. In response, radical transdisciplinary analyses of power can provide crucial insight for patriarchy's deconstruction and movement toward postpatriarchal patterns.

At its core patriarchy is fear of the feminine. The institutionalization of patriarchy is self-perpetuating and self-reinforced by groups and persons invested, unconsciously or consciously, in preserving a false dominator narrative based on unconscious fear of internal, repressed feminine qualities (in all genders and culturally). In this way, patriarchy dys/functions as the shadow of empowerment and agency, poisoning psychic, communal, and environmental spaces where hierarchy and "power over" (others) is perpetuated as the primary and unconscious operating system.

When unconscious fear is projected upon an Other, in this case the feminine, particularly what may be defined as the "divine" or "sacred" feminine, the resultant conflation requires careful unpacking. Psychologically, patriarchy's main action has been to systematically suppress persons, ideas, and movements expressing qualities *other* than those of folk who possess institutional power (i.e., possessing qualities and privileges that are sanctioned by dominant groups, including white/light skin, wealth, male gender identity, physical mobility, and education). This act of suppression is foundationally internal; by denying and rejecting challenging, vulnerable human qualities and actions—such as emotions, nurturance, and relationship building—internal oppression is outwardly expressed as fear of an-*Other*. In Jungian psychology an "Other" carries reflections of our own disowned darkness, our personal injuries unconsciously projected onto those around us as we demand they carry our wounds. Within otherness, the potential for creating conflict is enormous, yet it also holds both enormous energy and the necessary dynamics for potential healing, integration, and reconnection.[14]

This practice is beautifully articulated by Aleksandr Solzhenitsyn in *The Gulag Archipelago: 1919–1956*. He writes: "If only it were all so simple! If only there were evil people somewhere insidiously committing evil deeds, and it were necessary only to separate them from the rest of us and destroy them. But the line dividing good and evil cuts through the heart of every human being. And who is willing to destroy a piece of his own heart?" (746). Solzhenitsyn reveals the deep work of integrating our projections. This ability to turn from othering toward our-Selves comes after reconciling our emotions—in his case via physical exile and suffering—and is what is called for in regeneration.

Under patriarchy daughters are often Others within their own families. Close examination of the relationship between Christianity and "classical" (Greco-Roman) mythology reveals their common patriarchal foundation, allowing their influence over us to loosen. In *Daughters of Saturn: From Father's Daughter to Creative Woman*, Patricia Reis opposes James Hillman and other post-Jungians who elevate Greco-Roman mythologies without critical feminist analysis. She writes: "I find that the goddesses of classical Greek myth represent not a recommendation *for* women's behavior, but an analysis of Western women's resistance to being swallowed by a culture based largely on classical Greek ideals and of how that resistance is named by the culture as 'pathological'" (94). Reis points out how classical Greco-Roman goddesses are always operating within a patriarchal framework. Rather than romanticizing their disempowerment, they survive by developing specialized, unique "pathologies" and strategic responses to

---

14. For a comprehensive conversation on the intersecting roles of shadow, projection, and Other, see Connie Zweig and Jeremiah Abrams, eds., *Meeting the Shadow*. This volume goes beyond theory to practical, mythopoetic responses such as Sam Keen's "The Enemy Maker" (197–98).

being abused. Here, Reis offers an important clue as to how healing and regeneration can occur through struggle for survival in less than ideal (nurturing) environments. For Reis, when patriarchy, via Saturn as the enforcer father, swallows his daughters they go missing. Unconscious longing for the feminine leads to first othering, then attempts at colonization, consumption, and murder/filicide.[15]

It is difficult to identify what or who is missing in a culture or microclimate, what could not develop, create, interweave, thrive, or blossom in a hostile, necrotic environment. What and who went into exile and why? Within a cultural legacy of gendered shame and secrecy, women's absences are often unnoticed, quickly denied, or dismissed. Common techniques of denial employed to dismiss the void where the feminine might have been include hasty and disparaging statements such as: "Women simply don't like this particular field" (the sciences, for example); "Women do not have the physical strength" (in sports); "There is no madwoman in the attic" (while simultaneously barring entry to said attic); "That missing black sheep daughter/sister/lover is not birthing her baby abroad, alone—she is visiting her aunt"; and "Mary Magdalene was never very significant anyway." In light of such fervent, repetitive, and committed denial and clumsy incurious amnesia, how can we best detect the missing presence of the feminine and invite her return?

In her author's note to *The Book of Longings* (2020), a novel imagining a dynamic wife of a very human Jesus, Sue Monk Kidd contemplates: "How would the Western world be different if Jesus had married and his wife had been included in his story? . . . Perhaps women would have found more egalitarianism. Perhaps the relationship between sexuality and sacredness would have been less fractured. . . . How does imagining new possibilities affect realities in the present?" (411). Kidd's wondering sparked her work in the imaginal realm crafting a narrative that revisions human potential. Joining other feminist novelists revisiting Christianity's birth, Kidd creatively amplifies her questions of "what if?" via storytelling.

By applying a creative, dynamic, and playful array of sleuthing techniques from a feminist revision of history, archaeomythology, the arts, ecofeminism, and depth psychology, we can excavate and identify missing shards, learn to recognize and feel a void, sense that waft of forgotten fragrance, and reclaim our lost history.

---

15. See chapter 4, "Exiled and Underground," for a detailed discussion of tending such vampiric acts.

BRIDE AND GO SEEK: DYSFUNCTIONAL MARRIAGE IN THE WASTELAND

Central to understanding the sacred marriage from an alchemical perspective is the imagery of the Vesica Piscis, a visual expression of Jung's theory of the *coniunctio*. Two circles overlap so that the center of each rests on the circumference of the other; the central intersecting area or borderland, the *mandorla*, represents and suddenly contains a new and elegant third space, also referred to as the *tertium quid* and divine child. When the union occurs, it carries grace—so the divine third is potent, dynamic, and arrives bearing gifts.

When the feminine is removed from the sacred marriage—whether by unconscious abandonment or willful exile—we lose much more than half of the sum of two connecting parts. By removing the feminine circle from the Vesica Piscis, the entire mandorla (its central core, the elegant third/divine child) is also lost, leaving only the incomplete crescent of the masculine longing for wholeness. The patriarchal, desertified wasteland was left barren not only from the loss of feminine power and its aqueous emotional, relational potentialities but also from the incompleteness of a deeply wounded and incapacitated masculine.

The damming up of the emotional waterway (flow) against the fear of the feminine results not only in a masculine, solar desertification and the risk of drought and fire, it creates an-*Other* side—a corresponding flooded feminine wasteland, a swamp where fertility has become submerged and waterlogged, an emotional bog. Solar consciousness—the desertified, scorched result of imbalance and hubris, including valuing the masculine over the feminine and the disembodied disconnect of spirit from matter—cannot penetrate such a water-logged land flooded with grief. With the exile of the feminine, submerged as Black Madonnas under normally nurturing, healing waters that once flowed freely, fertility is replaced with pernicious dampness, deadly mold, and decaying rot.

Exile in either side results in different pathologies, archetypes, and tools. These adjacent, compound patriarchal wasteland realms require different, yet complementary, interconnected healing. What has been created is a shadow of sacred partnership; the Vesica Piscis has become concretized, static, and the mandorla, rather than embodying flow, is occupied by a shadowy separating, deadening dam ensuring death via either heated dehydration or drowning/decay.

Healing the paired complex wastelands requires a post-Jungian, ecofeminist, mythological response. Consciously deconstructing psychic dams first requires erosion control and elemental consciousness. Perhaps we are being called to the soul-making equivalent of planting willow trees, which thrive on the borderlands where grounding Earth and flowing water meet, while prioritizing aeration and flow mitigation—perhaps via a psychic equivalent of biodynamic flow forms used in gray-water systems. By tending internal and external elemental relationships, the compound wastelands may regenerate anew into an integrated healing vessel for individuation, cultural renewal, and Nature's paradise.

For example, it is worth returning to neurosurgeon Leonard Shlain's insights discussed in the introduction. His research suggests that the physical acts of typing, image making, and—most significantly—viewing, all have the potential to become regenerative acts of integration between separated (wasteland) hemispheres, simultaneously irrigating the desertified (left) logocentric cerebral region as the undervalued and exilic (right) erotic swamp is drained. In this way, simple acts might be effective regenerative tools.

The feminine is re/membered through the interrelated acts of: witnessing, recognizing, and acknowledging the effects of trauma and resultant addiction and dis/ease under patriarchy; attending the consequence of untended shards of abandonment and grief; and creatively moving toward a renewed, embodied wholeness. These movements liberate and release emotional moisture, irrigating the Logos-centered, desertified, solar Western wasteland, bringing both interconnected regions more fully into consciousness.

Much emphasis has been placed on the loss of the Great Mother goddess archetype and related mythology.[16] However, it was not only our mother who went missing; we also lost the mature and fertile Bride, the embodiment of woman moving toward sovereignty, equal partnership, and creative potentiality. The result is a psychological void where she might have been.

The erasure of Magdalene as Christianity's Bride—historically, but more importantly, mythologically—greatly impacted the development of Western cultures. Significantly, the severing and negation of evolutionary ties between Judeo-Christian "history" and myth with preceding Mediterranean mythologies resulted in a wounded "rugged individualist" masculinist stance, further isolating both partners, Bride and Bridegroom, and Western cultures from their fertile heritage. To best nurture the soul of the world, tending the lost and returning feminine is crucial. Recognition and active re/membering of Magdalene as the lost counterpoint of our incomplete world's soul, wounded under patriarchy, heals the compound wasteland.

---

16. For Jungian analysis on the necessity for reclamation of the "Great Mother," see Erich Neumann, *The Great Mother*. For a contemporary ecofeminist post-Jungian response, see Susan Rowland, *Jung*, 42–71.

HERE COMES THE BRIDE? CHRISTIAN SCHOLARSHIP AND
THE INCOMPLETE QUEST FOR MARY MAGDALENE

The public release in 2012 by Karen L. King, Harvard Divinity School's Hollis Professor of Divinity, of a papyrus fragment reading, "Jesus said to them, 'My wife . . .'" and (on another line), "Mary is worthy of it," suggests a *belief* by at least a segment of an early Christian population that Jesus was married and that Mary might have been the name of his wife. The week the news broke I noticed a public post online by a female graduate of my own Mythological Studies doctoral program suggesting this is interesting but what is truly important are the mythological implications. I found myself having an intense and visceral reaction to this simple statement, even though it was not dissimilar from comments I myself had made in the past while teaching women's history. I realized that as a feminist historian, I felt strongly that women's individual lives—as in the case of Mary Magdalene—*did* and *do* matter, even when we do not know much about them. Perhaps it is exactly that quality of "little historical knowledge" that supports their identification with archetypes. Perhaps it is their absence from our histories—and the resultant ahistorical perspective—that has served as an effective and particularly unattractive buttressing agent of patriarchy. I had also come to imagine, perhaps naively, that the importance and centrality of women's history had become accepted in academia. Even if Mary Magdalene was not an actual person, the resurgence of her story, her mythology, seems to be begging for our attention. As a mythologist I am also interested in running out of certainty, allowing space for the imagination to rush in.

Contemporary Magdalene scholars differ significantly in their discussion of her role and influence within Judaism and early Christianity. That Karen King was entrusted with this papyrus fragment by an anonymous owner reflects her public, academic profile within the elite environment of Christian-based Harvard University, where women with doctorates were, mere decades ago, denied any sustenance (entrée) in the all-male libraries and faculty dining hall.[17] Perhaps when we are new to the table, it is hard to get served.

---

17. See the documentary by Donna Read and Starhawk, *Signs out of Time.*

Karen King

King's book *The Gospel of Mary of Magdala: Jesus and the First Woman Apostle* examines the lost and recovered Gospel of Mary as the only existing early Christian gospel written in the name of a woman.[18] Her translation of this Gnostic text presents a more radical interpretation of Jesus's teachings as a path to inner spiritual knowledge, while rejecting his suffering and death as primal in the path to "eternal life." King's work focuses on analyzing how and why Mary Magdalene's apostolic role was systematically undermined over time and through various means in relation to the growing interpersonal and institutional power held by the male apostles, particularly Peter. Especially strong is her argument that the Gnostic texts—including the Gospel of Mary, Gospel of Thomas, Gospel of Philip, Dialogue of the Savior, First Apocalypse of James, Sophia of Jesus Christ, and the Pistis Sophia—offer evidence that earlier traditions venerated Magdalene and honored her authority (see especially chapter 13, "The Apostles"). Through intertextual comparison between canonical Gospels and Gnostic texts, King exhaustively and meticulously details how Magdalene held a valued and respected leadership role. Magdalene repeatedly, as King describes here in her analysis of the Pistis Sophia, for example, "appears to be preeminent among the disciples" (144). Simultaneously, King continually offers evidence that Magdalene's exile was rooted in unacknowledged envy from the male disciples who, in the Gospel of Mary, are "jealous and without understanding" (145).[19] The subsequent self-appointment to apostleship by these same men is in direct contradiction with their lack of leadership at pivotal historic points, especially during the crucifixion and resurrection where Magdalene, along with Mother Mary, are firmly grounded. King ends her book with a call for revision:

> For centuries, the master story has shaped people's imagination of the first Christian centuries; it has provided a myth of origins which casts the early Church as a place where true, uniform, and unadulterated

---

18. See Timothy Freke and Peter Gandy, *Jesus and the Lost Goddess*, for a discussion of the original intent of the Gospel of the Beloved Disciple (GBD) to describe Mary Magdalene; this work was later edited and renamed the Gospel of John. In *Unveiling Mary Magdalene*, historian and theologian Annine van der Meer offers an intertextual validation of this lineage from the GBD to the Gospel of John.

19. See chapter 4, "Exiled and Underground," for further discussion of the significance and cost of envy as patriarchal agent within Magdalenian mythology.

Christianity triumphed. This story has again and again fueled the fires of reformers who appeal to it to legitimize changes in Christianity as it encountered very different conditions and cultural settings around the world. Historians, however, have come more and more to understand the *Gospel of Mary*'s portrait—despite its imaginary elaborations—is in a number of respects more historically accurate than that of the master story. (190)

King calls for a polyvocal Christian dialogue, representing a postmodern commitment to diversity and historical context. Her juxtaposition of "myth of origins" with the concretized notion of a unified, singular "truth" supports open conversation and allows space for the reinterpretation of Magdalene's apostolic role.

But this is as far as King is willing to go in this book. She fails to unpack her use of the word "master" to describe the edified, mainstream versions of patriarchal Christianity. As Audre Lorde famously explained, we cannot use the master's tools to dismantle his house.[20] While King tells the story of the translated text, she fails to mentor us in the reclamation of what was lost of the divine feminine. Instead, she remains at the tip of the iceberg, never mentioning all that lies in the cold darkness below. Additionally, her use of the term "imaginary elaborations" countering a more valued "historically accurate" stance, denies and undermines the value of the mythic imagination and acts of remythologizing Magdalene and plops us back into hierarchical, concretized, dualistic thinking.

After the original 2012 revelation of the papyrus fragment, which debuted among splashy questions of "Was Jesus Married?" on national nightly news programs and in the mainstream media, the text was submitted to continual research and analysis on various levels. The *Harvard Theological Review* dedicated its April 2014 issue to a debate surrounding the "authenticity" of this papyrus, with many of the articles examining parsed, isolated components including: the papyrus structure via radiocarbon dating (forgers have access to ancient raw papyrus), the modern chemical composition of the ink (identifying it as a "forgery" from the seventh or eighth century), and inconsistencies in penmanship and the style and grammar of the Coptic language used.

An article appearing eight months later in *The Atlantic* (December 2014) presents these academic findings, along with subsequent and parallel conversations, in a manner exemplifying popular culture's hunger for news

---

20. See Audre Lorde, "The Master's Tools Will Never Dismantle the Master's House," in *Sister Outsider*, 110–14.

of Magdalene. Scholars Joel Baden, professor of the Hebrew Bible at Yale Divinity School, and Candida Moss, professor of the New Testament at Notre Dame, collaborate to digest the dialogue for mainstream readers and reward those awaiting word with an extensive, pithy rundown of recent findings. Though much of the article emphasizes the authors' belief that the findings are consistent with forgery, while recounting King's continued optimistic open-mindedness as to the value of the fragment, the authors also question whether the text could be an excerpt from either the Gospel of Thomas or the Gospel of John.

While discussing several scholars' proclamations of gut reactions that the "text just felt wrong—or perhaps, too right," Jim Davila of St. Andrews is introduced as saying the fragment represents "exactly, *exactly*, what the Zeitgeist of 2012 would want us to find in an ancient gospel" (78). Supporting his suspicion, the authors continue: "Put it this way: if an ancient Christian text describing Jesus as having a wife and elevating the status of women in the Church had emerged in 2004, just after *The Da Vinci Code* was published, it would have been laughed out of the room" (78). Baden and Moss identify an active academic decade for biblical scholars and feminist studies. Most interestingly, by alluding to a post–*Da Vinci Code* canon just ten years in the making, yet minimizing the value of said scholarship while also ignoring the extensive related creative output within the arts, they cast subtle doubt onto the validity of other fragments of research and creativity, effectively ignoring the imaginal realm.

In the summer of 2016 *The Atlantic* published Ariel Sabar's "The Unbelievable Tale of Jesus' Wife," a thorough investigation tracking the fraud behind the fragment. The trail he uncovered contained a range of shadowy components from the exile of an Egyptology dropout to forgery, channeling, and pornography. Sabar went on to publish his findings in book form, *Veritas: A Harvard Professor, a Con Man, and the Gospel of Jesus's Wife* (2020). In an interesting move, *Harvard Theological Review* stood by King citing the primacy of academic discourse over certainty; neither had ever fully authenticated the papyrus. If the artifact initiated dialogue, perhaps its "authenticity" or value lies in its mythology rather than in its provenance/history.

Jane Schaberg

Another branch of Magdalenian scholarship can be found in Jane Schaberg's *The Resurrection of Mary Magdalene: Legends, Apocrypha, and the Christian Testament* (2002), an analysis of archaeology, Gnostic texts, legend, and apocryphal traditions within a progressive feminist framework. Schaberg, a religious scholar who also taught women's studies, suggests a case for a theological resurrection of Mary Magdalene, whom she identifies as "Mary of Magdala." Her excellent analysis and deconstruction of the conflation between Mary Magdalene and the penitent sinner in her chapter "Silence, Conflation, Distortion, Legends" bears special note.[21] But perhaps her greatest contribution to Magdalenian scholarship is her use of the imaginal and theoretical work of Virginia Woolf as counterpoint to both religious studies and her own eloquent and persuasive language. She describes Woolf's significance to the conversation:

> Her questions about gender, about the boundaries and lack of boundaries between persons, about death and survival ("perhaps—perhaps") can redirect our attention from the ways issues are treated traditionally. A flawed and experimental spirit, she dealt with anger, the desire for dominance, women's "ancestral memory," the outsider's split consciousness. What she was after was a radical transformation of culture and society, for men as well as women, and she began an analysis of classism as well as sexism. (11)

Here, Schaberg calls upon Woolf's well-known and thorough deconstruction of patriarchy, including an analysis of what has become intersectionality. Schaberg also notes the messiness inherent in Woolf, the emotional woman, the mythopoetic writer. The dynamism of Woolf is a powerful tool to borrow and swing on behalf of one's own agenda.

Sadly, Schaberg herself is not such a heavy hitter, not as deeply committed to liberation. We find mixed messages in both her original work and the pared-down, "popular" version of her scholarship, published as *Mary Magdalene Understood* and coauthored with Melanie Johnson-Debaufre. This book was created to make her research and writings more accessible to a wider audience, though oddly stripped of the harmonic accompaniment of Woolf. In the introduction to this edition, Schaberg makes a declaration I find myself in agreement with, a feminist historian's standard proclamation: "If you are willing to engage in the process of sifting, you can learn something about both Mary Magdalene

---

21. See Marina Warner's analysis of Magdalene and the Bride in *Alone of All Her Sex*. Warner's chapter "The Penitent Whore" examines the genesis and mutation of Magdalene mythology, including: the second-century Gnostic celebration of love between Jesus and Magdalene, Origen's early Christian writings, Western folklore portraying her as a "hermitess," and the significance of the apocryphal Gnostic Gospels. While newer texts take these theories deeper, Warner's early work—in fine ecofeminist spirit—exposes the underbelly of a Catholicism constructed on the phallacies of the virgin/whore dichotomy and power-over-Nature drive (337).

and yourself, about one woman and about every woman's struggles to be heard, taken seriously, understood" (10). And then something altogether different: "If you don't care about women's history, or think all history is meaningless, or think Christianity and religion itself are unevolved, best ignored, I can't tell you why you should care about Mary Magdalene" (10). Well, I can.

Though Schaberg casts a wide interdisciplinary net suggesting the magnitude of interconnecting influences and impact of Magdalenian scholarship, while appealing to popular culture's valuing of history and the current political correctness of women's history—her intention is to illuminate how powerful and apropos a study of Magdalene is, both individually and collectively—she fails to make the larger leap, missing the opportunity to make crucial cultural and interfaith connections with just how broadly the lack of bridal representation in the Christian myth impacts us all—for one surely does not need even an interest in history, or in women, for that matter. Though exalting creativity, Schaberg fails to expand from religious studies (and here I suggest she is limited to mainstream Judeo-Christian theology) and women's history toward Magdalene's enormous influence on Western cultures. What begins as a maverick approach to feminist research falls short in the end. She also lacks interest in Magdalene as Bride and the impact of her resurgence, limiting her research to a Logos-concretizing, (unconsciously) nostalgic (sentimental) historical frame. She remains looking back, melancholic. What a curious limitation considering the title of her opus, *The Resurrection of Mary Magdalene*. She claims support of future feminist scholarship as a goal. "It is my hope also that this book will be a crossover, from feminist Religious Studies/Biblical Studies to Feminist Studies in general" (12). Yet by neither acknowledging the damning wasteland dam nor assisting in its deconstruction, she simultaneously muddies the water and leaves the trail difficult to follow.

It is worth noting that decoding Schaberg's work is further muddied by the lack of indices in either of her books, leaving us to plod through cumbersome biblical books as the only key to her legend. This archaic publishing style, which remains standard practice in biblical scholarship, limits access to these works of feminist scholarship as it becomes extremely difficult to track threads via themes, theorists, places, or historical figures; advanced (insider) biblical knowledge is necessary to wade through the (murky) waters. Under these practices, each writer remains isolated and disembodied within this new canon. Since allowing the masculinist Bible to be their only commonality, these disparate strands evolve without intertextual, transdisciplinary communication, remaining isolated—colonized and colonizing.

Jean-Yves Leloup

Jean-Yves Leloup, a French Orthodox priest and theologian, offered the first complete translation and commentary of the Gospel of Mary from the Coptic in his book *The Gospel of Mary Magdalene* (2002). Leloup presents the text as an illumination and a renewal of the sacred feminine in the Western spiritual tradition. He argues that the reclamation and practical application of these lost mystery traditions has the power to reinvigorate living spiritual traditions. He develops his theory further in *The Gospel of Philip: Jesus, Mary Magdalene, and the Gnosis of Sacred Union* (2004) and *The Sacred Embrace of Jesus and Mary: The Sexual Mystery at the Heart of the Christian Tradition* (2006). For Leloup, the central role of these texts is the restoration of Jesus's healthy human sexuality to the core teachings of Christianity, where Magdalene is also celebrated as an embodiment of the archetypal feminine. In *The Sacred Embrace of Jesus and Mary*, he writes:

> We must live our own sexuality fully before we can speak of true androgyny. As at the level of psychotherapy, at the higher level of spiritual evolution, we need to develop an ego structure that is as sane and stable as possible before claiming to have access to what we call—sometimes too glibly—the self. This is related to the significance the *Gospel of Mary* gives to the fact that Jesus must have been a normal, male human being who was at least capable of having a relationship with Miriam of Magdala as a prerequisite for becoming the archetype of synthesis, the Anthropos.
>
> Our path as individuals is the same in that we are called to become whole and therefore capable of loving—not from our lack, but from our fullness. . . . By the same token, Miriam of Magdala first had to become truly woman, in all the sexual dimensions of her femininity, accepting and integrating her masculine nature as well before realizing her status as speaker and knower (a status that many refuse to recognize). It was only after all this long and patient work to become fully human that she, too, could truly join her Master as anthropos, in a humanity complete and open to the divine, transparent, like he who was "more than Being: a Gift of the Good." (126–27)[22]

For Leloup, Magdalenian scholarship becomes useful in its ability to support individuation and subsequently the potentialities embedded within

---

22. See chapter 4 for further discussion of "the good" in relation to envy and Magdalenian mythology.

partnership, which is ultimately a tool for becoming *anthropos*, whole and fully human. His central thesis focuses on how the fusion of love and sexuality at the core of the partnership/sacred marriage that connected Jesus/Yeshua and Magdalene/Miriam is a psychological movement toward individuation. He also takes a Jungian stance in identifying the necessary internal parallel of cultivating a woman's inner masculine and a man's inner feminine. Leloup sees the relationship between these two leaders as both a template and container for individuals and partnerships to reach synthesis. By bridging religious teachings and psychological perspectives, Leloup offers a psychospiritual attitude backed by his extensive scholarly research in both the canonical and apocryphal Gospels. Unfortunately, in describing Jesus as her "Master" rather than beloved partner, he replicates the dominator paradigm.

Cynthia Bourgeault

Cynthia Bourgeault, an Episcopal priest and prolific writer, explores how Mary Magdalene became one of the most influential symbols in the history of Christianity. In *The Meaning of Mary Magdalene: Discovering the Woman at the Heart of Christianity* (2010) she examines the Bible, Church tradition, art, legend, and newly discovered texts to focus her scholarship on a tripartite Magdalene as teacher, apostle, and beloved within a lost and reclaimable wisdom tradition at the heart of Christianity. Highly popular with Christian practitioners, Bourgeault speaks to the radical (r)evolutionary potential of Magdalene mythology within institutionalized Christianity.[23] Curiously, she assures her readers that she is approaching the material "not as a feminist . . . but from the perspective of wisdom Christianity" (x) and that "I derive my observations not from contemporary Jungian categories but from traditional wisdom teachings on the human soul as a bridge between the visible and invisible realms" (xi), which happens to sound a good deal like Jungian psychological navigation. With such fertile correlations between the conscious and unconscious, as well as the Self and Other, she limits herself to literal interpretations within her exploration of wisdom teachings. Why does Bourgeault invest so much

---

23. For an earlier example of (r)evolutionary potential, see Marjorie Malvern's *Venus in Sackcloth*, perhaps the first major postmodern, ecofeminist remythologizing of Magdalene in religion and culture. Malvern's pre–*Da Vinci Code* scholarship, written in the decade immediately following the second Vatican Council, hypothesizes that the metamorphosis of Mary Magdalene—from maligned "prostitute" to the reclamation of her as Magdalene-Bride—resolves dualism, links her with antiquity's goddesses of love and wisdom, and offers reunion with the Earth.

energy in distancing herself from both feminism and Jungian theories, especially when the power and impact of her work seem derived from and congruent with both traditions?

When any person—let alone a white, educated, *preaching* woman, who has the ability to make an enormous social impact—apologetically denies a feminist stance, it sets my teeth on edge, especially when she clearly *behaves* and *writes* as a "feminist" while enjoying privileges won through feminist movements. While I imagine she might be attempting to reach a broader audience, one which might be fearful—afraid of power, their own and that of an imagined, perhaps potentially devouring, shadow feminine—I am disheartened to have to navigate such a quagmire of mixed messages.

Regardless, Bourgeault has much to add to the conversation on Magdalene, especially her perspective on her role as the Beloved. However, if she wants to support the return of the Bride, more conviction is required. She repeatedly offers powerful evidence, then backpedals, lest she seem too "Jungian" or too "feminist." In a particularly challenging section entitled "The View from the Gutter," she writes:

> The question of Mary Magdalene and Jesus has been little better than scandalmongering. Amid the flurry of gossip and speculation emerging from the current plethora of scholarly and pseudo-scholarly studies, we are really presented with only four options:
>
> 1. That Mary Magdalene was Jesus's mistress;
> 2. That theirs was a politically arranged marriage, strictly for dynastic purposes;
> 3. That they were sexual consorts in some gnostic Mystery religion, ritually reenacting the sacred *hieros gamos*, or union of the opposites;
> 4. That the whole story is purely archetypal, a great Sophianic myth depicting the integration of the masculine and feminine within the human soul. (88–89)

Bourgeault argues the problem of the Christian wisdom tradition as incomplete tableau created through dodgy scholarship. She brings forth the problems inherent with residual conflation of Magdalene and the penitent sinner, still lingering decades after Vatican II's exoneration without offering clarity. For Bourgeault, these four options are not comprehensive enough to encompass her perspective on what she defines as ancient wisdom teaching, yet somehow this brilliant scholar has used her energy to portray these themes as dirty—contaminated in a Protestant sinful sort of way—rather than inviting us to explore why they are part of the conversation related to elements of her own theories (see especially parts II and III). Her use of "myth" and "archetype" attempts to leave them devoid of spiritual integrity, sacred weight—quite the opposite of Campbell and Jung. Since much of her material is interesting and provocative within the Christian framework, why then go to such lengths to bring in a tone of dismissal and shame (a patriarchal and damaging move) when she is attempting to bring aspects of Magdalene into the conversation in the second half of her book? Bourgeault mirrors and reproduces the problem she has identified, projecting it outwardly as "scandalmongering" and "poor scholarship."

Pope Francis

During the summer of 2016, Pope Francis—in an unforeseen move—formally elevated Magdalene's status within the Catholic Church from saint to that of apostle, validating her title as "apostle of the apostles." The statement issued via the Holy See Press Office, "Mary Magdalene, Apostle of the Apostles, 10 June 2016," proclaims that Magdalene's traditional saint's day, July 22, is now to be celebrated as a feast day in the Roman Catholic liturgical calendar on par with those of the other (all male, self-appointed) apostles, recognizing her dual role as both the first to witness Jesus's resurrection and through "true and authentic evangelization" by announcing his resurrection "like the other apostles" (Holy See Press Office). Here we find the Catholic Church answering the call of many progressive Christians—including King, Schaberg, Leloup, and Bourgeault—as well as the swelling global Magdalenian movement, which overflows religious boundaries.

But is this new title large enough to reflect the magnitude of what Magdalene carries? The Church goes on to state its intention that "the special mission of this woman be highlighted, as an example and model to every woman in the Church" (Holy See Press Office). To be an apostle means to witness as a disciple, to follow. Here the Church is content to ascribe a clearly delineated and relatively mild role for women—what feels like a demotion. Is Magdalene's role that of witness, disciple, informant, follower? Is that the role of womanhood? And what of the more dynamic acts of leadership, healing, and creativity?

Is the very nature of religious scholarship incomplete without transdisciplinary dialogue? What can depth psychology, literature, film, and the arts offer this incomplete quest? Can a mythological perspective bring understanding and—more importantly—curiosity?

THE ARCHETYPAL BRIDE, FORETOLD AND EXPECTED:
CONSIDERING MARGARET STARBIRD

From outraged Catholic laywoman to radical insider and feminist historian, Margaret Starbird became a Magdalene scholar to negate controversial theories put forth by Michael Baigent, Richard Leigh, and Henry Lincoln in *Holy Blood, Holy Grail* (1982). Instead, the evidence she found radicalized her, leading to the publication of *The Woman with the Alabaster Jar: Mary Magdalen and the Holy Grail* (1993) and four subsequent books. Starbird draws transdisciplinarily on evidence in history, archaeology, symbolism, medieval art and heraldry, mythology, Jungian psychology, alchemy, and religious texts. Identifying Magdalene as having fulfilled a more radical role she terms the "Lost and Returning Bride"—which extends beyond the Christian tradition, having a deep impact on Western cultures—Starbird argues for Mary Magdalene as Jesus's partner and legitimate successor. Central to Starbird's quest is the assertion in *Holy Blood, Holy Grail* that the Provençal legend preserved in Old French emerges as early as the fourth century, telling of an exiled Mary Magdalene teaching and preaching a "purer" egalitarian form of Christianity in the south of France (23). A version of this legend is preserved within Jacobus de Voragine's 1275 collection of hagiographies, *The Golden Legend*, a late medieval Latin bestseller (1993).[24]

Starbird argues that Magdalene's mythology and teachings—including a displaced and beloved Bride as the bearer of the royal bloodline, the *Sangraal*, traveling to and settling in the south of France after the crucifixion, perhaps the existence of a child or children from her marriage with Jesus—have been perceived as threatening and subversive, and that her story and wisdom teachings survived by going underground, becoming outsider heresy, deeply influencing European culture and religion for millennia (23).

Despite being subjected to centuries of extreme violence and genocide, these pockets of spiritual practitioners throughout Europe emphasize the centrality of the feminine in balance with the masculine and continue to consciously honor Mary Magdalene as the Bride who was denied and abandoned by the male apostles who became early founders of the Catholic Church. Starbird contends that by encoding their heritage at different historical points through art, alchemy, grail and Black Madonna lore, the tarot, and folklore, Magdalenian mythology survived by going underground. It is worth noting here that this diasporic movement—along with Magdalene's possible

---

24. See *Holy Blood, Holy Grail*, page 826.

motherhood and leadership—is echoed repeatedly in literary fiction and throughout the arts, a significant aspect of her renewal.

By identifying and expounding upon the importance of the expected archetypal Bride in Hebrew tradition, Starbird reveals and amplifies the importance of Mary Magdalene's role then and now. Exploring how the heresy of Mary Magdalene as the exilic Bride influenced Western cultures, she continues to be one of few Magdalene theorists attempting a depth psychological analysis of Magdalene as the Lost and Returning Bride. This insistence on Magdalene's role as archetypal Bride is a crucial mythological contribution to understanding our compound wasteland crisis.

Diverging from other Magdalene scholars on several points, Starbird argues that it is not enough to recognize Mary Magdalene as "the apostle of the apostles" and that she embodies an *even more radical* identity as the Lost Bride. In *Mary Magdalene: Bride in Exile* she disputes the relationship between Mary Magdalene and an obscure Hellenic town in Galilee known as Taricheae until its destruction in CE 67, only later renamed Magdala (52–55). This is a significant divergence from the assertion of many prominent scholars—including Schaberg and Leloup—who proclaim the town of Magdala as the onomastic root of Mary Magdalene's name and identity, perhaps deriving comfort through a historical geographic "certainty." The town that was later built upon, or perhaps reconstructed from, the remains of Taricheae (post-CE 67) was called Magdala Nunnayah, a name meaning "tower of the fishes" in Aramaic. With the fishes being a well-known symbol for Jesus and Christianity, is it possible this resurrected town was instead named for both Magdalene and Jesus?

Several theorists consider Mary Magdalene's name as "Mary the Magdalene" to have been a title, perhaps linking her with a priestess lineage. In *The Woman with the Alabaster Jar*, Starbird discusses how the "messianic promises of the Hebrew Scriptures would someday be fulfilled in the descendant of Jesus" (71) and investigates the Hebrew prophet Micah and his vision of the restoration of Jerusalem (50). The prophecy beginning in Micah 4:8 becomes central to understanding an anticipated and central role of the Lost Bride:

> As for you, O [Magdal-eder], watchtower of the flock,
> O stronghold of the Daughter of Zion!
> the former dominion will be restored to you;
> kingship will come to the Daughter of Jerusalem.
> Why do you now cry aloud—
> have you no king?
> Has your counselor perished,

that pain seizes you like that of a woman in labor?
Writhe in agony, O Daughter of Zion,
like a woman in labor,
for now you must leave the city
and camp in the open field. (Starbird 50)[25]

Starbird asserts that "Magdalene" is an epithet for the same Mary who anoints Jesus at Bethany. "The place name *Magdal-eder* literally means 'tower of the flock,' with 'the promise of the restoration of Sion following her exile'" (51). The Golden Legend acts as primary source, telling of the exiled "Magdal-eder" seeking asylum on the southern French coast. She traveled with "Martha and Lazarus of Bethany, landed in a boat on the coast of Provence in France" (51). For Starbird, the tower is a recurring symbol used by heretics for centuries preserved within religious art history, Provençal legends, folklore, watermarks, and the tarot, which Starbird refers to as a flashcard catechism of the heresy (116).

Starbird also supports the theory of a dynastic marriage between a royal daughter of the Benjamites and Jesus of the tribe of David, whom she anoints, the only event recorded in all four canonical Gospels (40), uniting an occupied nation (49). Such anointing, which Jesus declares is for burial, is "the unique privilege of a royal Bride" in Hebrew tradition (30). The exile of a wife of a politically radical and threatening Jesus post-crucifixion—especially

---

25. The Bible used in *The Woman with the Alabaster Jar* by Margaret Starbird, unless otherwise noted, is the *Saint Joseph New Catholic Edition*. In comparison, the *Jewish Study Bible* version of Micah 4:8 through the middle of verse 10 follows:

And you, O Migdal-eder,
Outpost of Fair Zion,
It shall come to you:
The former monarchy shall return—
The kingship of Fair Jerusalem.
Now why do you utter such cries?
Is there no king in you,
Have your advisors perished,
That you have been seized by writing
Like a woman in travail?
Writhe and scream, Fair Zion,
Like a woman in travail!
For now you must leave the city
And dwell in the country—

one who was a mother or was about to be—seems plausible, especially with accounts of her exilic journey beginning in Egypt, then seeking "an even safer haven on the coast of France" (60).

Mary Ann Beavis

In "The Deification of Mary Magdalene," Mary Ann Beavis considers Margaret Starbird a feminist "mythographer" who makes two significant contributions to Magdalenian conversations by critically challenging biblical scholars—on points such as Magdalene's identity as the sister of Martha and Lazarus and the import of the title "The Magdalene" versus a name grounded in the place/landscape of Magdala—and because "her central thealogical assertion is highly relevant to Christian feminist theo/alogy" (147).

Significantly, Beavis identifies Starbird as a radical thinker who is calling for a profound transformation in Christian mythology. While Beavis cautions that Starbird's "Magdalene Sophiaology" runs the risk of being "overly romantic, essentialist, [and/or] heterosexist," she also discusses the impact of Starbird's work, especially how Mary Magdalene as the sacred Bride "captures the popular ('of the people') imagination in a way that other feminist christologies don't" (151). Identifying as a Christian and locating herself within feminist thea/ology, Beavis dialogues with both Rosemary Radford Ruether's question "Can a male savior save women?" and Jane Schaberg's "Magdalene Christianity" to identify the significance of Magdalene's resurgence (151). Ultimately, Beavis finds Schaberg's scholarship limiting (though Schaberg's concept of Magdalene is not that of a full feminine counterpart to Christ, she acknowledges a striving for Christlike qualities), and her answer to Ruether's question a resounding No.

Tracking trends in Christian feminism, Beavis suggests the growing usage of terms such as "Jewitchery" and burgeoning online discussion groups—with listserv names including: Asherah, goddesschristians, magdalene-list, thechristianwitchcourse, and sisterhoodoftherose—reflect a significant and developing "Goddess stream" (151). Beavis herself believes that identifying Mary Magdalene as *a* Christian goddess—as opposed to *the* only possible one—allows a plurality of goddess narratives to emerge. While Beavis identifies the pervasive and persuasive pull of Starbird's research and resultant popularity, missing from her analysis is a depth psychological perspective valuing the interconnected imaginal, communal, and cultural impacts and importance of remythologizing Magdalene. Unlike Starbird, Beavis has yet to make the restorative Magdalenian leap in her own scholarship, though that she may in the future is worth monitoring.

THE MYTHOLOGICAL LINEAGE OF "FERTILITY CULTS"

Situating Jewish history and traditions within the lineage of Near Eastern and Mediterranean "fertility cults" contextualizes Hebrew mythology within a larger matrix where cyclical sacrifice and resurrection offered redemption for the land and her people. In *Pagan Christs* J. M. Robertson suggests the complexities of such a legacy:

> Among the Semites there is a tradition that the sacrifice by a king of his son is extremely efficacious. The reference in Matthew 27.16.17 to Barrabas was long accepted in the primitive church to read "Jesus Barrabas," and this is translated "Son of the Father." There are grounds for surmising a pre-Christian cult of Jesus (Joshua), associated in remote times with human sacrifice. Other influences were also at work in fashioning the Christian mystery drama, notably the widespread myths of a dying and resurrected god and the sacrifice of a mock-king at Rhodes at the feast of Kronos. In Semitic mythology Kronos "whom the Phoenicians call Israel" sacrifices his only son after putting upon him royal robes. (11)

Robertson locates Christianity within a historical framework of interrelated, regional spiritual traditions, identifying interconnected threads of surviving tapestries. By linking Greek, Semitic, and Christian stories, Robertson illuminates the heritage of Christian mythology. In contrast to King, Robertson focuses on the sacrificial *and renewing* rite at the core of Christianity, amplifying the religion's connections to what was also primal to earlier traditions and—contrary to the concretized teachings of the contemporary Church on sacrifice—not unique to Christianity: the sacrifice and resurrection of a male god-king. Robertson's focus, however, remains solely on the role of the male savior god-king, missing the larger context and goal of these "fertility" rites as mystery traditions. To do so keeps us limited to the patriarchal realm of God the Father/God the Son, completely leaving out any representation of the divine feminine. Perhaps he never read our oldest surviving epic poem, the Sumerian *The Descent of Inanna* dating back four millennia, which describes how that goddess hung on a hook for three days before returning to renew the world long before these male deities appeared on the scene.[26]

---

26. See especially Diane Wolkstein and Samuel Noah Kramer, *Inanna, Queen of Heaven and Earth*.

In her exploration of the "Cults of the Sacrificed King," Starbird finds Mary Magdalene's role firmly alongside the Bridegroom:

The anointing by the woman in the Gospels is reminiscent of the love poetry connected with the rites of the "Sacred Marriage" celebrating the union of a local god and goddess. It is not impossible that the true meaning of the anointing at Bethany was the same: the Sacred Marriage of the sacrificed king. Its mythological content would have been understood by the Hellenized community of Christians who heard the Gospel preached in the cities of the Roman Empire where the cults of the love goddesses were not completely extinguished until the end of the fifth century A.D. . . .

It is always the Mary called "the Magdalen" who is pictured in Western art carrying the alabaster jar of precious ointment, and it is on her feast day that the Roman Catholic Church traditionally reads from Canticles (Song of Songs 3:2–4) the story of the Bride searching for the Bridegroom/Beloved from whom she has become separated. In medieval and Renaissance paintings, it is invariably the Magdalen we see, her hair unbound, at the foot of the cross with Mary, the mother of Jesus; and it is she who kisses the feet of Jesus in paintings of the Disposition. . .

These paintings recall for us the mythologies of several pagan sun/ fertility gods (Osiris, Dumuzi, and Adonis) who were slain and resurrected. In each case, the bereaved widow (Isis, Inanna, and Aphrodite) poured out her grief and desolation over the corpse of her beloved, bitterly lamenting his death. . . . In each cult it is the *Bride* who laments the death of the sacrificed god. In poetry used in the cultic worship of the goddess Isis, some lines are identical with those found in Canticles and others are close paraphrases. (31)

By connecting the mythemes of anointing, grief, and sacred poetry to the *relationship* between the Bride/Widow and the Bridegroom/Sacrificed King, Starbird's focus supports the reclamation of Christianity's lost Bride. By reframing the traditions in terms of "love," grief, and the female role as "love goddesses," Starbird both redirects focus to Jesus's central teachings and places Christianity in line with early mystery traditions. Identifying the Song of Songs (Canticles) as surviving sacred poetry dedicated to Isis, she cites specific, plausible examples of the role of the Bride within Jewish culture as descending from a rich regional heritage, emphasizing the vital, ritualistic significance of anointment and grieving.

Here we see how Starbird's writing embodies the goals of sacred partnership: balance in reporting on historical events, oscillation between
(supposed opposite) gender roles and experiences, and the location of the
mythological context of Christian mystery rites within a Mediterranean
"fertility cult" lineage, which is rooted in ancient partnership models seeking bounty and renewal. In her scholarship Starbird successfully holds the
tension between masculine and feminine, divine and human, knowing and
inquiring. Starbird's inclusion of both women and men, goddesses and gods
not only offers a fuller representation of historic and mythological events
but also invites resonance with a broader audience. Women are no longer
outsiders in the conversation. As Mary Daly famously stated, "If God is
male, then male is god" (19).[27] We can no longer afford to tell only part of
the story or negate the validity and necessity of the retelling, both of which
deny women's history, heritage, and power. The reclamation of such dynamic
agency clarifies the vital role an expected Bride might have historically held
in the collective psyche, especially within an exilic and occupied legacy.[28]

The mythology of sacred marriage is examined by Anne Baring and Jules
Cashford in *The Myth of the Goddess: Evolution of an Image* where they identify the Song of Songs as a surviving model for sacred marriage carrying the
seeds of earlier Mediterranean partnership traditions:

> The Song of Songs, the most beautiful of the sacred texts that have
> come down to us, was written down about 100 BC. Solomon is
> believed to have lived and built his great temple in Jerusalem in the
> tenth century BC. Whether or not this text, said to be his bridal song,
> descends from this time is impossible to say, but there is certainly
> much in it that relates to an earlier era and to the imagery of the
> Mother Goddess, who may have been his "consort"—mother, sister
> and Bride—in a sacred marriage rite similar to the Sumerian one. The
> richness of the sexual imagery and the abundance of earth's "fruits"
> suggest that its origin is not Judaic, but can be placed in a time when
> earth and sexuality were not split off from the divine. The fact that,
> although it was not excluded from the canon of Jewish and Christian
> scriptures, it really belongs within the mystical tradition of Judaism
> and Christianity may indicate that the aspect of life rejected by the

27. See Mary Daly, *Beyond God the Father.*
28. One scholar's writing on the feminine mysteries of the Bible was in limbo for seven years
as she contemplated Magdalene's return. Eventually placing her as the necessary epilogue to
her research, Ruth Rusca (like Malvern) cites Magdalene's primary function as overcoming
duality. See Rusca, *Feminine Mysteries in the Bible.*

orthodox tradition "goes underground" into the unconscious and reappears as mysticism, only to be rejected again by orthodoxy. (479)

This movement underground, and subsequent misinterpretation as depotentized "mysticism" is a powerful insight into the dismissal of dangerous heresies and the unconscious. Baring and Cashford support Song of Songs as evidence for the mystery traditions at the heart of Judeo-Christian roots, identifying Solomon as an incomplete component of a larger story—a sacred marriage union with his Sister-Bride. While noting the centrality of the bridal mytheme and sexual potency of the text, the authors suggest these components are reduced from greater mystical meaning. Since the Christian church maintains a disembodied stance, partnership and sexuality remain outside their sanction.[29]

Starbird describes the Song of Songs as an evocation of the sacred marriage and relates Mary Magdalene to the black Bride whose "hidden state [as the] unknown queen" correlates with the "deposed Davidic princes of Jerusalem" in Lamentations 4:8 (61). "Brighter than snow were her princes, whiter than milk . . . now their appearance is blacker than soot, they are unrecognized on the streets" (61). Here the Sister-Bride, "black but beautiful," seeks the lost Bridegroom (165).[30] Starbird asserts that the seeking of this union of opposites is indeed primary within Judaism:

> Jewish rabbinical tradition teaches that the Ark of the Covenant kept in the Holy of Holies of Solomon's Temple on Mount Sion contained not only the tablets on which the Ten Commandments were inscribed, but also a "man and a woman locked in intimacy in the form of a hexagram." This tradition articulates the fundamental basis of Hebrew society, the tablets represent the precepts of the covenant, and the hexagram symbolizes the *hieros gamos*, the intimate union of the opposites. (164–65)

Starbird emphasizes here the lost centrality of the sacred marriage to the Jewish tradition. For her, reestablishing the links between the hidden mystery tradition with the evocative symbolism identified with the Ark of the

---

29. For critical work on archaeomythological evidence of, and the necessity for, partnership models, see Riane Tennenhaus Eisler, *The Chalice and the Blade*, and Riane Tennenhaus Eisler and David Loye, *The Partnership Way*.

30. This portion of the Song of Songs 1:5 is translated as "I am dark, but comely" in the *Jewish Study Bible*.

Covenant, the Ten Commandments tablets, the Star of David, and Solomon's Temple refocuses the bridal import and potency of these archaeomythological items and spaces. Missing from Starbird's scholarship, unfortunately, is a clear citation of this "Jewish rabbinical tradition," hampering further inquiry.

Relatedly, Baring and Cashford go on to discuss the relationship of the Song of Songs to Inanna's sacred marriage mythology and "blackness as an image that was always associated with the Great Goddess: Isis, Cybele, Demeter and Artemis" (480):

> The sacred marriage came to be understood by Jewish and Christian mystics as an image of union between the soul and her luminous, or "heavenly," counterpart. In Jewish mysticism the sacred marriage was contemplated as an image of the union between Yahweh and his divine consort, the Shekhinah, and between the soul and Wisdom. The imagery of Gnostic myth took the union of the two aspects of the godhead as a metaphor for the union of the awakened soul with her Bridegroom. These, the sister and brother, were the "daughter" and "son" of the transcendent Mother and Father. In the Middle Ages the poets of the twelfth century transcribed the image of the sacred marriage to the Grail legends. Alchemy, in the marriage of sun and moon, king and queen, made the sacred marriage one of the central realizations of the Great Work, the prerequisite of the birth within them of the priceless philosophical gold, or the divine child, the "son of the philosophers" who were the lovers of Divine Wisdom. (484)

Layered, interconnected, intertextual symbolism abounds between Sumerian, Babylonian, Egyptian, Greco-Roman, and Judeo-Christian (including Gnostic) literature and is later translated into grail lore and alchemy.[31] By tracking how ancient mysticism resides at the heart of Judeo-Christian traditions, a previously disembodied Logos-oriented approach to the Christian tradition can become rooted.

---

31. Contentious new research links Magdalene to Artemis and bees via archaeomythological finds, including a Galilean mosaic possibly depicting sacred alchemical partnership, and a reimagining of the symbology of the statue of Artemis at Ephesus. See Simcha Jacobovici and Barrie Wilson, *The Lost Gospel*; and Stephanie Hagan, "Time, Memory, and Mosaics at the Monastery of Our Lady Mary." Interestingly, recent restoration at Rosslyn Chapel in Scotland, made famous in *The Da Vinci Code* book and film as a Magdalene site, revealed six-hundred-year-old beehives built into the roof's stonework. See BBC, "Rosslyn Chapel Was Haven for Bees."

The union of the chalice and the blade remains the visual symbol of the state of Israel embodied in the Star of David, perhaps as a testament to this longing for integration and balance. Yet how is this union, this equilibrium, achieved? How can such harmony be found between the masculine and feminine, between historical "knowledge" and mythological "perspective"? Perhaps the returning Magdalene, as change-seeking agent, might offer such a path toward balance.

The more fixated on a particular story or point in history we become, the less sense it makes in isolation from its surrounding sociopolitical and psychospiritual settings; it is the larger contextual container that gives—and makes—meaning. Perhaps situating Mary Magdalene within a larger frame allows a fuller grasp of who she is as archetypal Bride and what she brings, enabling a broader approach and study via mythological and archetypal meaning making.

MAGDALENE IN THE IMAGINAL REALM

Myriad novels depicting the life of Mary Magdalene have appeared over the past several decades. These fictionalized accounts range from historical fiction to what can be termed a "guest appearance" in Rob Brezsny's wildly creative, visionary *The Televisionary Oracle* (2000). Others, like Elizabeth Cunningham's extensive *Maeve Chronicles*, straddle both realms. Rather than prioritizing an interest in historical accuracy, some of these, including Brezsny's imaginal story, serve more as an invocation of the relevancy of Magdalene in history and contemporary culture. Chapter 3, "Bridal Agency: How Women's Literary Fiction and Memoir Crash the (Patriarchal) Wedding," digs into this material in depth. Unique among the myriad depictions of Magdalene's story within the imaginal realm is Kathleen McGowan's *Magdalene Line* series.

Kathleen McGowan's Magdalene: Archaeomythological Integrity via Creativity

Former journalist, Hollywood studio public relations agent, and Disney marketing representative turned novelist, Kathleen McGowan, traces evidence of Magdalene's impact in France as the diasporic leader who introduced Christianity to Europe, specifically in a more authentic and progressive form. McGowan's *Magdalene Line* series—*The Expected One* (2006), *The Book of Love* (2009), *The Poet Prince* (2010), and *The Boleyn Heresy* (2022)—is mythologically unique and pivots around sacred union and embodied spirituality.

The exilic threads of Magdalene's mythology are not limited to origins in the Golden Legend. Like Starbird, McGowan is distinctive in her attention to art history and archaeomythology, especially asserting that it is the art of Botticelli and not Leonardo Da Vinci (whom she identifies as a misogynist) that offers sacred, encoded Magdalenian symbolism. McGowan's assertion of the existence of a gospel written in Mary Magdalene's own hand—as well as one written by Jesus himself, *The Book of Love*—includes a claim that the trilogy is historical as well as autobiographical, citing that she cannot divulge her sources, for their own safety. Writing this trilogy became her (subversive, radical) way of sharing this knowledge with the world.

McGowan tracks the survival of progressive attitudes toward women and the feminine in modern-day southern France and a pocket of Italy, specifically Occitania and Tuscany, via oral traditions, (the ever-revealing realm of) economics and property rights, and encoded symbolism in the material culture—via art history, architecture, and archaeomythology—as having roots in the Magdalene heresy. Additionally, a widespread acceptance and dissemination throughout Europe of this history and/or mythology of Mary Magdalene's exile in southern France and her preaching can be traced through European art history. Especially of note is the painting *Saint Mary Magdalene Preaching* by the Netherlander known as "Master of the Magdalene Legend," circa 1500–1520. Currently housed at the Philadelphia Museum of Art, this was originally part of a larger altarpiece now divided between Denmark, Hungry, and Germany.

By investigated the lasting Magdalenian legacy via pockets in Occitania, Lucca, Italy, and royal lineages in France and England, McGowan addresses the impact of the underground teachings while uncovering well-researched and misunderstood layers of women's lost histories. Especially in *The Book of Love* and *The Boleyn Heresy*, the use of little-known primary sources—including letters, material culture, and art history—grounds her books, enabling them to paint worthy reinterpretations of relevant legendary historical women, including Matilda of Canossa and Anne Boleyn. This focus on the cultural impact of the Magdalene heresy over time on women's history is a vital, unique thread of scholarly potentiality.

Unlike the scholars discussed here, McGowan cultivates ongoing engagement leading tours to these regions and creating an ongoing online lecture series. In this way, and without an advanced degree, her work is more "of the people," and perhaps more accessible than most Magdalenian scholarship. Clearly identifying as both a feminist and a former pagan, turned Catholic Christian, she speaks openly about her commitment to telling her story, her truth, and how she has been personally attacked, even receiving numerous death threats since publishing.

In a 2006 interview with *The Guardian*, McGowan discusses this in depth:

So why didn't she write all of this up as non-fiction? McGowan looks at me as if I am mad. "Are you kidding? It's dangerous! Incredibly dangerous! There are still situations where people die under mysterious circumstances down there in the Languedoc, all to do with this stuff. There are societies down there who do not want this story to come out."

Who?

"It's too dangerous to say! That's been my conundrum all along. Everyone wants me to give the proof. But I can't put people down there in danger by identifying certain things. I can't do that. That's why I've had to write this book as fiction, in order to tell the truth. It was the only way to tell the story. I mean, I've just got back from the Languedoc myself, and I was followed all the time. I'm used to it. It happens all the time." (Aitkenhead)

Highlighting both her experiences and status as an insider within the Occitan tradition, the article goes on to clarify her first book (first proposed in 1997) was an antecedent to *The Da Vinci Code* (2003). After originally being turned down by publishers, she fictionalized her story and self-published in 2005. Citing danger to her sources, McGowan has continuously protected them and her knowledge.

CINEMATIC SIGHTINGS: MAGDALENE ON SCREEN

Two influential films, the iconic *Jesus Christ Superstar* (1973) and Martin Scorsese's *The Last Temptation of Christ* (1988), both repeat the conflation with the penitent sinner, oversexualizing and misrepresenting her, leaving an unfortunate and lasting cultural aftertaste. More recent films, including Mel Gibson's conservative *The Passion of the Christ*, have so far limited her portrayal to that of a disciple, not even moving toward apostolic integrity. Even the much-anticipated *Mary Magdalene* (2018) focuses more on male apostles than on the potency of Magdalene. Real-life partners Rooney Mara and Joaquin Phoenix—both famous for their grit and energetic performances—star in this film yet oddly bring little vitality to their depictions, which in and of themselves are neither original nor revitalizing of the myth, other than to portray Magdalene as an intelligent woman who gave up tradition to follow Jesus. Similarly, Abel Ferrara's *Mary* (2005), which stars Juliette Binoche as an actor playing Magdalene, attempts to creatively wrestle with questions of faith and filmmaking, and becomes muddy, ultimately failing to move the needle of Magdalenian depictions forward.

Several notable surveying articles have been written in the past few years, all from (spoken and unspoken) Christian perspectives. Biblical scholar Joan Taylor's "Mary Magdalene in Film" is worth noting, especially for her attention to issues of intersectionality and representation. Besides being oversexualized, Magdalene is nearly always portrayed as a white woman, with few exceptions, including the French film *Magdala* (2022), which sadly also falls into a conventional/patriarchal crippling Magdalenian trope/phallacy of the isolated hermit, limited by her nostalgic longing for what was lost.

Within the edited anthology *Mary Magdalene from the New Testament to the New Age and Beyond* (2019), Erica-Lyn Saccucci's "From Disciple to Deviant: The Magdalene in Contemporary Popular Film" offers a survey of what she identifies as archetypal Magdalenian expressions across four films: *The Da Vinci Code* (as partner), *The Magdalene Sisters* (as prostitute), *Mary: This Is My Blood* (as devout disciple), and *Chocolat* (as "Feminine Spirit") (318–36). Notably, Juliette Binoche stars in both *Mary* and *Chocolat*.

Citing conflation at the heart of Magdalene's (finally evolving) misinterpretations, Saccucci begins to pull apart the stories of four historical women: Mary of Bethany, Mother Mary (whom she calls the Virgin Mary), Mary of Egypt, and the unnamed "sinful" woman in the biblical account in Luke, chapter 7 (319). However, Saccucci nonetheless continues to muddy the waters by attempting to apply the terms "myth" and "archetype" outside of a depth psychological perspective. Likewise, she uses descriptive terms like "scandalous" (in describing *The Last Temptation of Christ* 320) and "mystique" uncritically, leaving the material ungrounded and (most disturbingly) doomed to repeat patriarchal patterns of confusion and shame. Using words like "scandalous" further perpetuates sweeping shadow projection of normal human relations and sexuality, especially considering the normalcy of partnership—the cultural requirement even—for a Jewish rabbi in Jesus's time. By neither clearly identifying her perspective within Christianity (though she seems to be situated within an unspoken Christian lineage) nor critiquing it, Saccucci's inquiry so far remains cursory. As I reader I felt hungover from contact with a Magdalenian identity crisis.

Chocolat is a fascinating example for several reasons. Saccucci's interpretation of Vianne in *Chocolat*, identifying Vianne's Magdalenian expression as the "Feminine Spirit," notes how "in addition to wearing red, which is described as a fiery, passionate color, Vianne also opens her Chocolaterie Maya during Lent, does not attend mass, and has an illegitimate child" (332). For these reasons, Vianne is demonized by ultra-self-sacrificing Mayor Reynaud. While Vianne stays balanced, withstanding his own shadow projections, Reynaud eventually implodes from his lack of (grounding) balance. Vianne invests her energy in nourishing support (via her chocolates), tending and mending relationships. Saccucci sees this as mostly "sexual" in nature, diminishing an expanded, empowering sense of Eros, as well as negating outsider Vianne's positive impact on a range of parental relationships.

The duel with Reynaud culminates in his meltdown (amidst her chocolate display window) on Easter Sunday. Like Eros, Reynaud is pricked by his own (shaming) arrow, tasting the very chocolate he'd intended to destroy—it is his very undoing, a necessary (and ultimately regenerative) collapse. Rather than out him, Vianne releases him from his shame, promising to never tell a soul. Saccucci identifies this movement as Magdalenian. For her, Vianne is "a strong woman who is passionate and sensual, but also transformative and merciful," a parallel to Magdalene's mythic identity carrying the "transformative power of love" (332).

Lasse Hallström's re-imagined setting for the film (a *Chocolat* transported back to the 1950s–1960s) differs from Joanne Harris's original novel set in contemporary times; Harris has gone on to develop what has become a remarkable four-book series—covering vital topics from shadow projection to othering, immigration, trauma, grief, community building, and regeneration. I have long wondered what sequel films could evoke and if they would be in the historical past or our imaginal present. Outsider Vianne could certainly be a remarkable evocation of Magdalene as a fully embodied leader in service to love, brought to life by Binoche's craft and skill.

Mary Ann Beavis makes a meaningful contribution to the conversation in "Mary Magdalene on Film in the Twenty-First Century." Examining *Son of God* (2104), *The Chosen* (2017), *Mary: This Is My Blood* (2005), and *Mary Magdalene* (2019), Beavis takes care to clearly identify faith-based productions and their target audiences (in the first two films) while discussing them effectively from several critical angles. She writes: "Unfortunately, however, these productions tend to find another way to situate the Magdalene as abject relation to Jesus and inevitably downplay the role of other women disciples in the Jesus movement. In addition, although most eschew the 'penitent whore' stereotype, they tend to reiterate the 'martyr/love story' narrative associated with prostitution in film."

Despite some progress, Magdalene continues to be depicted in conflating, disempowering, limiting expressions. Beavis identifies the problematic aspects (from demonic possession to a complete lack of stage presence)—and historical inaccuracies—in these depictions of Mary Magdalene, as well as noting the research holes left by the lack of diversity and feminist scholarship in research teams. Beavis spends a solid chunk of the article painstakingly pointing out how though some of the filmmakers understand some of the problems with Magdalenian representation, they continue to fail to make the leaps necessary to truly portray her in her fullness, dooming these cinematic representations to the shadowlands.

Differentiating Abel Ferrara's film *Mary: This Is My Blood* as clearly "influenced by feminist research, especially its focus on the Gnostic Mary" (11), Beavis dialogues with Saccucci's summary of the film's significance and notes the import of using Elaine Pagels in the film, uniquely grounding it in feminist Gnostic scholarship. However, she identifies how even this attempt at depicting Magdalene falls quite short of the twenty-first century norm of dynamic, expanding archetypal representation of women cinematically.

Wonder women are exploding on screen with remarkable impact. McGowan has publicly discussed her intention to produce either a television or film series of the books in her online communities via social media. This could be a significant contribution to the limited and limiting existing canon of cinematic depictions of Magdalene, none of which yet depict the potential of a fully engaged Bride and coleader of the original Christianity.

RE/MEMBERING MAGDALENE

Both Starbird and McGowan, while intending to relate Magdalene's historically layered stories with detail and accuracy, reach for the imaginal potentialities of mythological lineage, honoring sociopolitical context and reporting on how it might inform underlying psychic and cultural implications. Through metaphor meaning can be made, usually even more deeply than on an overreliance on facts alone. Perhaps it is in the *relation* between history and mythology—that mysterious gap—that we find support for our quests. Maybe the relationship itself suggests the potentiality of an elegant third emerging. In this case the reunion of Bride and Bridegroom might inform a rebalancing of our relationships within our-Selves, with each other, and within our larger environment by birthing something new.

Feminist scholarly methodology that seeks to embody the divine feminine is quite a commitment, involving no small leap of faith. With dedication to erotic principles of relatedness, as well as honoring Logos, these embodied practices could be at the heart of our best feminist postmodernist sensibilities and skills, an invocation to the returning Bride herself. Such skills are needed now to deconstruct the conflation between the archetypal Bride and patriarchy's shadow projected upon her. Returning to the difference between the original and a copy, the worth of a copy depends upon the intention and consciousness with which it is created. When Western media blatantly conflates a name of the archetypal Bride with a terrorist organization—just as Magdalene was mistakenly but intentionally (sinisterly) portrayed as the penitent sinner—they reduce Isis to cr/isis, diminishing all that she truly is and leaving her—and by this I mean the divine feminine in us all—grief-stricken over what is supposedly being done in her name.

SEPARATE, THEN TOGETHER: SACRED MARRIAGE ORIGINS IN EGYPTIAN ALCHEMY

The relationship between Egyptian alchemy and sacred marriage yields rich material focusing on funerary and resurrection mythology. Many eminent theorists, including C. G. Jung, Marie-Louise von Franz, and Edward Edinger, stress the centrality of the Isis–Osiris pairing in the philosophical and physical science of alchemy, as well as within the core psychological understandings of sacred marriage as growth/evolution, the *mysterium coniunctionis*.[32]

By identifying the roots of alchemy in the fertile loam of the regenerative Nile Valley, depth psychology has developed some of its richest, regenerative material within the study of Egyptian mythology. Though often filtered through Greco-Roman classical interpretations, these theories have had continuous impact, informing modern and postmodern cultures and psychology. They continue to do so because the integrity of the mythic structure, inherent in the archetypal pairing of the sacrificial year-king with his Sister-Bride, is effective in generating healing as the couple moves through the stages of dismemberment, containment, and regeneration. From its earliest days in Sumer, Babylon, and Crete to the Greco-Roman (partial, incomplete, corrupted) love goddess-consort incarnations, this ancient partnership lineage forms a foundation for the Christian myth. As such, inquiry into the importance of sacred partnership amplifies the parallels between Isis and Magdalene as archetypal Widow-Brides.

---

32. An earlier version of this section appears as "Separate, Then Together: Sacred Marriage Origins in Egyptian Alchemy," in *On the Wings of Isis*, edited by Trista Hendren, Susan Morgaine, and Pat Daly.

Much analysis of the mythology of Isis and Osiris seems to hinge solely on their relationship, principally on Isis's search for her beloved, her labor, and her action toward him. Instead, perhaps Isis and Osiris serve as prototypes of our inner masculine and feminine simultaneously moving toward *each other* in the radical act of individuation. I suggest that they do so independently, then jointly, and that they can come together only after each has completed his/her respective task. To better understand this rich process requires an examination of three distinct episodes of Egyptian mythology which uniquely inform this psychological alchemy: Isis's securing of the alchemical mystery, the function of Osiris's lead coffin, and their reunion as *coniunctio*.

Isis as Tricky Prophetess

In her investigation of alchemical history/herstory of women alchemists, *Searching for the Soar Mystica: The Lives and Science of Women Alchemists*, Robin Gordon writes that Jung "noticed that the process that an individual undergoes in the course of the individuation journey was mirrored in the alchemical operations" (43). This interpretation of alchemy as metaphor for psychic development correlates alchemical *prima materia* with an undifferentiated (leaden) unconscious and defines psychological development as the personal transformation toward the gold of our differentiating, distilling essence. As such, alchemy becomes a rich, transformative mythological realm.

Marie-Louise von Franz, perhaps the preeminent interpreter of Jung, brings much to the discussion of alchemy, and her analysis spans several works, flourishing in her landmark book *Alchemy: An Introduction to the Symbolism and the Psychology*. Though typically referred to as Western medieval studies in the chemical, and sometimes philosophical, transmutation of lead into gold and a search for the elixir of life, the roots of alchemy can be traced to ancient texts and practices arising from various world traditions. While analyzing the amalgamated Hellenic text, *The Prophetess Isis to Her Son*, von Franz explains several essential plot details that show the alchemical value of the myth. She begins with a marginal note in the text—appearing in the same hand as the scribe—relating that Isis's trip to the town of Hermes is metaphorical, translating as "she means that in a mystical sense" (44). Isis is in the land of the magician, of alchemy, of mystery. The use of the Greek work *kairoi* here describes attending to the astrologically right time. This is significant, since "the alchemist is the [wo/]man who must not only know the technique, but must always consider these constellations" (44). S/he must discriminate and pay attention. And, perhaps most significantly, von Franz links Isis's motivation in putting off the angel, who wishes to engage with her sexually, with her desire to strike a bargain with him, "getting the alchemical secret out of him" as only a trickster can (45). She goes on to say that whenever the mystery is told, either from the angel to Isis or from Isis to her son or best friend, the two become one to form a mystical union (46). The text is grammatically ambivalent here, and Horus may also be her best friend, or there may be two to whom she may tell the mystery. Then, after several paragraphs, she writes, "Isis is frequently referred to as the widow in the text and therefore from the very beginning in alchemy the philosopher's stone, the mystery, is called the mystery of the widow, the stone of the widow, or the orphan's stone; there was a connection between the widow and the orphan, but it all points to Isis" (50). Here, von Franz locates the widow archetype, Isis, and Egyptian mythology at the core of alchemical lore. Isis's identification as the archetypal widow is especially significant as the inescapable fate of Sister-Brides within the ancient partnership traditions.

Part of the widow's journey is to develop a transformative and mystical practice of grieving—moving through the grief of one who has lived the *unio mystica* and then resides in the deep grief of the *separatio*. Uniquely, the widow—and here I wonder if we might add the widower, divorcée, and divorcé (regardless of legal marital status)—experiences these acts *in this particular order* on her path, pointing us to the cyclical, regenerative life cycle. Psychologically we can fall into the trap of believing individuation to be a linear path through the alchemical process, one with a definitive and rewarding "ending." (Perhaps this occurs because we seek guaranteed relief after such an arduous journey.) Rather, individuation is the spiralic development of a lifetime.

And does the orphan not also follow this archetypal pattern? How interesting that the archetypes of widow and orphan appear in the text together. For what do we know of orphanhood but that, through birth, a child is (hopefully) received into blissful union (as the divine child, the elegant third) and risks losing their very sense of connection through the *separatio* of death or abandonment. To be alone, even forgotten, after having known love—to be solely responsible for one's own path—perhaps this too is a prerequisite for individuation.[33]

When first one angel, and then his superior, approaches Isis asking for hasty sexual relations, she delays them, for she is interested in the alchemical mystery. Delaying him in order to trick the secret out of him, she barters, promising to "give herself to him if he first tells her all he knows about that" (45). "Alchemy was born through Isis's resistance and the fact that she

---

33. See Carol Pearson's analysis of the archetype of the orphan in *Awakening the Hero Within*, 82–93.

did not cede quickly, at least delaying the sexual process, if not stopping it altogether. We do not know what she did in the end; she very discreetly won't even tell her own son" (57). This act of attaining the secret "implies we have made great progress, we have got this secret out of the angels, something so immense" that it must remain a sacred mystery (54). "When Isis succeeds in getting the secret from those angels it is seen as a great achievement. . . . The female element, the feminine principle, gets it from deeper layers and then is the mediator who hands it on to [humanity]" (51). Here, von Franz acknowledges Isis's trickster action. Though seemingly passive at first blush, it results in acquiring increased consciousness—quite a radical act. Isis's specific actions in the myth via the archetype of the widow—including right cosmic timing, her trickster skills, and her resistance to hasty sex—are key to her alchemical success.

Lead Containment, or Osiris Was a Twelve-Stepper

Elaborating on the *coniunctio* as the union of conscious and unconscious attitudes, von Franz points toward the leaden component of Osiris's coffin within the myth:

> Seth killed Osiris by first making a leaden coffin and then getting people when drunk at a party to enter it under the pretext of find-ing out whom it would fit. But when Osiris got into the coffin, Seth promptly put the lid on, covering it with lead, and threw it into the sea. Therefore, it could be said that Osiris was suffocated in lead, so you can think of the tomb of Osiris as a lead coffin, or a coffin sealed up with lead within which lies the dead god, or the divine spirit, in the form assumed in death. (84)

As von Franz describes how Seth and Osiris act out their psychic duel, the dance between our shadow selves and our consciousness, her amplification of the raw, leaden qualities of the coffin point to containment of the *materia prima*, raw material necessary for alchemical transformation. Stressing the necessity for containment, she continues:

> The vessel is a symbol for the attitude which prevents anything escap-ing outside; it is a basic attitude of introversion which, on principle, does not let anything escape into the outside world. The illusion that the whole trouble lies outside oneself has to come to an end and things have to be looked at from within. That is how we "suffocate"

the Mysterium of the unconscious. We do not know what the unconscious is, but we suffocate it through this concentrated treatment by which all projection is stopped, intensifying the psychological process. It is also the torture of fire, because when the flow of intensity of the psychological processes becomes concentrated, one is roasted, roasted in what one is. Therefore, the person in the tomb and the tomb itself are the same thing, for you roast in what you are yourself and not in anything else; or one could say that one is cooked in one's own juice, and is therefore the tomb, the container of the tomb, the suffocated one, and the suffocator, the coffin, and the dead god in it. (87)

Through the transformative motif of cooking, von Franz applies alchemy psychologically. She suggests that transformation requires appropriate heat and a beaker/cauldron/container. Containment provides a place for creativity to unfold; to make soup a pot is required. Von Franz is emphatic that in order to overcome our projections we must be somewhat trapped with them to claim them as our own (the antidote to projecting out), and then to "suffocate" them, an intense form of self-examination. Similarly, this alchemical step works within seasonal gardening mythology, with the compost bin standing in as transformative container. Without waste, we have no compost.

While this might seem to be a simple alchemical step—perhaps one of the most straightforward in the Egyptian myths surrounding Osiris—it is, at least in postmodernity, an exceptional challenge to remain still within (or committed to) our bubbling caldrons, our personal alchemical containers. Perhaps this is why our global pandemic was so very painful—and potentially healing for those who could bear to steep in their own juices.

With our physical and psychic containers having withstood so much harm done through physical, emotional, and sexual abuse, many have cracked and ruptured, some beyond repair. Not only do we leak moist psychic energy and libido (erotic life force as Jung describes it—prana or chi), we are frequently unaware of doing so (unconsciously). We have normalized leakage, creating puddles of projected drama and trauma in our wakes, and the resultant internal desertification and/or flooding of our souls. I suggest this is a tremendous global postmodern post-traumatic stress disorder (PTSD)—our *other* pandemic—severely hampering healing and our ability to seek support in rebuilding our containers. The subsequent development of addictive behavior in avoidance of *feeling* the resultant deep pain and grief delays the now-monumental healing process. Subsequently, it becomes necessary to fight through defensive, destructive armor to reach the root of dis/ease. To feel is to begin to heal. Like Osiris—steeping in his own juices, stuck there with nowhere to run, no way to avoid himself—in order to be revived into renewed psychospiritual life, we must endure that steeping.

Jungian theory and psychoanalysis have greatly influenced how addiction is viewed and treated in contemporary Western cultures. Offering a unique synopsis of this phenomenon is Sheri Parks, who examines the impact of the dark goddess as "a psychic or spiritual internal presence" (26) in *Fierce Angels: The Strong Black Woman in American Life and Culture.* Especially relevant is her exploration of the significance of the Sacred Dark Feminine, one personification of which is the Black Madonna, perhaps the aspect of the divine feminine most associated with the ancient lineage of Inanna-Isis-Magdalene as Sister-Brides. Parks describes how Jung "thought the Sacred Dark Feminine to be the oldest archetype. He believed she was so commonly occurring that she was inherited into our collective consciousness—hardwired into our brain chemistry" (5). She writes:

> Jungian therapy holds that one can transcend traumatic circumstances only by facing them. An addict can be cured only after going into the darkness to bottom out. But, according to Jungian therapy, the person is not alone in the darkness, because the Dark Feminine is there with them. She represents endurance and the hope of transformation. She is the guide who will lead the sufferer out, the psychic presence necessary for transformation and a new personal beginning. Jungian therapists and writers routinely use the goddesses and Black Madonnas as references. The popularized version of Jungian therapy is even more far reaching: it is the basis for 12-step programs and all the bestselling self-help books that build upon them. Americans believe in redemption. It is one of the culture's major narratives, and American authors borrow liberally from Jung, who believed that people were always developing and that they could grow out of their past problems; self-help programs and related books borrow directly from Jung to teach us how. Bill Wilson, who cofounded Alcoholics Anonymous, wrote Carl Jung a letter in 1961 to tell him of the organization based on Jungian principles. As the basis of AA and the 12-step programs that followed, Jungian therapy has had a tremendous impact on Western culture. The Sacred Dark Feminine has directly or indirectly become part of therapy and self-help of people across the country and around the world. (26)

Parks reveals how powerful the Dark Feminine was for Jung, and how present she is in the collective un/conscious. By acknowledging the impact Jungian psychology has had on twelve-step programs and within the entire genre of self-help psychology, Parks identifies the tremendous value and near omnipresence of the Dark Feminine as psychopomp in a modern therapeutic sense. The unique qualities inherent in the Dark Feminine are earned from her own alchemical, individuating journey of endurance and offer hope throughout time spent in cryptic exile. Parks's cultural excavations attribute the accessibility of archetypal understanding to Jung as one of psychology's founding "fathers," while naming the Dark Feminine as a primal recovery support. Perhaps it is she who anoints us at the darkest hour.

Depth psychology practices faith in transformation on these underworld journeys. In "Surrendering to Psyche: Depth Psychology, Sacrifice, and Culture," Glen Slater describes how psychic dismemberment, if we can survive it, ultimately leads toward wholeness. Working within Greek mythology, he suggests that when faced with underworld tests and tasks, "a psychological dismemberment resembling Dionysian ritual will occur—a chaotic, symptomatic sacrifice that, through courage and perseverance, turns into a rootedness in psychic depth" (186–87). For Slater, this rootedness evolves through the depth psychological ritual of tending psychic experiences and feelings. Key to understanding alchemical transformations is the need to turn *toward* feelings and grief—to acknowledge their leaden gifts, to lie within them, surrendering.

In *The Mystery of the Coniunctio: Alchemical Image of Individuation*, Edward Edinger writes that "very gradually we will collect our scattered psyche from the outer world, as Isis gathered the dismembered body of Osiris, and in doing that we will be working on the coniunctio" (18). He goes on to describe how the sacred or chemical marriage is the culmination of the alchemical process. "According to alchemical symbolism, the *coniunctio* is the goal of the process: it's the entity, the stuff, the substance that is created by the alchemical procedure when finally it succeeds in uniting the opposites" (18). Edinger views the *coniunctio* as the destination of the often long, arduous, and ultimately mysterious journey of individuation. Such expression of union within the psyche is at the heart of the interplay between Isis and Osiris and is possible only after each has done his/her individual work.

Von Franz suggests that the end of an age might be marked by a radical shift in consciousness. It is the end of the Egyptian civilization that amplifies the mythology of Isis, so much so that a rich and extensive "cult" dedicated to her develops and spreads throughout the vast Roman Empire. Beliefs exhaust themselves and come to an end, providing space for something new to come into being. In the case of civilizations previously dominated by severe laws, dogma, or rigidly structured social norms, a time generally arises when the pendulum swings to the other side. "Because these things come to an end, to an enantiodromia, the masculine mode of consciousness tires. That is a typical archetypal event, and then the feminine, or the unconscious and nature, the chaotic, have to take back the light" (62). For von Franz, this movement symbolizes a movement back and forth between poles. "Enantiodromia" describes the tendency of something to become its own opposite. This rebalancing actions evokes pendulum swings, arcs moving from extremity to extremity. Another interpretation might allow for a more integrative and holistic synthesizing, as Isis gathered and re/membered her beloved, as both Isis and Mary Magdalene retrieve, anoint, and tenderly wrap the bodies of their beloved partners with spice and fragrance.[34]

With such a transition time again upon us, the integrating skills of Isis as priestess of light and darkness might be called upon. She searches for her entombed beloved, attends the dismembered one, uniting with him as two who have individually labored to become whole. Together they bring forth a new kind of wholeness (queered, if you will). Resurrection means change—dramatic, painful, awe/ful change from death—the kind that often renders us unrecognizable, especially to ourselves. Resurrection does not mean returning to life as usual. It is not coming *back* to the life we once had but, rather, traveling forward. For Osiris, it was *life* in a completely different form. From flesh-and-blood king he became immortal, a god of the underworld, leaving his body behind. This motif repeats with other sacrificial year-kings, including Dionysus—who shares with Osiris regenerative grain symbolism—and Jesus, who left the earthly plane for a seat at his father's right hand. I can only imagine a highly charged and animated conversation between these newly regenerated ones, transformed toward a healing masculine.

---

34. See Margaret Merisante, *Tears and Fragrance for the God's Death and Resurrection.*

CHAPTER 2

GIVING AWAY THE BRIDE?

JOSEPH CAMPBELL, THE S/HERO'S JOURNEY, AND THE GRAIL QUEST

Answering the question, "What ails our society?": "We suffer from the absence of one half of our spiritual potential—the Goddess."

—JEAN SHINODA BOLEN, "THE WOMEN'S MOVEMENT IN TRANSITION: THE GODDESS AND THE GRAIL" (8)

INTRODUCTION: WHAT IS THE RIGHT QUESTION?

Mary Magdalene's historic and legendary role as the lost and returning Bride can be found embedded within the motifs and symbols of grail mythology, alchemy, Black Madonna lore, tarot, and folklore. Joseph Campbell's scholarly study of grail lore, Mediterranean and Western mystery traditions, and—especially in his later work—goddess mythology form the core of his writings. His study of these topics is generally considered to be exhaustive, attentive to polyvalent complexities, and thoughtfully analyzed for their depth psychological perspectives. In his four-volume *The Masks of God* series (1968), he fluidly applies the work of Jung, Freud, and Edinger to Judeo-Christian scripture, the Gnostic Gospels, and multicultural symbols.[35]

---

35. Campbell's scholarship on the grail and mystery traditions permeates most of his publications. See especially *The Masks of God, Volume 3: Occidental Mythology* and *Volume 4: Creative Mythology*, as well as "In Search of the Holy Grail: The Parzival Legend." For his later analyses of goddess mythology, see his posthumously coauthored text with Charles Musès, *In All Her Names: Explorations of the Feminine in Divinity*, his foreword to Marija Gimbutas's *The Language of the Goddess*, and *Goddesses*, edited by Safron Rossi.

Yet his only mention of Mary Magdalene is in a brief comment on her presence at the resurrection of Christ, a significant omission worth exploring. Particularly relevant is Campbell's own fascination with Parzival and that knight's longstanding inability to ask the correct question that promises to heal the (prevailing concept of a singular, masculine, solar) wasteland. Like Parzival during his first encounter with the grail cup, Campbell fails to recognize that which he has been questing after as it passes him by.

In this chapter I join other feminist mythologists and post-Jungian theorists who have been analyzing Joseph Campbell's "hero's" journey model to better understand how it relates to women's experiences. Does his well-known model apply equally for women? If not, what is different or missing? Do more-effective models exist to explain women's journeys and guide us, or do we need to create them? And how might these issues directly relate to Magdalene's absence from Campbell's tremendous body of work? Which essential questions still require tending—including suppositions about Campbell's scholarship and grail lore in general—to effectively identify and support Magdalene's regenerative return?

Joseph Campbell's extensive contributions to mythological conversations on aspects of the grail legends, the tarot, alchemy, and folklore fill many of his books and recorded lectures. Deeply influenced by Jung, Campbell's core theoretical work pivots around mythology's ability to convey vital encoded psychic and communal information via metaphor. In *The Power of Myth* (1991), both a book and landmark interview with Bill Moyer, famously accessible and influential in popular culture, Campbell describes how "a god is a personification of a motivating power or a value system that functions in human life and in the universe—the powers of your own body and of nature. The myths are metaphorical of spiritual potentiality in the human being and life in the world" (22). Campbell taught that the gods and goddesses who populate mythology are none other than our own inner forces. Foundationally, Campbell proclaims myth as the underlying organizing structure within psyche and culture and that the two are constantly interweaving.

Campbell saw myth as communication from the unconscious, both personal and collective. The essence of his life's work can be summarized as a quest to explain how mythology supports personal transformation. Campbell not only explored existing world mythologies but suggested that it is by working out our personal myth that we find psychological understanding, release from suffering, and transcendence. Campbell is known primarily for his masterwork *The Hero with a Thousand Faces* (1949), in which he identified a universal cyclical (or spiralic) pattern inherent in world mythologies, what he termed the "hero's journey." Applying a feminist revisioning of

Campbell's work on the s/hero's journey to Magdalene's regenerative cycle enables a deeper dialogue on both her return and the experience of the feminine principle.

Especially relevant are Campbell's theories on the survival and impact of shards of earlier religious practices. In *The Masks of God, Volume 3: Occidental Mythology* (1964), Campbell's analysis of the theological, archeological, and artistic mythological evidence across Western cultures reveals roots in goddess-centric mystery traditions. In *The Masks of God, Volume 4: Creative Mythology* (1968)—the culminating volume of Campbell's four-part series focusing on modernity's inheritance from our philosophical, spiritual, and artistic history—Campbell addresses Arthurian mythology and the legacy of the wasteland, central components for Magdalenian mythology. In his audio recording of the lecture "In Search of the Holy Grail: The Parzival Legend," Campbell discusses his key teachings on grail mythology, focusing on the centrality of Arthurian mythology within Western cultures. While Campbell never mentioned Magdalene, his broad range of scholarship on these topics provides fundamental understanding of underlying depth psychological and mythological potentialities in grail lore, as well as theories of subsequent authors. Conversely, his lack of scholarship and reflection on Magdalene also leaves hidden clues.

Campbell's theories on goddesses at the heart of classical mystery practices are developed from Jane Ellen Harrison's groundbreaking work *Prolegomena to the Study of Greek Religion*. Originally published in 1903, Harrison's work provides core evidence of the relationship and lineage between Mediterranean traditions. Also influential in Campbell's later work was Lithuanian feminist archaeologist Marija Gimbutas who pioneered archaeomythology as a methodology. Her watershed books *The Language of the Goddess: Unearthing the Hidden Symbols of Western Civilization* (1989) and *The Civilization of the Goddess* (1991) evaluate material archaeological evidence cross-fertilized with her expertise in and curiosity about folk traditions and linguistics. Significantly, Gimbutas identified a primary three-fold pattern of the cycle of life in the natural world as birth, death, and regeneration and saw this continuously reflected archaeomythologically. Like Jung, some of Campbell's most potent work originated with the brilliance of women scholars whom he valued.

If gender inclusivity is an invitation to relate more deeply with each other, I suggest the need for a more gender-inclusive term to describe our personal grail quests towards wholeness, perhaps the compound pronoun s/he supports a s/hero's journey. Knowing some men might squirm at the thought of an S before the noble H, I invite them to breathe. Women have been listening for our silent S's for a long, long time.

FATHER OF THE BRIDE? CAMPBELL GIVES MAGDALENE AWAY

In *The Hero with a Thousand Faces* Joseph Campbell illuminates the gifts at the heart of a mythological perspective:

> Whenever the poetry of myth is interpreted as biography, history, or science, it is killed. The living images become only remote facts of a distant time or sky. Furthermore, it is never difficult to demonstrate that as science and history mythology is absurd. When a civilization begins to reinterpret its mythology in this way, the life goes out of it, temples become museums, and the link between the two perspectives is dissolved. Such a blight has certainly descended on the Bible and on a great part of the Christian cult. To bring the images back to life, one has to seek, not interesting applications to modern affairs, but illuminating hints from the inspired past. When these are found vast areas of half-dead iconography disclose again their permanently human meaning. (213)

As Campbell articulates the loss of mythic vitality through the Church's mishandling of Christian mythology resulting in desiccation and concretization, his mythopoetic stance is revealed, offering story as cocreative acts—ever fluid, ever vital, ever evolving. While locating Christianity firmly within the realm of mythic imagination, he reveals the deadening effects that concretization has had on its deepest value as mythological meaning maker. Most significantly, he tells of the possibility and necessity of regeneration through detecting and decoding, as ways of attending to the past.

Such imaginal investigations into the mythology of Mary Magdalene, celebrating her reflexive and mythopoetic offerings, are surfacing alongside an examination of her historical shards. Curiously absent is any contribution, barely any mention at all, from Campbell on Magdalene. As the father of mythology's resurgence, Campbell's commentary on Christian mythology is vast in scope and depth and includes Gnostic texts, correlations with the ancient Mediterranean partnership lineage, grail lore, alchemy, and tarot, and the underlying principles of mystery school teachings. Campbell delves deeply into these mythemes in two of his *The Masks of God* series, *Volume 3: Occidental Mythology* (1964) and *Volume 4: Creative Mythology* (1968). Yet, even though he fully understands the partnership model lineage from which Judeo-Christian mythology evolved—including the sacrificial elements and regenerative potentialities inherent in union, which he stresses—he fails to mention Mary Magdalene *at all*. He fails to inquire about the missing Bride, whom some refer to as Christianity's lost goddess. Why? What does it mean for mythology's father to not notice a daughter's absence—especially one who could really use his help returning?

In part, Campbell was a product of his time, significantly impacted by his Catholic roots and sociopolitical perspectives. During most his lifetime (1904–1987), the Catholic Church's conflation of Mary Magdalene with the penitent sinner remained the dominant aspect of her mythology in popular culture, effectively defacing her identity, agency, and power. It was only in the late 1960s that Vatican II repealed Pope Gregory the Great's sixth-century conflation in the equivalent of a newspaper's tiny retraction buried at the bottom of page 8. Yet Campbell was a preeminent scholar and researcher—a man described as a maverick, continuously on a personal and professional quest for mythic truth. The discoveries of the Nag Hammadi texts (1945) and other caches of Gnostic Gospels all took place during Campbell's lifetime.[36] While fragments of the Gospel of Mary were initially rediscovered in 1896, they were not recognized as such until 1955.[37]

Campbell, evoking Jungian psychology, suggests that when we are stuck and in pain, it is through working out our own personal myth that release, understanding, and transcendence can be found. "What we're focusing on here is pulling yourself together" (*Pathways to Bliss* 92). Here, Campbell's use of pithy, straightforward language, steeped in the first half of the twentieth century, strengthens his teachings. His comments are often no-nonsense, crisp, distilled.

My devotion to and respect for Campbell is deep and old and has guided my professional career and personal life for decades. As a wise and charismatic father figure teaching on the importance of following our individual, individuating path, Campbell has guided me through many an abyss. Nevertheless, I felt betrayed by some chasms in his concepts. For years I had been able to tolerate his gender-biased language and content; Campbell, like all of

---

36. See Elaine Pagels's exhaustive analysis of *The Gnostic Gospels* describing the political and historical context within which these Gospels were discovered, analyzed, and secreted from public discourse. Pagels offers the first frank feminist-oriented academic conversation on controversies surrounding the Gospels and how access to them was originally restrictively controlled. As a thorough investigation of the Gnostic Gospels and other secret texts contextualized within the sociohistoric landscape of the emerging Church, Pagels's research has also resonated within popular culture, influencing the contemporary debate about these lost and found texts. Pagels's impeccable reputation in the broader field of biblical scholarship broadens the impact of this feminist revisionist.

37. See Karen King's *The Gospel of Mary Magdalene* for a contextual description of the three existing fragments of this Gnostic text: the Berlin Codex, Papyrus Rylands 463, and Papyrus Oxyrhynchus 3525.

us, was a product of his culture(s), and, situating his theories and writings within this context, he remains a dynamically radical thinker, often light years beyond his peers. However, his assumptions about women in relation to his masculinist "hero's" journey range from essentialist to exclusionary to downright gentlemanly. He is also capable of saying very different things at different times. It often seems as though he is saying: Oh, you gals don't need to go on a journey; you *are* the journey. You are the reason *we men* must journey.

Meeting the visionary work of Marija Gimbutas late in his life expanded Campbell's understanding of the feminine principle and goddess mythology; he incorporates her groundbreaking scholarship, especially in archaeo-mythology, into his later work.[38] Perhaps he simply ran out of time before finding the feminine counterpoint within his invaluable scholarly contributions, including the "hero's" journey. Was it too little too late for his work to reflect this new dimension? Or, perhaps more realistically, is this the work he has left for us, his lacuna?

The Opus Archives are a treasure trove of Campbellian research material, including many preserved lecture series. My research there revealed only two potential lectures on the topic of women and the "hero's" journey, one entitled "The Woman's Journey" in the *Myths and Mysteries of the Great Goddess* series, delivered at La Casa de Maria in Santa Barbara in 1983. This lecture focused on how a group of women in Jungian analysis created visual images based on vegetative motifs, repeatedly expressing spontaneous vitality, whereas men tended to draw and paint mandalas with jewels and fortresses. Here, Campbell discusses his belief that women have been unable to develop the intellectual sides of their lives due to their domestic responsibilities—too many children, too many chores, too much to do in the home have kept women too damn busy, a popular theme within second wave feminism prevalent at the time. (And mightn't vegetative motifs with spontaneous vitality be more highly evolved intellectually/logically than fortresses and jewels?)

Campbell's second lecture was "The Emergence of the Heroine" in *The Feminine in European Myth and Romance* series, delivered in New York City in 1985. Here, Campbell does all genders an incredible disservice by suggesting that it is perhaps only *through the physical components* of giving birth and motherhood that a woman works through her "hero's" journey. Not taking the time to unpack this essentialist phallacy, Campbell fails to acknowledge the myriad ways humans "mother" and nurture and how being

---

38. See especially *Goddesses* and *The Mythic Dimension*, both from his collected works series published posthumously.

one is not dependent on physically birthing a child. Though I do agree with Campbell's position that the embodied physical act of giving birth can be a journey deep within, he believes that through giving birth (and here he adds menstruation as a sidebar) a woman "becomes something else," that we "are transformed." He suggests that "nature does it for us," that we "have no control" over this process, and that through it we "acquire wisdom." (What about women who cannot or choose not to have children?)

Sadly, this statement also perpetuates dualistic concepts separating humans from Nature, rather than identifying us as part of and deeply inter-connected with Nature. The claim that women are closer to Nature because of biological generative abilities has been hotly contested by feminists and falls within wasteland distortions; with such theories we all end up being reduced. By limiting women to our reproductive bodies and/or roles, what might be celebrated is instead used to imprison. Excluding men from the life-giving interconnections with the birthing process and Nature risks returning to outmoded dialogues of disconnection.

Returning to the Campbell tape (these were recorded on audiotapes when I was originally researching them in 2011), he then reiterates his declaration, "A man has to go in search of something intentionally." Again, I am perplexed. Is he suggesting that pregnancy cannot be intentional? Are such deep physical experiences not available to men? And what of women who desire to search intentionally? Are we really so different? Campbell believes "man comes to know what nature is through women." Is this heteronormative stance true? And, if so, what are women, gay men, and other LGBTQ+ community members learning on our individual journeys and how? Are women's quests really any different from men's? Can men know Nature only through women? Are they all journeys toward regeneration? Or toward something else? And how does all this relate to Mary Magdalene, every woman's individuation, and the feminine writ large?

Though Campbell's own language reveals his stance and model to be masculinist and essentialist, he leaves me wondering how my journey might be different *because* of my gender. Many women before me have attempted to understand Campbell's approach and the absence of a female counter-point. Some have added their own contributions to the canon, crafting new names, including "heroine," "female hero," or Hera paired with "journey," "quest," or "adventure." As culture evolves around female representations of "the hero," meanings of these words also shift. "Heroine," which once described a woman passively awaiting princely rescue, has now been revi-talized, reemerging as a more fully active, feminine actor in her own life—a fantastic example of the power of our living languages.

One of the best-known early revisionist Jungian contributions is Maureen Murdock's *The Heroine's Journey: A Woman's Quest for Wholeness*, originally published in 1990 and revised in 2020. Some sister scholars differentiate a descent as the quintessentially female version of the "hero's" journey—such as Sylvia Brinton-Perera's *Descent to the Goddess: A Way of Initiation for Women* (1981). Yet both Murdock and Brinton-Perera's work seems complementary to Campbell's work on the journey, and not a different genre per se. Murdock's heroine's journey follows the cyclical movement defined by Campbell, flushing out the motion as individuation stages for women (5). While amplifying depth and darkness in the directional movement of the descent, Brinton-Perera nonetheless reinforces Campbellian theory by emphasizing both the need to journey to the underworld and the necessity of return to home and community. Emerging is a collaborative, inclusive, and "multidisciplinary" study at Brandeis University, "The Heroine Journeys Project," led by lawyer, poet, and artist Nancer Ballard. Its mission includes: "gathering, discussing, and analyzing literature, film, and life experiences that follow a different path than the conventional story arc referred to as the 'Hero's Journey.' Our goal is to help people of all ages and backgrounds to explore, understand, and give voice to personal experiences and stories that cannot be adequately expressed within the traditional 'Hero's Journey' narrative arc" (Ballard).

Recognizing diversity is a tremendous and vital polyvalent and polyvocal goal. Such research could further benefit from depth psychological and mythological perspectives as new trends, mythemes, and archetypes emerge and/or resurface.

Harvard-based folklorist Maria Tatar's exhaustive survey *The Heroine with 1001 Faces* (2021) offers ample evidence of the cumulative explosion of the feminine across the page and screen through the twenty-first century, the first such resource of its kind. Tatar's response to Campbell is rigorous on a sociological level. Perhaps the greatest contribution of this encyclopedic canon is in how it's used by subsequent scholars to add to the conversation.

These resources each offer tremendous scope for the expansion of the s/hero's journey. Moreover, they are scholarly indicators in and of themselves as to the importance of these themes within our collective psyches. Such research could further benefit from depth psychological and mythological perspectives as these (new and timeless) trends, mythemes, and archetypes emerge and/or resurface.

A fresh perspective can be found in Jody Bower's *Jane Eyre's Sisters: How Women Live and Write the Heroine's Story* (2015). Bower begins by thoroughly discussing revisionist models of the "hero's" journey for women, certainly quests in and of themselves.[39] We write to understand and, hopefully, to leave at least the hint of a trail which eases the journey for subsequent travelers. *Jane Eyre's Sisters* does this by shining a light on long existing patterns in feminist literary fiction and autobiography. Bower identifies how women are drawn to one of two distinct paths: descent and wandering. For Bower, women who received good-enough parenting were primarily drawn to the descent model— perhaps because a safe childhood gifts them with the self-assuredness and self-centeredness necessary to embark upon a trip into the dark. Here, I use "self-centered" in Jungian terms as a positive and grounded state cultivated by ongoing, embodied self-knowledge in tandem with personal centering and meditative practices. In this way being centered in the Self supports move-ment out into the world coming from a grounded perspective and practice.

Bower suggests that women who identified as having survived a less-than-ideal upbringing are drawn toward wandering out in the world. This woman, the Aletis (Greek for "wanderer") already knows darkness; she has grown up in it. Abandoned to childhood troubles, including "incest, abuse, death of loved ones, loss of family and home," this daughter already knows the dark intimately and instead needs a different psychic remedy: "the free-dom to be themselves—the freedom to get out of the cave of an oppressed childhood, and often a subsequent stifling marriage, and be the queen of their own lives" (63–64). For Bower's wanderer, an outsider who has always been alone anyway—perhaps a variant of the orphan archetype, fear is in staying in an abusive situation/home, and the idea of leaving offers hope (64). Unlike the hero who hears a call, the Aletis needs resolve to escape (66). The wanderer carries a "different kind of bravery," and Bower differentiates her travails from those of the hero (67). The hero's journey is dependent upon a return, yet the Aletis cannot, for her journey is dependent upon moving away from what has become unbearable. She must keep wandering, to find a place where she "can be more fully herself" (69). A creative act—for Bower, it is home-making—is necessary on the Aletis/heroine/s/hero's journey.

Bower uses these female storytellers and autobiographers to uniquely illuminate the trail, necessary markers, and helpers along the wanderer's path. Most significantly, Bower depathologizes the act of leaving intolerable situations. Instead, she acknowledges the courage necessary in such leave-taking and the gifts inherent in the resultant journey. Significantly, these Aletis women who know the pain of the dark, who choose—or who are cast out—to wander, are moving toward a more embodied ecofeminist—and therefore Magdalenian—form of resurrection: regeneration.

---

39. See especially chapter 3, "Heroic Quests and Feminine Journeys."

The act of wandering is dependent upon the land, movement on the Earth, through Nature. This somatic movement is healing in and of itself and offers opportunities for reconnection with—and re/membering our place within—Nature. This ecological, ecofeminist movement also evokes the Latin phrase solvitur ambulando, it is solved by walking.

Through various texts—purporting to offer history rather than the valuable speculative mythopoetics of mythology, legend, and literature—we are told that Mary Magdalene wanders at least three times. The biblical Gospel of Luke describes her wandering with Jesus (Luke 8:1–3). Some retellings suggest she left the intolerable political unrest after the crucifixion, first for sanctuary in Egypt. Medieval and oral traditions report her leaving for exile and preaching, perhaps eventually leading a contemplative life in a cave in the south of Gaul/France (*Golden Legend* 375–83).[40] Perhaps she was on her own Aletis quest, first in search of equal partnership, then sovereignty, then her own home.

NOT *ALL* FATHERS GIFT GRIT

The true grit of Mattie Ross in the 2010 film remake by the same name is revealed as she embarks on her s/hero's journey, moving from undifferentiated girl across the liminal threshold into unknown Choctaw territory. It is the story of two interconnected main characters, whose journeys and interdependence are key to understanding another element of the s/hero's journey: how our own individuation has the potential to support others in their personal transformation. This tale of an unexpected pair, and the lost feeling function in our collective unconscious, especially focuses on the necessary reclamation of the brutal side of our shadow nature.[41] Rooster Cogburn is an unlikely incarnation of Odin, carrying the redemptive value of the All Father, a powerful archetypal male principle for a daughter.

What is it that fathers have to teach their daughters? In *Pathways to Bliss*, Campbell believes "the father actually plays the educator to the spirit, he transmits the goals of the society, he informs the child of the adult role he or she is expected to assume. The mother gives birth to the physical body; the father, to the spiritual being" (82). According to Campbell, a daughter develops, through her relationship with her father—as primary link between

---

40. See Kathleen McGowan and Elizabeth Cunningham for speculative trajectories of Magdalene's wanderings, in chapter 3 on bridal agency. Also see McGowan's examination of Cathar oral histories as a living, feminist wisdom tradition.

41. For a discussion on the need for brutality, see Daniel Ross, "True Grit." CGJungCenter. org, July 24, 2011.

daughter and her public sphere—her public presence, her sense of how she is perceived in the world, and even perhaps her sense of personal agency. Unfortunately, this reinforces the patriarchal, Cartesian dualistic split of private (feminine) and public (masculine) spheres, and the echoing split of Nature from culture.

What might a more integrated, embodied model of fathering look like? Perhaps a little messy. And perhaps well-traveled. Odin's very name conjures madness, fearlessness, and love of battle; Rooster Cogburn embodies him well. As a god Odin came upon his power honestly, his battle-weary body having roamed the Earth, willing—though at first reluctant—to sacrifice much for wisdom. He also takes responsibility for the killing he has done. His lost eye, his voluntary surrender to death and subsequent resurrection, his deep weariness, are all signs of a singular commitment to his path. He is worthy of our attention because he has lived fully, uniting his internal opposing forces, and because he does not apologize for his life. He cautions us that a body without scars indicates a refusal of the call, of sacrifice, of death and the accompanying grief necessary for regeneration—and results in a life unlived.

Mattie is young to be propelled on her s/hero's journey. Through the death of her birth father, she is called to complete his unlived life—his interrupted life a cautionary tale, his unfulfilled quest becomes her own. But she is not alone. Cogburn, as the All Father who has wandered the world and both is painfully aware of its brutality and has learned to negotiate it, activates Mattie. He also teaches her discernment—how to eliminate that which does not serve. Embodying reflexive potentiality, he is an archetypal father who adapts beyond patriarchal limitations and grows as needed. In this way Cogburn surprises us with his nurturing skills.

A daughter must develop both sovereignty and nurturance; that these are interdependent is one of life's mysteries. This story is about a man willing to confront himself on a much deeper level than most are willing to go, and a girl needing him to do so for her own individuation. Perhaps this is a necessary aspect of our s/hero's journey as daughters, witnessing a messy, complex archetypal father commit to his own growth. Campbell identified "atonement with the father" as an integral step on the hero's journey. For a woman, this component might pivot around re/membering and reconciling what our fathers had been willing to do for themselves and for us as daughters.

When Mattie makes her dark descent, her *nekyia*, she encounters vines that bind her, a male corpse, a blade with which to free her-Self, and sacred serpents eager to inject her with the venom of consciousness. She has reached her personal *pharmakon*, for the poison and cure are one and the same, allowing her transformation toward womanhood. Perhaps if there is a necessary cost for what we need to complete our lives—a sacrifice—the primary function of our s/hero's journey is to act as guarantor for our ability to pay. When Cogburn rescues this courageous s/hero from the underworld, it is akin to Eros's final support for a road-weary Psyche, who had already completed so much on her own; (though not her lover, but instead the archetypal father) it was his love that did the work and also brought him his own redemption. Likewise, this action does not in any way diminish the tremendous labors already accomplished by Mattie herself. Simply, this is the action of a healthy father figure.

I suggest the gift is in the grit. Granted through the masculine, it is Odin's divine courage, acceptance of his own brutality, and commitment to his path that support Mattie's own learning and sovereignty—ultimately saving her life. He sees her for who she is and teaches her skills and tricks, but it is his consistent, sacred, and nurturing love that makes the difference.

WOUNDED, LOST, AND REPUDIATED: MAGDALENE AND THE FISHER KING

Central to grail lore is the interconnection between the physical body of the king—in this case, the Fisher King—the well-being of the people, and the health of the land. When the king is ailing, the whole realm suffers, the land is barren, and the people fail to thrive. Indeed, no one can thrive when the divine masculine is wounded. According to Ken Johnson and Marguerite Elsbeth in *The Grail Castle: Male Myths and Mysteries in the Celtic Tradition* (1995), the Fisher King, wounded fighting in the service of love, suffers endlessly, is in constant agony, cannot walk or attend to his body, people, or land (98).

Feminist interpretation of grail symbols, relationships, and synergies within the relatively young disciplines of depth psychology and mythological studies contains powerful, unique perspectives on the grail legend for women. Two such guides are Deldon McNeely's *Animus Aeternus: The Inner Masculine* (1991), and Marion Woodman's *The Ravaged Bridegroom: Masculinity in Women* (1990). In *Animus Aeternus* (curiously published by Fisher King Press), Deldon McNeely synthesizes various Jungian and post-Jungian theorists, offering a concise five-stage development model of the masculine principle in women. Evolution proceeds from Alien Outsider (symbolized by a stranger and/or abuser/abandoner/monster), to Father (as king/god, a patriarchal complex), to Hero (as lover/leading man and patriarchal partner), to Partner Within (as creative man/healer/magus), and finally an Androgyne stage (of integration and individuation) (66).

For McNeely, the Fisher King dwells around stage 2 and embodies a call for healing and an integration of women's inner wounded masculine. In these decades of what I suggest is the fourth wave of the women's movement, this integration cannot be overlooked as parallel to our cultural development. This model might also clarify the development of the masculine principle in general, whether in a woman or a man, an individual or a community.

In Wolfram von Eschenbach's retelling of the tale, *Parzival*, the Fisher King is named Amfortas, meaning "he who is without power" (Johnson and Elsbeth 19). Why is the king powerless? Significantly, the dolorous (painful, wounding) stroke the king received is from the Staff of Destiny used by the Roman centurion Longinus to pierce Jesus/Yeshua during his crucifixion; the linking of the Fisher King and Jesus/Yeshua is inescapable.[42]

Marion Woodman describes the ineffectual attempt on the part of the church to fill the void left by the abandoned Bride with a (nonsexual) mother-in-law. Perceval—this time in Chrétien de Troyes's grail writings— embodies the immature stage of male development. Perceval's adolescent unconsciousness is driven by the

wounding of the phallus in the pursuit of a luminous feminine vessel. So long as the masculinity is trapped in the fantasy of the mother, puberty rites (at whatever age) are in danger of becoming castration rites. The failure to ask the question—Whom does the Grail serve?— leaves Perceval in the unconscious grip of the outworn mother whose sole desire is to protect him against life, to keep him psychically bonded to her withering womb. The failure also leaves the old Fisher King impotent. (53–54)

Mother essentially dooms him into believing the phallacy—a falsehood located within the larger context of corrupted patriarchal systems, especially designed to reinforce patriarchal influence—of scarcity. Woodman identifies a key wounding of the feminine and how it plays out in a morbid, repetitive familial cycle through a corrupted relationship between mother and son. A woman unable to actualize her own inner masculine (including agency)

---

42. Significantly, Kathleen McGowan suggests Longinus himself as a healing Fisher King in her *Magdalene Line* series, which she asserts as autobiographical. Taking the name Destino, he was cursed to atone for his violence, living for millennia, originally teaching Magdalene's heresy in both France and Italy while tending the hereditary Magdalenian Expected One and Jesus/Yeshua-like Poet Prince as they repeatedly reincarnate as the sacred lovers. He eventually becomes the wise man, healed of his wound and released from the punishment of immortality.

projects it onto her young son, dooming him to remain an eternal boy tied
to her psychological apron strings—or, more accurately, trapped within
a vampiric relationship where she feeds on his youthful vitality and masculinity rather than cultivate her own—which manifests in repeating
patterns of mistreatment and disrespect of the feminine he encounters in the
world at large.[43] Perceval's mother is also the widow incapable of grieving;
having lost her husband and other sons to war, she tries protecting her son
by codependent management, controlling him to keep him ignorant of the
world at large and the ways of men and war. His growth and independence
would leave her alone, abandoned without her unholy source of stolen life
force; indeed, when he finally leaves her, she drops dead (Eschenbach).

As an eternal boy, he cannot ask the correct question of the wounded king,
whom he later discovers to be his uncle. Indeed, he can barely take care of
himself. It is only because Perceval/Parzival is dedicated to his own (wandering) quest that there is hope of his maturation. Marion Woodman suggests,
"The king is sick because consciousness and the unconscious are split apart;
therefore, the psychic life of his country has stagnated" (192). For Woodman,
a Jungian analyst, healing this split is the journey of a lifetime; the very act of
individuating occurs through attending this divide. It is when we fail to notice
that the king is ailing—perhaps by unconsciousness or willful ignorance, or by
propping him up on a throne of fantasies—that we stagnate and fail to thrive.[44]

We must also take into account the patriarchal landscape itself, where the
persecution of women and girls is a direct consequence of the wounding of
the masculine—indeed, the repeated injury of the feminine occurs *because*
the masculine is already wounded, impotent. They are deeply interrelated,
both inside us and all around us. Through the Fisher King we are offered
a unique opportunity to re/unite these distinct and interconnected parts:

> Bringing together the worlds of timeless and time, spirit and
> matter, is the problem of the Grail King who "corresponds to an
> imago Dei [image of God] that is suspended, suffering, on the
> problem of the opposites. . . ." The Grail King in most of us is also

---

43. We find remnants of this incestuous corruption in the propagandized relationship between
Mother Mary and Jesus as core of the Christian Church and within the modern mythology
of the relationship between an archetypal overbearing, omnipotent Jewish mother and her
impotent, *puer* son. See the segment "Oedipus Wrecks" in the film *New York Stories* and "'I'll
Have Whatever She's Having,'" by Nathan Abrams, in *Reel Food*.

44. From a personal conversation with Dennis Slattery on the political expression of psychic
wounds (2016).

suspended, his feeling and ideals not grounded in his body. . . . For centuries he has been cut off from his own matter, from what has been considered the dark, serpentine feminine side of himself. . . .

Attempting to transcend his own nature has not worked. Nature herself is beginning to rumble. Our very survival depends upon spirit embracing embodied soul. (Woodman 216)

Woodman identifies the state of the Fisher/Grail King as a form of paralysis. His stasis—like God's—echoes what Campbell, Jung, and James Hillman all describe as calcification, occurring in institutions or in the shadow of the archetypal old man, the *senex*.[45] Particularly significant for Woodman is the need to address the disembodied quality of solar Logos, desertified consciousness; to liberate our-Selves from such paralysis requires movement and moisture. The Fisher King needs yoga and a steam bath.

Woodman writes, "Real masculinity is not interested in copying the old king parading his empty power in robes and crown. Real masculinity is interested in genuine empowerment grounded in the instincts" (196). For both Woodman and McNeely real masculinity means Jesus/Yeshua who, in his role as shaman—a more evolved inner masculine image according to McNeely—emerges as a spiritual healer, offering embodied *access* to the divine. Woodman explains that "Patriarchal fear of the feminine can be overcome by building a conscious feminine container—a receptive soul that no longer needs to fear either spirit or matter" (27). This conscious act may be the work of a lifetime for both men and woman.

Self-containment that is strong enough to withstand true masculine penetration is central to Woodman's theories. Physician, and Jungian ana-lyst/theorist Esther Harding interpreted the Greek word *parthenos* depth psychologically as "a woman whole unto her-Self," perhaps an admirable goal for all those who choose to individuate (125).[46] Perhaps this is the underlying movement of a s/heroic journey—to come home to her whole Self, albeit in a new form.

Jesus/Yeshua can be seen as having such a container, as having come to terms with his inner feminine and with the feminine principle at large in the world. Perhaps Magdalene's return pivots around creating complimentary

---

45. See especially James Hillman, *Senex and Puer*.

46. For a detailed related conversation on the depth psychological impact of the *Parthenos* archetype, see Safron Rossi's *The Kore Archetype*.

containment. It is only after both are contained—as we saw with Isis and Osiris—that there can be conscious and sacred union. Woodman relates how, through the mature union between Jesus/Yeshua and the Bride, the (singular, in her definition) wasteland is irrigated: "She is Sophia, Wisdom, mother, Bride, Shakti, Shekinah. She is the love that radiates in, through and around the new king—enlightened matter opening to embody spirit. In their marriage, conscious and unconscious are united. Water is restored to the Waste Land, the Fisher King is healed" (203–4). Woodman clusters these archetypes together to show the power and eminence of the divine feminine. She is worthy of the new king, as he is of her. She identifies what has been missing from a desertified and barren (singular) wasteland: the aqueous, erotic qualities of emotion and relatedness. But this prevailing concept of the wasteland is incomplete.

This marriage between the masculine and the feminine principles not only irrigates what most theorists refer to as "the" wasteland, it offers clues revealing it for what it truly is: the desertified, *masculine* portion of a more complex wasteland realm. An adjacent realm lies secretly portioned off behind a patriarchy-made dam separating divine from human, masculine from feminine, Logos from Eros. This fetid, flooded swampland is the veiled (and denied) feminine wasteland. Neither barren realm bears fruit, yet their qualities are cruelly complementary; his is emotionally sterile and hers saturated by too much feeling. Through the potentialities of healing via individuation and the internal sacred marriage, the dam (originally built to prioritize and man/age Logos over Eros, thinking over feeling) can be consciously deconstructed, releasing swampy, stagnating water, irrigating the complementary desertified lands.

Mary Magdalene—with her unique gifts as Bride—is returning to this post-postmodern, dysfunctional Judeo-Christian compound wasteland, including now separate, secular "Western" cultures seemingly devoid of spirit, yet still insisting on disembodied, intellectual transcendence. Campbell describes this as the "dissociation of professed from actual existence and the consequent spiritual disaster which, in the imagery of the grail legend, is symbolized in the Wasteland theme: a landscape of spiritual death, a world waiting, waiting" (*Creative Mythologies* 5). Rising out of this waiting, barren landscape of moral corruption, environmental devastation, amnesia, and deceit comes an ecofeminist, postapocalyptic s/hero for a world reeling from more than two thousand years of unconscious madness: Mary Magdalene.

Campbell believes mythology serves four functions, the first being that a myth must evoke an experience of awe, humility, and respect as we recognize some form of sacred mystery (*Creative Mythology* 609). "The second

Table 1. Compound wastelands
Personal and Collective Wounds
Eros and Our Wounds
Logos and Our Wounds
Wounding over Time

function of a mythology is to render a cosmology, an image of the universe"
that explains our relationship with everything around us (*Creative Mythology*
611). The cosmology of a patriarchal, capitalistic military industrial machine
is one of rape and pillage, of power over Others. The missing feminine within
a patriarchal system signals ecological destruction. The emergence of ecofeminist principles, with the second wave of feminism, is syncopated with the
rediscovery and translation of the Gospel of Mary in 1955, which enabled an
in-depth analysis of her presence across newly discovered texts collectively
known as the Gnostic Gospels.[47] The returning Magdalene embodies key elements healing abandonment and grief.[48] Tending our personal and collective
wounds and resultant grief regenerates the compound patriarchal wasteland.

The third function of mythology is "the validation and maintenance of an
established order . . . an all-inclusive unity" (*Creative Mythologies* 621–22).
Here, Campbell suggests that healthy social cohesion depends on mythology
for its existence. Citing the grail legend as "the great mythos of the modern
European world," stressing its emergence as *secular* literature between the
years of 1150 and 250, Campbell identifies key symbols within this sacred
European tradition, including: the grail vessel, the Fisher King, and the
(singular) wasteland (*The Grail Legend*). All of these mythemes are found
within Magdalene mythology of the medieval era. Scholars have been examining translations from Provençal and Old French twelfth-century poetry
describing a grail family (or vessel) using the word for royal blood, *sang raal*
or *Sangraal*, which also translates to "royal blood" (Starbird 26). Here, Mary
Magdalene's body itself acts as the grail, a vessel carrying the bloodline of

---

47. Though the *Gospel of Mary* was first rediscovered/excavated in 1896, it lay dormant in
pieces in two disparate museum archives, abandoned and undervalued. It was after the
Nag Hammadi texts were discovered in 1945 (revealing related texts suppressed by the early
Roman organizers of the Catholic Church, most famously through the Council of Nicaea in
325 CE), that attention was paid to other remains of early texts, now known collectively—and
perhaps incorrectly—as the Gnostic Gospels. Leloup and others argue that the Gospels of
Mary and Thomas differ significantly in both content and scope.

48. For further discussion of grief, see Lesa Bellevie, "She Moves in Mysterious Ways."

Jesus/Yeshua and potentially two royal Judaic families, depending on her family lineage. The modern embodiment of bloodline theory—whether mythologically, historically, or some fusion of the two—is inclusive in its scholarship and vision, describing a vast Europeanized (Western cultural) lineage of royal descent effecting a majority rather than minority identity.

Through various clues in *Parzifal*, Eschenbach identifies the Fisher King as Jesus.[49] According to Campbell, there is a singular "theme of the grail legends: the king is powerless and impotent without his consort. The problem of the grail romance is to heal the Fisher King; the problem of the grail hero is to heal that wound" (*The Grail Legend*). Campbell reminds us that it is the knight whom we must keep our eye on; it is only Parzifal as *puer* who is capable of action, not the wounded (calcified *senex*) king. He clearly acknowledges the erotic relationship at the heart of the grail riddle and the impotency caused by the missing consort. So how is it that Campbell could not imagine Jesus and Magdalene as the divine couple at the heart of the quest? The heart of the grail legends pivots around the loss of Magdalene.

"It is the loss of the feminine counterpart of the god that causes the wound that never heals, and the stricken Wasteland reflects the woundedness of God" (Starbird 86). If Christianity without the Magdalenian half of the story renders Jesus/Yeshua as a Fisher King—wounded in his grief at the loss of his Bride—his leadership (and that of his patriarchal church by proxy) becomes impotent, because he is but half of a greater whole. The return of the Bride, therefore, is not for her alone but also for the partnership, the sacred union at the root of Western traditions, Jung's *coniunctio* embodied in divine partnership, and the healing of the land/Nature.

The final function of mythology is to offer psychological meaning: does a story bring us to our own center, and in harmony with life? For Campbell,

---

49. Eschenbach's clues are numerous. "The identity of the Fisher King of the Parzifal legend of Wolfram von Eschenbach is obvious: the wounded king is called Anfortas, a corruption of *in fortis*, which means 'in strength.' This is the Latin name for the left pillar of the Temple of Jerusalem, called Boaz in Hebrew. The name of this pillar, which is also the name of the ancestor of King David, is a clear and obvious reference to the promises made to the Davidic bloodline, the line of the princes of Judah, that the dominion of its princes would be established forever 'in strength,' since Judah was the *strongest* of the twelve sons of Israel's patriarch Jacob. The name Anfortas is thus associated with the broken left pillar of the Temple of Jerusalem, which is symbolic of the broken Davidic succession" (Starbird 86). Starbird goes on to describe the Black Madonna at Chartres, known as Our Lady of the Pillar, as another link with Mary Magdalene as the widow of Jesus (148). Particularly interesting is the iconographic symbolism in the High Priestess card of the Major Arcana in the tarot, where she is framed by the two pillars of the Temple.

myth calls us again and again from the wasteland motif of a "world of people living inauthentic lives—doing what they're supposed to do," toward regeneration and the commitment to making our lives authentic (*Transformations of Myth Through Time* 214). For Woodman, healing the cultural trauma of abandonment on such a grand scale is also always personal; healing demands attending the archetypes. "The individual now has to connect with the inner laws, the inner love. That is the Grail Castle" (191). Such sincere movement toward liberation embodies regenerative consciousness.

Myths are alive; living myths themselves are inherently regenerative. The Magdalene as returning the feminine principle is an especially unwieldy myth to track and describe, since it is alive and is being cocreated simultaneously around the world through scholarship, literature, and visual art, as well as via the World Wide Web. Could Campbell ever have imagined such a dynamically unfolding conversation? Yes, I believe he could, for though he could not see Magdalene in her role as Bride, she embodied nothing less than the regenerative properties of psyche and the collective unconscious, which Joseph Campbell understood well.

For Campbell the function of the grail knight in relation to the realm is to "restore its integrity to life and let stream again from infinite depths the lost, forgotten, living waters of the inexhaustible source" (*Creative Mythology* 5). This rising, uncontainable font contains the vital, erotic individuating moisture Campbell recognized and celebrated repeatedly. Yet, like that other grail knight he so thoroughly studied, Campbell failed to ask the correct question as the grail herself passed him by.

CHAPTER 3

BRIDAL AGENCY

HOW WOMEN'S LITERARY FICTION AND MEMOIR CRASH THE (PATRIARCHAL) WEDDING

> Psychological interpretation is our way of telling stories; we still have the
> same need and we still crave the renewal that comes from understand-
> ing archetypal images. We know quite well that it is just our myth.
> —MARIE-LOUISE VON FRANZ, *THE INTERPRETATION OF FAIRY TALES* (45)

INTRODUCTION: HERE COMES THE BRIDE

This chapter shifts the focus toward the significance of emerging, pervasive
regenerative bridal consciousness—including new forms of agency—appearing in new literary fiction and film. In these emerging expressions, these
appearances, the Bride does not always arrive in a horse-drawn carriage
or white limousine, or on the arm of a man. Here she might appear unan-
nounced, unheralded, unattended, alone, often unexpected—even broken.
She is sometimes a wedding crasher, a pest at her own nuptials—and it ain't
easy to crash your own wedding.

   It is worth noting here that I repeatedly attempted to shake this archetype
off my trail, preferring instead to write about the feminine principle, which I
had originally considered more broadly "useful," palpable, and valued. What,
I wondered, could a Bride have to offer? I attempted to write about historical
and archetypal Mary Magdalene—who certainly would not leave me alone—
in a "greater" context, including her other "more empowering" attributes and

84

attitudes, those of a leader and teacher. Yet the Bride haunted me. I continued to wonder: was not marriage inherently a patriarchal institution? In a world striving for postcolonial, postpatriarchal potentialities, are conversations about marriage still valid? Instead, would energy be better spent restructuring sacred partnership into completely new language and practice, making space for more radical, and ultimately healthier, acts of love and relationship?

When dismissing the Bride ultimately failed, I stopped running and turned to face her. By committing to her in this way, as well as to her missing partner, I began a new devotional trajectory ripe with synchronicity. (See chapter 6 for a discussion of synchronicity as healing modality.) Her own unique path and gifts began to unfold before me, one revelatory step at a time. I began to see her everywhere; Bridal "mysteries" appeared in unexpected literary and cinematic places and spaces, and I wondered if the authors themselves had noticed her presence.

Discussing the Bride can be problematic on several levels, especially in cultures where unconscious longing for the feminine and attempts at commodifying her are ubiquitous. The false virgin/whore dichotomy still terrorizes women globally in the twenty-first century. The Bride has been appropriated as a glamour gloss for capitalism and male fantasies all balled up in deceptive lies about womanhood, the feminine, and sexuality. Her real power cannot be commodified or commercialized. Nor can she be sacrificially sold by the patriarchy/wounded father principle as payment for his own undeveloped feminine and refusal to individuate.

Contemporary corrupted formats of bridal preparation include "purity balls," an extreme take on debutante cotillions, where historically girls were formally presented to society, neatly packaged, marketed as future wives—sometimes pawns between wealthy families seeking financial alliances. Produced in ultraconservative Christian pockets of American culture, "purity balls" partner daughters unnaturally with their fathers, to whom they then pledge their sexual "virginity."[50] This legacy of perverse female disempowerment is supported by patriarchal motherhood, as it continues to feed vampirically on their daughters' life force. Eros is a wild and uncontrollable power, which, if trapped within patriarchal mutations, produces shadows of objectifying porn, r/ejects the feminine, and turns us all into sexual machines. Rather than member/ship, its greatest achievement is jerking off.[51]

---

50. For an in-depth analysis of how this affects women's agency, see *The Purity Myth* by Jessica Valenti.

51. See chapter 4, "Exiled and Underground: The Lost Bride in European Fairy Tales," for an in-depth look at the vampiric nature of patriarchal motherhood.

Instead, Bridal stories advocating regeneration are re/appearing every-where, calling us to carry on. They are telling us that to heal the compound wasteland—in its complex, intersecting masculine and feminine forms—the movement required is away from the corrupted, incomplete patriarchal model toward more sustainable, regenerative ways. Women are being called upon to tend their wounds and leave extended maidenhood, deconstruct the phallacies of inflated and imprisoning martyr motherhood and the realms of evil false queens, and step toward sovereign self-centeredness and their own internal, Erotic weddings and coronations.

When the archetypal Bride's sovereignty is intact, she shows up of her own free will—a mature woman whose primary relationship is with her-Self. The archetypal Bride is that feminine part of ourselves and our cultures willing and enthusiastic to partner, both with the healing masculine principle and with the world. She ripens through relationship internally. This alchemical process requires the Other, someone/something different from herself and about whom she must remain open and curious, vulnerable, and present. The Bride is one-half of life, arriving, flowing, and holding the receptivity and capacity for love and healthy relationship.

THE HONOR OF YOUR PRESENCE IS REQUESTED:
INVITING THE BRIDE CONSCIOUSLY

Despite shifting social norms and expectations around marriage, bridal motifs continue to be exceptionally popular themes in literary fiction and biography and provide an invaluable lens for social analysis. The Bride appears in countless acts of fiction as a redemptive figure whose actions pre-pare her for the container of sacred marriage. Stella Gibbons's *Cold Comfort Farm* (1932) has become a wasteland until the arrival of the Bride as Flora Poste, who brings fertility and healing; through her the bloom/fertility of the farm and land is restored. The novel culminates in her union with a worthy, individuating man who recognizes her worth. Kate Beckinsale's performance as Flora in the 1999 film production highlights how her ambi-tions as a writer inform her open and curious stance, facilitating growth, insight, and relationship building.

Often multiple Brides appear in a novel, amplifying the trajectory toward marriage as *coniunctio*. Elizabeth von Arnim's *The Enchanted April* (1922) is a movement toward individuation for all four protagonists, with end-of-life resolution for one and union/reunion for the other three. The 1992 film adaptation is particularly effective in depicting the process of making space for awareness and growth as the women move from emotional saturation in cold and wet London toward their solar and maturing Italian retreat.

The same multiplication of bridal presence holds true for Louisa May Alcott's *Little Women* (1868–69), where one sister faces her health crises and end-of-life resolutions while three Brides encounter their tests, practice discernment, and ultimately meet worthy mates. With numerous extremely popular film, television, stage, and even operatic adaptations to date—including two released in 2018—Transcendentalist Alcott's gals have consistently resonated across 150 years.

Alcott, more than any other female writer, shaped my childhood. As Anne Boyd Rioux discusses in *Meg, Jo, Beth & Amy: The Story of Little Women*, within this quintessential book on growing up, we all either recognize ourselves in Jo or want to become her. The book fuses sensations of positive domesticity while evoking the dynamic electricity of the "cozy" village of an Agatha Christie novel where something must be solved. Jo is the detective in her own mystery. Alcott's subversive creativity—born out of her life within the Transcendental community of Concord and her family's somewhat painful legacy of utopian adventures at Fruitland—nudge and drag us through a civil war, the death of a sibling, the deep and painful call to social justice as vocation, and the quiet daily erosion of dignity that is genteel poverty.

Greta Gerwig's 2019 adaptation of *Little Women* amplifies Alcott's own graceful revealing of the power of tending grief while tipping her hat stylistically to the 1994 film. The casting of all the sisters is quite powerful. Emma Watson—famously known as Hermione Granger in the Harry Potter series—faithfully portrays Meg, remaining true to her somewhat milquetoast character (akin to Austen's traditional Jane Bennet). This unexpected depiction challenges us to witness "Hermione"—certainly a courageous Jo herself—cower in the face of fear. Perhaps the most riveting line of Gerwig's adaptation is spoken by Marmee, played by Laura Dern. "I am angry nearly every day of my life, Jo." It's both her acknowledgment of her rage and what she does with it—not allowing it to move her to lash out at others and the world in further injuring/traumatizing, but rather to meditate on it and utilize that acknowledged energy to transform her realm, as an agent for social justice.

Alcott's familial heritage is central to both her storytelling and her own use of the pen for social justice, her fictional sisters famously grounded in her own three siblings. Moreover, the individuation of the daughters could be studied as pivoting around the centrality of Marmee, a sturdy tent pole for the movement of the girls' diverse growth. Alcott's mother, Abigail May, was herself the great, great granddaughter of Salem witch trial judge Samuel Sewall. Sewall and his family experienced a series of tragedies they attributed to the injustice of the trials as their awareness emerged; Sewall offered a public apology for his involvement in the deaths and went on to become an abolitionist and early colonial advocate for women's rights (Salem Witch Trials Documentary Archive). Abigail May's multigenerational legacy of social work can be contextually understood as having emerged from this epic patriarchal trauma of colonial North America.

Conversely, in *A Hunger for Home: Louisa May Alcott's Place in American Culture*, Sarah Elbert identifies how Alcott attributed to Professor Bhaer qualities her father, Bronson Alcott, lacked: "warmth, intimacy, and a tender capacity for expressing his affection—the feminine attributes Alcott admired and hoped men could acquire in a rational, feminist world" (Elbert 164). What a powerful, individuating move to both evolve the father archetype while crafting a worthy—compassionate, brilliant, liminal, capable, present—partner for her own biographical Bride!

Returning to Jody Bower's *Jane Eyre's Sisters: How Women Live and Write the Heroine's Story* (2015) as a feminist revision of Joseph Campbell's masculinist "hero's journey" supports navigation in this literary territory by recognizing signs, portents, and players encountered while following female protagonists on their adventures. This provides a type of psychic location service, akin to GPS—perhaps a psychic positioning system, or PPS? Applying Bower's work here tracks the Bride as she is propelled out into the world. Like Patricia Reis, Bower's study depathologizes women's lived experiences, particularly the act of leaving dangerous and otherwise unhealthy situations.

Most significantly, leaving intolerable situations, enables s/heroes to move toward what Bower identifies as the healing outcomes for wanderers: the creation of a home of her own—a core theme for Brides—and mature partnership. As Hestian priestess—a seemingly paradoxical identity—the Aletis is a pathfinding seeker, wandering in search of home, integrating her experiences in service to soul.

Most importantly, the individuating wanderer—the *Aletis* in Greek—learns to pinpoint and track her geographic location. Like finding the "You Are Here" dot on a map, tracking her own movement across interior and exterior landscapes brings perspective and relief, enabling her to become her own psychic cartographer and take the long view of her journey. Imagine the impact of teaching young girls this essential psychological skill.

Bower identifies sacred marriage as central to the Aletis's regenerative movement:

> The hero of the Aletis story is a man who recognizes the value of partnership with the right woman; the man who can and wishes to

embrace the feminine both within himself and in another person. Perhaps we are spiraling back to the idea that the ultimate goal is marriage with the *other*, the formerly disavowed or unappreciated self; but this time we are coming to it with the goal that both people are able to be fully themselves both in the world and in the relationship. In other words: true partners. (245)

Bower describes the necessary preparatory, healing steps for conscious partnership, which occur only after earlier exposure to unconscious alternatives. For Bower, what is necessary for an individuating woman is self-awareness and sovereignty, and a male hero who is also actively individuating and prioritizing sacred union. (And here I want to stress that rather than a heteronormative model, what heals the complex wastelands in and around us is tending the feminine and masculine principles in each of us across polyvalent expressions of gender.) Sacred, mature partnership develops only after these conditions are cultivated, providing a dynamic container for deepening healing while supporting sovereignty for each partner. Sovereignty includes self-determination and access to personal power, as well as the ability to effect change—agency.

A dynamic body of literary fiction about Mary Magdalene as archetypal Bride has developed since the 1980s, accelerating especially after the blockbuster novel and global phenomenon *The Da Vinci Code* (2003) and film adaptation (2006). Much of this emerging canon appears to be self-reflexive, building on itself with both feminist and depth psychological themes. Simultaneously developing during these past few decades within the fields of literary criticism and depth psychology are emerging theories exploring the psychological potential and impact of our interaction with these written forms. Applying these here to literary fiction and memoir supports tracking the Bride who wanders forth toward sacred marriage via patterns of bridal agency and individuation in Jane Austen's six canonical novels and Elizabeth Gilbert's memoir *Eat, Pray, Love*. Both authors offer creative, embodied, regenerative models of Magdalenian literature that have also developed into effective and beloved films.

READING/(W)RITING THE FEMININE

Mary Magdalene has appeared overtly in numerous early twentieth-century literary fiction and poetry. H.D.'s epic poem *Trilogy* (1946) and Leonora Carrington's *The Hearing Trumpet* (1976), for example, both developed creative feminist narratives and identities for her, though neither takes the radical step of identifying her as the lost Bride of the Christian myth. The

1980s brought two fresh literary fictions, both of which locate her firmly as sacred Bride: Clysta Kinstler's *The Moon Under Her Feet* (1989) and Michèle Roberts's Jungian-inflected *The Wild Girl* (1984).

In the 1980s post–Vatican II politics were barely beginning to unravel the conflation between Mary Magdalene and the penitent sinner. Significantly, both *The Moon Under Her Feet* and *The Wild Girl* attempt to redeem and redefine Mary Magdalene's sexuality, as well as depathologize women's sexuality in general. Roberts explores the theme of prostitution, while Kinstler recasts her as a sacred priestess of Jerusalem, bearing the title "The Magdalene." Kinstler uses sacred sexuality, centered around the Sister-Bride and sacrificial year-king lineage of the Mediterranean "fertility cults"—which are more accurately termed ancient partnership models and mystery traditions—as the core of Judaic mystery traditions.

In *The Reflowering of the Goddess*, Gloria Orenstein identifies both *The Moon Under Her Feet* and *The Wild Girl*, along with other feminist matristic texts and scholarship, as actively remythologizing biblical, classical, indigenous, grail, and ecofeminist cycles. In her chapter "Cycling: Restoring Matristic Storytelling," Orenstein spots revolutionary motifs in both novels, placing them within a lineage of highly creative feminist mythological reclamation emerging from ecofeminist and revisionist scholarship. Ornstein suggests such revisionary texts require combining "the arts of the scholar with those of the visionary artist, showing us how only the combination of these two kinds of knowledge can help us piece together a past that, while conceived by the imagination, can also be rooted in the evidence of the real, and grounded by the workings of inspired intelligence" (152).

By acknowledging how the intersection of creativity and grounded scholarship is vital to our ability to reimagine, to remythologize, Ornstein, like Audre Lorde, is suggesting that the "master's tools" alone will never build an effective and innovative house; instead creativity must be applied to develop new ways and means. The vitality of story, of myth itself, gives our psyches more than scholarship alone can provide—itself sitting within a mandorla born of an erotic/logical *coniuntio*. This conscious cultivation of creativity as psychic healing agent is central to Magdalenian regeneration. Magdalene's return directly benefits from—perhaps even depends upon—our ability to tend the process from such a creatively informed and grounded stance.

In *C. G. Jung and Literary Theory*, Susan Rowland suggests the impact and significance of Roberts's *The Wild Girl* as a cutting-edge feminist Jungian text that simultaneously critiques Jungian theory while adding to it by creating a new form. Examining how Roberts shows embodiment and sexuality as significant and central to spiritual experience, relating individuation and sacred marriage within the context of Magdalene and Jesus (100–101), Rowland describes how Roberts gives us a Magdalene whose primary movement is "the marriage in the soul" (104), while providing an empowered model of a privileged activist, Jesus, as a leader who "rewrites images of gender separation as Jungian images of conjunction, of differentiation between male and female" (103).

With individuation as the structuring dynamic of the novel, Rowland explores Roberts's treatment of the unconscious (105) and the location of Christianity in relationship to its "pagan (m)Other" (104). Significantly for this study, Rowland identifies the novel's significance as due to the centrality of pain and shadow as change agents, "the source of her [Mary's] songs, her teaching" (103). Crucially, in this book Rowland develops a dynamic model for examining literary art and creativity from a feminist post-Jungian perspective, making a significant contribution to literary theory by exposing a deep function of reading and writing fiction:

> Reading (w)rite is a term coined . . . to signify a concept whereby Jungian active imagination is absorbed into reading and/or writing fiction. If active imagination relies upon spontaneous unconscious fantasies in the processing of images, then the same idea could apply to images provoked by words or groups of words. The more fictional or poetic a text, the more the active imagination might apply because of the greater scope for images likely to stimulate unconscious fantasies. If reading fiction can be construed as active imagination, then reading enters the individuation process in the continual re-forming of subjectivity; it becomes a rite of the subject. Similarly, if writing fiction occurs when the writer desires to romance the Other, to be open to fantasy images from the unconscious before choosing words, then writing also becomes a (w)rite of individuation. (227)

When reading and writing are understood and valued as forms of active imagination, entire worlds of potentialities open. As we engage with the structure of the written word as readers, we infuse the scene with meaning from our own very personal imaginal realm. A story then comes alive as reflexive medicine, a tonic for our souls, supporting the development of personal trajectory. This form of active imagination also supports identification with the characters and an expansion of our range of feelings, including empathy and empowerment. This transformative, alchemical process (like dreaming) activates psyche as we interact with images and symbols and becomes a radical act of psychic growth and development.

In this way, when evaluating Roberts's book, for example, as a creative act of literary fiction with reading/(w)rite as a tool, and reconsidering Mary Magdalene's pain and shadow as central to the narrative, we can imagine the potentiality for griefwork activated within readers of the story. Rather than dismissing emotions that arise while reading as ersatz feelings, they are instead recognized for their potential as central to psychic movement! Such activations by a text then become a signpost toward healing. By interacting with the novel, we renegotiate our personal myth. By actively engaging with Magdalene's narrative movement, we too move.

Returning to the lineage of Magdalenian literary fiction, the following decade brought significant contributions in both *The Magic Circle* by Katherine Neville (1998) and *The Televisionary Oracle* by Rob Brezsny (2000). While neither book features Mary Magdalene as the central figure, both introduce radical interpretations of her as Bride, linking sacred partnership with the mystery traditions while redeeming sexuality as natural and expansive. Additionally, Elizabeth Cunningham's award-winning Maeve Chronicle series also began in 2000. This four-part epic continues Roberts's thread of redemption with the themes of sexuality and prostitution, while also identifying Mary Magdalene—this time as a redheaded Celtic woman originally named Maeve—as the sacred and sensual Bride with divine partnership and individuation as central, humorous themes. Cunningham—an interfaith minister, counselor, musician, and poet—fulfills Orenstein's call for creatively infused scholarship as imaginal fecundity.

That so many of these emerging novels have made bestseller lists, captivating large audiences internationally, paired with the empowerment implicit in the act of the reading/(w)rite, implies these books are having significant personal and cultural impact. Further application of reading/(w)rite theoretically to bridal literature—where Magdalene appears both overtly and more covertly—excavates this body of work's potential for deep theoretical and psychological impact on readers.

These books were followed by Margaret George's *Mary, Called Magdalene* (2002) and *The Secret Magdalene* by Ki Longfellow (2005), neither of which identifies Mary Magdalene as the lost Bride; both focus instead on her apostolic role. Two other significant contributions to the emerging bridal canon include *According to Mary Magdalene* by Marianne Fredriksson (1997), and Kathleen McGowan's very relevant *Magdalene Line* series, beginning with *The Expected One* (2006).

Narrating the living heresy and history of Occitania, *The Expected One* depicts how Mary Magdalene hid scrolls containing a gospel of her own version of the events of the New Testament within the French Pyrenees foothills two thousand years ago. These sacred scrolls could be uncovered only by a unique seeker, a woman fulfilling an ancient prophecy as "the expected one." Protagonist Maureen Pascal is led synchronistically toward Magdalenian clues and sacred partnership with grail lore keeper Berenger Sinclair. *The Book of Love* continues with Maureen as a leader in the field of women's history, researching eleventh-century warrior countess Matilda of Tuscany, whom McGowan suggests was secretly married to Pope Gregory VII. The book's "Outtakes" section further illuminates McGowan's scholarship and access to primary sources, both as documents and archaeomythological material culture.

Maureen discovers a second branch of Magdalenian heresy surviving in Italy through Matilda's story and a connection with the sudden building of European cathedrals, possibly using previously lost ancient technology dating back to King Solomon and the Queen of Sheba, linking Magdalene with the Song of Songs and a Cretan labyrinth found in medieval Tuscany. McGowan connects Magdalenian mythology with Ariadne, Asherah, Saint Modesta, Joan of Arc, Teresa of Ávila, and Lúcia Santos (a prophetess of Fátima) in an effective and radical mythopoetic retelling of history she asserts as authentic and autobiographic. The series' third book, *The Poet Prince*, uncovers a how the Magdalenian heresy survived via the de Medici family's Florentine Renaissance, particularly through the encoded art of Botticelli, rather than a misogynist Da Vinci's. This volume is centered around a prophecy calling forth men as "the time returns," evoking a complementary sacred responsibility for the embodied masculine toward sacred marriage; significant here is the poetic nature called for in men—nurturing, sensitive, embodied Eros, central to the internal feminine principle in men.

McGowan reports the series to be a biographical firsthand account that she had been both living and developing for decades, submitting her first proposal for a book recounting a marriage between Jesus and Mary Magdalene in 1997, six years prior to the release of Brown's *The Da Vinci Code*; she was laughed out of the publisher's offices. It all began with a dream where Magdalene appeared to her pleading for her help; she went from being a Little League mum of three boys to traveling to Jerusalem and then the French Languedoc, experiencing an extensive embodied synchronistic quest.[52]

---

52. See McGowan's afterword in *The Expected One* and her interview with Decca Aitkenhead, "Mary and Me."

With the tremendous resonance of *The Da Vinci Code*, *The Expected One* was then picked up by Simon & Schuster the following year, immediately becoming an international bestseller, as have the subsequent books. Notable in McGowan's treatment of Magdalene is her assertion of the bloodline theory, particularly regarding prophecy. For her, Magdalenian ancestry offers women psychic insight and a gift for expansive vision, perspective, and clarity (qualities of Logos). Male descendants carry the complementary gift of tending the expected one and creative mythopoesis (in the realm of Eros). McGowan has created an empowered, remythologized offering of Magdalene as archetypal Bride and psychic guide on several levels, complete with a *coniuntio* with potential to tend the compound wasteland on several levels.

In her fourth novel, *The Boleyn Heresy, Part 1: The Time Will Come* (2022), McGowan again tracks the survival of progressive attitudes toward women and the feminine in historical France and England, excavating the story of Anne Boleyn's time within the French court. Herself a descendent of Boleyn's lineage via the Howard family, McGowan's unique contribution to this discussion pivots around insider status—both within her heritage and within the Occitan Magdalenian heresy community. Paying particular attention to the formation and influence of Europe's elite female royal leadership and links with the Magdalene heresy, the book amplifies Boleyn's education by three existing and future queens: Margaret of Austria, Louise of Savoy, and Marguerite of Angouleme (later known as Marguerite of Navarre).

McGowan's author notes illuminate her reliance on primary sources, some of which were previously unknown or even misinterpreted by scholars, including Anne's personal Book of Hours on display at her home, Hever Castle; records from the Dominican monastery at Saint Baume documenting the royal pilgrimage; and various archaeomythological evidence—in both architectural features and art—in the chateau fictionalized as "Chateau Sabra." A ramshackle property discovered deep in the Cathar region, which she was contemplating purchasing when her husband suddenly became ill and died, the historic property has since been purchased by a German group, becoming a boutique hotel. McGowan writes: "The backup research details for the historic choices I have made in this series can (and will) fill a non-fiction book of their own, which I have been working on simultaneous to the fiction, entitled *Avenging Anne Boleyn*. Some articles and expansions will also be available on my websites, www.anneboleyn.com and www.anneboleyn.co.uk."

Such crucial research breadcrumbs can be critical to establishing the legitimacy of a nontraditional scholar such as McGowan, who continues her prolific lectures via Patreon. Even remarkable challenges in the publication process of this series reflect the depth of research, study, and meaning making. This continuing mythopoetic engagement with our collective quest for the meaning of the Magdalenian heresy in Western religious traditions and cultures over time is worthy of our attention. Learning how Anne Boleyn's initiatory life in France may have shaped her experiences as queen reshapes our understanding of embodied female leadership, feminine archetypes, and the shadow of a dying patriarchal fear. The time has indeed come.

JANE AUSTEN'S BRIDAL AGENCY

Jane Austen—along with several other nineteenth-century women authors, including the Brontës (Ann, Emily, and Charlotte), George Eliot (Mary Ann Evans), and George Sand (Amantine Lucile Aurore Dupin)—pioneered placing women at the center of narrative interest. Shifting literary focus toward women's experience was a radical act. Protagonists created by male authors had, by and large, been male, created for supposedly male audiences, a male gaze. These women wrote profound stories, imbuing their s/heroes with sovereignty, intelligence, wit, and agency—radical acts at the time. Choice always is.

In her six completed major novels, Austen offers the consistent, invaluable gift of clear descriptions and warnings of the dreaded unindividuating person, often the first and false love interest of her s/heroes. Each woman must choose between two men: one who either refuses to grow or cannot (a deeply unconscious, unindividuated/unindividuating man), and one who is developing a strong character and integrity, coming to consciousness (achieving individuation). Ironically, although Austen takes great care with character development, I believe she suggests that some people—men and women alike—are simply incapable of deep psychological development. Perhaps she would agree with Joseph Campbell that a significant jump is required for such growth to occur, an often terrifying leap not everyone might risk in this lifetime (*The Power of Myth* 1991).

Austen repeatedly delineates the danger of entering into partnership with an unindividuating man, including the loss of energy for a woman's own individuation process. Historically, economic and personal power for Regency women of the middle and upper classes teetered on a knife's edge of respectability through social connection and education. Strict social morality codes also left little room for women's behavior or creativity to flourish

Novel	S/Hero	Unindividuated Man	Individuating Man
Persuasion	Anne Eliot	William Eliot	Captain Wentworth
Pride and Prejudice	Jane Bennet Lizzy Bennet	— (Mr. Collins) George Wickham	Charles Bingley Fitzwilliam Darcy
Sense and Sensibility	Marianne Dashwood Elinor Dashwood	John Willoughby —	Colonel Brandon Edward Ferrars
Emma	Emma Woodhouse	(Mr. Elton) Frank Churchill	George Knightley
Mansfield Park	Fanny Price	Henry Crawford	Edmund Bertram
Northanger Abbey	Catherine Morland	John Thorpe	Henry Tilney

Table 2. Jane Austen on bridal agency, individuation, and partnership

outside narrowly prescribed standards. Gendered laws and social practices, including primogeniture (property is entailed away toward firstborn male heirs, however tenuous their relation), had enormous impact on women and girls. This is one of Austen's favorite topics affecting her personally, so significant when most women lived perilously close to poverty, abuse, abandonment, and early death. However, even when faced with the possibility of economic ruin, Austen is loyal to partnering for love. This stance not only made Austen radical for her time but has kept her relevant and influential, a (r)evolutionary. Crucially, she urges us to fall in love with one who is *worthy* of it, he who has been or is willing to be—perhaps is even in the process of being—tempered by the alchemical fires of transformation, as her s/heroes themselves are.

Austen demands that her women strive for partnership with men who are cultivating their inner life, strength, and nurturance. It is from that this self-centering commitment that all else, including economic stability and deep partnership, evolves. Such a partner will ultimately be well equipped to fully participate in a dynamic marriage while supporting the Bride in her own alchemical transformation. And, perhaps most valuable of all her gifts, Austen *shows* us what these men look like, how they act in the world, the choices they have made, and their future trajectories.

For two of her s/heroes, Austen adds an additional clergyman foil. In *Pride and Prejudice*, Elizabeth Bennet is highly pressured by her family, especially her mother, to marry cousin clergyman, Mr. Collins, to whom their estate (and somewhat temporary home) of Longbourn is entailed away from the family line of five daughters (due to the law of primogeniture). This man is a buffoon, incapable of matching her intellectually, socially, or spiritually. His narcissistic grasping of her further indicates his own incapacity to truly know and comprehend her true nature.

Similarly, Emma Woodhouse in *Emma* endures and refuses the attentions of another inflated clerical suitor, Mr. Elton, who misunderstands her match-making attempts on behalf of her companion, Miss Smith; he reveals his true character by describing Miss Smith as someone of no fortune and therefore of no value to him. Having the impotency of their character exposed by these refusals, both clerics scurry off to immediately propose to and marry other (economically wealthy) women. In *Emma* Mr. Elton returns to the small community of Highbury gloating at having secured a different heiress; he and the new Mrs. Elton snub and repeatedly attempt to humiliate Emma and Miss Smith. In *Pride and Prejudice*, Mr. Collins succeeds in marrying Lizzy's friend Charlotte Lucas. Charlotte defends her choice, giving voice to the disempowered "marriageable" woman in a speech that amplifies the economic plight of "unwed" daughters seen as burdens on their families with few resources or options; sadly, for her Mr. Collins is good enough.

These women attempt to attain sovereignty and create homes of their own via loveless marriages and, in the case of Charlotte Lucas, the codependent management of her domestic situation. But Austen shows that sovereignty must be earned. Lizzy eventually visits the Collinses, and, though Charlotte continues to express an improvement in her status, happiness, and freedom, she ultimately joins her husband in decidedly disempowered, deferential—even comically bumbling—behavior toward the "evil queen," Lady Catherine de Bourgh, onto whom they have each projected much personal power.[53] In this decidedly unsovereignly stance, Charlotte remains occupied territory. These clerical, secondary false-grooms for Austen's s/heroes appear as the warm-up act to craftier and more confusing suitors.

Speculative analyses of Austen's characters in relation to her personal life have proliferated; while her father was a clergyman, much focus lies on the mother problem.[54] Almost all of Austen's mothers are highly prob-

---

53. See chapter 4 on the dangers of evil, usurper, and narcissist queens.
54. See especially the historical biographical film *Becoming Jane*. The film's speculative treatment of Austen's individuation and movement toward sacred marriage is embedded within an analysis of gendered economics. As Austen's father was a clergyman, her varying

lematic or absent. Some are numb or collapsed and ineffectual—including Mrs. Dashwood in *Sense and Sensibility* and Lady Bertram in *Mansfield Park*—or conniving as Mrs. Norris is in the same novel, or absent altogether as *Emma's* deceased mother. *Pride and Prejudice* features Mrs. Bennet as a frenzied, frivolous mother who might easily be dismissed or forgiven her stress due to the economic hardships of entailment; she might, like Mrs. Dashwood, lose her home at any time. Here it is worth noting that *Pride and Prejudice* was Austen's first novel, most likely written in 1796 when it was provisionally titled *First Impressions*; Austen returned to the manuscript only after publishing *Sense and Sensibility*, uniquely pairing these two novels, echoing various themes. Perhaps Austen was gaining traction in order to do justice in her storytelling relating the dangers of unconscious motherhood.

Austen shows how collapsed and malicious mothers are dangerous to individuating daughters, especially as they step into their Bridal role. Their action—or inaction—is primarily vampiric, siphoning and living off their daughters' stolen life force. Mrs. Bennet has never individuated, and her unconscious projections—from her reminiscence of her youth to her discomfort with Lizzy's courage and agency—repeatedly thwart her daughters. This comes to a head in the misadventures of young Lydia—whom she identifies as so like her own young self—who is ultimately seduced by shadowy George Wickham (after he is rejected by a waking/individuating Lizzy).

The novel's other peripheral mother, the demanding Lady Catherine de Bourgh, siphons off her own daughter's (erotic) life force, drastically and actively damaging her psychic and social vitality and wellbeing. Her "sickly" daughter, Anne, can neither speak nor act. She is drained. Much psychic energy is consumed/lost when a woman's own mother is a true adversary.[55] This vampiric action is deadly and interrupts the potential for individuation.

Perhaps Marianne Dashwood is Austen's most surprisingly courageously embodied s/hero. Her personal regeneration in *Sense and Sensibility*—even more than that of Lizzy Bennet, Emma Woodhouse, or Fanny Price—is located within what may be Austen's most physical, life-threatening scene. Like Lizzy Bennett, she has a deep relationship with Nature and heads there when suffering. Marianne's story is mirrored by the cautionary tale of the lost Eliza Williamses, mother and daughter—neither of whom is able to survive,

---

treatment of the clergy, sometimes as less-than-capable partners, sometimes as a liberating occupation for individuating Bridegrooms, merits examination.

55. See chapter 4 for further discussion. See John Wiltshire, "Mrs. Bennet's Least Favorite Daughter," 179–87, for a study of the dangerous impact of Mrs. Bennet.

much less individuate—in a patriarchal world where women are routinely abandoned and lost, their stories silenced. A similar pattern appears in *Pride and Prejudice*, though it is less brutal since merely women's reputations (particularly those of Georgiana Darcy and Lydia Bennett) are at stake, rather than illegitimate pregnancy and death.

Deserted by unconscious, unindividuating, and duplicitous Willoughby, Marianne is catapulted into an abyss of grief. Could the profundity of her collapse pivot around her earlier grief and abandonments: the unspoken loss of her father, her beloved home Norland, and her previous privileged life? She has been abandoned by both father (through his failure to provide for his second family upon his death) and mother (who abdicates her power and agency to her eldest daughter, Elinor, who becomes the economic voice of reason of the remaining feminine family). Marianne becomes untethered, losing the very ground of home and hearth that was the estate entailed away from the Dashwood daughters. It is partially Elinor's movement that saves the family through her sense and industry as she steps into the caretaking void left by her grieving and childlike (unconscious, collapsed) mother, who is shocked at expenses and fatigued by plans.

After Willoughby's abandonment and betrayal, Marianne is suffering. That she turns toward this extensive mourning somehow enables her active grieving; and she undergoes a bottoming out, ultimately inviting healing. When it seems she is unable to "progress" in her own individuation process— an often invisible, immense, and gestational process—Austen has Marianne willfully lose herself in a terrible storm, bookending her initial accident in the rain when Willoughby seems to "rescue" her. This alchemical washing of a soul can be all-consuming; for Marianne her tears are amplified in the storm. Colonel Brandon searches for and finds her on the ground, soaked to the bone with a terrible life-threatening fever. Elinor sits vigil, providing genuine nurturing care, attending her sister's regenerating soul. Marianne emerges exhausted, raw, open—washed.

The purifying potential of alchemical whitening—the *albedo* stage—lies in feeling our grief, allowing the washing of our souls with powerful tears. For Jung, water can purify and reunite body and soul, in an internal *coniuntio* of Bride and Bridegroom.[56] Tears carry albedic power, carrying away the released pain formerly trapped on a cellular level. Ginette Paris describes this active grieving as essential in her book *Heartbreak: New Approaches*

---

56. See especially page 85 in Edward Edinger's inquiry into Jung's poetic alchemical theories in *The Mystery of the Coniunctio*.

to Healing—Recovering from Lost Love and Mourning (2011). "Those unconscious contents which invade the ego can be summarized in a brief formula:
it is everything you failed to mourn" (147). Until we turn toward and attend
these contents—events, feelings, murky waters—they can rule malevolently
from our (flooded) unconscious. Care must also be taken to ensure we have
a *vas bene clausum*, a well-sealed vessel with structural integrity. Cooking
with a cracked cauldron simply does not work; the soup leaks out.

Austen's unindividuating, stuck men accurately represent the wounded,
incomplete, and festering masculine. I call them villains, for *evil* occurs when
someone *remains* stubbornly unaware of their motivation and complexes,
doomed to blindly repeat their harmful actions. Angry and flailing, they
unconsciously inflict pain on those around them in the guise of charm and
victimhood. Such an incurious attitude is dangerous.

The profusion of Austen fan fiction and biographies created within the
past few decades testifies to and further amplifies the resonance the characters and stories have with readers. Remarkably, these archetypes stay
true to form time and time again. Archetypically wicked Wickham is never
reformed; Willoughby is always a rogue.[57] In short, they remain forever
untrustworthy and capable of great harm, both to individual women and
to entire communities. In *Death Comes to Pemberley*, Wickham has continued to gamble and have affairs outside his marriage to Lydia Bennet,
creating massive tangles of hurt and misunderstanding, resulting in murder.
In *Bridget Jones's Diary*, charming Daniel Cleaver as the Wickham/unindi-
viduating male archetype, blames/projects onto Mr. Darcy his own act of
sexual betrayal, retelling the story to Bridget as the Lizzy Bennet character.
This classic martyr stance dooms him in perpetuity.

Finally, when Austen introduces us to individuating men, she allows them
to have flaws and foibles, casting them as rich and complex personalities. The
task of Austen's women is to get to know them over time, to measure their
choices, language, and actions within the context of society. Austen sets the
bar high. Colonel Brandon, Mr. Darcy, Mr. Knightly, and Captain Wentworth
are particularly well initiated into their individuation process. *Persuasion*
begins with the return of Captain Wentworth, who was refused by his

---

57. See especially: Amanda Grange, *Mr. Darcy's Diary: A Novel* (2007); P. D. James, *Death
Comes to Pemberley* (2011) and film (PBS, 2013); Shannon Hale, *Austenland: A Novel* (2007)
and film (Sony Pictures, 2013), Helen Fielding's two books and film trilogy *Bridget Jones's
Diary* (1996, Universal film 2001) *Bridget Jones: The Edge of Reason* (1999, film 2004) and
Bridget Jones's Baby (film 2016), and the made-for-TV series *Lost in Austen* (Image, 2009),
and the films *Bride and Prejudice* (Touchstone, 2004) and *Becoming Jane* (Scion, 2006).

beloved, Anne Elliot, eight years ago when her family believed that his lack of fortune reflected his value as a suitor. At the time a young Anne decided not to marry against her family's wishes. Austen's creation of his name reflects both the void his absence creates and Anne's inability to find another man of his caliber; his actual *worth* was not valued, so he *went* away. His return as a naval officer who has made his fortune offers them both renewed opportunities.

Repeatedly, Austen offers evidence of and stresses the importance of healthy containment possible within sacred partnership. As Bower relates, "Darcy and Elizabeth both grow as individuals as a result of knowing each other" (214). Each challenges the other; surely Darcy's first clumsy and inflated proposal and Lizzy's eloquent rebuttal dissecting his conceit is one of literature's great examples of this potential within (eventual, mature) partnering. Additionally, Austen's women regenerate as they move from stuck and festering options and homes toward curiosity and the vitality of true partnership. In response to her initial confusion as to Darcy's true character over time, Lizzy cultivates an open and curious stance—an invaluable regenerative tool for the wandering Aletis and s/hero.[58]

Like Bower, Austen is especially helpful in terms of identifying what her heroines must address, discern, and overcome on their respective journeys toward regeneration. The development of bridal agency within the pairings of these six novels, with the unfolding of eight individuating partnerships, reveals patterns of potentiality when the archetypal Bride commits to a partner worthy of her, as well as the transformative, regenerating nature of her own individuation; this is regenerative consciousness.

EAT, PRAY, LOVE: A BRIDAL ~~SHOWER~~ REGENERATION PLAN

Prenuptial events are designed to prepare the Bride for married life, provide tools for her journey, and honor her place within community and family. In the twenty-first century, bachelorette parties have become bloated, showy, and expensive destination journeys, where the explicit goal of sisterhood is overtaken by the shadow realms of excessive consumptive partying, economic competition, and inflation. Current bridal shower custom now demands gifts equivalent to wedding presents, burdening bridesmaids and leaving the

---

58. See chapter 6 on the regenerative function and centrality of an open and curious stance.

Bride malnourished, unprepared, and psychically hungover. When the Bride is unrehearsed/unprepared, or otherwise lost and repudiated, she might take a more meandering, wandering (Aletis) path toward her sacred marriage. Cancel the shower; we need a different sort of initiatory rite.

Along with literary fiction, Bower reveals how women's biographies tangentially illuminate the path of the Aletis (54). Tracking the threads of women's experiences as adept wanderers, Bower examines various memoirs and autobiographies, including the writings of Nancy Mitford, Jill Ker Conway, Maya Angelou, Katherine Hepburn, Margaret Mead, and Elizabeth Gilbert.

Gilbert's memoir and feminist travelogue *Eat, Pray, Love* has created a popular (again: of the people) cultural movement as evidenced by remaining on *The New York Times* bestseller list for 187 weeks, with over twelve million copies in print, and a high-grossing, internationally distributed Hollywood film production (elizabethgilbert.com). Perhaps the story's success could be attributed to its being a retelling of the ancient myth of Ariadne, still vital and relevant to postmodernity. This resonance with individuating woman reveals deep, archetypal patterns inherent within the bridal lineage of Magdalene, whose roots lie within the ancient mythology of Ariadne.

The current resurgence of Ariadne's mythological storylines—threads, if you will—in (very) popular culture might reflect the stamina and popularity of her myth and indicate revelations from the collective unconscious. Ariadne has been sighted recently in bestselling books *The Titan's Curse* by Rick Riordan and *The Book of Love* by Kathleen McGowan, the Hollywood blockbuster film *Inception*, and most recently in *Ariadne: A Novel* by Jennifer Saint. Classical sources of Ariadnean mythology include Homer's *Odyssey*, Hesiod's *Theogony*, Diodorus Siculus's *Library of History*, Plutarch's *Life of Theseus*, and Quintus Smyrnaeus's *Fall of Troy 4*. Both Karl Kerényi and Robert Graves relate multitudes of summaries as well as variations on themes found in these early tellings.[59]

At the core of the myth, Ariadne is a princess of Crete, daughter of Queen Pasiphaë and King Minos. Her adolescent situation on Crete pivots around her father having secretly sold her in a prearranged marriage to a stranger—the powerful and (initially) shadowy god, Dionysus. She is uninterested in this agreement, repelled by Dionysus's drunken reputation, insisting—in true Austen fashion—that marriage must be rooted in love. Instead, she becomes infatuated with a different stranger.

---

59. See Karl Kerényi, *Gods of the Greeks* (1951), *Heroes of the Greeks* (1974), and *Dionysus: Archetypal Image of Indestructible Life* (1976), as well as Graves's *The Greek Myths* (2012).

Immediately charmed when Theseus arrives on Crete, leading the Athenian tribute destined for sacrifice in the labyrinth, Ariadne (having barely, but fatally, seen him) supposedly falls in love (or is it simply infatuation?). Captivated by his beauty and princely ways, she devises a plan to help him slay her disowned half-brother, the terrible and devouring Minotaur imprisoned at the center of the labyrinth (perhaps her own imprisoned masculinity?). She supplies a sword with which to slay the beast, and thread—a remarkable offering crafted from her own hair—which they tie in a bridal knot at the entrance of the labyrinth; this ingenious locating device allows Theseus to know where he is at all times, enabling him to find his way in and out of the labyrinth.

Theseus is successful in slaying the Minotaur and with Ariadne frees the other Athenians. Together they flee the island on his ship. On their way toward matrimonial bliss in Athens, they stop at a neighboring island, either Naxos or Dia depending on the version. While Ariadne is sleeping, Theseus abandons her. Various reasons are given for Theseus' actions, from intimidation by either Dionysus or Artemis on his behalf, to his own lack of character. Ariadne awakens alone and marooned. She grieves.

After some time, a lovestruck Dionysus appears, inviting her to marry him. He is successful in persuading her to take a chance on partnership with him. Some suggest he matures because of her. He gifts her with a crown of stars and then petitions Zeus to elevate her status to that of a goddess, making her immortal, an equal partner.

In *Pagan Grace: Dionysos, Hermes, and Goddess Memory in Daily Life*, Ginette Paris points out that it is Ariadne who chooses Theseus, making her "not at all a passive woman, but quite a fascinating heroine" (42). The initiation and execution of a brilliant plan to face both labyrinth and Minotaur—with or without Daedalus, as designer, depending on the account—identifies Ariadne as a daring and creative genius. No victim, she chooses her fate consciously and with intention (43). Staying up all night weaving a golden thread from her very own hair, she shares insider secrets with the newly arrived hero, providing him with a shortcut to his own heroic task. Thus begins her codependent bargain. Theseus becomes a hero overnight, a terrible burden for him, because all the brilliance is hers—the creativity, skill, and problem solving, the extraordinary effort—ultimately setting him up to fail her. Ariadne projects her own qualities and power onto him; he never has to develop the skills himself. Psychologically, she overfunctions, forcing him into an underfunctioning role. Ariadne gave everything to Theseus so he would rescue her, saving him so he would love her.

Marion Woodman explains that Theseus as "the [wounded] masculine side often lacks the strength to penetrate; terror of losing oneself in another overwhelms the initial thrust that could lead to deeper intercourse" (Woodman 168). Theseus, unable to penetrate, remains an immature *puer*, at risk of remaining an eternal boy. It is this aspect of a man that abandons Ariadne on Naxos. While Theseuses might be well intentioned, charming, and enthusiastic, they are, nonetheless, emotional adolescents. By describing a man as carrying Theseus's characteristics, I mean he is not yet emotionally mature. He chooses to abandon women rather than face his own festering fear of abandonment or engulfment resulting from earlier trauma (which drives him unconsciously) and blames his relationships or his Ariadne(s) for his own projected failings. He remains, at least for now, sadly unaware of his own need to individuate. The dropped golden thread, once a promise of partnership, becomes a knotted mess.

This raises the question: considering all her skills, energy, and creativity, why couldn't Ariadne get *herself* off the island of Crete and away from her abusive father and dysfunctional family system? Ariadne was the power source of intelligence behind Theseus, rescuing the Athenian contingent from the Minotaur in the labyrinth, but she cannot rescue herself. Perhaps it is the erotic jolt of Theseus's arrival that stimulates her s/heroic capacities and sets her on her wandering journey. Perhaps the promise of potential partnership provides necessary alchemical containment.

The Ariadnean/Magdalenian qualities of Gilbert's wandering path reveal key elements of bridal movement toward regenerative agency. Gilbert's memoir reveals how her globetrotting s/hero's journey addresses her struggle to overcome anima dependence—a type of performance through which a woman identifies with a (false, constructed) sense of identity through men.[60] Early in *Eat, Pray, Love*, Gilbert describes her own immature Ariadnean patterns as they appear within her relationships:

> I have boundary issues with men. Or maybe that's not fair to say. To have issues with boundaries, one must *have* boundaries in the first place, right? But I disappear into the person I love. I am the permeable membrane. If I love you, you can have everything. You can have my time, my devotion, my ass, my money, my family, my dog, my dog's money, my dog's time—*everything*. If I love you, I will carry for you all your pain, I will assume your own insecurity, I will project upon

---

60. See especially Woodman's analysis of the father's daughter under patriarchy in *The Ravaged Bridegroom*.

you all sorts of good qualities that you have never actually cultivated in yourself and I will buy Christmas presents for your entire family . . . I will give you all this and more, until I get so exhausted and depleted that the only way I can recover my energy is by becoming infatuated with someone else. (65)

This messy conflation of love, empathy, and codependency—and the resultant collapsed, confusing fog and psychic depletion—can be experienced by Ariadnean women. Her needs, aches, and desires pose as love and gifts; this is erotic corruption. Psychologically we might define this as a form of altruistic narcissism. Or, as Taylor Swift asks, "Did you hear my covert narcissism I disguise as altruism?" ("Anti-Hero," 2022). Both the song and music video play ironically (à la Austen) with the tension between the cost of othering shadow projection and self-perception, an effective application of Jung's transcendent function; holding the tension of these (supposed opposites), an elegant third reality appears through the grace of her creative act. Creativity—inherently courageous—is regenerative and rewarded with healing movement.

Gilbert's approach to her lovers is classic Ariadne. Chronically optimistic, she mistakes their *potential* for their character. While she may appear to have an ability to see the beauty inherent in another's soul, having excessive empathy and patience for them can be a form of distracting, dazzled stargazing in (unconscious) service to her own (again, self-perpetuating) wound; this keeps her focused on the Other, not yet able to do her own deep work.

Gilbert's extreme sadness and depression was the catalyst that ended her marriage; she found herself in an unequal partnership with a husband who refused, or was unable, to self-nurture and mature into his Dionysian self (with her and within their marriage). To overlay Austen's model with Ariadne's myth: Theseus is stuck and Dionysus is individuating, moving toward his god-king, Bridegroom self. As such, a Dionysian man is actively growing, becoming his god-self with emotional intelligence and full access to his soul. He may even be a former Theseus; Theseus and Dionysus are potentially and frequently two aspects of any man willing to go through the journey of regenerating individuation. Otherwise, he is doomed to remain a wicked Wickham, a worthless Willoughby.

As often happens, Gilbert encounters two Theseuses simultaneously: her ex-husband and her new lover David, both of whom *portray themselves as Dionysian*—an interesting plot twist performed by many Theseuses wanting desperately to be their future individuating selves but who have yet to develop sufficiently. Gilbert writes:

All the complications and traumas of those ugly divorce years were multiplied by the drama of David—the guy I fell in love with as I was taking leave of my marriage. Did I say that I "fell in love" with David? What I meant to say is that I dove out of my marriage and into David's arms exactly the same way a cartoon circus performer dives off a high platform and into a small cup of water, vanishing completely. I clung to David for escape from marriage as if he were the last helicopter pulling out of Saigon. I inflicted upon him my every hope for my salvation and happiness. And, yes, I did love him. But if I could think of a stronger word than "desperately" to describe how I loved David, I would use that word here. (18)

Gilbert finds new infatuation the (temporary, ineffectual) solution to keeping her pain at bay and begins dating the young and spiritually earthy David, with whom she quickly moves in. Multiple Theseuses tend to enter a woman's life sequentially until the pattern is revealed. In *Anima: An Anatomy of a Personified Notion*, James Hillman defines how an anima woman—an individuating woman who as yet derives her primary sense of self through her relationship with men and their anima/inner feminine projections upon her—makes herself empty and therefore available to fill herself up with whatever her lover might want or need her to be, consciously or unconsciously, so that *he* is comfortable (in his own unconsciousness) (15). She is willing to do this in order to maintain connection, to get love because she has a breach in her containment. Perhaps early, emotionally shattering abandonment has left her leaking. Again, this is an unconscious codependent bargain.

In *The Goddess: Mythological Images of the Feminine*, Christine Downing proposes that "only after a Theseus has left and after an Ariadne has been left, only after both of them have really integrated that separation, is there the possibility of either having his or her own connection to soul" (56). Downing firmly locates the individuation process and maturation through regeneration at the heart of this myth, with Ariadne transforming from anima figure to individuated woman, symbolized as an immortal goddess. "Anima dependence must be overcome. Theseus cannot stay with Ariadne; he has to be able to leave her behind. It is just as important for Ariadne that she be left behind, so that she might leave behind her dependence on playing the role of anima" (56). It is by committing to exploring this dependence—where it came from, what its gifts might be, and how to leave it behind her—that sets Elizabeth Gilbert on her wanderer's road toward individuation.

With the pressure of the events of September 2001—Gilbert lived in New York City at the time—and the increasing stress of her divorce, Liz Gilbert cracked. She could no longer ignore her grief. David, with whom she is living at the time, responds in quintessential Theseus fashion:

> This is when he started to retreat, and that's when I saw the other side of my passionate romantic hero—the David who was solitary as a castaway, cool to the touch, in need of more personal space than a herd of American bison. David's sudden emotional back-stepping probably would've been a catastrophe for me even under the best of circumstances . . . but this was my very worst of circumstances. I was despondent and dependent, needing more care than an armful of premature infant triplets. His withdrawal only made me more needy, and my neediness only advanced his withdrawals, until soon he was retreating under fire of my weeping pleas of, "Where are you going? What happened to us?" (20)

Rejecting Gilbert after their explosive and brief passion, David pulls away emotionally and physically. This is the core of their immature dynamic. This is Theseus sailing away, abandoning Ariadne on her island. Gilbert's description of the pairing of (his) evasive and (her) clingy behavior and how it intensifies in reaction to each other is symptomatic of the Ariadne/Theseus dynamic, the dance between the twinned fears of abandonment and engulfment. Both are triggered, caught in reaction to each other's pain; neither is yet capable of mature and reflexive responses. Ariadne is beginning to realize she was already abandoned, living alone within a failing relationship. It is not until she receives the homeopathic poison of Theseus's abandonment that she can begin to rescue herself; it becomes a vital catalytic *pharmakon*.[61] If the healing is in the poison, sickness is necessary for the remedy. Abandonment could be fatal, but it evolved into an initiatory

---

61. While Gilbert does not pursue this revelatory theme in *Eat, Pray, Love*, for many women such an experience enables them to reconnect with earlier (frozen and denied) abandonment experiences, often within their family of origin. Such original woundings can be the source of the Ariadnean archetypal pattern. In Ariadne's myth this could include the emotional absence of one or both parents and the betrayal of her patriarchal old king/father. Possibly it is in desperation to free herself from such an island of familial abandonment and captivity that she sees potential freedom and (her own disowned) agency embodied in a handsome stranger. The act of leaving an intolerable situation becomes erotically charged. See Bower for further discussion on the wanderer, unconscious marriage, and depathologizing leave-taking.

rite that saved her, preparing her for regeneration and, later, sacred marriage with a mature mate in Dionysus.

Deciding to spend a year exploring three foreign countries, Gilbert creates space for psychic healing. (Imagine if Ariadne's original myth had included a year full of this type of detail—a roadmap for regeneration.) The title of Gilbert's memoir distills her plan into three actions. She begins in Italy, seeking to regain her appetite for life by eating incredible amounts of pasta, drinking wine—Dionysian acts of embodied, erotic pleasure—meeting new friends/allies, and resting. She is hungry and learning about and tending her own desires, finally. Free from old numbing agents, Gilbert is committed to feeling her feelings and grieving, no matter what. She cries and sobs. When the anima woman/Ariadne releases all that emotion she was carrying for her Theseus, her feminine wasteland begins to drain. What was once a saturated bog regains fertility.

Setting off next for India for four months of embodied, somatic practices—meditation, chanting, and yoga—Gilbert tends her need to surrender, sit, and be present. Resistance is futile as the isolated ashram echoes the self-containment of Naxos itself. By turning toward stillness with attention, such conscious containment can function as an antidote to abandonment/marooning. Here she sits and has revelations, finding God (her word) in herself. Realization dawns as this Ariadne gains perspective on her former ways:

> I have a history of making decisions very quickly about men. I have always fallen in love fast and without measuring risks. I have a tendency not only to see the best in everyone, but to assume that everyone is emotionally capable of *reaching* his highest potential. I have fallen in love more times than I care to count with the highest potential of a man, rather than with the man himself, and then I have hung on to the relationship for a long time (sometimes far too long) waiting for the man to ascend to his own greatness. Many times in romance I have been a victim of my own optimism. (285)

Such realization of previously unconscious material is for Bower a key step on the wanderer's path toward individuation. "Recognizing one's own unconscious behavior, naiveté, and complicity is the key to finding one's power" (130). While it seems an obvious component of individuation, the act of *becoming* self-aware is very often missing and/or grossly underdeveloped.

Grieving can be a solitary process, and Ariadne, isolated on an island, must learn to tend her own wounds. We grieve that which we have not yet accepted;

seemingly paradoxically, saturation and steeping in our grief can bring acceptance. By fully mourning what was lost, Ariadne can finally recognize that
what is done is done; it is over. She can no longer search outside herself for
the s/hero within; she can no longer deny that Theseus was capable only of an
emotional one-night stand. On Naxos she must take care of her-Self. No one
else is there. "She is not just the young maiden holding the spool of thread at
the entrance to the labyrinth, but . . . she occupies its center. To attend to this
Ariadne was to attend to my own soul, not to serve as anima for another"
(Downing 28). If codependency is prioritizing another over Self—in that crippling, self-perpetuating altruistic narcissistic pattern—this return to center is
crucial. The process of individuation requires us to relocate our-Selves to the
center of our own lives. By taking her time, being present to her feelings, and
embodying her grief, Ariadne transforms. Her individuation unfolds as she
practices radical Self-care, embracing her own presence *for herself.*

Woodman offers that Ariadne recognizes and loves "the powerful masculine figure who . . . lives outside the limits of the establishment in order to
protect himself from the bludgeoning of patriarchal power" (167). On Bali,
Elizabeth Gilbert meets such a Dionysian figure in the form of Felipe, a fifty-
two-year-old divorced Brazilian expatriate (a counterpoint to her thirty-five
years). She realizes who he is, "an actual grown man. The adult male of the
species—a bit of a novelty in my experience" (275). What a devastating yet
necessary commentary.

Woodman asks: "How then do we make our Bride-to-be strong enough
to receive the groom? "(169). Ariadne's original abandonment wound can
be expressed as a leaky container; she cannot hold her power, her energy.
"Ari's [Ariadne's] receptive feminine energy is not strong enough or flexible enough to open herself to the power of masculine otherness" (168).
Here, Woodman describes the necessary chronological investment in taking the time to heal a woman's container. What makes Dionysus so special
for Woodman is his potential for love and full penetration. "Unless there is
sufficient love and integrity between the container and the penetrator, fear
will hold the container rigid and render the phallos impotent. The greater
the integrity, the stronger the container, the more powerful the penetration"
(Woodman 169). Dionysian embodiment of mature masculinity is essential
for a healthy partnership/marriage, a radically cocreative act based on two
individuals coming together in their fullness.

Finally, Gilbert, like Ariadne, has been tempered through her grieving
process and has transformed her life into a strong container capable of receiving full Dionysian love and penetration. After such tremendous commitment

to personal growth, only a mature Dionysian male is worthy of Ariadnean love, each having learned how to approach each other in fullness, individuating.[62] This is the fullness described consistently throughout the ancient mythological lineage of sacred marriage and alchemical partnership between Ariadne/Dionysus, Inanna/Dumuzi, Isis/Osiris, and Magdalene/Jesus. Ariadne's tale might itself be the origin myth, the oldest surviving evidence of what spread throughout Mediterranean cultures.

The film version of *Eat, Pray, Love* ends with a very relevant voiceover of Gilbert's character speaking directly on the power of questing, a codicil that does not appear in the original book:

In the end, I've come to believe in something I call the physics of the quest, a force in nature governed by laws as real as the laws of gravity. The rule of quest physics goes something like this. If you are brave enough to leave behind everything familiar and comforting—which can be anything from your house to bitter old resentments—and set out on a truth-seeking journey, either externally or internally, and if you are truly willing to regard everything that happens to you on that journey as a clue, and if you accept everyone you meet along the way as a teacher, and if you are prepared, most of all, to face and forgive some very difficult realities about yourself, then the truth will not be withheld from you. I can't help but believe it, given my experience. (Murphy)

Gilbert echoes both Campbell and Bower here in her description of the quest as an individuating journey punctuated by encounters with guides, tests, and magical helpers. Likewise, she conjures Jung's work on synchronistic encounters, which arrive with potent timing and encoded messages. She also addresses the importance of cultivating "beginner's mind," an open and curious stance where we are more likely to accept what comes to us and respond from our center, our core. These markers and attitudes on the road to individuation support the wanderer and augment synchronistic opportunities, crucial components for regeneration.

---

62. See Gilbert's sequel *Committed* (2010) where she charts her journey toward sacred partnership. Gilbert's later public separation (2017) and subsequent relationships imply further developments on her path while (Dionysian) re/membering reflects that "the only way I can recover my energy is by becoming infatuated with someone else" (65). I anticipate ongoing insights via Gilbert's literature.

Perhaps a power of Gilbert's manuscript, also evident in the film, is the way in which her personal myth splays vulnerably wide open. Gilbert reassures us: "I was not rescued by a prince; I was the administrator of my own rescue" (329). Ariadne does not need rescuing; she needs her soul back. *Eat, Pray, Love* maps how it can be done. The popular resonance of this memoir—a roadmap of timeless mythological truths in the lineage of Sister-Brides—has created a new wave and culture of wandering Ariadnes because the method works. That Gilbert repeatedly takes the time to reflect and report back in a defining act of ritual (w)riting is central to her popularity; she, like a war correspondent, is (w)riting from the front. This fourth function of her Ariadnean roadmap suggests a retitling of her memoir as: *Eat, Pray, Love, (W)rite.*

Having barely vaulted out of the first century of psychoanalysis, popular journal writing, twelve-step groups, and self-help psychology, it benefits us to note how these reading/(w)riting tools yield radically effective, and sometimes excruciating, acts of liberation. As a representative of Ariadne's Sister-Bride lineage, Magdalene is undergoing her own re(w)rite of passage. Both Austen and Gilbert support Bridal agency via psychic cartography, the art of discernment, and the ever-renewing ritual of reading/(w)rite—crucial support for the individuating, wandering, regenerating Bride practicing regenerative consciousness.

CHAPTER 4

EXILED AND UNDERGROUND

THE LOST BRIDE IN EUROPEAN FAIRY TALES

Hiding is creative, necessary and beautifully subversive of outside
interference and control.
Hiding leaves life to itself, to become more of itself.
Hiding is the radical independence necessary for our emergence into the
light of a proper human future.

—DAVID WHYTE, "HIDING," IN *CONSOLATIONS:*
THE SOLACE, NOURISHMENT AND UNDERLYING MEANING OF EVERYDAY WORDS

INTRODUCTION: HIDE AND GO SEEK

Hiding can be a very effective survival technique. Conscious hiding—as
the Abenaki/Wabanaki nation did to survive colonial genocide—or even
unconscious fleeing compelled by dissociative acts can save our lives.[63]
Going and being underground can generate unexpected benefits, including
tremendous growth. Hiding can also have unforeseen costs to our personal
and collective psyches. What might be the lost—our visibility, access to
our/Selves, power, voices, reflections in the world writ large, traditional
forms of support? How might we best consider this while cultivating trust
and holding the long view through such darkness? How do we know

---

63. See *The Survivance of the Western Abenaki in Vermont—Middlebury College and the
Western Abenaki,* https://sites.middlebury.edu/abenaki/the-survivance-of-vermonts
-western-abenaki/. Accessed 6 Mar. 2025.

when it is safe to return?[64] What structures and rituals might support the re/membering and re/ensouling of what seemed lost, what's been masked, shrouded, and veiled?[65]

In *The Woman with the Alabaster Jar*, Margaret Starbird unpacks the ways the Magdalenian heresy survived in Europe via various underground living cultural streams, providing effective regenerative models. Identifying Black Madonna mythology, the troubadours, heretical artists, and tarot—which she describes as an encoded catechism of Magdalenian teachings—she constructs a complex web of curious evidence and interdisciplinary scholarship.[66] Perhaps Starbird's most significant contribution comes through her analysis of folklore identifying a distinctive, repetitive pattern exemplified in four popular European fairy tales commonly known as "Cinderella," "Sleeping Beauty," "Snow White," and "Rapunzel" as retellings of a quest completed by the wounded and healing/maturing masculine as the bachelor prince seeking his true partner, the wounded and lost/imprisoned Bride. "'Cinderella' embodies the belief that when the Bride is found and restored to the bachelor prince, the realm will be healed" (150). Starbird correlates mythemes and symbolism between these stories and Magdalenian mythology, including Magdalene's royal identity.[67] In "Rapunzel," these symbols include her famously extravagant hair and imprisoning tower.[68] Sleeping Beauty, also known as Briar Rose, was "pricked by a poisoned spindle and sent to sleep for a hundred (some say a thousand) years," suggesting the heresy continues in the form of a necessary—potentially even regenerative—retreat, where the feminine divine goes underground until it is safe and/or the right time to return (150).[69]

---

64. See "Something About Phryne" in chapter 5 on the importance of right timing.

65. See chapter 6 on effective regenerative practices and tools, including indigenous truth and reconciliation practices.

66. For a further elaboration on the tarot as Magdalenian heresy, see Starbird's *Tarot Trumps and the Holy Grail* (2000).

67. Starbird discusses Jesus's royal lineage as the Davidic messiah-king (50–64), while identifying Magdalene as a Benjamite princess, elevating their relationship as a union between two ancient houses of Israel. Novelists Dan Brown (citing *Holy Blood, Holy Grail*) and Kathleen McGowan also identify Magdalene specifically as a Benjamite princess, further relating her with the Merovingian bloodline claim/legend. For counterclaims, see Bart Ehrman's *Truth and Fiction in "The Da Vinci Code"* (2004) and Jacobovici and Wilson in *The Lost Gospel* (2014, with the later duo identifying Magdalene as Phoenician.

68. Significantly, Starbird argues that Saint Barbara, whose symbols include remarkable hair and the tower, is a foil for Magdalene (149–50).

69. Along with these four fairy tales, the Robin Hood/Maid Marian pairing—as a geographically British tale with French roots centered around a shepherd and shepherdess—may also be an underground retelling of the Jesus and Magdalene partnership, including radical gender roles, socioeconomic justice, and trickster traits.

Identifying Cinderella as lost, scorned, and exiled, Starbird links her with the Black Madonna, suggesting that the "dark" or "sooty-faced" girl is also the "black" Bride in the Song of Solomon, both enduring separation from their lovers (149–50). Starbird's interpretation suggests that the dismissal of these tales as merely descriptive accounts of disempowered damsels awaiting external, male rescuers is missing the (feminist) boat. She widens the focus to include the action of the searching, wounded—and here I would add immature/healing/individuating—masculine as critical to understanding the value of the pairing.

Perhaps the extreme popularity of these fairy tales and their continual retelling/renewal through literature, the fine and lively arts, and contemporary film repeatedly captures our imagination because they embody regenerative potentialities coming to consciousness, offering layered clues and teachings. From a depth psychological perspective, they suggest a psychic living tradition where the maturation of internal princess and prince results in a sacred marriage, which also plays out culturally through the ritual reenactment of the returning lost Bride and subsequent reunion with the beloved.

Fairy tales are considered written versions of orally shared folklore stories passed down within, and across, cultures as shared tradition. Fairy tales differ by having known authors and storytellers who may originally have been collectors of regional folk tales but who may have altered them for a variety of reasons. Often the most famous chroniclers have overshadowed a rich and varied legacy of what was traditionally more localized lore.

The most well-known accounts of these four tales include Charles Perrault's version of "Cinderella" (*Histoires ou contes du temps passé*, 1697), though she was also popularized by the Brothers Grimm, who also collected and published adaptations of "Snow White" and "Rapunzel." "Sleeping Beauty" was retold by both, with the Grimms' version told as "Briar Rose" (*Fünfzig Kinder-und Hausmärchen*, first in 1812 and finally in 1857). The Grimms also recorded a related story, "The Glass Coffin," which mirrors significant elements of "Snow White."[70]

Analyses of these tales from a range of angles, disciplines, and scholarly insight yield startling insights. Three such guides include literary

---

70. Contemporary to these writers is the highly original work of Marie-Catherine le Jumel de Barneville, Comtesse d'Aulnoy, whose fairy tales reveal much information about her era and the significance of fairy tales generally. A new collection, *The Island of Happiness: Tales of Madame d'Aulnoy* (2021), translated and introduced by literary and cultural critic Jack Zipes, makes her work broadly accessible for the first time.

critic and cultural historian Marina Warner, folklorist Maria Tatar, and Jung's primary interpreter, Marie-Louise von Franz. Warner has much rich material to add to our understanding of the function of fairy tales, including how they perhaps arose and multiplied as stories told by the general population, potentially serving as a type of Esperanto or global shorthand of our collective imagination (see especially *Once Upon a Time: A Short History of Fairy Tale*, 2014, and *Fairy Tale: A Very Short Introduction*, 2018). Similarly, much can be gleaned from Tatar's extensive study, *The Fairest of Them All: Snow White and 21 Tales of Mothers and Daughters* (2020), which shows the extent to which these particular stories pervade our collective cultures. Trained in literature, Tatar primarily analyses folklore and myth for cultural perspectives.

Amongst early Jungian scholarship, von Franz offers intertextual analysis of fairy tales and folklore, particularly in relation to alchemy and sacred marriage. Her findings in *The Interpretation of Fairy Tales* (1996) and *Shadow and Evil in Fairy Tales* (1995) are invaluable in unpacking theories relating European fairy tales with Magdalenian heresy and the depth psychological insights available within such a connection. These deeper psychological layers are begging our investigation. Von Franz's significant legacy continues to reverberate via contemporary feminist post-Jungian theories and practices, offering unique tools for unraveling the significance of these four folktales.

ONCE UPON A TIME, RIGHT NOW, AND EVERY TIME

The impact of cinematic representations of fairy tales is enormous; it is particularly necessary to address Disney's legacy and influence over these dynamic aspects of the tales in any analysis of contemporary film and popular culture. Disney's first animated feature-length film was *Snow White* (1937), followed later by *Cinderella* (1950), and *Sleeping Beauty* (1957).[71] Their often infantilized and commercialized portrayal of "princesses" diminishes these tales' inherent psychic and communal liberating power. In both its animation

---

71. Evolving gender, racial, and ethnic representation of and for women and girls in Disney can be tracked via two versions of *The Little Mermaid* (1989, 2023), two versions of *Beauty and the Beast* (1991, 2017, coproduced with Mandeville), *Pocahontas* (1995), *The Princess and the Frog* (2009), *Mulan* (1998, 2020), *Brave* (2012, coproduced by Pixar), *Frozen* (2013, 2019), and *Moana* (2016, 2024). While racial and ethnic representation expands, perhaps only *Brave* and *Moana* significantly broaden depictions of female agency and leadership, cultural roles, and opportunities for sovereignty.

and live-action features, Disney often falls into a fetishizing trap, where the princess/Bride is objectified, sanitized, and homogenized rather than dialogued with and listened to. Animation as an artform may add to this infantilization, as it has been successfully used in the production of films designed specifically for children's entertainment. Disney's earliest films also unconsciously reproduced and reinforced cultural hegemony and gender stereotypes from their eras of origin.

Tatar extensively studies the intention and impact of Walt Disney's overhaul and rebranding of Snow White in both *The Classic Fairy Tales* and *The Fairest of Them All: Snow White and 21 Tales of Mothers and Daughters*. In the former she writes:

> When asked why he did not stay closer to the Grimms' script, Walt Disney responded, "It's just that people now don't want fairy stories the way they were written. They were too rough. In the end, they'll probably remember the story the way we film it anyway." There is indeed much "rough" stuff in earlier cultural inflections of the tale, though one could argue that Disney, rather than lightening up the story, preserved much of the blood and gore. (84)

Stories are alive. Tatar amplifies how Walt Disney intentionally deviated from the Brothers Grimm's version (itself codified, solidified in their final 1857 publication) to suit his own purposes, yet might have unconsciously reproduced quite a bit of shadowy content. Similarly, the Grimms most likely deviated within many, if not most, retellings of the tales they collected, for various reasons over time.

We retell stories in new contexts to amplify current conditions and emerging patterns. Potent stories spun around vital truths offer both structure and fluidity; they have a way of maintaining their potentialities even through attempted sanitizing. Recent cinematic reimaginings of these tales, including *Ever After* (reimagining "Cinderella," Twentieth Century Fox Films, 1998), *Ella Enchanted* (reimagining "Cinderella," Miramax, 2004)—based loosely on the Newbery Award–winning novel by Gail Carson Levine—and *Tangled* (reimagining "Rapunzel," Disney, 2010), offer more empowered variations on the interconnected themes of gender, power, and agency in relation to sacred marriage than either the seventeenth-through-nineteenth-century or Disney versions of the fairy tales' depiction. Other films, including Disney's newest *Cinderella* (2014), rehash outmoded Disney values from the last midcentury; directed by the Christian and seemingly cryptically conservative Kenneth Branagh, this film reinforces patriarchal gender roles while missing the mark of what a Magdalenian Bride is capable of.[72]

Between 2011 and 2012 three major film or television productions featuring Snow White appeared: *Mirror, Mirror*, the popular and syndicated television series *Once Upon a Time*, and *Snow White and the Huntsman* with its prequel/sequel, *The Huntsman: Winter's War*, released in 2016. What is happening in the collective un/conscious that we are calling out to Snow White so loudly?

All three productions, especially the latter two, amplify Snow White's forest warrior aspect. Portrayed as a fierce, courageous, and vital Bride, she accepts her primary need to face and overcome the evil queen (her stepmother) in order to heal what the realm has become under a usurper's rule: a wasteland. Relatively independent, she is aided variably by dwarves, the huntsman, and, less frequently, the prince.

Once Upon a Time represents a recent trend in elaborate, composite film and television adaptations that overlap and interrelate fairy tales within a collective fictional geographical territory, in this case centered around the Enchanted Forest, where numerous European and other fairy tales are interwoven.[73] Life in the Enchanted Forest pivots around magic, both light and dark, principally as extensions of power and agency. Our own world is juxtaposed as one oddly devoid of magic, though it is later revealed that the series' hometown of Storybrooke, Maine, was artificially constructed by the evil queen/Regina. As the series progresses, this imaginary realm expands to include other interconnecting literary fiction territory, including Wonderland, Neverland, Camelot, and Oz.[74] The interconnectedness of the

---

72. Curiously, Branagh's larger-than-life cinematic trajectory seemed destined to chronic inflation through both his autobiographical *Belfast* (2022) and his dual roles as both director and detective, a hypermustachioed shade of Agatha Christie's narcissistic Hercule Poirot. However, in the 2023 film *A Haunting in Venice*, we find a much-evolved, vulnerable portrayal of the sleuth—a valuable embodied example of regenerating masculine.

73. Other examples include *Into the Woods* (2015), *The Librarians* (2014–16), and the *Shrek* (2001–2010) series. Amalgamated approaches to fairy tales sometimes succeed in creating enlivening, bricolaged tales; at other times the results can be incoherently muddy when the story arc is lost or archetypes are pulled out of alignment.

74. This becomes problematic in season 4 when the magical, reflexive book *Once Upon a Time*, the core storytelling device in Storybrooke, suddenly has an author. It is revealed that the author is a role that is passed on via a magical pen and that s/he is charged with only recording what happens (as "history") and creating action. The previous author, Isaac, had become corrupt, manipulating the stories for personal gain. Teenage Henry, Snow White's grandson, becomes the new author, because he, more than any other, *believes*. In season 5 Henry himself repeatedly uses the pen to effect change. This denial/repression of the creative (and erotic) act interrupts regeneration and continues into season 5.

tales, such as the discovery that Oz's Wicked Witch (Zelena) is the half-sister of Snow White's stepmother (Regina), and that their exiled mother became Wonderland's Queen of Hearts (Cora), supports depth psychological theories of transgenerational consequences of living with unresolved shadows, projections, and trauma—in short, without healing and individuating.

Some peculiarities are never fully explained or resolved. Sherwood Forest is curiously located within or sometimes next to the Enchanted Forest. Characters like Cruella de Ville, (masculine) Greek gods, and mermaids weave in and out of regions, seemingly without a grounded mythological movement theory. We also later find Mary Shelley's characters from *Frankenstein* in Storybrooke, though their original geography is unclear (i.e., everyone else originally in Storybrooke was relocated from the Enchanted Forest). Characters from two other stories made popular by recent blockbuster films, *Brave* and *Frozen* (based on Hans Christian Andersen's original tale "The Snow Queen"), also appear and are subsequently woven in, with the effect of additional strong female s/heroes who drive the story.[75] At the end of the fifth season, a new realm is introduced, a place where disenchanted and disgruntled misfit characters have gathered.

Regardless of the seemingly ever-expanding boundaries of this imaginal realm, and the ever-increasing cast of characters—these do include Cinderella, Sleeping Beauty, and Rapunzel—Snow White, as Snow/Mary Margaret, remains the primary s/heroic figure, along with her daughter Emma, and partner Charming. Similarly, partnership is at the heart of the series' resolutions. It is Snow who first individuates, acknowledging and integrating her own shadow.

Andrew Bard Schmookler writes in "Acknowledging Our Inner Split," in *Meeting the Shadow* (Connie Zweig and Jeremiah Abrams, eds.), "In the dance before the mirror, we find a false inner peace by demonizing the enemy. But recognizing even a truly demonic enemy as made of the same stuff as we is part of the true path toward peace" (190). Perhaps the most pressing danger is not recognizing, then consequentially externalizing our personal shadow, those disowned, unvalued parts of us. The mirror itself functions as a reflective surface in which to see our-Selves—personally and collectively—and continues to be a predominant symbol in these Snow White tales, reminding us to recall our projections. Schmookler relates how

---

75. Another underlying theme explored in the series is the lasting effects of trauma of childhood abandonment (especially on villains, either through the death, negligence, or betrayal of a parent). These include Snow White, Emma Swan, Henry, Charming/David, Rumpelstiltskin/Mr. Gold, Killian/Hook, Cora, Neil/Baelfire, and Zelena.

the redemptive path depends on compassion. This is Snow's main movement; she both recognizes the good in her enemies and acknowledges her own misdeeds, including the murder of a dangerous usurper queen. Her prince, Charming/David, is more often locked in a polarized war "between good and evil"; instead, Snow is integrating the two.

Charming/David's repeated archetypal proclamations, variations on the theme of "we are heroes and that's what heroes do: sacrifice" becomes predictable and pedantic. We learn in a backstory that it was a young woman (Anna/Joan from the *Frozen* storyline) who taught him to fight for himself and his home, the value of boundaries, and to recognize his inner strength and worth. Interestingly, in that same season the patho/logical Ice Queen/Elsa attempts to artificially reconstruct a broken mirror and, in tandem, her broken family without doing the necessary healing work to create something *new* and different out of what has shattered. She creates a false wholeness that cannot adhere.[76]

Conversely, Snow/Mary Margaret holds the Magdalenian regenerative energy. It is she who acknowledges her heart has been blackened by a murderous act; she killed Cora, an evil usurper queen, her own step-grandmother (the Queen of Hearts). Similarly, daughter Emma works this type of deep integration. Charming comes along, but he is not the fierce and compassionate regenerative leader that his partner and daughter are each becoming. It is their willingness to know and integrate their own shadows and accept others in tricky ways that enlivens the series. Snow believes in Regina, the originally loving woman who came to be her stepmother. She tells Regina her worldview that the universe rewards us for making good choices ("Smash the Mirror," season 4). She retells the story of the woman (Regina) who had saved her as a girl by risking her own life and how that act changed her. When Regina (in disguise) asks Snow what happened to this woman, Snow says, "She's gone. Oh, but I hope she comes back someday" ("The Evil Queen," season 2). Snow describes how someone's potential for goodness never ceases, even when their goodness leaves for a period of time. She also cites her (birth) mother's advice to keep goodness in her heart at all times as a mantra to draw upon. Though she sometimes falters, Snow continually renews her practice of relentless support and healthy boundaries while enemies are acting out.

---

76. This psychic pathology is the antithesis of bricolage, where the act of consciously creating a mosaic from shards requires steps of bonding (integration and acceptance of the breakage) and accenting the fault lines through the grouting of grief work. See chapter 6 on tending trauma and grief via bricolage.

By offering relentless support to "enemies" (and in *Once Upon a Time* they are all potentially future friends), after creating healthy boundaries and fighting for themselves and the health of the realms, these s/heroes support the conversion of countless villains to emerging s/heroes learning to make better choices. Snow, Emma, and their family fold them into their community, and, collectively, the realm heals and progresses.

KEEP YOUR EYES ON THE PRINCE: MASCULINE AGENCY

All four fairy tales offer us princes worth watching. In "Rapunzel" the prince—after being blinded by the evil witch—wanders into the woods, unable to see, wounded and vulnerable. As Starbird identifies in the tale of Sleeping Beauty (also known as Briar Rose), the prince must "hack his way through the hedge of briars that has grown up around the Beloved, hiding her very existence" (151). This necessary act reflects a deeper psychic movement: "Only sheer determination on the part of the prince unites this pair. The image of the impetuous prince slashing his way through the thicket of thorn bushes is significant for our modern world. The wounded male recklessly brandishing his sword is not only hurt and frustrated, he is also dangerous. The sooner he is united with his own lost, scorned, and repudiated feminine side, the better!" (150). For Starbird, these radical acts on the part of the princes express their movement toward their inner feminine. Their own quests are fraught with danger. They are also highly significant indicators of what is necessary on both personal/psychic levels, as well as what is required culturally to move beyond patriarchy. Like Betty Friedan's problem with no name, the prince's dilemma is a vague awareness that something is askew and missing, yet he does not yet have the skills or emotional maturity to identify what he is setting out to find—this deep longing for the lost and repudiated feminine, his primal wound.

One particularly weak interpretation of these collective themes, *Princess: A Modern Fairytale*, a made-for-TV-film, does, however, illuminate a particularly shadowy attitude (2008). The princely character William first meets the princess at the ball. While all around her hush and stare, his inadequate best friend explains, "You see how the men are looking at her? As if she's proof alone that there's a god? She's a fairy tale virgin princess. Women want to be her; men want to possess her. . . . She's the ultimate conquest" (2008). This character is capable of seeing a princess only through his tyrannical, hypersexualized, colonizer, unquenchable male gaze. Her sexuality becomes part of an unblemished, fresh, public, and "pure" fantasy of the feminine. This distilled quote reveals patriarchy's vampiric shadow fantasy, where young women are lusted after as personal property via other women's envy and men's anima projections, dis/embodied as objects of desire. By also revealing his colonizing mentality, objectifying a "marriageable" woman as Other—rather than potentially knowing her powerfully erotic—she is merely "exotic," some*thing* to conquer.[77] Clearly this pal is no prince and unworthy of such a Bride himself.

On this princely patter, Jodi Bower writes, "if a prince has to go into the forest to rescue the lost or sleeping princess, I believe that means it is his story, and the princess more likely represents his repressed feminine side that he needs to retrieve from his own unconscious" (154–55). Bower amplifies a necessary act of individuation in men—an act crucial not only for personal individuation but also for collective healing. Perhaps a man must physically approach that dam between the masculine and feminine complex wastelands and deconstruct it with his bare hands, rebalancing his internal emotional flow and recognizing it in his external world—his own s/hero's journey. But I do not believe that these stories are only about, or for, princely maturation. That they all end in marriage further supports *both* the central drive toward individuation for all people as the movement of the archetypal Bride toward her partner and vice versa, their healing and growth completely interdependent. Moreover, since these tales highlight the masculine searching for the lost and degraded feminine, it seems at least half of the action must originate from the wounded/healing masculine.[78]

Starbird's own vision of a healed (singular) wasteland where "the desert shall bloom" is itself incomplete, as she tends only the desertified masculine aspect of the complex wasteland (157). She posits that it is the wounded masculine who will be healed by reunion with the lost Bride. However, she fails to fully discuss where the Bride might have been (in exile), the conditions of her exile (saturated, bogged down), or how the Bride redeems and frees herself from imprisonment by patriarchal fear and oppression. In chapter 6, I track the journey of a very real contemporary, powerful, and dark Bride and the public healing movement with her grieving English prince to heal the complex wasteland.

---

77. For an analysis of the "exotic" within gender and postcolonial frames, see Cynthia Enloe's *Bananas, Beaches, and Bases.*

78. Gender-inclusive language relates to individuation for all genders, including questioning polarities and continuum models. My goal is queering (troubling, questioning) heteronormative language, rather than promoting it, as a function of the ongoing process of re/generating empowering concepts of the feminine and masculine principles.

CINDERELLA: ENVY AND CONFUSION
AS PATRIARCHAL COUNTERINTELLIGENCE

In their book *Cinderella and Her Sisters: The Envied and the Envying*, Ann and Barry Ulanov tackle the under-researched topic of envy and its intrinsic relationship with confusion. Starbird relates the origins of Cinderella as ninth-century Europe, the general era of the Merovingian deposition, placing it firmly within the Magdalene heresy timeframe and geography. The Ulanovs widen the origins of "Cinderella" beyond Charles Perrault's most familiar seventeenth-century account, reporting "tellings that reach back in time as much as a thousand years and across the world from the Indians of North America to the peoples of Africa and China" with more than "seven hundred attempts to tell this tale" (15). Regardless of origin, much can be gained by locating the Ulanovs' study alongside Starbird's thesis; a significant pattern concerning the role envy and confusion play in coming to regenerative consciousness is revealed.

The Ulanovs explain how envy objectifies a person, pulling them radically off-center, leaving them feeling utterly helpless. They identify the importance of acknowledging when someone is indeed the target of an envious attack. This complicated process warrants a close study, especially considering its psychologically destructive capacity. The Ulanovs argue that the envier escapes the identification and exploration of their own feelings by projecting them onto the envied one, believing the cause of their suffering lies firmly with the Other. "Accusation substitutes for self-examination" (20). For the Ulanovs, the action begins when the *envier* perceives a form of attack, that somehow the envied one (Cinderella, for example) is depriving them of what the Ulanovs define as "the good." This belief is rooted in the patriarchal phallacy of scarcity and its secret agent, fear. In this belief system there is never enough "good" to go around. It is the basis of divide-and-conquer warfare; fighting over breadcrumbs keeps the loaf safe.

It is then that the envier lashes out. The effects of such an *actual* attack leave the envied one (Cinderella) disoriented, invalidated, "cut off at her roots" (21). The envier's perception and good opinion/approval then may become for a time disproportionately important, amplifying the need for an external locus of control, as she (Cinderella) has lost her own center.[79] The

---

79. As more research develops around our pandemic of narcissistic abuse syndrome (NAS), correlations become clear that envy (along with interlocking shame, trauma, and grief) can be a core component in a narcissist's vampiric motivation. See Leonard Cruz and Steven Buser, editors, *A Clear and Present Danger*; Vickie Howard's "Recognising Narcissistic Abuse and

persecution of the envier is distorting in nature (as in Stockholm Syndrome) and may dangerously assume grand proportions in the envied one's psyche. The Ulanovs relate this type of interaction to an invasion and annexation by enemy forces. "Envy attacks, envy denies, envy eviscerates" (29). To be the object of such intense threatening projection is disorienting and potentially debilitating; recovery depends upon the resilience of the envied one. When a person cannot find her own vitality and recover her own center, her psyche risks invasion, resulting in feeling a pervasive powerlessness.

Dennis Slattery distinguishes between jealousy (wanting what someone has) and envy (wanting who someone *is*) in *The Way of Myth: Stories' Subtle Wisdom* (see chapter 8, "Envy's Corrosive Power as Soul Sickness," 87–102). By identifying how envy is a product of a lack of imagination, Slattery illuminates the very real dangers in inherently vampiric laziness. When we fail to question this moody shadow projection and instead be (unconsciously) moved by it, we risk losing our own mythic movement and psychic center.

There are two types of enviers in Cinderella: the stepsisters and the stepmother/false, usurper queen. These relationships are at the core of this fairy tale, as well as central to the other three. By examining them we gain insight into Cinderella as archetypically representing Magdalene's mythology, both as she has been treated historically, and how her return reignites healing.

Repeatedly in both the canonical and Gnostic Gospels, Magdalene is described as the object of envy by the apostles (stepsisters/stepbrothers), who try repeatedly to diminish and silence her; she also carries centuries of conflated projection as "the penitent sinner/whore" by the apostles' church (stepmother or false usurper queen).[80] Within corrupted Christian mythology, the void left by Magdalene as Bride is subsequently replaced by three very different entities. The church, and sometimes Israel, is often described as the Bride of Christ in scripture and colloquially.[81] In terms of partnership, Jesus is presented as relating only to his mother Mary; something is wrong in the realm when a nice Jewish boy/prince/rabbi is portrayed as having been married off to "the church" or, in a bizarrely incestuous twist,

---

the Implications for Mental Health Nursing Practice"; and Marina Litinetskaia and Julien Daniel Guelfi's "État amoureux normal et pathologique," 280–85.

80. See especially the Gospel of Mary and the Gospel of Philip. For analyses of the relationships between Magdalene and the other apostles, see the work of Karen King, Jean-Yves Leloup, and Freke and Gandy.

81. Consider especially the canonical Gospels, Revelations, Ephesians, and Corinthians.

his mama.[82] Lastly, novice Catholic nuns take their spiritual vows as "Brides of Christ," requiring a commitment of chastity, a supposed "sublimation" of sexual energies into their spiritual devotion. Christianity has a bad habit of attempting to usurp and replace Magdalene's erotic bridal power. Magdalene, instead, offers a case study in resilience, regeneration, and agency—the true nature of Eros. She is playing the long game.

The Ulanovs cite a case study involving sisters where the envying one described feeling superior when her sister was not doing well (21). Again we find an external locus of control; the envier's very self-worth is externally located, dependent upon someone else's misfortune. For the envier to feel good about herself, she needs her sister to fail. In such a lazy, vampiric paradigm nurturing sisterhood is impossible. Unconscious vampiric feeding (forever unsuccessful) on our sisters is at the core of this distorted scarcity trap, leaving everyone depleted, hungry, and malnourished.

The next developmental step might seem counterintuitive and surprising since misleading ideas about feminine behavior and power conflate "nice" with true kindness and ignore the need for healthy boundaries. According to the Ulanovs, as long as the envied one (Cinderella) is concerned with mending a relationship with her envier, she is doomed to fail. Trapped, she "cannot reach through the thick wall of projection the envier has thrown up against her" (21). They suggest it is necessary to completely break connection with the envier, as all attempts at reparation amplify the corruption, leaving her vulnerable to the vampiric acts of the stepsisters/stepmother. If she does not break with them, the envied (Cinderella) runs the risk of forever seeking (external) approval from her persecutor, another form of disempowered vampiric relating, a codependent bargain.

There is (initially) a powerlessness inherent in being envied. The magnitude of disconnect is tremendous. All attempts to tend and repair the relationship on the part of the envied one fail and, instead, cause additional harm. Knowing the predictability of this pattern can be extremely helpful in moving towards a new strategy for survival, especially in relation to a

---

82. See, for example, the ceiling painting at the Benedictine monastery of Downside Abbey in Somerset, England, depicting a crowned Jesus crowning his mother, Mary. Symbolism of this incestuous corruption of partnership—where the son steps into the void left by an absent father while the mother attempts to get her unmet and unconscious emotional/psychic needs through her son—can be seen repeatedly in Judeo-Christian iconography and mythology. Also follow the encoded traumatized, necrotic movement of the mother in Eschenbach's *Parzival* (thirteenth century) and Campbell's analysis in "In Search of the Holy Grail." Living vampirically through her son, she drops dead on the doorstep when he leaves.

"stepmother" or other type of person with power over the envied one. Step away from the envier. Doing so interrupts the energic bond.

With no obvious provocation for the crisis, the envied one may go through extreme bewilderment. Responding with kindness and patience can have no positive effect. Being helpful and actively supportive cannot protect the envied one. She may feel she is on the brink of madness. All seems topsy-turvy—illogical, neurotic, and necrotic. Unpacking this phenomenon, the Ulanovs cite Helmut Schoeck's sociological study of international loans to the Global South being destructive rather than redemptive. "Rather than receive, envy wants to destroy the giver, pushing for a leveling down so all will be equally miserable" (22). Kindness is met with resentment, ingratitude, and envy. It is Cinderella's very being and cheerful attitude towards life that is the core of the problem. In a patriarchal world it is not safe to be kind, compassionate, productive, and optimistic. Cinderella is the perfect target for envy, a "vulnerable" scapegoat, attacked as Other.[83]

In *Meeting the Shadow*, Marie-Louise von Franz writes, "The shadow usually contains values that are needed by consciousness, but that exist in a form that makes it difficult to integrate them into one's life" (36). These deformations require our attention. When left untended, projections risk becoming a cheap way to displace onto another what we cannot yet accept about ourselves. It is, however, costly, condemning us to a type of half-life until we reclaim those missing shards. Instead, by accepting the wall of projection, and ceasing all attempts to get over it, the envied one surrenders to the situation, exploding the fantasy that simply continuing to be "good" is an effective antidote to envy. Cinderella is in danger not only of losing her chance for a full life but also of becoming that which she is victimized by: an envying, calcified "stepsister" or "stepmother." And thus the next traumatized and re/traumatizing generation is born.

Perhaps the toughest knot to untangle when envy strikes is the debilitating confusion that may take hold of the person being envied. Quoting Julia Segal's book *Melanie Klein*, the Ulanovs reiterate, "Envy attacks the good object and, by projection and fragmentation, makes it bad; therefore, it produces a state of confusion between good and bad, which is at the root of many psychotic confusions" (181). Here they explain how envy's resultant disorientation makes both identifying the problem and solving it extremely difficult. The envied one, in a form of post-traumatic stress disorder (PTSD),

---

83. For further discussion of fear and hatred of the feminine, see Ann Ulanov, *Receiving Woman*.

conflates her own connection to the good with the trauma she is suffering, resulting in corruption and confusion. "Wouldn't it be better to be less talented, less virtuous, less subject to envy?" (27). This collapsed posture becomes a defense mechanism. It is no longer safe to be her full self—which an Other is attempting to take.

There are few things more confusing or more powerful than intermittent reinforcement. The inconsistency of elusive rewards, including love and nurturing attention, and/or the enforcement of rigid or invisible boundaries, creates conditioned dis/eased responses. A classic and inhumane example from behavioral psychology is the imprisonment of an animal (usually a rat or mouse) in a Skinner box. Once conditioned to depress a lever to receive food pellets, the "experiment" progresses to have pellets intermittently released; the frequency with which s/he depresses the lever increases dramatically as the inhumanely treated "laboratory" animal searches for food that was freely rewarded only moments ago.

Culture is infused with intermittent reinforcement. Watch anyone new to owning a smart phone as they quickly become trapped with a high frequency of checking it. The intermittent reinforcement of love and attention in family systems can similarly be dangerously traumatizing. Healthy parenting and relationships are built upon consistency and healthy, clear boundaries. When sisters, mothers, and Others sometimes love us and other times abandon and/or terrorize us, we can become extremely disoriented. Real trust cannot develop in such a toxic environment. Additionally, when the home is unsafe, it sets a dangerous pattern, potentially replicating this as a lifelong narrative if a woman cannot call on her wandering Aletis self and leave intolerable situations.

Thus confusion becomes a subtle, pervasive, and corrosive agent, especially between women under patriarchy. When envy and confusion infect the mother-daughter relationship, it is in danger of becoming the next patriarchal wound. An unconscious agreement can form between them: let's stay here in the "bad"; at least we will be together. Cinderella's stepsisters have entered into such a disempowering pact with their birth mother, extending the mother's wound poisonously for another generation and out laterally between them and toward Cinderella, their shadows becoming vomited projections upon their sisters. Is it any wonder they have no energy left to question their lazy projections upon Cinderella?

The extreme confusion that can result from envious attacks by those closest to us, especially parents and siblings, is threaded throughout these four fairy tales. Daughters become submerged, in danger of drowning in the fetid, swampy waters of the feminine wasteland as air (Logos, the ability to think clearly, to reason) is lost, replaced by flooding water (Eros, in this case too much debilitating emotion—grief).

In "Rapunzel" we see how the paltry price of lettuce in exchange for a daughter's life is a clue left by collapsed parents.[84] Whether disempowered, dissociated, or dismissed, such lack of protection signals hollowed-out evidence of patriarchal motherhood. When cheap and nutritionless baubles have often been exchanged for the true power of the Bride, she is unsafe; the realm rots.

I find the Ulanovs themselves to be intermittent reinforcers of feminist theory. Sometimes they function as tremendous guides: "She needs it all—the incompleteness, the sacrificial role, the energies elicited in her by desertion and betrayal. They prepare her for the machinery of her deliverance" (43). Here they clearly identify the necessity for the entire arc of the s/hero or Aletis's journey, like those who must be abandoned in order to individuate, as Ariadne was abandoned by Theseus, and Magdalene was abandoned by so many, personally and culturally—even by Jesus himself through death. Yet they seem to abandon us in act 2 of an unfinished play: "Erich Neumann notes that the scapegoat can sometimes be a superior figure; Cinderella plays that role here, like a female Christ figure, a suffering servant" (41–42). As Christian Jungian theorists, the Ulanovs perpetuate here a common tenet widely found in some post-Jungian studies: the conflation between suffering and value. Suffering might be a component of the journey, but attachment to it, as either the destination or the worthiest task, denies the cyclical regenerative nature of life and leaves us with a Christ figure as the impotent and lonely Fisher King. It is not Christ whom Cinderella represents; it is regenerative Magdalene.[85]

A BRIDAL CROWN OF HER OWN:
OVERCOMING THE EVIL USURPER QUEEN/STEPMOTHER

The Bride's procession down the aisle is one of coronation, symbolized by her bridal crown. With internal union as the culmination of individuation, the transformative act of sacred marriage includes the Bride/princess becoming her own queen as the Bridegroom/prince becomes his own king, sovereigns of their own lives. Yet the Bride might first have to battle a feminine shadow—in

---

84. For another example of the cost and consequence of parental collapse, see the fairy tale "The Handless Maiden," in *The Complete Grimm's Fairy Tales*.

85. See chapters 5 and 6 on sacrifice versus regeneration, especially Megan Rose Woolever's treatment of Magdalene as returning Christa.

the form of another woman—for the right to wear her own crown. In each of the four tales, the princess/Bride is cursed and/or held captive by such a shadow figure of corrupt feminine power, the combined usurper archetype of wicked stepmother/evil queen/wicked witch.

In her dissertation *Sovereignty: Reconciliation, Rupture, or Retaliation*, Leona Marie convincingly argues that representation of the feminine via an archetypal triad of maiden, mother, and crone is incomplete and that for a woman to develop sovereignty, what is required is a coronation. Marie utilizes three fairy tales to amplify the necessary movement from maiden to queen: "One-Eye, Two-Eye, Three-Eyes" (which I suggest is a variation of "Cinderella"), "Rapunzel," and "Snow White." In each case the maiden must confront corruptions of motherhood: an envious mother, a kidnapping evil "witch," and a usurping stepmother, respectively.

Western cultures lack models for mature, erotic womanhood. Inherited and reinvented archetypes of a triple goddess have been routinely stripped of their power, demoted, and projected upon as shadow figures. While Gimbutas's triple goddess symbolism depicts the interconnections of birth, death, and regeneration, another highly popular neopagan version centers around the maiden, mother, and crone, stages based on biological reproduction (essentialism). Traceable directly to classicist and mythographer Robert Graves, this version may represent another expression of (unconscious) longing for the feminine. Maidens have been portrayed as powerless, mothers as corrupted by their power, and crones as decaying, feeble, invaluable remnants of life.[86] As a neopagan and masculinist construct the maiden-mother-crone triple goddess also echoes the Christian Trinity—both strategically constructed, albeit perhaps unconsciously, with patriarchal intentions of limiting women's roles.[87] Of course this also limits access to and emulation of cultural archetypal roles of leadership and agency.

Rob Brezsny, whose novel *The Televisionary Oracle* revolves around the second coming of Mary Magdalene, suggests Magdalene carries the missing archetype of sovereignty: "Magdalen, alas, was too far ahead of her time to succeed in being seen for who she really was. Her archetype was not permitted

86. See especially Patricia Reis's extensive treatment of patriarchal pathologizing of the feminine in *Daughters of Saturn*. For a history of the maiden, mother, crone mytheme, see Carol P. Christ, "Maiden, Mother, Crone. Unfortunately, here Christ also dismisses the queen archetype, which need not be a hierarchal term describing dominion over others but, rather, reclaimed as a benevolent, mature ruler of her own soul, representing internal sovereignty reigning over formerly fragmented, occupied, and unconscious parts.

87. During an archaeological research trip to Tunisia in 2005, while discussing the local contemporary tradition of symbolically representing the Trinity above doorways, our guide stated that, for the Berbers, Mother Mary, along with Jesus and God, formed the Trinity.

to imprint itself deeply enough on the collective unconscious. Sadly, the divine feminine barely managed to survive in the dreams of the race through the defanged, depotentized image of the Virgin Mary—Christ's harmless mommy, not his savvy consort" (60). Brezsny invites contemplation on the enormous cost of a missing archetype of feminine sovereignty and the damage done by replacing her with a disempowered corruption of Mother Mary, as if a "depotentized" nurturing guide could ever replace an embodied lover, equal partner, or our full inner feminine strength. The roles are quite different. Without such models we are left not knowing how to clear our minds of confusion, fight envious projections, and get ourselves to the altar of individuation. The cost of Magdalene's loss has been enormous. Yet threads of her resilience remain encoded in the world at large, as they are here in these fairy tales; reclamation of her archetypal image promotes courage and agency.

Starbird discusses the primary murderous movement within Snow White as it relates to Magdalene mythology: "The princess Snow White is ordered murdered by her evil stepmother. There is almost always a malicious, jealous stepmother or an ugly old witch trying to keep the prince separated from his counterpart; she is trying to keep the Bride from replacing herself. This wicked mother sees the beautiful princess in her magic mirror and tempts the maiden with a shiny apple, which poisons her" (151). The false usurper queen is murderous. What she most fears is the Bride attaining sovereignty, including the union of the Bride/princess and the Bridegroom/prince, since both events will expose and topple her. Starbird associates the stepmother with the wounded and incomplete Catholic Church that murderously forced the Magdalene heresy, the Church of Amor/Love, underground.[88]

It is a mistake to underestimate how serious this drive to annihilation is. This form of patriarchal stepmotherhood is a corruption of power and parenthood. Born out of trauma, it is fear-based, and the formidable energy behind it is archetypal, generational, and deadly. This older woman has usually married the ruling king under some false pretense and has then killed or otherwise incapacitated him. This is her first vampiric act; she seizes the good king/nobleman's (Cinderella's father is often a duke) throne, home, and realm.

The stepmother/evil queen/old witch shadow archetype brings with her a legacy of trauma. In the films *Maleficent*, *Maleficent: Mistress of Evil*, and *Snow White and the Huntsman*, we learn painful backstories of how this

---

88. See especially Starbird, Dan Brown, and Kathleen McGowan for various treatments of the Albigensian Crusade against Occatanian Christians and the trans-European, papal-ordered Templar massacre on Friday, October 13, 1307. See Gerda Lerner's *The Creation of Feminist Consciousness* for a feminist historical analysis of the impact this strategic persecution had on Cathar women and culture. Both McGowan and Lerner track evidence in material culture; McGowan also works with art history, while Lerner traces economic agency.

archetype became deeply wounded, having herself survived trauma and abuse, patriarchal fear, and scarcity. Hers is a cautionary tale: heal or become a vampiric usurper, someone who cannot generate or contain energy for herself. She must endlessly suck it from Others, often daughters and other vulnerable women. Turning other women into "the Other," she simultaneously drains them of their life force while projecting her own unacceptable traits upon them. This envious act poisons the daughter and the realm.

As we see in both "Snow White" and "Cinderella," the loss of the good father leaves a gaping wound for the Bride, who has already lost her good mother long ago. Enter the vampiric stepmother. The Ulanovs identify how parental envy can be extremely debilitating. The loss of the good parents (which can also manifest as the loss of "the good" in our parents) is a heavy burden. However, both Snow White and Cinderella are seen as courageous and good precisely because of the healthy parenting they received from their birth parents. Again, it is precisely their inherent "goodness" that makes them targets for the invading patriarchal shadow mother.

These fairytales caution: beware the corrupt queen/witch/stepmother/ stepsister figure who attempts to annihilate her daughters and sisters— stealing "the good"—condemning them to either eternal maidenhood in servitude or a corrupt "marriage" with the wounded (and stagnant) masculine, continuing their legacy of abuse. But these are not merely cautionary tales—which, as a genre, are fear-based, tragic, and incomplete. Instead, these mythic stories represent the full comedic cycle (including life's inherent and necessary comedy and tragedy) of regeneration.[89] As such, they lay a path for healing. They also share elements with an older myth, that of Psyche, which provides vital clues for how to achieve sovereignty through the initiatory act of defeating corrupted sisters and queens.

PSYCHE/CINDERELLA/MAGDALENE

The triangular story of Psyche, Eros, and Aphrodite lies nested within the second-century CE Roman novel *The Golden Ass*, or the *Metamorphoses*, by Apuleius. The myth of Psyche and Eros is popular among depth psychologists and mythologists and has inspired a range of interpretations.[90]

---

89. Louise Cowan's study of the epic cycle in *The Epic Cosmos* provides a tool for literary theory aligning with both the s/hero's journey and Gimbutas's study of regeneration. Cowan frames life's encounters as the culmination of styles and skills gained via lyric, tragic, comedic, and epic structures and realms. See especially "Epic as Cosmopoesis" (2014).
90. See James Gollnick, *Love and the Soul*, 1992), 114–15.

Several theorists, including von Franz and Ann Ulanov, see this primarily as a story of male individuation and/or anima relationship. Robert Johnson begins deconstructing the myth in *She: Understanding Feminine Psychology*, yet leaves us hanging for further interpretation. I suggest this myth relates a patriarchal initiatory journey for women by other women. Psyche is a Bride who, like Cinderella on her way toward sacred partnership, must first confront traitorous sisters and a wicked queen within a patriarchal paradigm in order to attain sovereignty and sacred marriage. Like Psyche, Cinderella, when assigned overwhelming tasks (including sorting vast quantities of seeds) receives mysterious and timely aid from Nature.

The story begins with the birth of Psyche, the third daughter of a king and queen. Not only has she been newly proclaimed as the most beautiful human woman, Psyche is compared favorably with the goddess of beauty and love herself; worship has dropped off at Aphrodite's temples. The general population, so struck by this princess's stunning beauty, redistributes its worship (away from the goddess of love and beauty, Aphrodite), disproportionately toward Psyche (as if she were a goddess). Born beautiful and worshiped for this alone, through no fault of her own, then abandoned by her family and followers alike—with little if any self-knowledge, training, or skill—she is uniquely vulnerable to the Aphroditic shadow.

I could not imagine a worse mentor than what we see in the *Metamorphoses*. Their relationship begins on terrible footing. Aphrodite's shadow aspect takes repeated revenge on the royal princess. Psyche is perceived as Other, the usurper. Aphrodite enters fear-based thinking, feeding her shadow. She is in scarcity mode, where she believes "there's not enough for me." Whether her fear is realistic or not, it is real because she feels it. Like Aphrodite, many mentors and mother figures hold tightly to power they fear losing, be it institutional or personal.

When women do not own and embody our power and agency, we attempt to get our needs met sideways, manipulatively, and we begin the unconscious act of othering. Projection becomes a convenient way to displace onto another what we cannot yet accept about ourselves. It is, however, costly, condemning us to a type of half-life until we reclaim those missing shards. Most significantly, the act of reclamation is revitalizing—life-giving—since it releases potential energy stored in those previously disowned fragments. In this way our shadow can be appreciated as a storehouse of potential energy, simply needing liberation.

Aphrodite's shadow is frequently depicted as her primary identity; she is often represented as self-absorbed, petty, and narcissistic. She is also portrayed as omnipotent; others lose their agency when near her, so captivating is her beauty and "charm." They want to possess her or be possessed by her; both are vampiric acts. Though she is meant to embody love—she is often portrayed as being reduced to manipulative seduction with her physical beauty and (untrustworthy) "charm," yielding her (almost) whatever she desires. This is not the goddess of love in her power; this is a patriarchal corruption and shadow projection of the fear of feminine power and Eros as erotic life force. It is from *this* place of fear and shame that Aphrodite attempts to punish and neutralize Psyche (soul itself).

It was while listening to a forgotten and unfortunately rare audio recording that I found confirmation of deep links between Magdalenian mythology, these four European fairy tales (especially Cinderella), and Psyche's story. Jean Shinoda Bolen's *The Myth of Eros & Psyche: Growth Toward Wholeness of the Archetypally Vulnerable Woman: The Tasks to Learn* delineates Psyche's path as one of psychic development for women. Significantly, Bolen identifies Psyche with Aphrodite archetypally, in the lineage of Sister-Brides:

> Psyche's story is the story of the soul who is connected to love. It is the story of—on a human level—a woman whose chief archetype is Aphrodite, the goddess of love. It's true that she seeks marriage, and she is pregnant and will be a mother, and yet her major archetype, the archetype that she has a strong issue with, is Aphrodite. And that means that Aphrodite has an enormous power to make her unconscious and to put her through something devastating again. (Bolen)

Locating Psyche within this erotic lineage (devoted to love) differs from the institution of marriage, firmly in the realm of Hera. Bolen, like many Jungians working primarily with Greco-Roman pantheons, does not automatically link love with sacred partnership.[91] Bolen also sees this experience as something only certain women need go through—those who primarily identify with Aphrodite. I suggest this separation between love and a sacred, healthy partnership is a patriarchal corruption. As discussed in chapter 1, the ancient Mediterranean partnership traditions held love and sacred partnership as their dual core, with interdependent functions. While I generally agree with Patricia Reis's interpretation of the Greek goddesses as diminished, pathologized archetypes fighting for survival against patriarchy, I also see great opportunity in reclaiming what is left of love and partnership within the Aphrodite–Adonis and Psyche–Eros mythologies. Therefore, I

---

91. See *Goddesses in Every Woman* and *Gods in Every Man* for Bolen's archetypal theories regarding love, marriage, and partnership.

see all three—Aphrodite, Psyche, and Magdalene—as regenerative bridal lineage holders.

As such, Aphrodite here behaves as an evil queen; traumatized by patriarchal scarcity in relation to beauty, and, conflating attention with love, she acts out of fearful envy. Young, mortal, and inexperienced Psyche is declared to be more beautiful than the goddess of (patriarchal) love; motivated by a narcissistic need for attention, Aphrodite is angered when the male gaze is no longer focused on her (she is abandoned by both the population at large, who have begun to idolize the beautiful human, then by her son, who falls in love with her). Psyche is then seen as a danger and a threat to society; not wanting to risk Aphrodite's rage, the king and queen cast her out to be sacrificed. Sent by Aphrodite to poison her with his arrows, Eros instead falls immediately in love with her, carrying her safely away to his palatial private home. Eros maintains his true identity a secret, and she only knows him in the dark privacy of their bedchamber. Jealous of her new home, her sisters prey on Psyche's trust in her mysterious partner and plant an insidious seed of doubt in Psyche toward her beloved; they tell her he is a monster about to devour her and their unborn child.

Armed with a lantern and knife, Psyche shines a light on her lover. Accidentally pricking herself on one of his arrows, she herself falls helplessly in love with Eros. Simultaneously he is awakened and burned by a drop of oil from her lamp; he flees. (In this way they are reciprocally injured by each other's tools.)

Surviving her sisters' betrayal, Psyche devotes herself to reuniting with Eros and seeks out Aphrodite as intermediary, experiencing terrifying abuse at her hands. Aphrodite assigns her four impossible tasks. Bolen describes each of Psyche's four initiatory tasks psychologically: sorting of seeds relates to priority setting; collecting of golden fleece illustrates right use of power while staying in right relationship to her feminine psyche/soul and Nature; collecting water in the crystal flask gives shape to the creative impulse and life itself; and focusing on task maintains healthy boundaries and conserves energy (Bolen). Psyche's initial response to each task is *I can't*. Each time she first collapses, cries, surrenders—perhaps a type of *albedo* washing via feeling her despair. She then finds the psychic energy to continue; it is only then that support arrives where there had previously been none.

Bolen proposes that through these tasks Psyche is asked to take care of her-Self, create something, or clarify her feelings for someone. By completing the initiation, she finds "strength, knowledge, and power within herself" (Bolen). The act of showing up and continuing onward—the simple act of movement—provides answers. These tales suggest that perhaps this shadow aspect of Aphrodite is exactly what/who is necessary for such a bridal initiation; perhaps individuation and sovereignty are possible only through such cauterizing tasks. Yet, when a Bride/princess is overwhelmed with poisonous projections and abuse, and lost in the confusing fog of envy, her success might also depend on trickier means, as investigated in chapter 5 on the Bride as detective.

The final task unfolds via Psyche's trip to the underworld. Instructed to journey there to retrieve Persephone's beauty cream for Aphrodite—who is feeling less than beautiful—Psyche is issued "standard travel agent's advice to the Underworld: three times you will be asked for help and each time you must harden your heart against compassion and go on" (Bolen). Bolen reports the tower's advice to harden her heart as unique, since "no hero in Greek mythology was ever given" such counsel. Bolen describes this last task:

> Like the maiden who does what other people ask of her, you must learn to say no, because only by saying no are you really able to be in life, able to say yes strongly as well as no. Otherwise, [you will continue] instinctively responding as you have been programed, either by culture or by archetype, to take care of everyone else's needs and not your own. The task of learning to say no is learning how not to be a codependent. It is a major step in leading an authentic life that grows out of what is important to you. And this is Psyche's task. (Bolen)

This is the initiatory movement a woman must make to own and repair her own container, heal from codependency, and attempt to learn new ways to regenerate her life force/chi/prana. The conservation of energy is stressed here. Effective containment of our psychic resources protects us against vampiric attacks. A mythopoetic expression of psyche's necessary containment can be found immortalized by Mary Oliver:

> though the voices around you
> kept shouting
> their bad advice—

> "Mend my life!" ("The Journey," in *New and Selected Poems, Volume One*)

Oliver amplifies how vital it is that psyche/Psyche withstand the vampiric offstage voices attempting to distract us from our journey, shouting, "Mend my life!" By divesting from outside voices, Psyche liberates her energy and capacity to complete her task.

The Bride/princess must find the healing action through the psychic fog and feminine bog, otherwise she is left fragmented and confused, preyed upon. This is where Magdalene makes her move from (our collective) unconscious, incurious amnesia toward agency—from codependent management to creativity. Rather than trying to reconstruct what has been shattered *as it was*, the Bride/princess is required to first surrender and feel. Next, using her sleuthing skills to get curious and search for clues among the fragments, she begins to create new patterns, fresh lively mosaics—symbols of her deepest nature. This is the action of bridal, regenerative Magdalenian consciousness coming to fullness.

MEETINGS ON THE BRIDAL MARCH:
THE MADWOMAN AND THE INTERNAL PATRIARCH

Linda Schierse Leonard takes on false, usurper queens and how they can colonize and live on in their daughter's psyches in her landmark book *Meeting the Madwoman: An Inner Challenge for Feminine Spirit*, identifying two types in her chapter "Mad Mothers, Mad Daughters," the Dragon Lady and the Ice Queen, variants of the usurper queen archetype. Though their styles differ—one rages while the other freezes—both are controlling, and a daughter cannot develop a healthy relationship with either. Since a Dragon Lady's burning fury and the Ice Queen's twisted responses can be so overwhelming, dominating a home and the relationships within, a daughter's own feelings can be quashed. She may not know what she feels; all she seems able to feel or experience is her mother's disapproval via disproportionate, manipulative emotional tides and tirades.[92]

Leonard discusses how these mothers, or madwomen, were most likely abandoned or abused themselves as girls and it is precisely their deadly fear of being hurt again that causes them to attack first. Though they wield power

---

92. Leonard discusses a third pattern, the Saint or Too Nice Mother. While she is not overtly present in these fairy tales, this archetype bears mentioning in relation to Magdalene and the corrupted, incomplete model of Christianity. This mother is not in touch with her rage, having, as Leonard puts it, denied the potent and threatening "archetypal energy of the Madwoman" in herself (27). This is the primary "model mother" figure put forth under patriarchy, primarily as Mother Mary (and historically for women writ large via the "Cult of True Womanhood" and the related "Cult of Domesticity"). Rather than a raging, grieving, and active woman—perhaps a religious leader and priestess in her own right—a collapsed, diminished Mary is offered, polite, pious, pliant, quiet, and ultimately powerless.

wildly and rule by anger, inside they feel helpless, powerless, afraid. This unconscious anger takes over the very core of the wounded mother's identity. Leonard writes, "Because she suffers from the memory of real or imagined slights or injustices, any attempts to soothe her feel like criticisms" (51). Here, Leonard describes what the Ulanovs have identified as "the good" feeling like poison. This is precisely the conflation a rejecting usurper queen creates by confusing her own fears with a daughter, a Cinderella/Snow White/ Magdalenian Bride. A colleague privately described navigation with her own (raging) narcissistic mother: "I visit her briefly as it seems my love and caring feels like poison to her after just five minutes and she begins to pull me apart." Perhaps further exploration of this *pharmakon* of love/poison will detect a remedy for such narcissistic wounding.

Leonard cautions that if a woman fails to confront such an archetypal mother (as Snow White does successfully), she may repeatedly meet her again as evil queens throughout her life. Secondly, she may come to recognize an internalized part of herself, a sliver of her mother's wounded animus/ masculine residing within her, as an inner controlling, rejecting, and punishing patriarch. Moreover, an unresolved mother wound can result in eternal searching for the unattainable and rejecting mother love in future (unsuitable, unavailable, unindividuating) partners, the type Jane Austen warns of.

The bridal march toward sovereignty depends upon the healing potential of a daughter getting in touch with her own anger and, possibly, even her own madness after surviving such a dangerous and confusing mothering experience. Again, unless the daughter recognizes her own patterns, she is in danger of repeating the morbid path she grew up with, continually projecting her power—and perhaps her madness—onto others. Rather than a true Bride, she becomes instead a necrotic one, akin to Dickens's Miss Havisham, forever wearing the wedding dress yet incapable of partnering. Powerless and ghostly, she remains a *puella*—an eternal girl—and in middle age she remains the antithesis of regeneration: a liminal maiden-crone who is neither.[93]

For Leonard, the Madwoman is a potent archetype, full of unlived, negated, and writhing emotions—trapped energy! Pent up in our unconscious, this inner feminine force, once integrated into our psyches, has remarkable liberating potential. By contextualizing her within culture that continually seeks to disempower the feminine, we can better understand how to guide her back toward sanity, while simultaneously inviting her guidance.

---

93. See Charles Dickens, *Great Expectations*. For a related critique of "traditional" marriage and exploration of two bridal regeneration opportunities, see Tim Burton's *Corpse Bride*.

In this way individuation comes through holding the tension of these (supposed) opposites, Jung's transcendent function. It is by trusting both of these two truths—she may be "crazy"/outside societal conventions/hurt, and she may be brilliant, cunning, surviving—that we invoke healing. Rather than a wishy-washy middle-of-the-road "resolution," holding the tension of opposites invites the active liaising between the two, offering two entire sets of archetypal tools for individuation that can now be in dialogue. Rather than each annulling the other, polarity builds bridges.[94]

A Bride regaining her strength after surviving vampiric (m)othering may encounter such an opportunity.[95] Leonard quotes a client who encountered her inner Madwoman: "I could no longer avoid the issue of power and anger and had to face my fear of confrontation. I had come to the point of no escape. I was damned if I didn't. In the abyss, you either die, go mad, or discover the strength and power to survive and transform" (59). This surprising extremity of choices an individuating daughter/Bride may face depends upon her first accepting her power and then allowing her formerly suppressed anger to arise, eventually to express it in healthy, constructive ways (though it may be messy at first). The key is *feeling* her anger; otherwise, it can be (unconsciously) weaponized.

Unhealthy Madwomen/usurper queens lack and break boundaries, cannot contain their feelings, and flood over their daughters. This is a primary wound in the feminine wasteland. This act overwhelms and drowns the daughter, condemning her to exile from her-Self, stuck instead in swampy confusion, going under, deprived of air (Logos).

Addressing confusion, Leonard describes a sick mother as having a fragmented ego. Though shattering is necessary for regeneration, this woman has (unconsciously) chosen to maintain and identify with her fractured state, attempting to operate from a disembodied, disenfranchised, and utterly discombobulated position. Leonard writes, "She throws her daughter into confusion because she lives in chaos. Split into pieces herself, she tries to divide the members of her family so that she can be the center" (61). The image is of a woman actively playing with sharp shards; rather than building a creative and healthy new mosaic, she repeatedly cuts herself and her daughter on her shattered inner mirror. The mother will "need her daughter to mirror

---

94. From ongoing conversations with Paulo Ricardo Ferrer on the value of polarity in archetypal integration. See especially Ferrer's innovative and transformative game based on Campbell's hero's journey, *O Jogo do Herói* (*The Hero's Game*), as an embodied practice of *homo ludens* via the s/hero's journey.

95. For an analysis of othering and (m)Other, see Susan Rowland, *C. G. Jung and Literary Theory*.

her in order to feel secure and centered" (61). This pseudo-self-centering technique results in more projection and confusion; imagine trying to mirror or see someone through shards. Again the daughter/Bride is required to liberate herself from the false notion that mother and home are safe and nurturing. Navigating space in such an environment can be like walking on eggshells, or rather, broken (looking) glass. Fear of becoming crazy or sick like her mother is another trap for the Bride, like quicksand along the bridal march. Such fractured attempts at manipulation and false mirroring happen in community as well, and a Bride might do well to guard against them in the world at large.

When women and men, under patriarchal misdirection, deny their intuitive feminine sides, naturally constructive energies can become destructive. Crucial to healing this is implementing a practice of creating clear boundaries and healthy containment, allowing internal energy to replenish and nurture body and psyche. Accepting our (potential for) madness within allows the daughter/Bride to digest her mother's legacy, taking whatever sustenance she can, eliminating the waste.

Leonard cites the mythology of Inanna—perhaps the primordial Bride—as embodying the healing remedy necessary for meeting the Madwoman. When Inanna was held captive by her enraged shadow sister, Ereshkigal, it was the compassionate act of two tiny beings, who simply bore witness to Ereshkigal's suffering and cried with her, that secured Inanna's liberation. Such witnessing tenderness is called for when we meet the Madwoman—or her curious double agent, the internal patriarch—on our path.

When a raging usurper queen is our primary feminine role model, power becomes a tricky topic. Since patriarchal culture devalues women's contributions, experiences, voices, and perceptions, it can also be difficult to even discuss what is happening; add to that the confusion inherent in abusive family structures, and it may take decades for the Bride to escape the patriarchal bog of the feminine wasteland, reclaim her breath, and regain her footing on the bridal march. Once she does, this reclamation of sovereign Bridal power further deconstructs the artificial dam interrupting the flow between the feminine and the masculine at the core of the complex wasteland.

One of the most powerful, practical antidotes to malignant stepsisterhood, where envy and jealousy are fostered, is the growing global phenomenon of women's circles, including the Red Tent movement.[96]

---

96. See Isadora Leidenfrost's documentary *Things We Don't Talk About* and Jean Shinoda Bolen's *Moving Toward the Millionth Circle*.

Nothing interrupts the cycle of fear faster than actively listening to another woman share her personal story/myth in protected, contained space—somewhere free of interruption and distraction, grounded simply and radically in a shared goal of trust building. Historically emerging through consciousness-raising groups during the second wave of feminism in the 1960s—while also drawing on the twelve-step tradition of deep witnessing—the elegant efficacy of women's circles has profoundly and positively affected the narrative of healthy sisterhood and sacred conversations, and embodies regenerative consciousness.

BRING OUT YOUR UNDEAD!
DISINVITING NARCISSISTIC MAMA ZOMBIES AND VAMPIRES

Once upon a time in an academic library, a group of female librarians and faculty collectively giggled over the question "Which are sexier, zombies or vampires?" Those on team vampire were shocked team zombie even existed. Some on team zombie scratched their heads and grunted. Decades later I take these monstrous apparitions seriously and recognize them as potential narcissistic expressions, often in the form of the evil usurper queen/stepmother archetype. (Our first group membership is within the family unit (traditional or nontraditional); our first encounter with the undead may well be within the family, it could be with our own mother.) Take evasive action immediately; if you've invited them to your internal nuptials, rescind the invitation.

Highlighting, discussing, and preparing for these archetypal behavioral patterns provide vital opportunities to tend and heal collective wounds. Again, we have long been in early stages of theoretical and practical understanding of these crises of vitality. Narcissism and narcissistic abuse syndrome (NAS) is being studied much more closely since the trauma of the Donald Trump presidency, along with the sweep of similar dangerous global leaders and the very close links with the global white power movement—including Russia under Vladimir Putin, the UK under Boris Johnson, Brazil under Jair Bolsonaro, Turkey under Recep Tayyip Erdoğan, Egypt under Abdel Fattah al-Sisi, India under Narendra Modi, the Philippines under Rodrigo Duterte, Hungary under Viktor Orbán, and Poland under Mateusz Morawiecki.[97] Narcissism is a patriarchal problem.

---

97. See especially historian Kathleen Belew's *Bring the War Home*; feminist scholar Jackson Katz's timely documentary on white male identity politics, *The Man Card*; and philosopher Kate Manne's research in both *Down Girl* and *Entitled*.

Pamela Pitman Brown in her humorous yet deadly serious research "Tales from the Academic Dark Side: Bringing Untold Realities of Academic Positions into the Daylight" (2013) amplifies encounters with dangerous undead archetypes and their effects on groups, in this case within a workplace group dynamic, academia. Brown describes four archetypes—ghosts, zombies, vampires, and shapeshifters—then recounts true horror stories and survival techniques in response to each.

Zombies are certainly among us. Though sometimes apparently shuffling, mumbling, or otherwise ineffectual and incoherent, zombies can be aggressive, strategic, adaptive, and deadly. Their primary mandate is to create more zombies—herd mentality at its most primal. Zombiism, as an expression of the collective unconscious, amplifies how something within may have become necrotic and cannot regenerate; force feeding on others' energy seems the only way to survive. Zombies lack empathy—one clear symptom of narcissism. They seem to lack critical thinking and nuanced understanding, appearing utterly unconscious.

Jung noticed how humans first work on unconscious material through dreams and fantasy (Collected Works 5, para 4–45). To become aware of this and to then do so intentionally (consciously) through active imagination marks an invitation for transformation. In her essay "Zombie Apocalypse: A Symbol of Collective Transformation" (2013), Jenna Lilla writes, "Film and art may present an unconscious attempt to work through collective transformation at the limits of reason and sense. In zombie movies and the growing zombie apocalypse movement, we may be seeing an attempt to dream 'apocalyptic' change." Exploring the zombie apocalypse—including the recent cascade of zombie fiction, series, and films—as a healing motif provides clues as to exactly what in our collective shadow requires tending.

Vampires, as Brown identifies, may hide their bullying behavior in their nocturnal patterns. Their confidence and beauty can be seductive, mesmerizing, making them particularly effective at gaslighting (those are not your feelings/experiences) and having their bidding done without question. Like zombies but with greater finesse, "they may also encourage these bystanders to participate in the bullying, creating a mobbing effect" (9). This manipulation and targeting within groups/families further concentrates vampiric power, leaving others wrong-footed and insecure.

Vampires need others to live. Unable to generate or contain life force, they invest what energy they do have (once creative and now damaged) in seeking external sources of nourishment. (In this way zombies are also vampiric.) Table 3 tracks such necrotic patterns; see chapter 6 to resolve them side by side with nutritious, generative practices as antidotes.

Psychotherapist Christine Louis de Canonville works extensively with NAS and illuminates the dilemma of the narcissistic mother applying Karpman's drama triangle.[98] She writes:

> The narcissistic mother takes pleasure in creating a situation where the siblings have to compete for her attention by unfair means. . . . Due to the deep emotional scars that the mother creates, there may be little connection between the siblings as they grow up. None of the narcissistic mother's children realises that they are their mother's puppets where the roles may switch at any time. Without any awareness, they will each take their turn of becoming either the persecutory villain, the victim or the rescuer in the drama triangle as their mother dictates the outcome of the family dynamics convoluted dance.

This confusing and terrifyingly fluid sick behavior allows the mother to feed off her children (and often the entire family). As such it is effective vampiric and narcissistic disorientation.

With an evil queen/stepmother at large, no Bride is safe, nor can she regenerate. Surviving through exile/seeking shelter underground in the arms of the primordial chthonic Earth mother, she may be lost to the human world. Refocusing on recalibrating, the underground Bride regenerates, one day to rise again.

Rising relates to the alchemical process of *sublimatio* and centers around creating elevation and regaining one's air. Buoyancy—floating up—becomes possible when we fill our lungs with air (Logos, a drying-out of the emotionally flooded bog). In traditional Chinese medicine (TCM) untended grief can take up residence in the lungs. Sublimation is a process of attaining height (perspective) through integration. Through breathing we inspire—etymologically from the Latin *spirare*, to breathe truth into. Tending personal grief, breathing in the truth of our experiences sublimates our pain, bringing buoyancy.

The Bride regenerates not only herself but the complex wasteland; she cannot do so leaking down the aisle, attached by a sanguine IV to a (stoned) vampiric or zombie narcissistic mama with a front row seat. Instead, a successful wedding depends upon healthy self-containment and bridal vitality, necessary precursors to sovereignty. Like our four fairy-tale regeneratrices— Cinderella, Snow White, Sleeping Beauty, and Rapunzel—she must face and disinvite the undead from the nuptials.

---

98. See updates of Stephen Karpman's landmark article "Karpman Drama Triangle" (1968–2021).

Table 3. Shifting from necrosis to regeneration practices	
Necrotic, Vampiric (Theft) **Living off the Energy** **and Effort of Others**	**Regenerative Move** **(Self-Generating, Sharing)** **Vital/Life-Giving, Revitalizing**
Gentrifying/Co-opting/Colonizing Taking/moving into Craving/devouring beauty, value created by Others	Creativity! Making something with our own hands and imagination
Unconscious copying, theft, longing	Poetic mimesis: metaphor as mythic meaning making
Vampires, zombies. *The Walking Dead* writ large	Gardeners, travelers, wanderers and Wonderers
Colonizing mentality Ecocide: global morbidity Civilization over Nature Move to Mars The male gaze	Interdependence Tending the Earth and elements Identify as part of Nature The female mirror
Power over	Power from within, power with
Avoiding/Creating suffering, trauma and grief Weaponizing feelings: anger, shame, and fear Creates addiction Nostalgic inertia Maintains cycles: suffering, trauma, and grief	Tending suffering, trauma, and grief Feeling our feelings Unpacking addictions Tending mnemosyne Interrupts cycles: suffering, trauma, and grief
Othering/Shadow projection, cancel culture	Identifying, reclaiming, owning our projections
Political apathy, elitism, anti-intellectualism separation, feeling disconnected	Social justice and community building Connection, interdependence
External locus of control, avoid responsibility and feel powerless: Psychological and communal health Spiritual bypassing Spiritual materialism	Internal locus of control, take responsibility: Psychological and communal health Feeling our feelings Tending personal and collective trauma Embodied, somatic healing

Shadow trickster to avoid accountability Manipulation of feelings	Trickster actions with integrity Manipulation of oppression
Fragmented	Bricolage as re/membering
Incurious, willful ignorance, amnesiac	Open and curious stance, cultivating synchronicity Utilizing Logos + Utilizing Eros
	Jung's transcendent function
Willful ignorance, amnesiac	Bricolaged re/membering
Personal trauma Personal Intergenerational/Inherited/Collective	Somatic and other meditative practices: *Solvitur ambulando* See tree of contemplative practices
Phallacy of scarcity I'm not enough, not enough time or resources Fear-based decision making	Synchronicity as Antidote *Homo ludens*: deep play, relaxation, creativity Wayfinding, s/hero's quest

(DON'T) *SPARE* ME:
HOW A PRINCE, A BRIDE, AND A TRAUMA TEAM DECONSTRUCT A DAM

Searching for the lost Bride occurs when all is not well in the realm. From the complex wasteland, the prince ventures forth to find his own missing inner feminine—his relationality, deep feeling, and erotic principle. His personal search and rescue mission is also undertaken (often thanklessly) on behalf of the collective. When haters come out in droves, it is clear that an archetypal nerve has been activated—(traumatized) zombie unconsciousness is unable (and stubbornly unwilling) to feel.

When word came that the Duke and Duchess of Sussex, a.k.a. Prince Harry (Windsor) and Meghan Markle, would be resigning their posts as senior (active, public) members of the British royal family, the (British and global) realm was shocked. Keeping our eyes on the prince is crucial; his movement tending wounded masculinity and the negation of his own inner nurturing feminine is central to regeneration. When a prince is grieving, it is a very, very good sign. It also makes folks extremely uncomfortable.

The television series *The Me You Can't See*, copresented by Prince Harry and Oprah Winfrey, is a sweeping interdisciplinary response to trauma and grief, a survey of best global healing practices (2021). It begins with the hosts' experiences, later expanding into various expressions of mental dis/ease and diverse successful approaches and techniques. Harry recounts how finding his Bride, Meghan Markle, was a turning point of his life—a catalyst for his pivot toward healing. Through his words and archival footage, the series reveals how the journey of an earlier lost and repudiated Bride of the realm, Harry's mother, Princess Diana, has become unfinished business requiring tending. Diana's death and the royal family's frozen treatment of it encased a young prince behind a wall of inexpressible grief (because it was neither modeled nor safe to feel and express) and resultant trauma. From relentless hounding by the press to correlations made between Diana's partner Dodi Fayed and Meghan Markle for "not being white," the series unfolds the story of Harry's journey of maladaptive coping into adulthood and the positive effects of his time in the army (away from the family and their handlers). Harry discusses this combined group as "the firm," emphasizing the institutionalized power and extensive enforcement beyond members of the family themselves. Exposing this crisis, this fault line at the heart of English culture, reveals a logocentric phallacy of "keeping [a] calm [persona] and carrying on" (without feeling). This action simply reinforces dissociative, compartmentalizing defenses, and is itself retraumatizing.

Locating his Bride outside the compound wasteland, the prince finds a healthy counterpoint to established/corrupt patterns, an ally and reliable witness who can confirm unhealthy patterns and behavior through her own experiences. In both the TV series and in his autobiography *Spare* (ghost written by Pulitzer Prize–winner J. R. Moehringer), Harry details his growing awareness through his relationship with Markle; his princely movement as (awakening) Bridegroom, pivots around his growing awareness of the (unconscious) vampiric nature of "the firm," the colonizing effects of racism, and commitment to self-discovery. For Harry, coming to consciousness—while often messy, unpopular, and shadowy—is the trajectory worth investing in. Moreover, by physically re/moving his new family from the UK with his Bride, he relentlessly supports her and locates their partnership at the heart of their new, uncharted quest in unoccupied territory.

At the 2021 Diana Awards celebrating youth leadership while raising funds for COVID-19 vaccine equality and gender equity, Harry reiterated his commitment to healing. "Never be afraid to do what's right. Stand up for what you believe in. And trust the way you live by truth, and in service to others, people will see that, just like they did with my mum." By invoking and practicing his inherited legacy of truth telling, using privilege to become an ally, and standing up to bullying, this prince further deconstructs the false patriarchal dam that once defined his complex wasteland. In this way Harry's willingness to be vulnerable and feel not only enables a reclamation of his personal agency, drains the emotional bog to irrigate our logocentric desert. The prince has made a move—a healing, regenerative move.

CHAPTER 5

WATCHING THE DETECTIVES

REGENERATIVE INDIVIDUATION VIA TRICKY SLEUTHING

"What exactly does she [Miss Marple] do?"
"Solves things."
—AGATHA CHRISTIE'S MARPLE: "SLEEPING MURDER," 2006

INTRODUCTION: THE IMPACT OF TRICKY FEMALE DETECTIVES

Apparitions are appearances of something remarkable. Creative apparitions of feminine regeneration in literary and cinematic detective fiction have been developing exponentially and are worthy of our attention. Some fit overtly within the genre of detective fiction; others are transdisciplinary crossovers illuminating how tricky feminine detection attributes might be employed out in the world. Just as the bride needs discerning and penetrating detection skills to stay alive and then thrive, detection skills can expand out into healing communities and the world, regenerating the complex wastelands. This chapter closely examines regenerative qualities and skills developed via successful detection by contemporary literary and cinematic detectives, taking care to track and examine patterns across transdisciplinary contexts— including historical, psychosocial, economic, and gendered landscapes.

The simultaneous appearance of the detective and psychoanalyst as archetypes, as discussed by Susan Rowland in *The Sleuth and the Goddess*, indicates the interrelated significance of how both search for clues to buried mysteries of modernity, for "truth hidden from view" (*Sleuth* 4). Locating such simultaneous and synchronous eruptions—a phenomenon known in the sciences as multiple discoveries or simultaneous invention—within their historical frameworks can offer insight into patterns and meaning making; by paying attention to their interconnections, we can amplify their information and efficacy. Within post-Jungian studies, the appearance of such clues and agents is recognized as messengers from the collective unconscious when culture is ready and evolving. For these reasons, I suggest the modern archaeologist as a third, interconnected archetype simultaneously emerging through the modernist movement, unified with the other two by their joint quest: digging for hidden truths.[99]

Add to this mix archaeomythology—the dynamically inclusive and complex cross-referencing study of mythology, archaeology, history, linguistics, and folklore—meaning making that is complex, cocreative, and messy by design. Pioneered by archaeologist Marija Gimbutas, archaeomythology has had a significant impact on both detective fiction and psychoanalysis.[100] As a methodology, it offers unique insights and applications transdisciplinarily.

At the conflux of this trinity of detective fiction, psychoanalysis, and archaeomythology, we find the dynamic mind of Agatha Christie, whose writing career was deeply influenced by her own archaeological work in Syria and Iraq beside her second husband, archaeologist Max Mallowen. That Christie remains the bestselling novelist of all time—second in sales only to Shakespeare and the Bible—is a remarkable achievement, testament to the gravitas of her work. Central to Christie's storytelling are both emerging psychological understandings and (possibly unconscious) highly creative imaginal insights providing layered meaning making. Her canon has been remarkably influential across genres, in both structure and content.

All three fields birthed tremendous innovation during World War I and flourished in the interwar years. The birth of Jungian analytical psychology (prioritizing the unconscious) can be traced to Jung's break with Sigmund Freud (and his modality, psychoanalysis) in 1913. Agatha Christie began writing her first detective novel, *The Mysterious Affair at Styles*, in 1916; it

---

99. Archaeology in the modern era is distinguished from earlier forms by its use of excavations, due in part to tremendous scientific advances. Also central to accessing ancient treasures was global colonization by first European nations, then former territories, including the Americas and the Antipodes. For evidence of vampiric consumption of the exoticized Other, see Claire L. Lyons and John K. Papadopoulos, editors, *The Archaeology of Colonialism*, and Sharon Waxman's *Loot*.

100. For detailed analysis of the significance of Gimbutas's development and application of archaeomythology, see Joan Cichon's "Archaeomythology from Neolithic Malta to Modern Poland," and her comprehensive opus *Matriarchy in Bronze Age Crete*.

was published in 1920. Howard Carter's search for King Tutankhamun's tomb extended from 1915 to its unearthing in 1920—perhaps the most immediately impactful event of the three on the collective psyche as stories and images filled contemporary news reports.

These three interrelated disciplines—literary detective fiction, analytical psychology, and archaeology—can also be discussed as realms, imaginal and mythological places. Not only was the ground of all three realms inhabited by women, but it was perhaps women who were digging most effectively. Their turning over of the ground, searching for meaning, was often pioneering and creatively transdisciplinary as they worked the fertile borderlands between three unique and interconnected ways of questing—all *grounded* through myth.

Trailblazers within both psychoanalysis and analytical psychology included women from the very beginning. Early on, innovative women, including Sabina Spielrein, Tatiana Rosenthal, Melanie Klein, and later Emma Jung, Anna Freud, Toni Wolff, and Marie Louise von Franz, among others, were marking their fields in deep ways that are only now being fully re/excavated and valued for their maverick contributions, which had often been mistakenly attributed to Freud or Jung. Both men's body of work benefited greatly from contributions from these women—both offered and taken (vampirically, at high cost, in the case of the pathologized Spielrein, for example). Freud at least originally credited Spielrein; his subsequent editors did not.[101]

These (personal and collective) losses are meaningfully amplified by renowned feminist psychologist Phyllis Chesler in her review of Angela Sells's penetrating study *Sabina Spielrein: The Woman and the Myth*—a convincingly argued reclamation of Spielrein's astonishing legacy (2017). Rightly shocked at the injustices Spielrein suffered, including how the theft and erasure of "Spielrein's intellectual legacy by the psychoanalytic establishment may be an even more troubling, long-standing crime," Chesler asserts:

> I did not know how hard Spielrein fought against concepts such as penis envy back in 1912 and that she—not Jung, not Freud—was the one who first proposed the existence of mythic archetypes in the human unconscious and the existence of a death wish which, as she understood it, was about death and rebirth. Spielrein also began to chart the psychological relationship between mothers and daughters, the nature of female sexuality, and the origin of human speech.

---

101. See Catrine Clay's biography *Labyrinths: Emma Jung, Her Marriage to Carl, and the Early Years of Psychoanalysis*; Nan Savage Healy's *Toni Wolff & C. G. Jung*; *Four Eternal Women: Toni Wolff Revisited—A Study in Opposites* by Mary Dian Molton and Lucy Anne Sikes; and Elizabeth Clark-Stern's play *Out of the Shadows*.

Imagine if such work had never been disappeared. Imagine if Spielrein's brief stint as a patient had not been used forever after to denigrate her as a "crazy" woman who fell in love with her psychoanalyst and "forced" him to cure her via a dangerous method known as the "love cure." ("New Bio of Sabina Spielrein," *Tablet*, 2017)

That this legendary leader in the interdisciplinary field of feminist psychology recognizes the impact of Spielrein's lost and undervalued work—including her frantic fight against the skewed and skewing phallacy of "penis envy"—is akin to Virginia Woolf's evocation of the aching loss of Shakespeare's sister's missing oeuvre. The excavation of Spielrein's recognition of the potentialities of mythic archetypes alone is earth shattering.

There are other painful parallels here with Woolf; Spielrein was also likely to have been an incest survivor with no language or container within which to heal in the early twentieth century. Both women also suffered the loss of close family members—Woolf's mother and half-sister and Spielrein's sister—as young women.[102] That Spielrein went on to develop complex and groundbreaking theories on the mother–daughter relationship, female sexuality, child psychology, and regeneration are vitally significant and deserve our attention. That she was repeatedly silenced, denied safety and the ability to earn an income because of her gender and for being Jewish, and even blamed as a seductress and for her own death is horrific. Sells's detailed account of these documented atrocities makes women's history accessible, supporting a re/membering and reintegration—excavating vast amounts of buried work by women.

Consider how Jung's life's work centers around the rich mythic and archetypal content in our unconscious, yet never once does he publicly recognize the origin of these theories—and as Spielrein's dissertation chair he had direct access to her original ideas. Perhaps he buried them, unconsciously, as the truth might have been unbearable (for him, though not for us). The dis/(re)membering and dis/missal of this woman's body of work, functions as (unconscious) attempts at colonizing women's experience, work, and "dark continent" of female sexuality (as termed by Freud)—a hostile takeover of chthonic territory—resulting in the annexing of Spielrein's groundbreaking

---

102. See Woolf's journals, Louise A. DeSalvo's groundbreaking *Virginia Woolf*, and the layered and meticulously researched familial biography by Gillian Gill, *Virginia Woolf*. For insightful analysis of the impact of domestic situations, relationships, and supportive community on the writing ability of Woolf, Sayers, and three other women feminist scholars—classicist Jane Ellen Harrison, modernist poet H.D., and economic historian Eileen Powell—see *Square Haunting* by Francesca Wad.

theories as well as the neutralizing of her protests against incomplete (uncon-scious) theories. Vampires strike again.

GROUNDBREAKING EXCAVATIONS: QUEENS, PUZZLES, AND SOLVING

Conversely, the powerful quartet known as the Queens of Crime had an immediate and tremendous impact on mainstream culture as popular and affordable books, though they were initially dismissed by academicians as lowbrow and somewhat disposable. It would be nearly fifty years before Brits Agatha Christie, Dorothy L. Sayers, Margery Allingham, and New Zealander Ngaio Marsh would be recognized for the full literary genius they contrib-uted to detective fiction and culture generally. Of the four, Christie and Sayers offer intelligent and extraordinarily capable female detectives—Jane Marple and Harriet Vane—who creatively solve and dissolve confusion, fear, and injustice. Like Woolf, Christie and Sayers are particularly innovative in narrative form and depictions of nuanced female experience. Archetyp-ally the queen symbolizes full female empowered maturation, agency, and individuation—aptly applied to these women (particularly in the case of Christie) and their two primary female detectives.

By locating Golden Age detective fiction—with its experimentation, sym-bolism, and effective methodology—firmly within modernist literature, its well-earned status within the modernist art movement writ large becomes clear. Moreover, detective fiction is celebrated as pleasurable—interactive and fun—solvable puzzles, opportunities to play. As Johan Huizinga's landmark text *Homo Ludens: A Study of the Play-Element in Culture* explores, human-ity has a primal need and desire for play (1938). Furthermore, play is—at its heart—a creative, highly effective methodology. Games solve puzzles. Consider a highly trained Olympic volleyball team assessing and competing, moving the ball together, looking for spaces. Play is also deeply interrelated with relax-ation and meditative practices. When we relax and play we make connections, building on what we know, as in collage and bricolage. The sheer fun and joy of solving can be solitary (as in reading) or communal (as in a cinematic or locked-room murder mystery where a group competes and/or collaborates to solve a mystery). In this way, detective fiction evokes Eros as Psyche plays.

The popularity of female literary detective fiction and a fascination with its Golden Age roots are explored in Caroline Crampton's meticu-lously researched and scholarly podcast *Shedunnit*, an edgy, feminist inves-tigation of the classic roots and contemporary application of this genre-bending and complex body of work (shedunnitshow.com). Using creative transdisciplinary detection skills herself, Crampton delves into a range of underlying dynamics, including the critical topics of: grounding in historical and geographical location, deduction before modern technology, psychological love of the puzzle, intertextuality, the complexity of nostalgia, queer subtexts, and intersectionality.

Each episode builds on evocative examination of specific books, cases, and historical factors—from murders that affected culture and influenced writers to Japanese whodunits to the repeated postwar phenomenon of "surplus women"—while hosting academic and popular writers. This unique, playful podcast brings literary detective fiction out into the world in accessible, cross-cultural, jolly ways via a formidable thinker, further amplifying the tremendous collective impact the Queens of Crime, and specifically Christie, have had on global culture and the collective unconscious. *Shedunnit* takes care to show how the Queens of Golden Age detective fiction have created subversive, feminist modernist artforms that have remained vital for a century.

Crampton's sleuthing addresses Christie across many episodes and overtly in "Is Agatha Christie a Good Writer?," "Agatha Christie's England," "The Many Afterlives of Hercule Poirot," "The Christie Completists," "Death Sets Sail on the Nile," "Mary Westmacott," "The Dispenser," "The Lady Detective," and "The Detection Club." Crampton studies the function of the Detection Club (whose founding members included the Queens of Crime), which sought to shore up and legitimize detective fiction (as its popularity soared) through the codification of the genre's standards of literary excellence. In this way Crampton tends the legacy and cultural impact of Christie and the other Queens in accessible, playful ways. The group formed a playful, intellectual, and longstanding (the club is still in existence) comradery amongst mystery writers—*communitas*. Similarly, in her exploration of Jane Marple in "Surplus Women," via a conversation with scholar Corinna Nelson, Crampton notes how everyone underestimates Miss Marple:

> **CRAMPTON:** Confidences are shared with her that would never make their way to a male detective's ears.
> **NELSON:** She's pink cardigan on the outside, but she's got a mind like a steel trap and the men in the books around her actually respect her. The policemen defer to her.
> **CRAMPTON:** She finds the solution to the puzzle when nobody else does because she pays attention to tiny domestic details like the toppings of a trifle, or how a curtain was hung. Because she's so involved in the village life of St Mary Mead, there's not much about human nature that she doesn't know. (Crampton, "Surplus Women")

Grounded in the community and landscape (especially via the garden), Marple responds from her lived experience—a wise woman. Like the archaeologist, Jane Marple digs for clues—often in the garden (hers and that of whomever she is visiting—she is flexible). Using preconceptions about spinsters to her advantage, her keen presence is rarely detected by the uninitiated. Able to pass in anonymity, cloaked in the invisibility of feminine age and (undervalued) quotidian domestic patterns, she listens and pays attention undisturbed. By tending embodied clues—as Marple tends her garden, crafts her knitting, and offers hospitality via English tea ceremonies—she pays a uniquely mature and detached attention and compassionately proceeds (as in procedural) to map out cases, bricolage data, and develop perceptions. She solved the puzzle which had troubled the cozy, reducing it to a (complex) wasteland; through her detection the garden returns. Here the detective, like the psychoanalyst, is healer.

I have always been drawn to detective stories featuring female sleuths (and a few very exceptional male detectives). I grew up savoring detective fiction, first the Nancy Drew and Trixie Belden series, later graduating to Christie and Sayers; I loved racing the literary sleuth to the solution. During my doctoral research I returned to re/view the large repository of Christie films—first as relaxing play, then as serious study as I began to grasp their remarkable, unique worth.

I noticed that my need to read and watch noncoursework material grew in proportion to my deadlines. It seems especially poignant that my soul—and eventually, my writing—benefited from the intense psychic medicine of actively *solving* something. Furthermore, I needed to work beside another woman. (While male detectives Lord Peter Wimsey, Hercule Poirot, Sherlock Holmes, and even the spy James Bond also fascinate me, they serve different functions, often as benevolent double agents in shadowy animus territory.)

My own reading rituals have often centered on how sleuthing generates movement and provides satisfying, straightforward, and regenerative endings. Mysteries provided therapy my studies could not: each book or film was a complete package, as a crossword puzzle is. Whenever I felt overwhelmed and emotionally exhausted from attempting to digest magnitudes of as yet "unsolvable" and seemingly unending, ever-expanding volumes of disparate information, the detective stories were gifts of wholeness. Ah—something can be solved! Puzzles are inherently moving toward resolution. Moreover, the nuances and vitality of these well-crafted stories are set in fascinating, "cozy" places while also exemplifying pithy storytelling excellence. These women writers practice a refined craft—not only experts in the art of the novel, but practitioners of revelation, redemption, and healing. Furthermore, as investigations inevitably reveal every character's shadow and dirty laundry, these detecting women (like Austen) neatly sort characters into orderly and digestible categories such as: unindividuating/needs redemption, individuating/often does bad things, and too good to be true. These digestible cases were an antidote to my confusion. And, as I applied their tricky ways, the detectives became psychic coauthors in my practice of reading/(w)riting, grounding my work as I solved my own puzzles.

In this vein, the practical application of four sleuthing techniques germane to the solving and dis/solving required in individuation supports discovery. They are:

1. Discernment: decision making via discovery and weeding out disinformation
2. The Function of the Trickster: creative problem/puzzle solving and survival
3. Re/membering: from death by nostalgia to mnemosyne's revivifying case map
4. Bricolage as memory clues, patterns and case maps

These interconnected practices inform a meandering, spiralic revelation (rather than a linear inquiry), revisiting mythemes and archetypes as layered meaning making takes shape—echoing the journey of the sleuth, following clues where they lead, reworking landscapes, digging again and again.

Discernment: Searching for Clues with the Shakti Principle

According to Indian physicist and ecofeminist Vandana Shiva, we have in the feminine goddess archetype of Shakti an agent of life/Gaia/the Earth herself. Shakti, one half of a grand partnership within the Hindu pantheon, is the dynamic dancer brought to life by her partner Shiva's groundedness. In the myth, unswayable Shiva represents consciousness; ever dependable, he is Shakti's rock, enabling her dance. In this way his namesake, Vandana Shiva, acts as his agent and grounds theory into practice as she explores applying mythology to animate decision making—discernment, amplifying the creative potency of the feminine as healing agents.

In *Soil Not Oil: Environmental Justice in a Time of Climate Crisis*, Shiva writes, "Energy is Shakti—the primordial power of creation, the self-organizing, self-generative, self-renewing creative force of the universe in feminine form . . . Shakti is power" (136). Responding to a call to deconstruct the crumbling and barren patriarchal, logocentric, mechanistic worldview, she offers the Shakti Principle as a simple, effective tool for measuring the health of human activities, a way of determining if they place us in right relationship with the Earth and life widely. Citing biological, chemical, and ecological processes occurring in Nature, Shiva grounds her theory in the body of the Earth and in the elements, identifying bounty and rejuvenation as primary functions of life (135–37).

For example, using the tool to discern whether to invest in "food for cars or people" via building a proposed giant automotive manufacturing plant, Shiva examines the cost to community and land (questioning cries for ultimately unhealthy "jobs") and the ecological perversity of the supposed "prosperity" of eco-imperialism. The overwhelming environmental cost and devastation, the increase in pollution from both the plant and more cars on India's already severely overcrowded roads, acutely outweighs any marketed so-called benefits from the plant.

Used to measure the sustainability and health of a system, the Shakti Principle amplifies existing wounds in order to better tend them. As a trim tab, the Shakti Principle can be applied with a relatively small amount of energy to effectively create enormous change. Tending local food communities, eco-refugees, and the suicide crisis of India's farmers, *Soil Not Oil* has evolved into an eponymous global movement, anchored by an annual scholarly and activist-oriented international conference and a practical pledge.[103]

As a dynamic tool to determine the health of stories and actions, and as an act of applied mythology and embodied ecofeminist practice, the Shakti Principle exemplifies two key functions of regenerative consciousness: discernment as necessary counterintelligence agent and antidote to confusion, and the import of choice/agency in turning toward ever-renewing life. Consciously exploring the necrotic shadow appearing in our psyches and cultures, and against Nature provides a deeper understanding of motivating factors, bringing us to a more dynamic, vital choice.[104] Applying Shiva's theory to personal, collective, and environmental events provides clear opportunities for informed decision making, supporting discernment between necrotic/vampiric and regenerative behaviors.

Vandana Shiva invites us to step out of the phallacy of lack by remembering how life itself, as an expression of Shakti, is an infinite reservoir of power (136). Reductionism, which focuses only on parts, cannot see or understand the unexpected creativity of natural processes (142). As in crime fiction,

---

103. See the *Soil Not Oil Pledge* with MoveOn.org: https://sign.moveon.org/petitions/sign-the-soil-not-oil-1.

104. See Robert Wonser and David Boyns, "Between the Living and Undead."

phallacies—falsehoods that actively prop up patriarchy—are predicated upon red herrings, false narratives, and bribes.

Equipped with this potent regenerative tool, tricky detectives can effectively discern—make excellent choices while weeding out psychic and communal disinformation—and move forward to assess clues and creatively solve puzzles. Remarkably effective is partnering discernment with an open and curious stance, inviting intuitive and synchronistic dialogue with life, as addressed further in chapter 6. Sleuths, take note.

The Tricky Detective: Creative Problem/Puzzle Solving and Survival

In *Big Magic: Creative Living Beyond Fear*, Elizabeth Gilbert discusses how being in right relationship with our creativity might be predicated on our ability to embody the trickster archetype. Quoting visionary wordsmith Caroline Casey, "better a trickster than a martyr be," Gilbert focuses on differentiating between the two (220). Offering a primer on consciously choosing which of these diametrically opposing archetypes to embody, Gilbert writes:

Martyr energy is dark, solemn, macho, hierarchical, fundamentalist, austere, unforgiving and profoundly rigid. Trickster energy is light, sly, transgender, transgressive, animist, seditious, primal, and endlessly shape shifting. Martyr says: "I will sacrifice everything to win this unwinnable war, even if it means being crushed to death under a wheel of torment." Trickster says, "Ok, you enjoy that. As for me, I'll be over here in this corner running a successful little black market operation on the side of your unwinnable war." Martyr says, "Life is pain." Trickster says, "Life is interesting." (220)

By differentiating between the shadow archetype of the tormented artist as an icon to martyrdom and suffering, and the regenerative qualities inherent in acts of creativity, Gilbert shows how martyrdom is ultimately draining and necrotic, while the trickster archetype is inherently fluid and regenerative.

While the trickster archetype does—like all archetypes—have a shadow, appearing when fear arises as manipulative and untrustworthy, Gilbert's assessment of the positive potency of maintaining a tricky attitude is especially significant in terms of problem/puzzle solving. A martyr attitude leaves us in the complex wastelands, dying by either drowning or dehydration, no closer to solving anything. Tricky detection is integral to and inherent within the creative process. Gilbert illuminates how a trickster *survives* to heal herself and the complex wastelands by creative movement, making art as solving problems/puzzles. In this way, tricksters make excellent sleuths, their creative detection a boon for individuation, culture, and the land.

Re/membering: From Death by Nostalgia to Mnemosyne's Revivifying Case Map

Detectives infamously ask witnesses, "What do you remember?" Etymologically, the word descends from Old French and Latin for "calling to mind"— certainly a potentially individuating psychic act. What and how we re/member impacts our individuation. Re/membering locates and grounds (existing/ old/known/forgotten) information together in a meaningful way to build something anew, as Isis re/membered Osiris.

Mythologically, memory is personified by Mnemosyne, mother of the Greek muses, and can be renewing, loving, connective or selective, malleable, and unconscious—even treacherously misleading. Mnemosyne's shadow includes the often-necrotic lure of nostalgia, especially significant since both primary detectives examined in this chapter (Maisie Dobbs and Phryne Fisher) echo Golden Age feminist detective fiction. For example, fans longing for a past that never was might ostensibly be drawn to cozy detective fiction as "escapist," a way to inhabit a (supposedly better) past while fleeing the present. Considering the potency of reading as individuation, they might be surprised at the psychic and communal merits of reading feminist literary fiction. With this in mind, memory's shadowy relationship with sentimental or romanticized nostalgia might develop a complex—clusters of unconscious feelings and psychological processes acting on us.

Differentiating between memory lane and memory drain, Svetlana Boym's landmark study *The Future of Nostalgia* (2001) shows etymologically how nostalgia (*nostos*—return home, *algia*—longing) can be a longing for a home that no longer exists or never did (xiii). Relatedly, in "Female Valor Without Renown: Memory, Mourning, and Loss at the Center of Middle-Earth," Sarah Workman applies Bohm to discuss nostalgic pitfalls of memory's shadow, "a sentiment of loss and displacement, but . . . also a romance with one's fantasy" (83). Here Boym and Workman tandemly highlight nostalgia's illusory qualities and potential shadow side for misremembering—particularly in terms of longing for what we have grown out of or for perhaps what never was. We are also at risk of becoming locked within our fantasy or false memory (against which reality cannot possibly compete). Recognizing this type of nostalgia as grieving our inability to find or return to that mythological home, parental imperfections, or the dream never followed can be a tremendous healing tool. With awareness, we can, rather than weaponize unprocessed grief and trauma internally or externally, instead turn toward and feel our emotions and allow true memories to surface.

Boym brings a richly Russian-inflected perspective to her study of memory's malleability via both her experience in the former USSR and her expertise in Slavic comparative literature. She describes a contemporary Russian saying that acknowledges how "the past has become much more unpredictable than the future" and that "the alluring object of nostalgia is notoriously elusive" (Boym, xiv). Longing for a past that never was—a fantasy of a long-distance love affair, the lost relationship that almost was, or the romanticized dead parent—keeps us from being present. Failing to grieve loss can freeze us in perpetual longing for what is ultimately unattainable and unsatisfying. For Boym, the dream of repairing our longing is deeply tied to "finally belonging" (xiii). Perhaps connection and belonging is the antidote to nostalgia, Mnemosyne's necrotic sticky shadow.

Remaining stuck, stagnant in ineffective longing can be remedied by actively excavating our feelings and memory for meaning. Our nostalgia can offer clues to where we need healing. Rather than becoming locked in memories, longings, or fantasies, we can apply regenerative models to unlock what draws us toward the past, creatively infusing the present with information once the grief locked into nostalgic reminiscences is acknowledged and *felt*—tended. Unpacking the elements of this longing provides information and tools for applying Mnemosyne's regenerative potential. In the case of nostalgia, we can build Mnemosyne's case map as questing detectives discover clues and solve the problem of nostalgia. Mapping reveals patterns, constructing regenerative connective tissue.

Creative possibilities for mapping are endless.[105] For example, an advent calendar model might be an effective beginning; by first turning toward and labeling the top layer with what we are nostalgically drawn to, we can trust the underlying buried content to surface. Searching for and finding clues in our personal and collective histories makes meaning of past events and can be a deeply fulfilling healing modality.

As trauma specialist Gabor Maté emphasizes, it may not be the traumatic event that causes the most pain but the way we respond to it emotionally, including how we re/member events over time.[106] With this in mind, deconstructing and reconstructing traumatic crimes and crime scenes can be

---

105. For a compendium of creative mapping over time, see Katherine Harmon's *You Are Here*.
106. See the documentary *The Wisdom of Trauma* by Zaya and Maurizio Benazzo, and chapter 7.

healing acts by individuating detectives. Moreover, from seemingly unrelated fragments, meaningful, and dynamically patterned patchworks emerge and revive. In this way, the tricky tending of Mnemosyne becomes an embodied, creative bricolaged methodology.

Bricolage as Memory Clues, Patterns, and Case Maps

Anthropologist Claude Lévi-Strauss suggests bricolage, where something new is created from disparate parts, is the primal pattern operating in mythology. Quilting, mosaics, collage, and jazz are all examples of how fresh and exciting art emerges via acts of re/membering, re/clamation, and re/newal. These collected slivers come together across mediums and genres; in this way, bricolage has an inherent transdisciplinary potential to collect, sort, and tend shards of grief, trauma, and hope.

Crazy quilts are a marvelous example of bricolage's function as *aide-memoire*. Historically they have been composed of fabric to hand—outgrown clothes, prize ribbons from county fairs, fabric from special occasions, including baby clothes and wedding dresses, as well as practical scraps chosen for their insulative properties. Inherently ecofeminist and sustainable, bricolage relies on "used" objects, ideas, and/or memories. These sophisticated art forms depend upon fragments to upcycle. In this way bricolage functions as a core psychomythological tool when fragments of the personal and collective unconscious require tending/recycling.[107] It is also the primary function of writers, artists, and cultural animators utilizing creativity and art as healing agents to re/member.

In this way my intention with the methodological and material foundation of this material is as a crazy quilt: a collection of researched fabrics—chosen for their individual power—stitched together with sturdy theoretical threads, then embroidered over time with colored silks in complex patterns designed to bring cohesive relaxing transdisciplinary function to integrate beauty, warmth, and memory. Curiosity, research, and meaning making build necessary regenerative connective tissue. As meaning breaks through and shards are recombined anew, psyche heals.

To re/member is to reunite the broken pieces of our lives—splinters of memory and personal history—seemingly disconnected segments of joy and suffering. Within the mythological legacy of ancient Mediterranean partnership models, this was a primary healing modality of grieving Sister-Brides, popularized through the myths, including those of Isis and Osiris and

---

107. See April Heaslip, "Bricolage."

Ariadne and Dionysus. For example, after her beloved is dismembered, Isis not only reunites his scattered remains, she also re/members him through pilgrimage, grieving, and cleverness—actions that culminate in their sacred re/union and the resultant birth of Horus as the divine child. Sifting through the shard mound of our lives and our disintegrating structures is grief work. Tending a mound of shards through which she must sift, Isis becomes the archetypal Widow who depends upon the healing potential embodied in her necessary ally, time. Here the Bride/Widow embodies detection, grieving, and creativity by making art; she becomes a tricky *bricoleuse*.

Master tea ceremonialist Christy Bartlett discusses the value of *kintsugi*—a Japanese bricolage technique for golden joinery accenting, rather than hiding, fault lines. "Accidental fractures set in motion acts of repair that accept given circumstances and work within them to lead to an ultimately more profound appearance."[108] *Kintsugi* images have been viral on the internet for the past decade, attesting to the sustainability and resonance within the zeitgeist. Most significantly, these "accidental" fractures offer underworld descents into previously unknown, chthonic darkness—integral to our individuation—containing gifts as they release the life force necessary for resurgence.

What is required for this release? The curiosity to want to heal—a call for discovery. Enter the sleuth. Piecing together clues, she discovers evidence, fragmented memories and feelings. In this way, building a case map is a creative act of bricolage supporting groundbreaking insights, revealing patterns that alchemically dis/solve disinformation and solve (psychic and communal) mysteries.

FROM HARD-BOILED TO COZY VULNERABILITY: HEALING WRITERS, HEALING DETECTIVES

When authors prioritize their healing, their characters develop and their audiences benefit greatly; in short, when authors individuate, so can their detectives and their readers. As we shall see here in the case of mystery writer Jacqueline Winspear, recognizing and facing traumatized mothers (acting out as usurper queens as identified in chapter 4) is an invaluable regenerative step.

Across literary fiction and subsequent cinematic depictions, hard-boiled detective fiction used to be a severely gendered wasteland populated by male, alcoholic, and perpetually wounded protagonists—as in Raymond

---

108. Christy Bartlett, "A Tearoom View of Mended Ceramics."

Chandler's private investigator Philip Marlowe, Dashiell Hammett's Sam
Spade, and Mickey Spillane's violent Mike Hammer. These PIs bore the nickname "dicks"—a stunning precursor to the derogatory nature of the word to
come and a shadowy echo of the incomplete wounded masculine longing
for wholeness, as discussed in chapter 1.

Now this form of stuck and unindividuating (or minutely individuating
at maddingly slow rates, like the devastatingly wounded neonoir Aussie PI
Jack Irish) detective has expanded to include (overtly wounded) female
sleuths. Watching wounded, traumatized humans compulsively repeat poor
choices and perpetuate self-harm is a challenging cinematic draw, yet financial empires have been built around so-called high functioning hard-boiled
detectives such as DCI Endeavour Morse and Commander James Bond
(spy and assassin).[109]

The root of my frustration with this particular subgenre is that the hard-
boiled detective is bogged down, unindividuating; their wound is festering.
In "The Wasteland and the Grail Knight: Myth and Cultural Criticism in
Detective Fiction," Susan Rowland unmasks the hard-boiled (usually male)
detective as a wounded Fisher King (*Clues*). Emphasizing the importance
of identifying literary detection as grail quests that tend "urgent political,
social, and psychological questions," we can study how they arise from the
collective unconscious, infusing detective fiction with meaning ("Wasteland"
44). Considering fiction and the imaginal realm as landscapes of cultural
transformation, detectives perform vital renewing functions through their
investigations; they respond to and move archetypally through the complex
wastelands as s/heroes, healing agents.

Grounding her study in Riane Eisler's 1987 landmark book *The Chalice
and the Blade*, Rowland argues that sociopolitically "modernity has suffered
from a surfeit of the masculine hero. Without his discriminating blade-type
consciousness existing in a dialogue with feminine connectedness, the male
hero turns desperate and predatory" (46). This negation and loss of the
feminine leads to the breakdown of the realm into our complex wastelands.
In the mid-twentieth century, when hard-boiled behavior was glorified—out
of balance with incomplete, swinging, traumatized, vampiric dicks—unappreciated, underground/chthonic, and undercover female detectives became
antimatter, invisible yet vital.[110]

---

109. See chapter 6 on the regeneration of James Bond.

110. For a peek into the erotic, creative, and practical functions of the female physicist as
detective, see *The Mystery of the Missing Antimatter* by Helen R. Quinn and Yossi Nir.

Table 4. Individuation within hard-boiled and cozy detective fiction		
	Hard-Boiled	**Cozy**
Location	United States: Chandler, Hammett, Spillane	British: Originated with Christie and Sayers
Style	A tragedy, stuck as incomplete cautionary tale	Regenerative, expresses the full comedic cycle
Realm	Flooded emotional bog in detectives Urban, barren, disillusionment Rotting from the inside, stagnant and sluggish, bogged down by untended and festering wounds	Bringing balancing Logos to Eros Rural renewal promised after the Great War Solving the crime restores the health of small communities; the garden/Eden restored with the discovery/removal of the problem/ murderer/serpent (Rowland 15*).
Fertility	The wasteland is not neutral real estate; it poisons. Neither the hard-boiled detective nor the wasteland ever heals in this genre	Gardening motifs—tending seeds, plants, harvests, com- post—reinforce spiralic regen- erative cycles of life (over time)
Consciousness	Unconsciousness (trauma and grief) is necessary for the wasteland. Traumatized: the "tough guy" is defended and ineffectual, a cor- rupted response to perpetually living in the wasteland.	Knowledge informs consciousness The cozy reveals that each character is hiding something. Conventional, rule-abiding life is not what it seems or ideal/glorified.
* Source: Rowland, Susan A. "The Wasteland and the Grail Knight: Myth and Cultural Criticism in Detective Fiction." *Clues*, vol. 28, no. 2, 2010, pp. 44–54.		

Unprocessed trauma becomes weaponized, either internally lodged (in our bodies as dis/ease, an unexploded bomb) or externally projected (onto others via shame, fear, and violence). Lodged or projected, untended trau- matic wounds can be deadly. Instead, tending experiences and *feeling* emo- tions—again, such a simple phrase for such a tremendous choice—is the tricky call to action. I often hope that endless elementary school classes in spelling (a futile effort in English at least) be replaced by courses in recognizing and feeling emotions. What might our world become when children are taught such vital life skills?

Enter Miss Marple. The cozy form of detective fiction—initially dismissed as diminutive, conservative, realistic, or artificial—is, instead, a regenerative model for the healing of the complex wastelands as a post-Jungian, eco-feminist, and s/heroic potentiality. The vulnerability, strength, and vitality of Christie's Marple, Sayers's Harriet Vane, and subsequent female detectives from the Golden Age onward are central to their archetypal potency as regenerative s/heroic sleuths.

When curious, attentive, and brilliant Miss Marple knits, gardens, and takes tea with suspects and witnesses, she's labeled an old gossip (when she's noticed at all—another of her misunderstood skills: stealth). Gossip—rather than merely a morass of morbid fascination, shadowy projection, and the fetishization of neighbors, colleagues, and frenemies—is also potentially generative. Gossip has the ability to build the connective tissue of understanding and meaning making via the sharing of information, building of relationships, and discovery of clues. Modernity's men's clubs call it networking. Marple pays attention and is indeed building complex systems—networking clues as to motive, means, and opportunity. Most importantly, Marple is open and curious—an invaluable skill and necessary precursor to synchronicity, according to Jung.

In *Nemesis* (1971) Marple becomes a container, an alchemical vessel, for transformation—holding the tension of opposites in Jung's transcendent function. Greek goddess Nemesis was the rebalancer of the scales of justice. In this way, when evil is committed in an act of il/logic (unconscious) patriarchal fear projected by a patriarchal double agent (a nun in the effective 2009 adaptation in "Agatha Christie's Marple: Nemesis") onto an open and vulnerable young woman, Verity (truth), Marple brings the full erotic truth of the murder (of Psyche herself) to light, honoring the story of divine lovers healing together after war and suffering. Lodged anger and poverty (of soul) are released through the expression of grief. By weighing Logos and Eros jointly, Marple holds the tension of opposites, rebalancing the scales; grace appears as re/solution—an elegant, harmonic, and regenerative third.

Marple's vulnerability is earned through a long life of experience, accumulated wisdom, and individuation. She is present, a very reliable witness, not trapped by past traumas and griefs. Paired with her open and curious stance, these qualities offer a transparency never available to a hard-boiled detective. Hers is a grounding invitation to become *cozy*—snug, sheltered, down-home (to her-Self).

THE CONFUSING CASE OF MAISIE DOBBS

I was so relieved to read that Jacqueline Winspear, author of the Maisie Dobbs detective series, had PTSD. What an odd sentence to write—yet it is true. More accurately, I was relieved she identified this, because it was permeating her writing and, I suggest, impacting her readers. Here is how my relationship with Maisie Dobbs and Winspear has played out over time.

When I first met Maisie, I was enchanted. Here was a detective series featuring a savvy, pioneering female sleuth who was also a trained psychologist utilizing intuitive deduction, meditation, and collaboration to solve crimes. I wanted her to find—or be!—the grail and heal the complex wasteland. The series developed into *New York Times* bestselling books with ardently devoted fans. With pithy accuracy and depth, Winspear's historical mystery fiction sketches rich social textures and philosophical explorations. Each mystery wrestles with themes of social justice, including the consequences of war and economic, racial, and gender inequity. Winspear also examines the danger of othering—unconscious projection, especially of our shame and fears onto others—across class, race, and gendered borders within a deteriorating toxic colonial framework. National Public Radio's literary critic Maureen Corrigan called the original self-titled novel in the series "a class-conscious feminist fairy tale about a woman without advantages finding autonomy" ("Maisie Dobbs").

The series originates with Maisie in her thirties in 1929 and, through flashback, reveals her early, impoverished years as the daughter of a London costermonger. Following the death of her mother at thirteen, Maisie was removed from school and placed "in service"—as a house maid—with suffrage leader Lady Rowan Compton. A voracious autodidact, Maisie's hunger for learning leads her to clandestine nocturnal study in the Comptons' library, where she is eventually discovered. Rowan and her confidant and advisor, psychologist and physician Dr. Maurice Blanche—who becomes Maisie's mentor and a father figure—recognize Maisie's brilliance and decide to sponsor her education. Unorthodox for the times, Maurice introduces Maisie to the mystic Khan for additional tutoring in meditation, which develops into a lifelong practice grounding her professionally and personally.

Earning a coveted place at Cambridge's Girton College for women, Maisie has barely arrived when she chooses to interrupt her studies and clandestinely enlist—she is underage—as a field nurse in the Great War. She falls in love with a dynamic young doctor, Captain Simon Lynch, who wants to marry her. Significantly, one of Maisie's primary movements is toward individuation through partnership, toward becoming a Bride. Highly intuitive, Maisie can see no future with Simon and delays her response. At the Western front, Maisie barely survives the artillery shelling of the casualty clearing station where they work together; Simon suffers severe brain damage and lives the rest of his life in a disabled state, a silent shade. After physically recovering, Maisie returns to nursing, eventually completing her degree and going on to further study in forensics and psychology. She regularly visits Simon yet cannot actively grieve her losses; they both remain trapped by their wounds.

Meanwhile, Maisie's detecting skills and practices are somatic, embodied. With Maisie as "part clairvoyant, part intellectual, part new age therapist," the series offers what Corrigan calls "a primer on holistic health" "Maisie Dobbs"). As a psychologist-investigator, Maisie requests time to sit in the rooms of individuals recently murdered, to feel the space and use her various senses to attune to their stories. She physically touches people to better connect and comprehend who they are. She uses the embodied technique of physical mimicry, echoing how people move in the world to better understand and even feel their traumas, resultant fears, and complexes. On wallpaper scraps Maisie builds physical case maps. Citing Maurice as the originator of the case map, Maisie explains:

> It's such a simple thing, really. Putting down every thought, every consideration, on a large sheet of paper to better see threads of connection. But he always used thick wax crayons in many colors—he said color stirs the mind, that work on even the most difficult of cases becomes akin to playing. And because a case map is an act of creation, we bring the full breadth of our curiosity to the task. (*In This Grave Hour* 20)

This new and colorful bricolage technique for creative visual sleuthing—de rigueur in contemporary cinematic detection series and films—evokes both *homo ludens* (humans foundationally as players) and creativity as healing. Case mapping builds the connective tissue essential for regeneration.

Maisie has regenerative potential on several levels. She is a wounded healer, a complex archetype that impacts her decisions, healing modalities, and professional acumen. As a trauma survivor who tends her afflictions reluctantly, incompletely, and only after extreme incapacitation, Maisie remains haunted by her festering wounds, particularly: the loss of her mother and her childhood, the traumatic witnessing of WWI, Simon's horrific trauma and loss of vitality, and her own severe head injury and near death. For Corrigan, Maisie is repeatedly challenged to "confront her own still gaping psychological war wounds. . . . Maisie Dobbs takes too many risks to be flawless . . . [Her] intelligent eccentricity offers relief" ("Maisie Dobbs"). This appreciation of Winspear's creation addresses her best intentions. However, under the surface of these stories, Maisie remains bifurcated; her emotional intelligence is bogged down, while her belief in a masculinist creed of rugged individualism and martyrdom leaves her isolated.

Maisie is generally incapable of real intimacy. Chronically prematurely terminating conversations rather than developing intimacy, her manner keeps her isolated, in a liminality of her own making and remaking. Despite ongoing connections with best friend Priscilla Partridge, her loyal assistant veteran Billy Beale, and others, only Maurice—serving as both mentor and psychologist—can penetrate her false, malfunctioning protective shell; he alone successfully sees how she is (unconsciously) driven by her trauma and successfully intervenes.

Maisie's class identity becomes the subject of later books as she spatially weaves in and out of her old impoverished neighborhood of Lambeth, the academic world of Cambridge, political subterfuge at 10 Downing Street, and two sudden and unexpected inheritances of vast fortunes and several homes, including a chateau in France. She has difficulty feeling at peace with her sudden wealth and does not fit in easily with either her working-class background or her extremely affluent friends. In this way she remains an outsider, liminally occupying space as both an ethical nonconformist and a lonely misfit. Though Maisie goes on to attempt partnership with several men, she remains solitary and lonely through several books. In many ways she resides restlessly between the worlds of past and present, poor and rich.

Battle-weary, Maisie is repeatedly enthralled by her post-traumatic stress disorder. In *Pardonable Lies* she collapses while revisiting the French site where she was injured by shelling. She is found by Maurice, who anticipated her breakdown—her psychic cracks had been showing, and he understands the power of pilgrimage, even when undertaken unconsciously. No longer capable of running, she is forced to convalesce and begin facing her wounds and resultant shadow. Corrigan discusses Maisie's role in healing the wasteland/s while rereading the original novel ten years later: "Unlike the Golden Age detective fiction it mimics, Maisie Dobbs doesn't restore order to a devastated post-war world" ("10 Years Later"). Nor is she yet creating something anew; her wounds still fester.

While Maisie's character certainly develops throughout the series, I argue that her wounds, like the Fisher King's, remain her primary identity. Her own psychic realm—although at times opulent and full of potential (not unlike Gilbert's Theseus heroes, ever full of potential and charisma)—neither nourishes nor effectively contains her. It remains a complex wasteland, and

Maisie, at this point in the series, is in exile (*A Dangerous Place*, 2015). As a detective, she remains hard-boiled.

Maisie's life unfolds during a potent period in European history where known economic and social structures are crumbling; the resultant socio-economic uncertainty becomes an (unconscious, pervasive) collective preoccupation. Later novels in the series foreshadow World War II with a heavy hand that prioritizes war, though the interwar years of the 1920s and 1930s were also a time of dynamic creativity, often referred to as a golden era, when regeneration (after the collective shock of the Great War) flourished and was vibrantly experienced and prioritized, as in England via the Bloomsbury group and within Germany's Weimar Republic via the Bauhaus school. Tremendous creative output, from literature, the fine and lively arts, liberating fashion, and modernist architecture, was evidence of modernity's renewal and cultural refocusing.

Yet Maisie turns consistently away from her own creative regenerative potentialities. In *A Dangerous Place* she is compelled to repeat her morbid re/turning toward patriarchal structures, which promote and insist upon suffering and "sacrifice." Maisie's eventual partnership with James Compton, cultivated throughout four books and promised at the end of *Leaving Everything Most Loved*, is reduced to six scant pages of disembodied telegrams and letters briefly narrating the last year and a half. In short, the author has (in an oddly discordant, premature move) murdered both the Bridegroom and the divine child. Readers are cheated out of a wedding, a partnership, and a birth! No wardrobe, flowers, last-minute cold feet, or vows.

After so much psychic investment, we, in our reading ritual, require a ceremonial celebration. Instead, potent content is presented in brief, almost incoherent shards. Winspear chooses this distanced modality to recount not only Maisie's agreement to the marriage and the wedding but also a move to Canada, a pregnancy, and Bridegroom James's shocking death while test piloting, an event Maisie witnesses at eight months' pregnant, inducing her loss of their child. These huge events are told all in one airless breath. This arid epistolary account contrasts sharply with Dorothy L. Sayers's successful comic application of this technique, relaying the juicy details—from diverse points of view—of Harriet Vane's marriage to Lord Peter Wimsey in *Busman's Honeymoon: A Love Story with Detective Interruptions* (1937).[111]

With this rapid reversal of fortune, the (barely) regenerating garden decays again into the complex wasteland, and Maisie is plunged back into

---

111. Sayers's contrasting lively treatment of nuptial news and reversal of fortune exchanged via correspondence begins a landmark work of women's mystery fiction, fertilizing the literary landscape.

grief and suffering. The horrific, repetitive compounding of trauma upon grief seems unnecessarily cruel. At first Maisie returns to India, where she had been between earlier books and for which we have no reference as readers (again, no storyline for either restorative trip, no lush landscape, merely the feeling that she has left the page). She returns (suddenly, to us readers) hollowed out: absent, curt, smoking cigarettes to smother grief and any feelings she may have. Even the mystery is lackluster, taking place between worlds on Gibraltar—itself a liminal place—where she is hiding out, ill-equipped to complete her suspended s/heroic return.

At this point Winspear seems to have calcified the series into a subtle (and confusing) glorification of war. For king and country. For duty. For sacrifice. Maisie is to be commended because she survives, *because* she suffers—a confusing glorification of sacrifice, an example of confusion functioning as patriarchal double agent. There is not much narrative substance between the traumatic beginning and the equally tragic ending of this novel. Maisie's family and friends repeatedly call her home; she continually refuses them. Rather than returning to heal, she turns instead toward the civil war in Spain and chooses to stay on, nursing soldiers in a dangerous foreign landscape for a cause that is alien, famously bewildering and disjointed, piling sacrifice upon sacrifice.

We could argue that it is precisely here, when Maisie's beloved has died "sacrificially" (as a test pilot in service to Churchill's seemingly inevitable war) and she has lost everything, that she is most like Mary Magdalene. But her action, an act of glorified martyrdom, reveals her addiction to suffering. That she is portrayed as honorable, self-sacrificing—as if this were noble—is utterly perplexing. Magdalene herself did not re/turn toward war and suffering. Her legends and myths are primers in the devotional arts—grieving, contemplation, love, reading, writing, and teaching. Repeatedly her iconography pivots not only around a skull and an alabaster jar but also a book—perhaps an archetypal amplification of the potential of writing and reading as individuating.[112]

---

112. See various artistic depictions of Mary Magdalene, especially those by George de la Tour, Ambrosius Benson, Rogier van der Weyden, Mateo Cerezo, and the Flemish artist known as the "Master of the Legend of Mary Magdalene," some of which can be found in *Searching for Mary Magdalene* by Jane Lahr. Kathleen McGowan suggests the symbolism of the book in Magdalenian iconography represents both a historic gospel written by Magdalene and another written by Jesus himself, which McGowan refers to as "The Book of Love." Additionally, she claims a copy was made of "The Book of Love" by the apostle Philip, known as the "Libro Rosso," followed by a second group of European "Cathars"/heretics in Tuscany. Significantly, McGowan notes that the Gnostic Gospel of Philip carries similar teachings (*The Book of Love*, 2009).

The subsequent four books—*Journey to Munich* (2016), *In This Grave Hour* (2017), *To Die but Once* (2018), and *The American Agent* (2019)—echo the morbidity of Maisie's compulsion; even the titles reveal a bias toward war and martyrdom. Yes, the act of her nursing service in Spain has supported her grieving process (though we have not witnessed it on the page). Yes, another war is looming. Yes, a terrified England expects invasion at any time as it witnesses European countries fall one after the other as the cataclysmic Nazi war machine rolls across the continent. Yet when do we most need regeneration if not during such terrifying times? Maisie seems incapable of happiness or full relationships. That capacity seems plausible only at the very end of her series, whenever that may come; then perhaps she might be at peace. Instead, it is during our very challenging times when we must regenerate, at least a little—investing in our joy, creatively.

At the beginning of *Journey to Munich*, Maisie has returned to England only because Priscilla found and brought her back. Though owning several houses and extensive property, Maisie is again homeless—firmly outside Hestian home and hospitality, unwilling to inhabit the structures she does own and careless about creating a place for her own self-care. She has lost her center; her internal hearth fire has been extinguished. Discussing the impending war and another woman's seemingly irresponsible travel, Priscilla self-righteously recalls, "I did not run away from my responsibilities. Neither did you. We knew what we had to do when the war came, and we did it. And you lied about your age" (*Journey to Munich* 4). Reinvesting in narrative patterns of martyrdom keeps characters locked in concretized, shaming patterns. Maisie seems ever more entrenched in the complex wasteland—both swampy martyrdom and its ever-present twin, the desertifying prioritizing of reason over feeling. Her manner terse, Maisie remains simultaneously swamped by unprocessed grief and shame while aridly detached in an il/logical Logos for someone so gifted, insightful, and trained.

Traveling to 1938 Munich as a Secret Service agent to extract an inventor critical to England's war effort, Maisie works with the Otterburn family, whom she holds responsible for her husband's death, and begins to face her anger. Also investigating the Reich is an American agent, Mark Scott, with whom she develops a tentative relationship in *The American Agent*. Infiltrating Nazi spaces at great risk, Maisie encounters the Gestapo and, predictably, Hitler.

The London Blitz begins, and Maisie remains entangled with the Secret Service, though she repeatedly decides their tactics lie outside her code of ethics. Redemptive hope comes in the form of Anna, an evacuee whom Maisie eventually decides to adopt, though she remains emotionally detached for quite a (painfully) long time, afraid to love again. The actual act of adoption, which occurs at the end of *The American Agent*, begins to melt Maisie's (long-fortified) reserve.

The Maisie Dobbs series, as it stood in 2019, was more confusing, incomplete cautionary tale than the feminist masterwork lauded by Corrigan in her "Ten Years Later" retrospective. Martyrdom, as Gilbert warns, is a morbid, risky business. And while the difference might initially seem subtle, we run the risk of replicating this addiction unless it is brought to consciousness. Applying Vandana Shiva's Shakti Principle as discerning detection tool serves us well. Here it is crucial to re/member that life's impulse is always *toward* feeling our feelings, toward life—regenerative.

With Maisie's vast training and experience, she could be an astonishing s/hero. I wanted to love Maisie; I *had* loved her. And then I had to break up with her, awaiting her evolution. Should she come knocking, I'd invite her in for a chat; hospitality is a regenerative practice. Sadly, Maisie Dobbs remained lost in the complex wastelands, not yet passing the Shakti Principle test. Rather than recommend the companion book *What Would Maisie Do? Inspiration from the Pages of Maisie Dobbs* (2019), I could not give her my endorsement. That would take an additional two years and the release of Winspear's own memoir.

Jacqueline/Maisie/Reader and the Case of the Quantum Healing Leap

A quantum leap can refer to a sudden and significant advancement of great magnitude. Winspear published her memoir with the prescient title *This Time Next Year We'll Be Laughing* in March of 2020, before the beginning of our global COVID-19 pandemic. It wasn't until I'd read the subsequent Maisie Dobbs novel, *The Consequences of Fear* (2021), the following spring that I picked up the memoir; reading them together was a gift, as Winspear had experienced a quantum healing leap, remarkably evident in this newest installment of Maisie's adventures. As Winspear turns her significant detection skills on her own life, we are reminded that literary detection writers—beyond their dazzling detectives—are themselves the primal sleuths.

After paralyzing fear repeatedly gripped her while horseback riding, Winspear worked with an insightful sports psychologist who identified her as having secondary PTSD originating from her mother's graphic accounts of World War II, which had begun when she only three. By contextualizing her memoir within the revelation—and finally beginning to come to terms with what at least one reviewer had identified as her wartime hauntings—Winspear prioritizes healing. There are other layers of very terrorizing trauma that Winspear poignantly discusses—without (yet) owning their full effects on her—from a legacy of trauma on both sides of her English family surviving the horrific effects of back-to-back world wars, to the acute intermittent abusive behavior of her (also traumatized) mother, Joyce. While applauding Winspear for her action calling her wounds to consciousness, I was dismayed she missed the next enormous leap to claim her family's as yet unhealed transgenerational trauma from both world wars—suffering very much alive in her. Let's give her time.

Like so many people across Europe and their colonized territories, Winspear's family experienced two exponentially linked generations of war. Her father, Albert, and his father (a costermonger whom Maisie's father was patterned on) lived their entire lives with untended war wounds that translated to lifelong, transgenerational traumatic patterns in both men and their families. Winspear's mum, Joyce, also survived both a traumatized veteran for a father—an alcoholic who weaponized his pain against his family—and her mother who reportedly told her she'd tried killing her as a baby (citing too many babies in the pre–birth control era), but that she wouldn't die. This saturation of pain from the world wars and their familial wounds explains so much of Maisie Dobbs's actions, including her brisk dismissal of her own needs and unconscious traumatized turning and re/turning toward war and suffering. It came from Winspear's own untended trauma.

What I wasn't expecting was in the memoir was her frank and elegantly simple account of her mother's intermittent abuse. Winspear's depiction of a loving, dynamic, and creative mother gains depth as she weaves in Joyce's shadow to better understand how a marvelous woman can (also, sometimes) become a dangerous usurper queen. Perhaps it is exactly the intermittent nature of her behavior that is most terrible—especially when the trigger is a daughter herself, and walking on eggshells becomes de rigueur. Surviving a usurper queen mother is inherently traumatizing, resulting in PTSD.

Joyce was gregarious, had a sharp intellect, and what Winspear defines as a "killer wit," the weaponization of which was indeed deadly (*This Time Next Year* 138). Living in a gypsy bardo and tiny cottages, courageously embracing gypsies and Roma culture in the 1940s, the newly married Winspears had escaped crumbling London after the Blitz for a grounded, agriculturally based carefree life close to the land. Young Jackie was born into this free and lush world. Her later years marked sharp contrast and polarized bifurcation in her mother's temperament.

Many of Winspear's family stories felt very familiar to me, including a sense of feeling "as if I were caught in a time warp, because my cousins had such modern lives and mine seemed so old-fashioned" (*This Time Next*

Year 288). With my own Victorian grandmothers—one of them British/ Anglo-Indian—and older parents who'd migrated from exotic Manhattan careers, my family's stories seemed otherworldly compared with my peers'. Both of our families could get caught in nostalgia's shadow side, attempting to (unconsciously) romance memory in an attempt to put a shine on even the bad times. Her mum (like my father) could weave a fascinating story, not necessarily based on truth. Reflecting on early stages of her reaction to her mother's cruel behavior, including her thyroid disorder and its effect on her, Winspear writes: "Worry had started to become my comfortable place; the place I knew where to be. My mother worried a lot; there was always something to worry about. But she was also a creature of highs and lows, given to dancing around the kitchen with John on her hip, or making people laugh, or shaking with fizzy energy, or shouting in a temper" (*This Time Next Year* 114). By pinpointing the birth of her own coping skill of worrying—a necrotic behavior (unconsciously) mirroring her mother—Winspear can begin to unravel what became an addictive behavior.

Similarly shaming was a common "parenting" and "teaching" tool in mid-century Britain and other Western cultures. When the young Winspear was learning to read at home, her mum both threatened her with being labeled "the dunce," including making her stand in the corner wearing the proverbial cap, and continually described how bright she herself was, winning a scholarship that her bully father refused to allow her to accept. The family also had a culture of being acclimated to things going wrong. Even in her own memoir, Winspear might wrestle persistent shackles as she primly spells out her teenage cousin's swearing education as "F**k you." I cringed reading how her mother uttered that horrible line "If you don't stop crying, I'll give you something to cry for," hearing the echo from my own home and father (131).

Winspear's father was a keen individual and planted the seed of lifelong successful problem solving and creativity by encouraging her to "think different, love—always think different" (*This Time Next Year* 222). Amid the trauma are bright retellings of bricolaged family creativity—from crafting a home out of nothing to the extended family on a beach holiday transforming into a spontaneous, joyous band with found-object instruments.

Winspear admits to a sense of liminality at home in California, "miles away from my roots—*neither here nor there*" (*This Time Next Year* 138). Though Maisie owns several homes over time and multiple homes in later novels, she shares this dis/placement, never rooting or feeling fulfilled with only one hearth. Living outside of Hestian hospitality can be exhausting.

In discussing how her brother was not the target of her mother's anger and envy, Winspear identifies how her mum treated the siblings quite differently, perhaps because of a critical illness John had as a child. "It seemed there was nothing he could do wrong . . . without a doubt he avoided Mum's temper" (*This Time Next Year* 219–20). "I realized Mum saw me as some sort of competitor, that I was no longer just a daughter, but someone she didn't quite know how to deal with, living in the same house" (222). Jackie became a target because of her gender.

It is worth a detailed close reading of Winspear's story, especially in connection with chapter 4, as an embodied example of surviving a mother in the grip of the usurper/evil queen archetype. When her father's work colleague good-naturedly compliments a teenage Winspear's beauty, her mother swiftly intervenes:

> "She'll never be as good looking as her mother." I wanted the ground to eat me up and never spit me out again, I blushed even more. . . . Bill winked at me, "She's getting there, Joyce—she's getting there." . . . While my mother could be my greatest supporter, one who I know loved me very much, it was as if . . . I became an enemy, the daughter who had to be shown who was boss, or who had to be taken down a peg or two . . .
>
> There was sometimes little warning of an incoming verbal missile, or a lie told about me in company, or an opportunity to make a joke at my expense. I would sometimes hear her talking about me to her sisters. . . . "You'll never guess what *it* had the cheek to say to me the other day. . . . And there would be a made up story of something I was supposed to have said, or done—or more accurately, what *it* had done." (223–24)

> . . . My mother would often stand in front of the mirror when she was shouting at me, staring at her reflection as if she had been drawn in by the furrowed brow, the flared nostrils, a hallmark of her temper. This fascinated me, the urge to watch herself losing her temper. One day . . . I said aloud, "Mirror, mirror on the wall, who's the—" . . . I think it was not long afterward that I dropped the mirror and it broke into hundreds of pieces. An accident. Just slipped through my fingers. Really.
>
> Yet amid all those verbal attacks, I adored her. I thought she was the most wonderful woman—witty and intelligent and I knew she had a capacity for deep compassion. (225)

Taking the time and space to reflect on this very real detailed account of living with a wounded and usurping mother can help apply and understand theoretical underpinnings. This mother attempted to publicly shame her daughter, diminish her rank in the family, demean her by calling her "it," and was seemingly mesmerized by her own reflection (or was she screaming at herself?). My heart broke for Winspear's confusion as, when she becomes a teenager, on some level her mother sees her as competition, a threat. This intermittent behavior locked Jacqueline into a necrotic bond through which she could neither receive sustained nurturance nor free herself.

Winspear's story reminded me of my friend Katherine's account of her mother's response to her winning a prestigious local beauty contest at the age of eighteen. When Katherine turned her back to say goodnight to the beau who had escorted her home, her drunken mother—who had failed to protect her from a physically, emotionally, and sexually abusive father—stole her daughter's (earned and brand-new, shiny) crown and red velvet floor-length robe. Katherine was mystified over the missing regalia, and then there was her mother before her, asking didn't Katherine think she looked good? Posing for pictures in a false coronation, declaring herself the (false, usurper) queen, she was a pretender in every sense of the word. As discussed in chapter 4, the false usurper queen is dangerous, even murderous. What she most fears is the Bride/daughter attaining sovereignty, including the union of the Bride/princess and the Bridegroom/prince, since both events may expose and topple her, robbing her of the (vampirically, stolen) source of her vitality, her unwitting and vulnerable daughters.

Tricky Katherine survived ongoing abuse by both parents. It was through therapy (re/membering via bricolage) that Katherine used her detection skills to identify her confusion, sadness, and the effects of her mother's dangerous envy. She illuminated numerous episodes in her life, making meaning of her (and her family's) transgenerational trauma. Healing these wounds supported Katherine in shifting toward compassion for her mother, eventually supporting understanding as to why her mother had had to hide her own light and enabling Katherine to mentor young women in their own struggles to shine. Through her account, a trail of clues is evident; tricky, creative detection skills of discernment, survival, and re/membering via bricolage directly support such a quantum regenerative leap.

Returning to Winspear, she continues:

The torment escalated with my new nickname: Fat Arse. My family thought it was just hilarious when she called me Fat Arse the first time. John then started calling me Fat Arse, and Dad laughed—and the fact . . . crushed me. I thought he would be the last person to add to my humiliation. They all laughed a lot about me being Fat Arse, then when I became upset I was admonished for not being able to "take it." You had to be able to take it in our family, whatever the *it* was. (*This Time Next Year* 226)

My mother stopped calling me "Fat Arse" when I'd lost so much weight she didn't quite know what to do . . . and sent me to the doctor . . Mum had no idea that I wasn't eating much for two reasons. Not only did I want to put a stop to being called Fat Arse—and, in truth, I was never fat at all—but I also felt guilty about the fuss she'd made about the cost of school meals . . . I withdrew my name from the meals list . . . I don't think she noticed because she only noticed things that were on the school bill, not things that were missing. (227)

Gaslighting and shaming a healthy child into considering herself to be overweight, paired with collective familial bullying, can be devastating to a daughter. Vampiric mothering survives on the (stolen) lifeforce of children, robbing them of nutrition. Winspear's insight into how her mother noticed charges but not voids (of care, nurturance) goes a long way toward understanding the usurper queen/pathological narcissistic dysfunctional blindness. Additionally, her unwillingness to invest in her child's nourishment—paired with her addiction to worry—left her daughter exponentially impoverished. That young Jackie stopped taking school meals is especially troubling, an internalization that she wasn't worth the nourishment.

Winspear's specific account of her mum's patterns has hallmarks of how untreated trauma and grief can become classic usurper queen behavior, augmenting as her daughter matures into a teenager. Joyce attacks her daughter, undercutting her voice and agency. She has predictable "attention-seeking behaviors" when gathered with her daughter within groups.

Joyce's jealousy extended to Winspear's wealthy and attractive employer. While working as a nanny, her mum forbade an exciting trip abroad with the family to Antibes, forcing her daughter instead into a horrific summer job at the local egg packing factory. Joyce also viciously goes for the throat when she mocks her daughter's singing—a particularly heartbreaking passage, since young Jackie was so enjoying herself and this shared activity.

I'd probably always had trouble finding my voice with my mother—to be sure we had words, but there's a difference in finding your voice, expressing what you really want to say in a measured tone, and being "on the defensive" against an incoming verbal missile. The issue of voice was something I'd struggled with since childhood and I dreaded being on the receiving end of what might at first appear to be witty repartee on my mother's part, but was really a cutting comment . . . And there had been the devastating critique of my voice when I was about eight or nine. I had started singing along with my mother while we were both in the kitchen—she would often sing as she worked. I was peeling vegetables and Mum was standing near the stove. She stopped singing, turned to me and said, "Jack, can you sing solo?"

I nodded and smiled, pleased that she'd asked, and began to sing the song with all my heart, stopping only when she held up her hand and shook her head.

"No, Jack—I mean, can you sing *so low* that I can't hear you?"

She didn't smile or laugh, so it didn't sound like something said in jest.

I never sang again.

I mimed in music class and I mimed in school assembly, moving my lips so no one knew I wasn't singing. I left the choir at the Congregational Church because I was sure I had the most terrible voice. I still don't sing, and I don't know if I'm really dreadful or just moderately bad. (279–80)

I read this passage while preparing for a PET scan, just after a potential diagnosis of throat cancer. Her account is eerily close to my memory of my own mother mocking me as a tiny girl who loved to sing. "You couldn't carry a tune with a handle on it." Why anyone would say that to another human is baffling. Singing is a universal gift, regardless of how we might sound to others. The act of singing raises dopamine levels; moreover, communal singing, as amplified during our pandemic, can be a balm for the soul.[113]

Unlike Winspear, I sang my little heart out far away from my mother, joining every school chorus I could. When home isn't safe, thank goodness for school. Still, decades later when I would sometimes feel my mother's crime against her daughter's voice, I lost the melody; clearly there was more healing to come for me.

Gabor Maté discusses how "people are a lot more isolated than they used to be. Literally it causes inflammation in the body and suppresses the immune system" (*The Wisdom of Trauma*). Trauma is isolating and promotes dis/ease. Winspear's account tracks her early awareness of her mother's

---

113. See Sarah J. Wilson et al., "Finding Your Voice"; and Sarah Keating, *The World's Most Accessible Stress Reliever.*

maladaptive behavior, which presents as violent, obvious outbursts complete with plate throwing and shouting. Counterbalanced by her father's calm and capable demeanor, the small nuclear (explosive, isolated) family of four adjusts, gaining support from connective tissue with the extended family that has more information and experience of the intergenerational trauma the family has survived. Perspective can grant the long view, a tremendous resource for resilience.

Like my own parents, Winspear's failed to advocate for her in preparation for college. Creative decision making around their daughter's education was outside their experience. They blandly endorsed a "safe route" into teaching, determined by a secondary-school aptitude test, ignoring her desire to become a writer. Winspear eventually becomes "almost mute in class, afraid to speak, afraid that I was socially unacceptable" (*This Time Next Year* 244). Feeling disempowered, Winspear "just got on with" college, echoing the very British sentiment of "keep calm and carry on," a motto adhered to by Maisie Dobbs (*This Time Next Year* 267).

As an adult, Winspear took to leaving the room when her mother attacked, including while in hospital and in front of extended family. Finally, she reaches a turning point:

> On this day, years later, I knew I had to find my voice and speak from my heart. . . .
>
> I sat down and reached for her hand. "I can't do this anymore, Mum. I can't do this fighting. I can't take the nastiness, and I just cannot have any of it any more. I'm fed up with the highs and lows—it's gone on my whole life. I'm exhausted and I'm done with it."
>
> She said nothing, just stared at me. Then she nodded. She had heard my voice, and she hadn't told me to shut up. (*This Time Next Year* 279–80)

Leaving intolerable situations is the healing action of the Aletis/wanderer (Bower). It's also sound advice when dealing with pathological narcissists who seem capable of standing only short periods (perhaps five minutes) of love, which then begins to feel like poison to them (*pharmakon*) and they lash out.

Following her mother's death, Winspear gained insight into the complexity of their relationship, clarifying both her loving and abusive behavior patterns:

> While walking alone across the fields, once again seeking solace in nature, I asked . . . "Why did she hurt me so much?" The answer came to me in an instant, as if a dear friend were walking beside me

offering counsel. "Because she knew you would always love her, that
you would never falter." And she was right. I would always love her.
As those words settled in my heart, a comfort entered my aching soul.
(*This Time Next Year* 287)

Winspear realized it was safe for her *mother* to act out with her; however, it
was never safe for her mother's daughter. Often humans act out with those
closest to us; conscious adults can sometimes recognize this pattern swiftly
and tend the human in pain in front of them.

Like Katherine, Winspear heals by following clues to her mother's behavior and her own feelings. Discerning, surviving, and re/membering via bricolage, she moves from hard-boiled toward cozy vulnerability—stronger for
her commitment to healing her wounds. Winspear is clearly grateful for her
loving—albeit flawed and very human—parents as she identifies and cher-
ishes childhood privileges and freedoms that shaped her character. However,
by concluding her memoir with a blithe and dismissive it was all "icing on
the cake" comment, Winspear indicates she is still healing.

I want to tend compassionately this brave and newly vulnerable living
writer's memoir, certainly a commitment to her journey of understanding
her family's legacy in a deeper way. What could have been Death by Mother
becomes, instead, The Case of the Quantum Healing Leap. I do believe writers have a type of obligation to allow their characters to grow (as opposed to
stretching out their unconsciousness, sometimes in an attempt to sell more
books over time—a phallacy, as interesting, individuating characters sell
books and there is always more growth to become aware of). However, we
are all only individuating as fast as we become conscious.

By the transitive properties of individuating writing and reading rituals,
when writers grow, characters and narratives grow (developing mythological
healing potentialities). As writers grow, readers grow. Literary wastelands
regenerate, and the garden blooms again.

Detection requires evidence. Maisie's most recent novel, *The Consequences
of Fear* (2021), offers ample clues to Winspear's and Maisie's individuation.
Contemplating leaving her work—passing her business to Billy and living at
her estate of Chelstone full-time with her adopted daughter Anna—Maisie is
again working for the Secret Service, screening agents for dangerous deploy-
ment with the French Resistance. Her deepening relationship with Mark
Scott teeters uncertainly when he is abruptly called back to Washington.
Readers get bare sketches of Scott in this book, perhaps at least in part due
to his archetypal nature as a particularly stealth spy. Nonetheless, it's hard
to get acquainted with this newest beau.

The novel generally remains formal and questions the British attitude of "getting on with it" as an (unconscious) antipractice (i.e., no emotions, please). Culturally, emotional responses are generally categorized as whining and not allowed (*The Consequences of Fear* 132). Maisie breaks this mold often during this case, meditating on how "some . . . carried the weight of their wounding in anger" (124). Maisie notes the cost of fear as she realizes she is "feeling another weight—that of doubt settling inside her as it prepared to take up residence, ready to sap her energy, slow her mental reflexes and bring down her defenses against that most powerful of emotions: fear" (165). Most importantly, she recognizes her maladaptive patterns. "Hatred, revenge—they're just as bad as trying to protect yourself from more hurt—they can make you brittle inside. And if you're brittle, you break" (170). Juxtaposing a necrotic concretized posture with an ability to embody flexibility and fluidity—and the necessary presence required—provides Maisie with a lodestone throughout this unique installment in the series.

Maisie's emotions finally threaten to explode with the death of Elinor Jones, Pricilla's decades-long-beloved Welsh nanny who'd been training secretly. Grieving for this tremendous familial loss, she realized she had "never trusted the world to keep herself or those she loved safe. From the moment of her mother's death, she had known that terror could be around the next corner at any moment" (*The Consequences of Fear* 196). Maisie finally identifies her original trauma—the terminal illness and subsequent death of her mother. (Though she does not yet identify this, bundled into this original wound is perhaps the loss of her childhood, including the collapse of her father, who removed her from school and placed her into service). Deconstructing her resultant learned and corrupt response is key to Maisie's healing. Recalling her numerous losses, she fears fate fooling her into ease, only to be devastated again. Struggling to remember a time untouched by fear, Maisie begins to wrestle with the devastating cost her ongoing terror has taken. Elinor, so integral to the family, taught Priscilla—racked by the loss of all three of her brothers to WWI—how to mother. After Elinor's death, Maisie is able to be present for Priscilla and grief as never before.

Winspear's work tending her own trauma appears clearly in the novel. "Experience had taught Maisie that drawing back from the work of facing up to tragedy could cripple a person from within. She knew only too well that any reticence to look grief in the eye might cause emotions to atrophy, as if the heart had been drained of an ability to feel even the most searing pain" (*The Consequences of Fear* 201). This turn of Maisie's toward trauma is a marked difference from earlier maladaptive evasive techniques. Maisie's emerging openness and vulnerability are now at odds with masculinist, logocentric nationalist policy focused on surviving and winning the war (at seemingly any cost), personified in sometimes gruff Robbie MacFarlane, her longtime link with the intelligence service. When discussing how "Justice is hiding out in a shelter somewhere, wounded, her head in her hands, but not yet beaten down" (292), Maisie remythologizes the masculinist/detached depiction of this archetype, relating more now with feminine/relational vulnerability and, ultimately, resiliency.

Recognizing her detection as "akin to creating a patchwork quilt," Maisie practices bricolage (*The Consequences of Fear* 219). She identifies how our intuitive responses (in this case, of pathologists) can really be "rooted in their depth of knowledge" (140). Her informed insights and decisions can appear as lucky guesses to the uninitiated unaware of either her level of training or the attention and informed discernment she invests in searching for clues and solving mysteries (225). In this way Maisie creates connective tissue. Again, Maisie pays attention to synchronicities (a term coined by Jung in 1952, though Winspear uses it here in 1941) as coincidence—which her mentor Maurice called "a messenger sent by truth" (101). By identifying and utilizing *bricolage*, informed intuition, and synchronicity within the detective's tool kit, Maisie begins to regenerate—finally.

In her embodied investigation, Maisie connects young messenger Freddie Hackett's compulsion to physically run with psychological running. Identifying how a bomb's impact can cause heart arrhythmia she responds, "I suppose the sad truth is that war can cause a heart to break, both literally and figuratively" (317).

Maisie has extensively trained in biology, forensics, and psychology over time. Yet in this novel there is a marked deepening of her skills. An emerging somatic linking via heartbreaks—as she does with psychological running—locates Maisie's healing firmly with the body, grounding her as she has not been in earlier novels. This recentering for Maisie signals a re/turning to the heart of her own matter, informed by Winspear's re/turning to her own (maternally wounded) *mater*.

When Scott returns and decisively proposes to Maisie, it is decades-long best friend Priscilla who is stunned at her acceptance (which takes place—again—off the page, disembodied). Maisie recognizes breaking the "habit of a lifetime. But if there's one thing about wartime—and indeed love—that I've learned the hard way, Pris, it's that you don't dither when it comes to happiness . . . it's not only my happiness, but that of my beautiful daughter" (*The Consequences of Fear* 311). Though there are shades of doubt here as to whether she would have said yes for herself alone (a type of martyr mother move), Maisie, in choosing happiness, clearly makes *does* make a regenerative move.

Discussing the loss of her title upon her second marriage, Maisie affirms, "I rarely used it anyway. Just occasionally when I needed to cross a tricky threshold here and there" (*The Consequences of Fear* 331). Ever a trickster, though a mild-mannered one, Maisie easily discerns which information and attitudes to share to best dis/solve blockages, enabling movement across liminal spaces. Her detection skills pivot around this crucial discernment.

Ending with her wedding brings much needed relief and healing to the novel's various personal and collective complex wastelands of mid-war Britain in 1941. That the vicar asks the congregation "to forever love and support the bride and groom as they move forward into a life together" grounds and locates the bridal couple firmly within *communitas*, with the community as further connective tissue (*The Consequences of Fear* 332). I laughed out loud reading Winspear's choice of dance music: "At Last." Indeed.

That Winspear interrupts the nuptials with the bombing of Pearl Harbor is perhaps predictable given her track record, though I was saddened by this ongoing compulsion of turning toward war. Could they not have had a week—or even a day—to enjoy this long-awaited *coniunctio*? The much-anticipated entrance of the USA into the war, now guaranteed, does promise relief for Britain and the allies, who have been fighting since 1939; especially poignant is Winspear's overlay of Scott's formal entry into Maisie's realm. I have high hopes that Jackie Winspear and Maisie Dobbs continue *digging*, tending their personal wars, bringing to consciousness traumas and grief. Meanwhile, let us turn toward a woman detective from Down Under with her own unique path toward individuation.

SOMETHING ABOUT PHRYNE: TOWARD THE REGENERATIVE ALTAR

Dynamic, creative, and stylish, the Honorable Phryne Fisher is a female detective operating in the latter years of 1920s Melbourne. Unmarried, she is no maiden but a full-fledged sovereign, sexual queen. Named for a historical Greek *hetaera* (courtesan) of the fourth century BCE who was tried for impiety and considered a priestess of Aphrodite, Phryne embodies sensuality and ease.[114] While the book series by Australian mystery writer Kerry Greenwood has been popular in its own right, the televised/cinematic series, produced by Australian national public broadcaster the Australian Broadcasting Corporation (ABC), was viewed seasonally by approximately one million Australians per weekly episode and is accessible internationally

---

114. See Helen Morales, "Fantasising Phryne."

streaming via Netflix and AcornTV. Miss Fisher has certainly been trending. The series has been followed up with a multiple-film deal, the first of which was released in 2020.

Notably, there is dissonance between the original books and storyline developed for the TV series and subsequent film. The television series episodes do not follow print publication order, nor do they emphasize the same characteristics of the Phryne of the novels. For example, in the books Phryne smokes and never avenges the death of her murdered sister, who, in print, perished from diphtheria and starvation.

One significant fact from the original books has (so far) been omitted from the cinematic production. Phryne's drunken father confuses his Greek goddesses in his addictive (trauma and grief-avoidant) state, mistakenly naming her Phryne; she was originally to have been named Psyche. Miss Fisher, having survived the imperial patriarchal co-opting of Aphrodite, Psyche, and marriage, represents instead the regenerative lineage of Magdalene. Moreover, Phryne reclaims the *hetaera* archetype as sovereign—not primarily identifying in relation to a man or to his anima/inner feminine projection—but as a self-centered, fully sexual, individuating Bride.

Series author Greenwood comments, "Phryne is a hero, just like James Bond or the Saint, but with fewer product endorsements and a better class of lovers. I decided to try a female hero and made her as free as a male hero, to see what she would do" (*Phryne Fisher*). By intentionally setting out to write with an open and curious stance, Greenwood engages the ritual of writing, allowing unconscious material to permeate her books; in this way writing is in service to both individual psyche and the collective.

Aussie actress Essie Davis, who portrays Phryne, clarifies her character's attitude toward sexuality and relationships with men, responding to conservative critics in the US. "She's just a woman who knows what she wants, and it's *not marriage*" (Meares). Yet it most certainly is individuation and perhaps even, eventually, sacred partnership. The movement of the series' three seasons and subsequent film has consistently been toward sacred union, both internally and externally, through her sleuthing encounters with criminals, the resolution of her past, and her partner in detecting.

Season 1 begins with formerly impoverished Phryne Fisher as a traveling heiress related to the king of England who has recently inherited the title of Honorable, a class privilege trumping many age and gender restrictions. Phryne experiences deferential treatment because of her newly acquired wealth. While the original book series is collectively known as *Phryne Fisher Murder Mysteries* the TV series was curiously renamed *Miss Fisher's Murder Mysteries*. Though the title of "Miss" is generally used to describe young unmarried women as a less-than-powerful maidenly honorific, it actually might lend the thirty- or forty-something Phryne clout because of her wealth. As the Honorable Miss Fisher, she is not attached to or beholden to any man.

Returning to Australia from Europe to establish herself as a self-described "lady detective," sophisticated Phryne follows up on the incarceration of the man she believes murdered her younger sister, a horrific act for which Phryne blames herself. She is welcomed off the boat by Doctor Elizabeth "Mac" Macmillan, who serves as Phryne's gender-bending gal pal and police pathologist. Mac serves at Melbourne's women's hospital and supplies a scholarly, feminist, and grounding (she knows the terrain) approach, which Phryne supports both financially and emotionally.

Season 1 pivots around Phryne tending a childhood wound: the death of her sister Jane. The series opener, "Cocaine Blues," like many subsequent *Miss Fisher*'s episodes, introduces elements of women's history, enabling viewers to penetrate intersectional problems of colonialism, empire, and patriarchy. This particular episode addresses back-alley abortions and the vulnerability of female domestic staff to rape, pregnancy, and dismissal.

Having grown up in poverty, Phryne is committed to thoroughly enjoying her new prosperity and status as she demonstrates her commitment to empowering others. The show's luscious palette of domestic and personal textiles, decor, and food amplifies Phryne's embodiment of Eros—ease, love of beauty, and generosity. While passionate, vital, and dynamic, she is never rushed or inclined to be bullied. She remains, above all, centered in her-Self. Her gun (carried for protection) is golden and pearl-handled. She uses a diaphragm. She also gives generously, and her kindness reverberates throughout the lives of those she helps. Unlike Maisie, whose efforts at helping others seems to unfortunately (and awkwardly) create codependent backlash, Phryne gives gracefully without attachment to outcome.

As she creates her team, Phryne seems to know what each member needs to help them along their personal paths. Recognizing Dorothy "Dot" Williams's skills, Phryne supports her transformation from a suddenly unemployed, displaced, naive, and homeless lady's maid to Phryne's efficient personal companion and sleuth-in-training. Fiercely loyal even while fearful, Dot follows Miss Fisher faithfully, against the advice of her Catholic priest. With Phryne as her sisterly guide, Dot goes undercover—pretends to be pregnant, allows herself to be taken hostage by Latvians, works in a factory, even learns to drive a race car in a road rally, all in the service of solving mysteries with Phryne. Dorothy's deep trust in Phryne infuses her initiatory training with Phryne with regenerative potential, a healing version of sisterhood.

In a house filled with Phryne's own joyous, sensuous approach to embodied practices—including bathing, feasting, music, dancing, and sexuality—Mr. Butler acts as devoted Hestian priest. Protecting her hearth and coffers, he feeds and otherwise nurtures Phryne and her guests with sensual cuisine within a clean, glamorous, and welcoming home—all while effectively guarding her doors and thresholds. Such a strong container protects Phryne's freedom. Cec/Cecil and Bert are working-class, communist "red-ragger" taxi drivers in need of a vehicle, which Miss Fisher provides as she invites them openly into her world of adventure, heavily populated by corpses and crime.

Detective Inspector Jack Robinson returned from the Great War deeply traumatized. In season 1 Jack soon reveals he is separating from his wife, whom he eventually divorces. Robinson wears his wound palpably, complementing his highly effectual and capable role of "official" detective (as opposed to Phryne's initially amateur/outsider status). While not particularly "hard-boiled," Jack's detective begins as a type of (wounded) Fisher King, yet he is not stagnant; he is healing. During the period of his marital separation, he uncharacteristically overworks, drinks at the police station, and becomes snappy; his feelings risk cresting over the dam of his personal complex wasteland.

Jack consistently maneuvers toward Phryne. Initially confused and put off by Phryne's "modern," up-front, and persuasive manners—and the fact that she consistently appears at murder scenes, consciously and synchronistically—the pair move toward sacred partnership in unexpected and cocreative ways, personally and professionally. Both are scrupulously honest with each other; Jack waits until he is practically and emotionally available before advancing toward Phryne; Phryne awaits Jack's move, though she continues to see other men.

Jack's assistant, stable constable Hugh Collins, provides comic relief and the working-class conservatism typical of a young man who—unlike his supervisor—has never traveled far from home or even been exposed to much outside of his family and neighborhood. Mentored by the inspector in both police matters and affairs of the heart, Hugh as *puer* plods along toward his own, more modest individuation and union with young Dot's *puella* (her own young/eternal girl). Throughout the series, their relationship serves as foil to the bold, accelerated healing, and more radical connection, between Phryne and Detective Robinson. Perhaps this counterpoint allows some viewers to identify with Magdalenian regeneration at this couple's slower-paced, less radical growth. It is always Phryne's attitude that is the most progressive, experienced, open, and accepting of the four, with Jack earnestly catching up. Yet at key moments he provides a different, essential component for her to succeed. He is often the rock of Shiva allowing her Shakti self to dance. She is the risk taker, he her ground.

Each episode reveals another of Phryne's extensive talents. A renaissance woman, she expertly tangos, shoots, picks locks, cracks safes, fan dances, races cars, uses martial arts, founds the Adventuresses' Club, and speaks several languages, including Mandarin, Russian, French, and Spanish. An accomplished pilot who owns her own plane, Phryne's character reflects a mixture of the safety and economic privilege of her acquired class, augmented by her singular daring as a modern woman in the uncharted territory of the late 1920s.

While unflappable in the face of corpses, criminals, and murderers, Phryne is an active and complex member of Melbourne society, in the habit of adopting people in need, especially orphaned and abandoned girls and young women. Besides exposing how vulnerable young women are to sexual predators, Phryne's deconstruction of perceptions of the feminine in relation to power—at a time when there were few models for such a theory—is quite radical and innovative. By acknowledging this shadow and the need for attending it, the series repeatedly addresses the necessity for the integration of light and darkness. Phryne's stories provide a breadth of social analysis, making the show an effective transformative tool.

The series introduces a variety of sexual partners, whom Phryne treats respectfully while meeting them on her own terms. In her book *The Moon and the Virgin: Reflections on the Archetypal Feminine*, Nor Hall describes how a *hetaera* "generates great excitement, and fear as well" (152). Being internally guided as well as self-centered, she is uninterested in conventional mores (fear-based projections about erotic desire, women's sexuality, and power) that ultimately do not serve her or the community, and contribute to the perpetuation of the complex wastelands. "The wise *hetaera* takes the relationship between love and freedom into account. She is the woman who would rather struggle to keep her loves unbound by convention" (152). Love and connection define the *hetaera*'s archetypal trajectory, grounded in a healthy relationship with her evolving self. Above all else, she keeps her own counsel, trusting her inner wisdom. She must, as a central quality, be in right relationship with love and freedom. By embodying her wise *hetaera*, the Bride approaches partnership in right relationship with her body, psyche, and sexuality. As a result, her capacity for connection and nurturance benefits and is ultimately more authentic and effective.

Phryne promotes open, empowering dialogue about women's sexuality and agency. Addressing Dot's concern for her sister's life as a brothel hostess, Mr. Butler, who has previously described his religious identity as a nonbeliever, relates Dot's sister, Lola, to Magdalene. "Mary Magdalene was a fallen woman and Jesus had no trouble forgiving her" ("Murder Most Scandalous").

Here, Mr. Butler speaks to Dot in her own Catholic language, with the common early twentieth-century, pre–Vatican II conflation between Magdalene and the penitent sinner. As an antidote to this misconception, Phryne supports Dot in gaining a more mature perspective on sexuality. "There's no shame attached to indulging in the sensual pleasures of life. I'm just not that interested in getting paid for it. Women have supported themselves this way since before antiquity" ("Murder Most Scandalous"). Repeatedly, Phryne discusses sexuality frankly with Dot and others. In doing so, she models an open and curious stance, as well as a healthy, active sex life without the shadow of Christian shame.

While Jack works on his political correctness and responsiveness within the changing landscape of newly liberated women and their sexuality, Phryne patiently clarifies, "You're never wrong, Inspector, just a little behind the times" ("Death by Miss Adventure"). The series repeatedly points to the importance of sovereignty and the dignity inherent in it. Phryne teaches young women to take care of themselves, while flamboyantly modeling a woman whole unto her-Self. Autonomous and self-sufficient, Phryne invests in charitable institutions that educate women, fortify their lives, and bring pleasure. She emotionally supports all her gathered, consciously constructed kin, blood relations and otherwise, yet she also allows them space to develop their own skills, desires, and self-reliance.

Phryne is deeply committed to the larger sisterhood between all women, reminding Dot, "Sisters are a precious commodity" ("Murder Most Scandalous"). Here, Phryne clearly speaks of her own lost sister Jane. Simultaneously, her actions throughout the series support global sisterhood as an antidote to patriarchal scarcity, a phallacy that wedges fear between women, fostering the shadow behavior of mean-girl stepsisterhood and evil queens/stepmothers, bitterly battling each other for crumbs that will never nurture, never sustain.

Rosie, Jack's ex-wife, and Lola, Dot's sister, provide examples of women living half-lives under patriarchy through their choices and reactions to what life brings them. Rosie has no profession and moves from man to man for economic security; Lola has become a sex worker for economic independence, becoming estranged from her family because of it. Both (unconsciously) choose shady criminals (demon lovers) as partners and are astonished when the true identities of their men are revealed—uncomprehending of their own wounded and shadowy inner masculinity. Neither woman is sovereign. Rosie is out of synch; she has terrible timing and seems to tumble in when Jack and Phryne are close, unlike Phryne, who is alert and has excellent timing. Disembodied, regretful, lost, wanting to impress—Rosie is off balance. With no career or interests of her own, she has simply attached herself to her father's next protégé (Jack was his first), swiftly becoming engaged to her father's godson, Sidney Fletcher, an oily, slick man lacking Jack's substance and finesse. Lola also attaches herself to men for a living; her own almost-fiancé turns out to have been a murderer. Rosie's father, police commissioner George Sanderson, also acts as shadowy, manipulative patri-archal agent and bully ("Murder Most Scandalous" and "Unnatural Habits").

Melbourne's Magdalene Laundry is the stage for "Unnatural Habits," where lost and repudiated young women, abandoned by their families and society, are imprisoned, many for the "crimes" of being orphaned or victims of sexual assault. Identifying them as "the fallen and friendless girls who do our laundry," Catholic Dorothy amplifies the (lasting, haunting, misunder-stood) legacy of the Magdalenian archetype as outsider ("Unnatural Habits"). Phryne's response to the horrific and exploitative working conditions of the asylum and the militant evil-queen nuns is clear, crisp, and unwavering. The nuns, of course, are terrified of Phryne and refuse to readmit her once she starts asking questions; detecting gals are dangerous to the patriarchy, echo-ing the brilliance of both Christie and Jane Marple (in *Nemesis*, for example).

The episode reveals that the "forgotten" "girls" of the laundry are being abducted by human traffickers and that both (of Rose's shadowy men) Syd-ney and George are involved in an international human trafficking con-spiracy. Only Phryne will listen to these Magdalenian sisters, and it is she who reveals the extent of the patriarchal corruption at the heart of their struggle.[115] This essential step both is powerful and highlights her willing-ness to be vulnerable. Through tricky detection, discernment, and grounded presence, Phryne re/members the Magdalene sisters.

The series offers complex contributions to the genre of literary detective fiction. "King Memses' Curse," the final episode of season 1, places the Phryne Fisher mysteries in the auspicious lineage of feminist literary mystery begun with Agatha Christie—at the intersection with psychology, and archaeo-mythology. This combination provides necessary clues as Phryne digs to

---

115. Primarily originating as a British, then Irish, movement, Magdalene Asylums spread throughout Europe, North America, and Australia. For a close examination of the Catholic Church's legacy of abuse through the Magdalene laundries, see Rebecca Lea McCarthy, *Origins of the Magdalene Laundries*, and the feature films *The Magdalene Sisters*, including the documentary on which it was based, and *Philomena*. Documentaries include *Sex in a Cold Climate*, *Magdalene Laundries*, and "Demanding Justice for Women and Children Abused by Irish Nuns." For a scholarly analysis of a creative response to surviving a Magdalene laundry in Australia, and continued contemporary censorship by the Vatican, see Adele Chynoweth's potent "The Stain Is Indelible," 48–58.

solve the mystery of her lost sister, complete with the help of a statue of Isis. This episode also contains the first appearance of a case map (à la Maisie Dobbs and Maurice Blanche), built by Jack to effectively track the emerging psychological connective tissue of patterns and a complex psychological profile. Phryne's successful quest and resultant psycho/logical liberation from the legacy of grief and trauma originating from her sister's abduction and death is akin to Inanna's journey to her own sister's underworld, again placing Phryne in the fertile realm and lineage of sister-Brides Inanna, Isis, Ariadne, and Magdalene.

Having solved the season's overarching mystery, Phryne's self-centering psychic energy is liberated for sacred partnership. The season ends on a celebratory note with a strong bridal image; Phryne's birthday falls on the summer solstice, and her team circles round her, offering containment, as she dances, Shakti-like, center stage with present, attentive Jack watching from the side, holding grounding space for her. Surrounded by her unorthodox tribal family, with the healing masculine by her side, the scene amplifies their personal individuation and joy as well as their deep connection, foreshadowing potential partnership. The series uses period music to great effect, and as the song foreshadows, Phryne and Jack are building an internal, sacred partnership.

As detective, Phryne consistently requests information as she fosters trust building with her team/constructed kin. Repeatedly she uses her detecting skills interpersonally to discover information when those with whom she is developing or deepening a relationship remain mute. To Dot when they first meet: "I can't help you if you don't tell me the truth" ("Cocaine Blues"). Upon meeting young Jane (whom she later adopts): "How can I help you if you won't tell me?" ("Murder on the Ballarat Train"). To her father (a question many of us would have been wise to ask): "Why aren't you telling me anything?" ("Death Do Us Part"). Phryne's penetrating ability to ask the right questions compassionately enables her to clear the fog of confusion, to succeed in her quests, and ultimately to heal the complex wasteland.

Season 3 revolves around the grand mystery of Phryne's father, Lord Fisher—himself a seemingly limping Fisher King—forcing Phryne to again tend her past, including her father wound, an initiatory act for inner *coniunctio*, necessary for partnership. But it was from her father that Phryne first learned her trickster ways, and Lord Fisher, like Jack, proves to be a model of the healing masculine. Phryne's father, who turns out to have been a savvy trickster, rather than the corrupt shyster he seemed to be, actually protected the family financially and emotionally. As the good father, he supports Phryne on all levels, and she recognizes his own investment in her. They are in new territory, together.

The season—and most likely series—finale, "Death Do Us Part," also moves toward the bridal altar for Dot and Hugh. It is Phryne who accompanies Dot down the aisle in her wedding to Hugh Collins, a remarkable move into unconventional territory. Phryne's mentoring has continually grounded Dot, and their sisterhood as constructed kin is a healed version for both women (each of whom lost their family-of-origin sisters). This new healthy connective tissue supports the Bride in innovative and tricky ways, so apropos for the era and the genuine erotic (of Eros, nurturing) spirit with which Phryne infuses life.

The final scene has Phryne preparing to fly her father back to England, toward a healing reunion with her mother—yet more regenerative connective tissue that Phryne supports. As she starts up her biplane in a rural field, Jack arrives. They move toward each other, consciously. She plans to continue her journey, and he does not ask her to stay. Instead, Phryne invites him along, "Come after me, Jack Robinson" as she prepares for takeoff ("Death Do Us Part").

The subsequent film, *Miss Fisher and the Crypt of Tears* (2020), opens with Phryne's supposed death in Jerusalem and a devasted Jack arriving in Britain to bid her farewell. When Phryne's golden biplane crash-lands at her own funeral (echoing Samuel Clemens's quip that reports of his death were greatly exaggerated), the reunited pair spar as shocked and grieving Jack cannot fathom Phryne's effervescence as she asks if he's not glad to find her alive instead. They ultimately investigate a sensitive international case touching on women's accepted roles in public life versus patriarchal expectations of marriage. The film's culminating scene depicts the couple's long-awaited, sensually portrayed erotic consummation, finally.

Savvy Phryne Fisher successfully embodies regenerative qualities as archetypal Bride and moves consistently toward sacred partnership, both in her personal individuation (especially with her inner masculine) and in support of empowering relationship with the beloved. Her role as regal, quick witted, sensual, evocative, tricky detective serves her commitment to support sisterhood while fearlessly dethroning false usurper queens. Her regenerative qualities inspire, nurture, and heal both the adjacent masculine and feminine wastelands, ushering forth erotic joy.

While Phryne's expected in at least two further feature films, her (previously unknown) niece Peregrine has her own (two-season) series set in the 1960s, *Ms. Fisher's Modern Murder Mysteries*. Upon Phryne's sudden death, orphaned Peregrine inherits her fortune and detective-skill legacy. Centered around the Adventuresses' Club, young Peregrine's emerging detection is grounded in courageous feminist mentoring. Again paired with a traditional, reliable detective,

James Steed—himself mired down with a corrupt DCI, a former nemesis of Phryne's—carefree outsider Peregrine's trajectory is at first toward engagement, then apart for reevaluation. In this way the couple—like Phryne and Jack before them—individuate interdependently, building their sovereignty and relationship through shared detection. Meanwhile, Greenwood continues to pen innovative novels depicting Phryne's newest adventures, which might translate into future cinematic opportunities to dance with Phryne.

DÉNOUEMENT: WATCHING THE DETECTIVES, CULTURALLY

Trickster detectives discern, creatively re/member, and embrace their vulnerability as they individuate via solving and dis/solving personal and collective mysteries. The impact of the Queens of Golden Age literary detective fiction—particularly Christie—can be seen in both the Maisie Dobbs and Phryne Fisher series (including Peregrine Fisher's spinoff). This broad impact on the genre in the books is evident in early mavericks of historical detective fiction—from the mythopoetic Ariana Franklin and Elizabeth Peters (the pen name of Barbara Mertz, whose PhD in archaeology became her *grounds* for writing and detecting), to the prolific and eloquent Anne Perry (herself convicted of murder as a teen, turned individuating writing sleuth), and current innovative novelists, including Deanna Raybourn and Elly Griffiths (the pen name of Domenica de Rosa). Each has created individuating female detectives worthy of our attention.

Moreover, this living legacy continually revitalizes via the sleuthing required to uncover lost women's histories—here in tandem with psychology and archaeomythology. It can be detected in the recent publication of numerous books on female codebreakers and spies, several of which have become films.[116] Emerging cinematic depictions of the female detective—so radical when *Cagney & Lacey* burst on the scene in 1981, followed by *Murder, She Wrote* in 1984—now include (cozy) *Enola Holmes* and (not-so-hard-boiled) *Jessica Jones*. Each exudes qualities grounded in their feminist heritage.[117] Most recently representation and diversity have exploded in cinematic depictions of crime fiction, including a wealth of British crime shows with diverse and individuating female detective inspectors.

---

116. See especially Sonia Purnell, *A Woman of No Importance*; Liza Mundy, *Code Girls*; Ariel Lawhon, *Code Name Hélène*; Jason Fagone, *The Woman Who Smashed Codes*; and the film *A Call to Spy*, directed by Lydia Dean Pilcher.

117. For proof of Jessica Jones's individuation, see Samira Nadkarni's outstanding "I Was Never the Hero That You Wanted Me to Be."

Expanding our scope outward from Western cultures, it's remarkably significant that decolonizing feminist series are emerging globally. For example, in formerly occupied territories, new feminist literary mystery fiction provides striking opportunities to deconstruct outworn paradigms while creatively crafting diverse, tricky mythic motifs. Witnessing the emergence of these fierce young female detectives within formerly historical colonial landscapes is momentous evidence of the clever detecting Bride, regenerating her-Self and the realm.

Sujata Massey's treatment of the impact of the (invading, disempowered yet colonizing) "fishing fleet"—young British women sent by the thousands by their families to "find prosperous husbands" and higher fortunes than possible in England (a direct result of the opening of the Suez Canal in 1869, dramatically easing travel to India)—shows the effects of weaponizing internalized oppression. Massey's unique literary detective fiction—featuring detective Perveen Mistry—addresses the complexities of colonialism, diversity, and inclusivity in 1920s India from a Parsi perspective (*The Widows of Malabar Hill*, *The Satapur Moonstone*, *The Bombay Prince*, and *The Mistress of Bhatia House*).

Ecology professor Harini Nagendra's clever and resilient young sleuth and scholar Kaveri Murthy and her supportive physician husband Ramu have a welcome and significant partnership worthy of our attention (*The Bangalore Detectives Club* and *Murder Under a Red Moon: A 1920s Bangalore Mystery*). Both of these female detectives are lively, vulnerable, and outside conventional norms. Kaveri teaches other women to read, regardless of caste or religious identity—remarkably courageous and vulnerable for 1920s colonial India. Moreover, the novels have ecofeminist groundings, evident in discussions on food and the nutrition of women writ large.

When writers are themselves individuating, they discern and creatively re/member clues; in this way they detect, regeneratively. As they grow, their detectives individuate; as we read and watch these female detectives—rather than neutrally escaping, we grow—our psyches actively go sleuthing. Whenever we look for clues and dis/solve puzzles, we are healing, regenerating, becoming our own detective.

CHAPTER 6

THE RECESSIONAL

REGENERATIVE PRACTICES IN SUPPORT OF BRIDAL QUESTING

Beauty is intimately engaged with darkness,
with chaos, with destruction.
You need to walk into the darkness and hold it in your arms.
Broken places are my canvases.
—LILY YEH, *THE BAREFOOT ARTIST*

INTRODUCTION: THE RECESSIONAL

The recessional is the final liminal act of a wedding ceremony, marking transition from one threshold toward a new one. The leaving of the altar begins when the newly joined couple turn to face their community, newly joined, changed; it is no less significant a component for the internal sacred marriage. The movement from ritual space and the quasi-intimacy of the (yet often also performative) altar back out into the world toward loved ones/community can be a type of s/heroic return, the couple newly infused with an elixir to share. Or, as Bower suggests, the beginning of a new phase of the quest, differing from "returning," a going forth into uncharted (matrimonial) territory, the primal healing outcome for wanderers: the creation of a home of her own—a core theme for Brides—and mature partnership.

Meaningful rituals change us. When we feel supported, energized, we have more access to our agency, are capable of making informed decisions and elevating our practices. The Bride now steps into such a space, renewed. Most importantly, she brings her regenerative potentialities into her new home and practices.

Feminine regeneration is simultaneously personal, collective, and ecological. Individual movement toward the altar of psychological individuation and internal sacred marriage leads us collectively toward regenerating the feminine. The interrelated, regenerative feminine archetypal expressions discussed at length in the preceding chapters—including the Bride, the Aletis/wanderer, the queen, the detective, and the *bricoleuse*—combine to support her return.

The Aletis skillfully navigates unknown territory, recognizing signs, portents, and players, providing vital internal psychic positioning—making meaning of her movement. As a Hestian priestess, she is grounded (of the Earth) in the remarkable value of home, capable of leaving intolerable situations, a (seemingly) paradoxical and misunderstood skill. She is on the move, a seeker. This regenerating wanderer learns to find her geographic location (crucial whenever we are lost), track her movement across interior and exterior landscapes, and become her own psychic cartographer. Conscious partnership can occur after the development of such bridal agency.

Queenly moves include surrender in the face of envy, clearing away the fog of confusion, and battling wounded stepsisters and vampiric usurper queens. Via healthy containment, the individuating Bride differentiates and learns to conserve her energy and vitality. By bringing these acts to consciousness, the bridal crown of sovereignty is won, and coronation becomes part of the sacred marriage act.

Sleuthing skills are required to identify, animate, and untangle a problem—all while staying alive and safe. As the detecting Bride searches for clues and solves puzzles, dis/solving unconsciousness (both personal and collective), she functions as mysterious change agent. Investigation as a tool for psychic growth inherently requires and supports an open and curious stance, a wondering attitude.

Finally, as this chapter highlights, as *bricoleuse* the Bride needs perhaps her most revitalizing set of archetypal skills: her creativity. Collaging together vast arrays of kaleidoscopic insights—effectively switching between her diverse skills as required—her archetypal nature is fluid, responsive. As artist, she is present with her process and her-Self. A *bricoleuse* flourishes because of her open and curious stance, ever asking regenerative questions such as, "I wonder what wants to come forth?" and "What could be the significance of this?" and "How might I best tend this material and process?" Her mantra might be "Show me, please."

BRICOLAGE: THE INHERENT CREATIVE POTENTIAL OF HEALING

Everything breaks. Bricolage is the craft of creating beautiful and functional art by piecing together what is at hand, constructed from shattered fragments of what came before. In "How Art Can Heal Broken Places," community arts activist Lily Yeh discusses how daunting inner-city problems can appear. "But if a person wants to learn to be creative, to be innovative, go to the heart of the problem—go to the broken places" (51). Yeh addresses how our contemporary desire to "be creative" may fulfill a variety of needs—from expressing something of ourselves as in a legacy, to improving our world, and participating in the joy of creation itself, alone or with others. Yeh continues, "In this broken but open space, people can bring their seeds of creativity as offerings" (51). Here an open and curious stance, and offering from a place of not knowing what will come from such an offering, provides a type of psychic lubrication for the healing process.

Sometimes what is most comfortable must be deconstructed and reassembled into a new (as yet unknown) form. This is a function of feminine consciousness: faith in the primacy of the regenerative cycle of life.

Mosaics, paper collage, jazz, and crazy quilts are all bricolage examples of how regeneration is possible through this art of re/membering. This turning, and continuous returning toward wholeness through integration, is actively revitalizing, erotic—an expression of life's full comedic cycle. Inherently full of healing potential, creativity is a phenomenal tool when we are stuck. By consciously shifting (out of a calcified state) toward creative agency, we actively re/member our-Selves. Re/writing and re/collecting our myths and personal collage in these ways therefore become acts of vital imaginal necessity.

Regeneration is the counterpose to calcification, whether in individuals or cultures. Remaining lively, relevant, and effective requires dynamic growth and change. Joseph Campbell discusses Christianity in this context in *The Power of Myth*: "We have a tradition that comes from the first millennium B.C., somewhere else, and we are handling that. It has not turned over and assimilated the qualities of our culture and the new things that are possible, and the new vision of the universe. It must be kept alive. The only people that can keep it alive are artists of one kind or another" (106).

Here, Campbell identifies the danger of calcification that Christianity, or any belief system that has become overly reliant on Logos, faces. If it does not grow and change with the times—incorporating, for example, shifting ethical norms such as ecological preservation and cultural standards of social justice and equality relating to gender, race, class, and sexual orientation—it runs the risk of obsolescence and death. Campbell identifies the key role of the artist as cultural interpreter and animatrix, s/he who asks the right questions and offers a (creative) glimpse of what is possible. If the return of the feminine signals vital potential for renewal, it is the creatives who are pointing out how. By studying how these expressions utilize bricolage as a primary healing methodology, we can more effectively apply their curative powers.

Brené Brown is a social scientist known for her research on shame, vulnerability, and wholehearted living; Brown's timely research sparked a global conversation on these topics, igniting much-needed growth transdisciplinarily. In a guest appearance in May of 2014 on *Chase Jarvis LIVE*, a podcast specifically designed for visionary creatives, Brown outlines her understanding of the importance of creativity and why she would be focusing on it in future research: "[There is] no such thing as 'uncreative people,' only those who use their creativity and those who don't. And it's not without a penalty. Turns out, unused creativity is dangerous—not benign—and metastasizes. It turns into grief and judgment, rage and poison" (Jarvis).

Understanding humanity's inherent creativity and the cost of not using it is invaluable. A corrupted worldview limits creativity to a small portion of the population, usually linking it with accompanying shadows of addiction and suffering. Such false cautionary tales warn people away from creative expression, robbing humans of our birthright. Just as the s/hero who becomes stuck in the tragic worldview, promoting it as "truth," contributes to the complex wasteland, the artist (and here, along with Brown, I mean every single person) who denies her or his gifts runs the risk of poisoning both themselves and the world around them.

Significantly, Brown's warning illuminates the consequences of codependent management. Codependency, prioritizing an Other over Self in distorted acts of "caring" and/or approval seeking in order to feed unconscious wounds, is akin to an exhaustive tennis match where we attempt to play both sides of the net. Ultimately this is self-defeating; the attempt to function and care excessively results in the chilling score of love-all, zeros all around. Again, this is a type of covert narcissism disguised as altruism demanding our attention. Continuously tending and unraveling such unconscious motivations can be daunting work; creativity can be a remarkable erotic, feminine tool for movement from codependent (mis)management to regeneration.

In her 2015 book *Rising Strong*, Brown discusses the importance of creativity, citing Steve Jobs's belief that "creating was connecting the dots between the experiences we've had, to synthesize new things. . . . Creating is the act of paying attention to our experiences and connecting the dots so we can learn more about ourselves and the world around us" (42). Creativity is mindful meaning making. By reminding us that we all know how to connect dots, Brown breaks down barriers between creativity and the phallacy of the caricatured suffering and distant artist, reminding us that we all do this daily. Quoting poet and writer William Plomer, Brown names a fundamental and mysterious property of creativity as "the power to connect the seemingly unconnected," highlighting the importance of how "connecting the dots of our lives, especially the ones we'd rather erase or skip over, requires equal parts self-love and curiosity: *How do all of these experiences come together to make up who I am?*" (53). Brown examines how a creative act can require a leap in order to bring together components which at first appear unrelated and irrelevant, suggesting that our resistance might indicate that an application of creativity might be just the required healing agent. Brown indicates that maintaining an open and curious stance, partnered with self-love and self-care, enables a healthy internal environment—containment—for creative exploration. Moreover, this is about making something new out of a sum of parts—bricolage indeed.

Brown continues, "The irony is that we attempt to disown our difficult stories to appear more whole or more acceptable, but our wholeness—even our wholeheartedness—actually depends on the integration of all of our experiences, including the falls" (43). She identifies the risk of remaining detached from our stories and our pain. When our worlds and selves shatter, the risk of remaining dismembered is quite real. In this way, she describes the absolute necessity of integration. Re/memberment occurs through integration by taking the seemingly unrelatable shards, piece by piece, and putting them next to each other. Each shard is really a clue, a part of a newly emerging mosaicked larger figure.

Riting Myth: Individuating Bricolage as Personal Practice

Dennis Slattery's depth psychologically charged literary theory, riting, offers an effective and radical transdisciplinary, decolonizing approach to understanding and applying psychological functions of literary and cinematic texts. In *Riting Myth, Mythic Writing: Plotting Your Personal Story* (2012) Slattery brings home theoretical concepts of writing as healing modalities. Through the practical application of exercises, which he has taught extensively in both classrooms and retreats, Slattery advocates writing/riting as personal practice deeply embedded with mythological potentiality. He writes: "Riting one's personal myth is a conspiracy. In the act it conspires to free oneself from what has not been conscious while embracing it at the same time, but with a field now constructed to make those memories manageable, in the sense that they do not any longer have the devouring power they did when left alone to chew on us little by little, for good or ill" (42). Riting offers the reclamation of an opportunity to conspire—etymologically, to breath together with—remythologizing our story as we recalibrate our relationship with memory. Like Rowland's reading (w)rite discussed in chapter 3, Slattery's riting harnesses the impact of writing and reading as active imagination sessions—dialogues with soul/psyche.

Regarding the dismembered self, Slattery relates, "dismembering is a mode of not wanting to remember" (102). He continues with questions. "What desire, dream, project, travel, skill, art that you know to be a part of you, has been taken out of your backpack? Framed another way, what outcast parts of your own psyche, carried within your personal myth, can you re-collect and acknowledge?" (103). Supporting this essential turning toward our disowned parts and creativity is itself necessary glue and grout for re/memberment—vital steps within bricolage. By offering probing questions as w/riting prompts, Slattery jumpstarts the process of re/membering through creative w/riting. As an embodied and proactive practice, riting grounds theory, supporting individuation via the cultivation of creativity, key regenerative qualities.

Isaiah Zagar, *Bricoleur*

Over thirty years ago, in the swiftly gentrifying South Street neighborhood of Philadelphia, one man began mosaicking vacant lots near his art studio, expanding into the excavation of tunnels and building of entire grottos and walls created from tiled and sculptured folk art. When the absentee property owner opted to sell his lot for skyrocketing prices, the community stepped in and formed a nonprofit museum space to protect what has fed the neighborhood for over a generation. Philadelphia's Magic Gardens is more than a sculpture garden; it is a visionary art extravaganza surrounded in each direction by Isaiah Zagar's many public murals, over thirty spread over a twenty-one-block area.

During an evening talk at the gardens, when asked about his freeform style, Zagar described how a reciprocity exists between artist and objects/shards (19 Nov. 2015). For him, mosaicking one piece at a time—trusting the pieces he has at hand—without a structured plan, is wholly organic and natural. When a piece finds its natural place, it *itself* feels good and feeds that sense of rightness back to the artist, even if it's simply a conversation going on in the artist's head with her/himself. In this process the "subject remains unknown to the artist." When Zagar was asked by a guest, "How do you manage?" he replied, "I don't manage. My work has been called visual pollution—on the brink of chaos. I don't have control because I don't want control." Here, Zagar embodies the healthy psychological move from (inherently codependent) management toward regenerative creativity's necessity for an open and curious stance.

Trained artists, Zagar and his wife, Julia, served in the Peace Corps in Peru. After a psychic break resulting in suicidal feelings and hospitalization, when none of his drawing or painting could soothe his soul, he pivoted (unexpectedly) toward mosaics. Naming his previous work as derivative of the European artists he had studied and loved, including Chagall and Matisse, Zagar went on to find his own pioneering style, a meditative method grounded in his open and curious fascination with and appreciation for the creative process.

For Zagar, the act of remaining present to what we do with our hands, while staying open and curious, aids us in tending what is coming through. In this way, he uses shards to create wholeness anew. Confirming our necessary movement from management to creativity, Zagar's body of work offers a living, revitalizing legacy, an homage to the healing potential of bricolage for psyche and *communitas*.

I Now Pronounce You: *Broken (for You)*

Jennifer Baker, in her 2004 review of Stephanie Kallos's novel *Broken for You*, has this work of art all wrong, suggesting it contains "powerful metaphors for . . . the need for personal sacrifice." Rather, Kallos points to a wholly different path, away from the corrupt and incomplete model of sacrifice and instead toward regeneration and renewal. Sadly, Baker's insistence on the sacrificial/tragic trap leaves us out in the wastelands, missing what this literary masterwork has to offer: a roadmap toward full comedic recovery, utilizing bricolage as remythologizing healing methodology.

Kallos's narrative begins around 1997 as Margaret Hughes, who owns a rambling mansion full of antique ceramics, where she has lived alone for decades, discovers she has a star-shaped brain tumor. Her diagnosis initiates her into action, and she impulsively advertises for a housemate. Wanda Schultz answers the ad, and the two sit down together for tea; a cup breaks at this first meeting, foreshadowing the underlying necessity of breakage in order to attend our wounds (Kallos 18–20). "Let me do this," Wanda insists regarding the broken cup. "I'm good at fixing things" (20).

While Wanda becomes an unlikely yet authentic Magdalenian Bride, both women uniquely embody Magdalenian consciousness. It is precisely Margaret's shattered life and her prognosis of a terminal disease at the novel's outset that enable her to craft an innovatively bricolaged final chapter to her life, while relentlessly supporting Wanda in developing a healthy, feminist relationship between women—part sisterly, part motherly. Kallos effectively uses breakage motifs throughout the book to amplify the power of the various steps of bricolage. She knows regeneration requires shattering.

Margaret and the Incomplete O: Daughter Born Out of Containment

Margaret's life began with the false fairy tale promise of "happily ever after" in the castlelike home built by her father, Oscar, known as King O. Margaret's world was all roundness, a celebration with sweets, hugs, and distractions designed to supply comfort to a little girl engulfed in a patriarchally constructed hyperfemininity. "Plump bounty" was everywhere, supplied in earnest by King O and the housekeeper (Kallos 45). Only Margaret's mother, Cassandra, was unhappy. Absent from the (potentially sacred) marriage (as Wanda's mother also was), Cassandra embodied darkness, mystery, and illness, and was "bewildering" with her chronic ailments (46). Beautiful, young, and thin, she lived liminally on the fringe of life in the round castle, speaking little—and when she did she was incomprehensible—even draped in liminal diaphanous peignoirs. She lurked, a shadow figure; she "watched and listened," observing, but not an *actor*, not fully living (46).

As an only child, Margaret rummaged through a box of photos, evidence of Cassandra's earlier happiness, freedom, and friendships. Margaret then decided something terrible must have happened and that she, as her daughter, must be the cause of it (47). Margaret developed a grand codependent preoccupation for a child: what is wrong with Mother, and how can I fix it? A child's relationship with a collapsed mother, including what Jasmin Lee Cori describes in *The Emotionally Absent Mother* as original loss, can result in the development of a preoccupied attachment style, a way of coping with Mother, her behaviors, and the greater family dysfunction. Cori defines behaviors children creatively cultivate as survival techniques in response to the mother's emotional absence, a way of managing their distress and trauma.

"So it was that Margaret's mother became a great stimulant to her creative powers" (47). Margaret identifies as a father's daughter. Her mother becomes Other, reappearing in the present as ghostly symptoms, manifestations of her pain, "a noisy headache" (46). When a daughter grows up without the wholeness of the parental/familial container—the Vesica Piscis formed by a solid and healthy union of the parents—no inner mandorla holds her. She is not safely contained between her parents. When the mother is absent and girls misalign as only father's daughters, they try to become the Other complete O themselves, attempting to overlay their littleness on the absent and mysterious shadow where Mother should have been. She is not there. I can do it. I can fix this. I can fix them. I can fill this space. I am big enough.

I can fix and carry this whole family; perhaps it was my fault anyway? Such circling dramatic thoughts dominate her thinking.

Children need to grow up within the safe embrace of both parents, whether or not they remain in partnership, and regardless of their gender identity.[118] A parental Vesica Piscis offers the alchemical containment of sacred marriage. As two parents continually recommit to their own individuation, the intersecting circles maintain cohesion and the resultant elegant third—the mandorla, where the divine child might reside and grow—is steadily contained at the intersection of their union. This is not a static place, but one with dynamism and flexibility.

Instead, Margaret learns to please her father, entering into a codependent bargain for love. Over time it is revealed that Margaret's father's vast antique ceramic collection was stolen from people living in France between 1933 and 1945 and that they were all Jewish (246). In flashback, he describes porcelain, aligning it symbolically with purity, indirectly linking it with the Aryan way—the Nazi wasteland. "Good girl. Remember always, my love, how important it is to recognize purity. Recognize it, and prize it. Papa O will not always be here to tell you what is the pure and what is the copy, do you understand?" (49). Like "the purity ball fathers" discussed in chapter 3, he reinforces her dependence with a twisted view of value. Racism and misogyny go hand-in-hand in such a patriarchal, capitalist, colonial conquest mentality. But in the present we meet a wise and savvy Margaret ready to break these chains with the past. Regarding the porcelain, she notes, "Some people like that sort of thing" (30), whereas the wanderer/Aletis in her prefers the stronger, more resilient secondary/sedimentary clays (31).

The Second Coming: Wanda as Renewing Christa

In her paper "Mary Magdalene: Dark Madonna, Female Christ," Megan Rose Woolever defines the phenomenon of Magdalene's return in contemporary culture as the anticipated second coming of Christ foretold in Christian theology, with Magdalene embodying a radical new "Christa." For Woolever, the emerging Magdalene is an embodied goddess, co-redeemer, and model for "empowered female sexuality amplifying what it means to be a fully awakened woman." She also rebalances the Christos–Magdalene relationship. I suggest that Wanda embodies just such an appearance, her own second coming.

A young adult and abandoned child of a broken, alcoholic family, Wanda is a survivor who tried to fix the broken pieces of her life via unhealthy

---

118. Queering heteronormative definitions of family and parents helps to shatter corrupt, stagnating, and incomplete patriarchal interpretations of gender.

technique of codependent management. When placed in the care of her aunt, Wanda "abandoned her own childhood to take on the oversight and management of her cousins'—becoming, one might add, a godsend to her aunt Maureen" (Kallos 43). In trade for affection, Wanda successfully—and trickily—managed her eight adopted sibling-cousins when their parents were collapsed. "It didn't even matter that it wasn't a real hug; Wanda knew that she had purchased this show of affection in the most shameful way imaginable" (43). Thus, Wanda enters into her own codependent bargain with her adopted family and primarily Aunt Maureen, her mother figure. Wanda bribes and manipulates her cousins to survive in what is mostly an unhealthy style of codependent management. It is also a tricky, cultivated skill allowing her to survive—though not thrive—when the adults entrusted to nurture her fail.

Determined not to be abandoned again, this little girl gets tricky. Foreshadowing her adult transition to *bricoleuse*, her aunt Maureen finds her one morning "asleep on the kitchen floor, surrounded by plates and bowls which she had apparently been trying all night to repair" (44). Coping skills serve a very real need; they keep us alive in the complex wasteland until we grow strong enough to shed them.

This feat, which awarded Wanda temporary "love" as well as some power and insider status within her adopted family, becomes her trademark for dealing with difficult and childish actors. Professionally Wanda becomes an overfunctioning and meticulously dependable, self-sacrificing stage manager. Privately she develops a highly dysfunctional codependency with her now-former partner Peter—going so far as to suddenly and secretly sell all their possessions when he suggests he wants to travel, an act that culminates in Peter also abandoning her. Wanda relocates to Seattle because she has received a mysteriously blank postcard from the city. She is sure that Peter sent it. Imagining Peter as a *bricoleur*—"He *restored* things, *made* things" (36)—Wanda projects her own disowned inner masculine as well as her creativity onto him.

Recognizing "she would have to be tricky if she was going to find him," Wanda develops the persona of Detective Lorenzini in order to search clandestinely for Peter (35). Donning a wig, glamorous gear, and lipstick, and lowering her voice, Wanda considers, "What kind of character would be most unlike her? What kind of person would Peter least expect?" (35). Wanda tries to catch him by being not-herself, embodying an/Other. This intense rejection of her-Self sends her directly on the path of further destruction.

Although she is propelled forward compulsively, her creativity begins to emerge through her role or persona as Detective Lorenzini. Embodying a form of guerrilla street theater, Wanda ruthlessly and comically interviews record store clerks as to whether they have seen a man fitting Peter's description purchasing certain jazz music. Having developed a practice of positive, daily affirmations—an act that she finally recognizes as futile—Wanda eventually realizes the value in shattering. "Affirmations couldn't save her. Wanda had faced the fact that she would have to keep cracking up, little by little, like a windshield, until she found him. She just didn't seem to have a choice" (36).

Regeneration presupposes collapse. Once-useful but now obsolete ways of being and understanding disintegrate as new archetypal content blasts through, making necessary psychic space for regenerative techniques.

Wanda continues to believe that her deepest work is to find her lost love in a large city: "the enormity of the quest she'd undertaken began to sink in" (36). But the magnitude of the quest is instead about her own individuation. What Wanda does not yet realize is that the "he" she searches for is not Peter, who carries the surrogate energy of her abandoning father, Michael. But her father is unavailable, lost, having followed her mother out into the world when Wanda was a young girl. In searching for his own lost beloved, who—suffering from mental illness—abandoned them both, Michael condemns his daughter to repeat the pattern. Wanda's family-of- origin story explains the roots of her codependent management. That Wanda adopts the name of Detective Lorenzini, her mother's family name, is a creative act of reclamation.

Along with the intersecting threads of Margaret and Wanda, Kallos weaves a parallel story of Wanda's Irish poet father, Michael, whose decades-long desperate and battered search for his lost Bride mirrors Wanda's search for Peter. In Seattle he finds unexpected containment working in a bowling alley; Wanda's mother, Gina, was a superb bowler, and he has moved throughout the world from alley to alley seeking her. Like his daughter, he committed his vital energy to seeking out the places where his lost counterpart might linger, abandoning himself along with his young daughter.

Gina was an artist, painting and repainting herself in a practice akin to that of Frida Kahlo. When Michael initially sees her paintings, Kallos offers the first connection with Magdalene. "He stood before the painting of her dressed as a nun, the funereal folds of cloth so realistic he could almost smell the sour sweat and suffocating steam of a magdalen laundry" (188). As in the Phryne Fisher stories, contemporary encounters with Magdalene often begin in the haunting realm of these laundry asylums, representing horrid examples of the flooded, sour, and suffocating feminine wasteland where women were misunderstood, systematically abused, and then left to rot or drown, forgotten.

Michael unconsciously reaches toward healing and his daughter. The movement of father toward daughter pairs with Wanda's movement toward

her coworker, Troy, and offers a healed version of the lost beloved. It was
Michael who sent the mysterious postcard from Seattle. He then unknow-
ingly witnesses Wanda's dismembering car accident. Finally, at the end of
the novel, Michael arrives to receive the single object in the vast collection
of Nazi plunder, on behalf of Irma Kosminsky, Mrs. K, his friend at the
bowling alley who has recently died, having left her final piece of treasure
to Michael in her will. Mrs. K is the one who takes care of the broken ones:
her dying husband, her three-legged black cat, and Michael—who now
calls himself M.J.

Irma survived the Holocaust but lost her first husband. Her young daughter died in a transit camp after they were forced to leave their Parisian home.
She has one surviving teacup that holds the memory of her daughter. Irma
teaches Michael/M.J. the meaning of *mitzvah*—a good deed, a religious
duty—and of *Tikkun Olam*: "Repair the world. Fix what you can" (273).

Meanwhile, Troy becomes devoted to Wanda in a grounded, spacious,
hands-off style, allowing her time and freedom to heal her body and psyche.
Wanda does not realize the depth of his presence and offerings. "She couldn't
help herself: she loved to watch him leave" (110). All men leave her. She tries
repeatedly to sabotage their budding relationship, to shake him through
cruelty, neglect, and rage. Discussing the arc of preparing for a stage production, she says, "Everything always falls apart before it comes back together"
(102). Despite her imperfections—or perhaps because of them—Wanda has
always been a *bricoleuse*.

On Easter—precisely the day Magdalene finds a risen Jesus and believes
him to be the gardener—Wanda suffers a catastrophic accident. Easter is
the time of encountering the resurrected beloved; Wanda's further breakage accelerates her regeneration. She is struck by a car when distracted by a
passing ponytailed man who reminds her of Peter; it is in truth her father,
whom she does not recognize. Michael, in turn, witnesses the accident but
also does not recognize his daughter. After Wanda's broken body is taken
away by ambulance, Michael—who had been comforting the driver and her
son—notices something remaining in the street:

> It was the girl's shoe, a foolish high-heeled thing, the kind of shoe a
> woman wears when she has no faith in her own beauty. M.J. won-
> dered again about the girl, what her reasons were for wearing that
> kind of fancy getup, in this neighborhood, on this night. Her sweet-
> heart cradled the shoe carefully in his two hands, as if it were a relic
> made of finest glass. And then he started to weep. (217)

Troy picks up this Cinderella's shoe, embodying the masculine longing for the lost, repudiated, and now-dismembered feminine. Michael considers standing in for Troy's dad but instead leaves, believing that "he should never have come out in the first place" (217). This scene holds the compound fractures that occur in transgenerational trauma. The wounded father dooms his daughter to roam in risky landscapes, searching for the abandoning Other who can be neither found nor redeemed. Indeed, that is not her job. Michael doubts his own ability to "father" Troy and leaves it to an older policeman, whom he assumes to be better qualified (217). That Troy cries publicly and later stays with Wanda—moving into the eclectic collective forming at the castle/mansion, building wheelchair-accessible facilities for her while tolerating the intensity of her emotions during her healing process—is a testament to the healing masculine and his own inner feminine. He is worthy of the archetypal Bride.

It is only through her complete collapse that Wanda is able to begin making something of her own that is new, creative, and soulful. When Wanda builds her first bricolaged piece, it is constructed out of trash. It is Peter's face, which she then throws away (36). Management gradually transforms into creativity, and Wanda's detective skills are liberated for a higher calling. The mosaics she creates, which first require the shattering of the old forms—as Nazi plunder, stolen, corrupted "treasure"—become, instead, learning opportunities and mythological symbols.

For weeks after the accident, Wanda sleeps and dreams as her body is tended in the hospital. Her dreams offer her leading roles, yet she rejects them, claiming, "But I'm not meant to be an actor!" (222). Here, Kallos describes the venues and productions as grand and, for the second time, alludes to Magdalene, this time within the context of "whole communities gathering to see the crucifixion of Christ, the resurrection. Where hundreds of townsfolk acted out the story of the Passion Play" (224). Here, Kallos utilizes not only the regenerative Magdalenian cycle but also the power of collaborative communal cocreation. Wanda regains consciousness after various procedures to immobilize her fractures; her jaw has been wired shut. She cannot speak and remains deeply depressed for a long time. Like Osiris, she must silently steep in her own juices.

From Management to Creativity: Margaret and Wanda Break Through

Relating to Bower's Aletis model, the novel begins with Wanda arriving at her new home, which provides a rich, newly bricolaged community. Within the container of this new structure, Wanda can allow herself to break down. "The enormity of Margaret's kindness engulfed her, not as a comfort, but as a shroud" (Kallos 229). With Margaret and Troy and the rest of their community, she feels safe enough to bring her shadow to consciousness. It is regeneration Margaret offers via hearth, home, and unconditional love. This Hestian movement enables and supports Wanda's healing and individuation.

Simultaneously, Margaret liberates herself from her own imprisonment within her parents' house. The literal smashing of her father's lingering profiteering shadow, the release of her mother's collapsed ghostly hold on her, together free her energy. After Wanda moves in, the ghost of Margaret's mother questions her about her new housemate:

> *What is it she does, exactly?*
> *She sits in a little booth,* Margaret replied, vaguely, *and . . . manages things.*
> *That's hardly impressive.*
> *She's very important, Mother. They couldn't do without her.*
> *That may well be, missy—and you needn't get so huffy about it with me!—but you can't convince me that she's doing anything creative. She's not an artist!* (120)

This internal dialogue illustrates the contrast between codependent management and creativity. Margaret has not allowed herself a creative life either. (Neither did her mother.) Rather than taking longed-for trips to Paris, she remains imprisoned in her father's house (as her mother had been trapped), fantasizing. Her creativity, her very life force, was subverted into managing his collection, meticulously dusting and shamefully, silently maintaining his stolen objects. Her midlife was lost in a confusing fog of immobilizing grief after the tragic death of her young son Daniel in a car crash and the subsequent abandonment of her alcoholic husband, whom she allowed—as a collapsed mother—to drive the car while intoxicated.

Meanwhile, Margaret has met retiring valet Gus at the French-themed hotel, a limited landscape of the extent of Margaret's knowledge of France. France itself lies beyond her known and imaginable cartography. They fall into a new kind of love; fluent in French and yoga, Gus teaches Margaret how to breathe. He also moves into her newly forming, eclectic home. Soon they are joined by her health team, including fellow outsider Bruce, a gay and Jewish chef, and Susan, a nurse, who becomes his best friend. This new tribal family grows, and relationship webs build between them all—chosen kinships. When Susan confides in Bruce her longing for motherhood, he offers to biologically donate and coparent.

Meanwhile, both Margaret and Wanda begin to actively and creatively grieve. Initially, Wanda expresses confusion and hesitancy around actively breaking with the past, asking Margaret if she is sure she wants to give the stolen collection away. "'I don't want to give it away. Or sell it,' Margaret announced, as much to herself as to anyone. 'I want to break it.' With that she let it go" (132). The outdoor patio becomes littered with shards of destruction as Margaret corrects her own thinking, "Not destroyed—reconfigured" (135).

Not only does Margaret nurture Wanda back to health by providing for her physical needs, she also tends to her psychic needs. In a novel where renaming shows progressive movement, Margaret renames Wanda as Tink. Wanda/Tink's recovery depends upon her reclaiming her creativity.

As Wanda teeters between the worlds, angry, stuck on painkillers, and contemplating suicide, Margaret intervenes by telling her the full story of her father's legacy. "When the Nazis began their work, he saw a great opportunity" and became "a broker of fine antique European china and porcelain" (240–41). She hands Tink an old and heavy letter from a dealer describing the inventory he is shipping to King O. "Ah, these kikes and their tchotchkes! The whole lot came from a Paris apartment of a French professor named Lazar, and the details, as always, you will find on the attached inventory" (240). When her father died in 1946 just after the war, twenty-four-year-old Margaret unwittingly took over his art dealership. One day "a man burst in. His face was awful. Haunted-looking. Skeletal. He was wearing a black wool coat and a yarmulke. He started yelling at me. His English was very broken. 'You are standing on the dead!' he shouted. 'On the bodies of the six million you make your fortune! I curse you! I curse your family!'" (241).

Shaken by this encounter, Margaret begins sleuthing and uncovers the truth about her father and the origins of his fortune, finding "the unthinkable" (241). Closing the shop, she stores everything at the house and goes silent, believing she can contain the horror herself. Later her husband discovers the truth, their son dies, and her husband leaves.

Though she tries to find the original owners, these sorts of objects are more difficult to return; unlike paintings or bank accounts, they are difficult to trace. She tells Tink that atonement has never been made. "These things have outlived their time, it seems to me. If all they do is sit on a shelf, no one will ever know their worth. I think it's time for them to die. . . . They should all be broken. I want you to do it" (242). This revelatory act between women is the first time Margaret has shared her burden and the weight and consequence of this man's curse, liberating her for action. It is only after her decision to break (with) her father's collection that effective restitution can be seeded.

Wanda/Tink agrees with Margaret, with one caveat. "These things need to have stories, even if the stories aren't true" (246). As mythologist, she is making meaning where it has been lost. Wanda breaks the first piece on the hearth, but only after Margaret creates a possible story for the dog figurine (247). This is significant since both women have come toward each other to re-create a healthy, containing home. Such growth requires release, remembrance, and reclamation. Wanda asks Margaret to write the stories down.

There is a vast quantity of objects in innumerable boxes within a massive mansion; the breaking goes on and on. Wanda discovers that smashing objects against "hearths guaranteed the most dramatic and thorough breakings" (249). Why? Because they are the center of family life, of home as container. These women use the containment of their new, regenerative home to heal. Breaking is not so hard. These simple acts of dropping—how easy—when the time is right, take "no effort at all" (249).

Wanda/Tink reclaims her voice by vocalizing her anger as she throws the ceramics. Again, she begins sorting the pieces, deciding that all her mosaics would illustrate a single subject and begins applying her tricky detective skills to the re/constructive act of researching Judaism and World War II. Continuing their commitment to remythologize the stolen objects, the stories pour out of Margaret. "Her dreams were full of the persecuted, the condemned, the dead—all telling their story" (251):

> She walked the rooms of the house with Margaret—who had imagined owners for every single piece, from the largest Chinese garden seats to the smallest snuffbox, from the most valuable and rare items in the collection of those which were more common, less dear. Sometimes Margaret's imaginings were scant: "Moshe. Widower. Wore garters. Fed pigeons. Shot in the head, in the night, in a forest." In most cases, though, her stories were full of details: "Adele, nine years old, sitting at a school desk, proud and straight, wearing a plaid blouse, white anklets, her hair in braids. She was going to be a journalist. She loved horses. She won the school essay competition and her grandmother gave her this as a prize. When she starved to death, she was holding a pencil. (251)

These women engage in a transformative act of imaginal re/membering. Even when the stories were lost to them, they remain committed to the possibility of atonement. They did not know what they were creating; they just kept going, reclaiming meaning.

As Tink applies her considerable detection skills, she uncovers stories of resilience and regeneration within the mythology of the Holocaust. She becomes inspired by the story of Jewish children in the ghetto-turned-concentration camp of Terezín, in the occupied Czech Republic. These children wrote, drew, and made collaged bricolage from scraps from 1942 to 1944 (252). Words and pictures—Wanda/Tink blends them in her art. She copies these children's words and uses her own house's shards, including Margaret's stories, to echo their breakage. As she allows these stories to incubate, she walks with shards in her pockets (259). Like her connection with Troy, they keep her grounded.

Wanda/Tink also uses paper with story fragments, the words are included in the mosaics along with bits of poems and drawings. When Troy becomes her technical assistant, Tink blooms into a full-blown artist, turning tesserae, these small components, to treasure. When she fears that her work looks poor, he challenges her: "Keep going. . . . It's all in the grout. . . . That's it. Take your time" (256–57). But grouting is risky business, a foray into unknown territory. "Grouting meant losing sight of the familiar. There was risk here, terrible risk. The risk of failing, again" (257). This blind step requires faith. Grout becomes her binding agent. Like the decorative finishing stitching in crazy quilts, this final step psychically sets the shards, committing them to place and relationship, as she alchemically re/integrates lost and reclaimed pieces of her own soul.

Tink realizes, "Troy was right. The space between the pieces, the *negative* space, was highly important, maybe even more important than the pieces themselves" (257). "Space made everything possible" (258). Troy makes crucial space for Wanda repeatedly. He does not react to her pain, instead remaining silent. He leaves when she lashes out, allowing her to contemplate her own actions. This is a mature act of the healing masculine. When the container is strong, spaciousness is possible. Tink begins to quiet her mind and let go of her need to control. Her previous codependent, list-making management style is replaced with "a kind of magic which only happened when she let go" (259). She transforms, metamorphosing from manager to creatrix.

Regeneration: Community, Home, and *The Magdalene Kitchen*

Soon the mansion co-operative takes on an additional dimension: a non-profit school of mosaics whose mission is "fostering community through artistic collaboration" (Kallos 281). This school of social and artistic bricolage becomes the Crazy Plate Academy. Volunteers collaborate with Wanda/Tink, Troy, Margaret, and the entire household to cocreate community artwork. Their first exhibition includes *Seder Plate*, *Holy Book*, and *Shoes of the Dead*, in response to the Holocaust Museum's exhibition of piles of victims' shoes. Instead of amplifying the horror and death, the vivid display is somehow an ingenious, "joyous affirmation of life" (279). Headlines respond with "The Hughes Collection Scandal: Desecration or Deification?" (278). Word spreads about Margaret's legacy and gift back out into the world. Wanda/Tink begins to establish her place in the art world as a serious mosaicist.

With the devotional act of a sociopolitical mitzvah, or good deed, *The Magdalen Kitchen 1972* is revealed as Wanda's first full-scale solo installation—slated to travel to museums around the country. It is the culmination of her vision, cocreated with the support of the Crazy Plate Academy, and provides a reinterpretation of her aunt Maureen's kitchen. Here, Magdalene shows up as her aunt/adopted mother, serving breakfast to the enormous family in a reimagined, nurturing space from Wanda's childhood. The broken scene is made whole by the remythologizing act of bricolage.

After living for two years in a state of vitality with her star tumor, Margaret actively begins to die. She decides to cross the known boundary of her previously confining life and finally take the journey she has always dreamed of; she travels to Paris with Gus and Susan. Consciously venturing into uncharted—and yearned-for—territory for the first time in her life, she synchronistically stumbles upon Le Centre de Documentation Juive Contemporaine, the Center of Contemporary Jewish Documentation, where she is able to finally, after much research, track one single piece of inventory of those possessions confiscated from Parisian Jews that ended up in her care: the green and gold chocolate service—the tête-à-tête—that is missing a single cup (306). It belonged to Mrs. Irma Mariska Sendler. Eventually tracing her via Holocaust research centers and oral histories, they discover her number in Seattle; she is now known as Mrs. Kosminsky, Michael/M.J.'s only friend, Mrs. K.

Margaret's atonement for her father's misdeeds responds to the Jungian tenet that we unconsciously leave our unfinished business for our children.[119] She has come out of the shadows, released her inherited shame, and reclaims

---

119. The young discipline of epigenetics is validating Jung's assertion by tracing the physiological impact of the intergenerational transmission of traumatic experiences and how they lodge physiologically. For a close examination of how inherited PTSD manifests physically—particularly via methylation, a vital physical process responsible for detoxification and maintaining equilibrium within the nervous system—see Tania L. Roth, "Epigenetic Mechanisms in the Development of Behavior."

Central to this discussion is tending the intersection of war and the wounded masculine; in this vein see especially Gadi Zerach et al., "The Role of Fathers' Psychopathology in the Intergenerational Transmission of Captivity Trauma."

Most significantly, see Krista Tippett's interview with psychiatrist and neuroscientist Rachel Yehuda tracking trauma markers in children of Holocaust survivors, "Rachel Yehuda: How Trauma and Resilience Cross Generations."

her lost pieces by coming to terms with the truth about her father and his legacy. She has also dealt with her ghosts—both mother and son. Now Margaret's star is bursting, her ghosts more defined and vivid. As she crosses over to their realm, her mother reminds her: "You didn't expect to stay in the shadows forever" (289). Margaret is finally leaving her own liminal prison.

The return of the (healing) father occurs on Thanksgiving Day. Michael/ M.J. is about to leave town after Mrs. K's death. She has bequeathed to him her only memory of her daughter, the single cup her daughter carried with her when they were interned. Michael receives a call from Mrs. K's lawyer summoning him to Margaret's mansion. Upon his reluctant arrival at the Hughes house, he is put through the rite all visitors undergo, be they "unsuspecting solicitor, substitute mail carrier, FedEx driver, or fledgling volunteer" (336). They are each welcomed, handed an object, told its story, and asked to break it before being allowed in. Having been successfully initiated at the threshold, Michael meets with Margaret and receives the tea/chocolate set on behalf of Irma and her daughter. Margaret begins to actively fade and invites Michael to stay. As he wanders the property, he finds Wanda's studio in the carriage house, recalling the image of his lost wife, Gina, in a sculpture. Recognizing his daughter, he understands it was she he has been searching for. Though she does not realize who this stranger is, Wanda/Tink invites him to Thanksgiving. He stays. Margaret dies.

Michael moves into the mansion without revealing his identity. He connects with and supports Wanda/Tink, enabling her to lay to rest her codependent search for Peter. As her energy is liberated for individuation, for becoming whole and complete in her-Self, she is finally able to both recognize her father and be present with and commit to Troy. The novel closes with their wedding. The community celebrates as the couple smashes Irma and Lucie's tête-à-tête in blessing. Both feminine and masculine wastelands are regenerating. Susan and Bruce's baby, Augie, arrives at the novel's close. He is a divine child beloved and held by the whole household.

Broken for You contrasts the worth/value of objects with that of human souls, both our own and those of Others. Kallos functions as an agent of the regenerating feminine in culture, accentuating the fault lines of conscious and unconscious breakage, examining how repair begins when we are present with our shards. Her depictions of time as an ally—it sometimes takes a significant span to heal—reveal our continual capacity for renewal—the repurposing and reconstruction of our mosaicked selves. Kallos utilizes feminist cocreative community building, a neo-Hestian matriarchal, nonhierarchical model that supports and welcomes a wandering Aletis. Kallos guides us through our reading/(w)rites as preparation for alchemical sacred marriage. Dismemberment, grief work, remythologizing remembrance, and the intersections between the wounded masculine and lost feminine are all required, as well as recognizing cultural wounds as personal and vice versa, including war, betrayal, and abandonment—all written on the body. Furthermore, Kallos addresses intersectionality, interlocking forms of oppression, including ageism, homophobia, class wars, racism, and sexism. From the shards of such shattering can emerge a complex mosaic that no single person could have crafted alone.

Repeatedly throughout my research on Magdalene, Nazism and Adolf Hitler cast an unexpectedly long and chilling shadow across the page and screen. Though I at first ignored these archetypal apparitions, then tried outrunning them, I finally learned—as we always do—to turn toward them. Is it all that surprising that an exploration calling for recognition of the regenerative and feminine principle of humanity, one born out of the historic and cultural Jewish tradition, would also nudge its shadow into the open? Nazism was certainly a massive, fear-based attempt at controlling and silencing the Other—Jewish, Catholic, queer, gypsy, feminine. *Broken for You* is part of a lineage of emerging literary fiction of reconciliation, repatriation, and regeneration in response to Nazism and Hitler in particular; this lineage includes *The Little Book* (2008) and *The Lost Prince* (2012) by Selden Edwards, *The Magic Circle* (1998) by Katherine Neville, and *Anna and the Swallow Man* (2016) by Gavriel Savit. Perhaps it has taken seventy years to fully grout the shards left by Nazism. Each of these books addresses the treatment of Jews, Roma, gays, intellectuals, differently abled, children, and other groups and individuals as Other.

All suggest new models, but *Broken for You* uniquely and specifically shows us how. This epic narrative is worthy of our attention. It is no wonder it took Stephanie Kallos seven years to complete such a masterwork. Kallos's method for healing and recovery is so effective because it illuminates the complex gifts of feminine regeneration in subtle, lyrical form. Mythologically, the novel narrates Magdalenian regeneration creatively and communally, mythopoetically embodying what can be called a handbook for regeneration.

Broken for You offers a feminine restitution motif, a powerful emerging literary and film trend. Films such as *The Rape of Europa* (2008), *The Monuments Men* (2014), and *The Woman in Gold* (2015)—all of which are based on books—document reparation/reconciliation/restitution as regenerative healing acts.[120] We tell stories of the return of what was lost because they provide a sense of wholeness, of right relationship. Before reconciliation we must first tell the truth, as exemplified by successful healing models

---

120. The film *Woman in Gold* is based partially on Anne Marie O'Connor's book *The Lady in Gold*; the other two films retained their original book titles.

developed in post-apartheid South Africa, the former Yugoslavia, and other war-torn nations.[121] *Broken for You* offers something more, something new, created out of what cannot be returned but must go forward; even when we do not know the truth, we can—and must—tell new stories to make meaning. In this way the imaginal realm offers truths that cannot adequately be contained within fact-based literal and forever-incomplete "history." What Campbell might call a failed return, Jody Bower calls going forth.

The Aletis who wanders and must find her own, new home is also a *bricoleuse*. When there is no home left, and family/old village are toxic and dangerous, she must move along and use the materials to hand and create something new, somewhere new, remythologizing her-Self. Kallos's Wanda and Margaret are unconventional pilgrims, and the narrative embodies their personal s/hero's journeys of renewal back to themselves while they wander on, cultivating new, dynamic expressions of community, hearth, and home. *Broken for You* is unexpected detective fiction with Wanda as an unlikely— and successful—regeneratrix.

SYNCHRONICITY: BRIDAL HEALING PRACTICE AND ECOFEMINIST STANCE

Expanding our understanding of life, from a concretized narrowness of linear causal experiences, to including acausal events, is akin to connecting the right side of our brain with the left, linking problem solving with creativity, bathing Logos in Eros. Jung saw the emerging knowledge base of new physics directly supporting his study of synchronicity as a more complex, comprehensive way of understanding life. By expanding out from a reductive, limited Newtonian understanding of cause and effect—one that dooms us to Cartesian dualistic repetition and a literal, inanimate world—to instead include synchronicities, Jung advocated for *incorporating* (adding to the body of knowledge, embodying) acausal meaningful events into how we understand the world around and within us. This tempering integration may be a core gem of Jungian theory and practice.

---

121. For a detailed account of a successful, multilayered approach via a truth and reconciliation commission after genocide and trauma in South Africa, see *The Book of Forgiving* coauthored by Archbishop Desmond Tutu and his daughter the Reverend Canon Mpho Tutu van Furth. Sadly, after her recent marriage to her longtime female partner, the South African Anglican church revoked the reverend's license to practice as a "priest," stating its policy on gay clerics is celibacy ("Tutu Chooses Gay Marriage over Church." *BBC News*, 9 June 2016, https://www.bbc.com/news/av/world-africa-36486908. Accessed 7 Mar. 2025.

A Dialogue of Interconnection: Jung, New Physics, and Synchronicity

Arguably one of Jung's most extraordinary contributions is his work on synchronicity, developed late in his career. Using the term to describe meaningful coincidences—seemingly acausal and highly meaningful and/or helpful events that offer clues to our relationship to the world around us—Jung believed synchronicity to be expressions of a profound, holistic, and interactive reality. In this way such events potentially provide a sense of connection with an *unus mundus*, a unified worldview based on a continuous, complex, multidimensional fabric of the universe, situating humanity firmly within Nature. In this paradigm synchronistic events support meaning making and even—quite significantly for this study—foster a sense of well-being. Perhaps synchronicity's most powerful gifts lie in its regenerative potentialities.

When Jung teamed with former patient and Nobel laureate quantum physicist Wolfgang Pauli to seriously study synchronicity, they identified a monumental shift in scientific thinking. In *Synchronicity: Nature and Psyche in an Interconnected Universe*, Joseph Cambray discusses the magnitude of this shift in perspective, which they amplify in their publications by relocating psyche as "embedded into the substance of the world" (1). Coinciding with the emergence of complexity theory, their inquiry parallels and interacts with a massive expansion in scientific knowledge and consciousness.

Most significantly, Jung and Pauli set out to scientifically track synchronistic occurrences; they were seeking to comprehend—and support—the conditions under which they thrive and augment. They believed synchronistic events can be invited, cultivated by an "open and curious" attitude of inquiry. Contrarily, they discovered how the frequency of these events drops during states of boredom and depression.[122] This information lies at the heart of synchronicity's radical potential for expanding how we experience and participate in life.

For example, synchronicities or "strange coincidences" tend to occur when we are relaxed and in a state of wonder, such as when we are traveling or otherwise on vacation, "away" from life's daily stressors. When I am fascinated by a new research project, interesting articles seem to "appear" out of nowhere, the right scholars "suddenly" contact me, and books have been known to fall off the shelves and open to relevant passages. Conversely, when I am stressed about a deadline, multitasking, or am afraid I won't find

---

122. See Cambray's chapter 1 in *Synchronicity* for a precise scientific discussion of their process. Cambray's doctorate in chemistry and training as a psychoanalyst inform a unique investigation into Jung and Pauli's original study.

the right material, it seems the flow of information and support dries up.[123] The question then becomes: How do we return to the beneficial "open and curious" state, reenter the flow?

Jung calls for nothing short of a complete overhaul of outmoded, one-sided Logos-centered (limiting, rational, conscious, masculine) thinking and acting, promoting instead a worldview that is complex, cocreative, and inclusive of essential feminine elements that Jung termed Eros (expansive, relatedness, feeling, feminine). This integration fosters a turning toward greater wholeness, including chaotic uncertainty, and supports an open and curious state.

As the feminine and erotic side of life becomes more valued—less feared as shadowy, denigrated, treacherous—it becomes safer to be more whole. The opposite—to morbidly repeat necrotic patterns—keeps us locked into doing the (fear-based) dirty work of the unconscious shadow, including the patriarchy. It has cost us dearly to have remained stuck acting as its reinforcers.

Two profound theoretical breakthroughs in relativity and quantum mechanics during the previous century launched the "new physics," and both revealed a holistic perspective quite different from the now-outmoded Newtonian, mechanistic worldview.[124] The resultant remarkable scientific shift enabled through these discoveries pivots around how interconnection is intrinsic to both relativity and quantum mechanics and is inherently cocreative. In *Synchronicity: Through the Eyes of Science, Myth, and the Trickster*, Allan Combs and Mark Holland identify this new, emerging myth, one that, due to the very nature of its complexity and lack of visual understanding of how quantum mechanics operates, "gives us absolutely nothing to hang an optical hat on. . . . Unlike its classical predecessor, quantum physics presents an open view of the world, one in which the outcomes of events are not entirely predetermined by fixed and inflexible laws. Quantum predictions do not dictate exact experimental results at all, but allow for a range of outcomes of differing likelihoods. In this sense quantum theory is probabilistic, mapping probabilities rather than specifying events" (xxxii).

---

123. For an extensive survey of related synchronistic phenomena from a Jungian perspective, see Phil Cousineau, *Soul Moments*.

124. For ongoing conversations toward a working understanding of quantum mechanics and the history of science, I am grateful to my lifelong friendship with theoretical physicist Professor Sílvio Renato Dahmen of the Universidade Federal de São Carlos, Araras, São Paulo, Brazil. Our shared experiences as teenage Rotary exchange students were deeply centered around our sense of wonder, which was supported through our travels; having, and being able to return to, an open and curious stance made all the difference for both of us, as we each cultivated lifelong practices in support of international travel/wandering in wonder.

By relating the impact of this radical new cosmology, one that depends upon the liminality of probability, Combs and Holland identify the magnitude of this shift, including how physics was suddenly grappling with several new astonishing discoveries, including: Albert Einstein's general theory of relativity with time as a new fourth dimension; Werner Heisenberg's uncertainty principle; and Niels Bohr's principle of complementarity, which identified how particles have the flexibility of becoming either waves or particles based on how they are observed. What a mind-bending time of inquiry! This is the uncomfortable realm of uncertainty. Or, as Virginia Woolf puts it mythopoetically, "I am rooted, but I am flow" (*The Waves* 102). Paradoxical indeed.

Even the physicists were terribly uncomfortable with such possibilities. Einstein himself rejected probability/not-knowing, denying that "God" would "play dice" with the universe (Combs and Holland xxxiii). Liminality is at the core of new physics; its open nature "is related to a certain willingness of many quantum physicists to tolerate paradox and ambiguity in their own lives". A suspension of disbelief and a bit of faith in what could not yet be seen was required. Yet how uncomfortable this can be—especially for those who might feel cheated, searching for grand theories and believing they were promised certainty and rewards for following the (obsolete, Newtonian) rules.

As a powerful counterpoint, feminist post-Jungian theorists have been further investigating the beneficial role of synchronicity, offering fascinating responses to and engagement with Jung's material. Most significant is an appreciation of the power of synchronicity as embodied potentiality, offering unique creative responses and integration. Theorists digging into this rich material extend the legacy of Jung and Pauli's investigation in fascinating ways.

Right on Time: Synchronistic Feminist Post-Jungians as Wonder Women

Jung was a proponent of cozying up with the unconscious—advocating, acknowledging, and integrating our previously unknown, shadowy parts, itself an energetically liberating act; this is the heart of individuation. He understood dreams and synchronicities as direct expressions of the unconscious. This more feminine, receptive, and inclusive stance is indicative of his general approach and promotes dialogue with the unconscious.

In *Jung: A Feminist Revision* (2002), Susan Rowland makes a potent case for Jung's work being deeply in line with the rising feminine and that synchronicity itself becomes a powerful agent for creative understanding and action. Rowland's analysis of Jung's (conscious and unconscious) actions and theories offers an understanding of his complexities, including theoretical limitations and problematic issues in relation with women, politics, and power. Her study includes a comprehensive survey of feminist thinkers in Jungian studies, directly contributing to the evolution of synchronicity studies. In her later work on synchronicity in *C. G. Jung in the Humanities: Taking the Soul's Path*, Rowland investigates the significance of Jung's scientific contributions in the field of emergence science (studying complexity):

> Synchronicity is a productive working together of the feminine (nature, dreams, and so on) and the masculine (the impulse toward consciousness and transcendence). Both feminine nature (in which nature is at once cosmos and psyche) and masculine meaning-making are active creative partners. . . . Just as the Jungian unconscious is androgynous, capable of producing feminine as well as masculine images, so is reality an on-going creation, with processes we have chosen to define as rational and masculine, as well as those of a feminine and creative nature. (116–17)

By sketching the holistic nature of synchronistic theory, particularly in uniting and remythologizing what have been portrayed as "opposing forces" and "gender differences," Rowland shows how Jung's synchronicity theory—in direct response to a mechanized worldview—is instead inclusive and radically re/unites all gendered qualities, including reclaiming lost and devalued feminine qualities. Feminist post-Jungian theory is rescued from essentialism because it advocates for the cultivation and integration of our full spectrum of skills and qualities through individuation—the work of a lifetime, ever integrating toward wholeness.

Emergence science studies how something new and meaningful arises from the interaction of complex collectives. Both Cambray and Rowland suggest Jung was a pioneer in emergence science. Also known as complexity science, this new, integrating field based on chaos theory (which, rather than "chaotic," is informed by spiralic, cyclical order) developed as a complex systems theory approach where entities are recognized as whole in and of themselves *and* interdependent, even altruistic. Moreover, these vital systems are ever evolving, intelligent—*learning* from their experiences.[125]

Jungian theory on (personal) individuation, where psychological growth might be experienced as a personal quest toward an inner union of feminine

---

125. For a thorough linking of post-Jungian theory with chaos theory, emergence and/or complexity science, see Rowland's complete chapter "Jung in the Twenty-First Century," in *C. G. Jung in the Humanities*.

and masculine qualities (for people of all genders), is perhaps widely known. Jung extended this theory out into the realms of culture (the collective) and science (the cosmos), reimagining "a world actively intervening in the psyche in an irrational yet ultimately meaningful way" (Rowland, *C. G. Jung in the Humanities* 19). Significantly, from his work on synchronicity, Jung developed his worldview into a paradigm of interrelationship of life whereby psyche (soul) is inherently connected with the cosmos, as are individuals with the collective, destabilizing all subject-object relationships. This returns us to quantum mechanics, chaos theory, and the patriarchal phallacy of objectivity—that we do not affect a scene or story by being present, witnessing, and reporting out. Instead, we are intimately interconnected with life on myriad levels.

In her early book *The Tao of Psychology: Synchronicity and the Self* (1979), Jean Shinoda Bolen discusses Jungian psychology's unique approach to synchronicity as an underlying principle of connectivity. Bolen identifies how Jung theorized a collective unconscious linking all animate and inanimate objects within:

> An interconnected cosmic web in which the human observer is always a participator emerges from quantum physics. At the atomic particle level, the world view becomes very Eastern and mystical; time and space become a continuum, matter and energy interchange, observer and observed interact. . . . Just as modern atomic physics acknowledges that the researcher affects whatever he or she studies at the particle level, Jung suggested that the psyche of the observing person interacts in the moment with the events of the outside world. (5–6)

Bolen utilizes physics to identify and illuminate the value of synchronistic events in promoting a deeper way of knowing, uniting experience with intuition, and providing a sense of agency, connection, and purpose. How enlivening to be active, participating actors within a mysterious universe!

Further relating synchronicity to the Tao, Bolen writes that both translate to "meaning," suggesting that "we feel ourselves part of a divine, dynamic, interrelated universe. Synchronistic events offer us perceptions that may be useful in our psychological and spiritual growth and may reveal to us, through intuitive knowledge, that our lives have meaning" (7). This is a mythological stance. By consciously choosing meaning making as a primary action (personally and collectively), synchronicity supports us. It is a way of returning to an open and curious stance, inviting signs as clues that we might follow along the journey.

How might we—both personally and collectively—return to a sense of wonder after being fearful, distressed, disenfranchised, traumatized, and/or depressed? How could we practice regenerative acts that return us to an open and curious stance, re/inviting synchronicity? We can begin by mimicking nature. Jung was a naturalist; he witnessed the wisdom of Nature's rhythms and cycles and encouraged his clients to realign with them. From winter's cold and fallow fields to the recovering octopus who has dropped her own arm in a life-saving act, to the silent and invisible caterpillar about to mutate into a completely new DNA expression as a butterfly—we can observe and follow natural paths back to wonder. Applying regenerative skills, synchronicity is an effective ecofeminist stance.

Case Study as Cautionary Tale: Narcissism Cannot Thrive Here

Synchronicity can serve as an antidote to and/or shield against necrotic behaviors and potential woundings. Phrased conversely, narcissism cannot thrive in a synchronistic state, cannot feed in the presence of an open and curious stance. Narcissistic personality disorder (NPD) is a more complex, nuanced, and widespread psychological disorder than previously understood. With the publication of *A Clear and Present Danger: Narcissism in the Era of Donald Trump*, Jungian studies explores these murky waters, previously uncharted territory.[126]

Narcissism is necrotic. Dependent upon the vampiric taking of others' energy (granting them narcissistic supply), narcissism can reign only in an unconscious wasteland, be it personal or cultural. Not only does narcissism thrive under patriarchy and fear, but it is also a patriarchal agent, seeking to prolong the life of a dying, hollowed-out shell.

Trump's presidency and a global rise in nationalism, racism, and misogyny compounded the urgency felt by many to better understand the cycle of narcissistic abuse syndrome (NAS). Other emerging literature offers crucial insight into the predictable patterns and deadly traps set by narcissism as a vampiric predatory wound, as well as the resultant, disempowering condition of narcissist victim syndrome (NVS) I believe we are experiencing on a vast cultural level.[127]

Recognizing when we are attempting to usurp something from the outside (psychic theft), rather than doing the seemingly arduous work of cultivating

---

126. Steven Buser and Leonard Cruz, editors, *A Clear and Present Danger*.
127. See especially the work of Christine Louis de Canonville, including *The Three Faces of Evil*, and Shahira Arabi's *Becoming the Narcissist's Nightmare*.

it from within, is a crucial step. Bringing our behavior to consciousness brings us to choice. Liberating our agency from unconscious forces of trauma and related shadowy nostalgia is at the core of regeneration.

A Return to Wonder: The Shakti Principle, Testing, and Tending

Jung's work was very much centered around bringing the feminine principle back into the world, reintegrating it into the incomplete, wounded masculinist worldview. Through embodied practice and intentionality, synchronicity can be seen as both a benevolent product of this integration and an opportunity to further develop our (personal and collective) capacities for cocreation. How, exactly, might we dance with uncertainty?

The first function of mythology, according to Joseph Campbell, is to return us to a state of wonder and "participation in the mystery of this finally inscrutable universe."[128] As such, mythology—the study of story as meaning making—supports synchronicity. What if, rather than developing newer more sophisticated, abstract theoretical (and dangerously disembodied) critiques—akin to outdated Newtonian physics—we developed flexible and reflexive mythologies that support a turn and return toward wonder? Such an open and curious stance then amplifies opportunities for synchronistic events, which are inherently connective and, I suggest, joy-producing. As Woolf would advocate, we return to amazement with life: "Perhaps . . . perhaps."

What if we fashioned our informed choices out of gossamer wonder and the uncertainty of not-knowing? For example, what if, in academic culture, the question mark replaced the period—while leaving adequate space for exclamations? Rather than regurgitating suspicious rhetoric and egoic debate—could we tolerate mythopoetics and liminal quests from and on the unconscious? Rather than gendered certainties, could we queer intriguing cocreative feminist potentialities? Might such an evolution better equip us to heal the enormous consequences of life under our patriarchal legacy—including personal and cultural complex PTSD and our pandemic of narcissistic abuse syndrome? How might we best hold the tension between the best practices of an evolved feminist wisdom (intersectional, transnational, transdisciplinary, ecofeminist) and a post-Jungian psychology of the unconscious (including an ability to tend the unconscious, acknowledge and recall our personal and cultural shadows, and resist othering)?

---

128. See Joseph Campbell, *The Way of the Animal Powers*, vol. I.

Table 5. Necrotic wounding and regenerative healing	
Necrotic Wounding	**Regenerative Healing**
Shadow projection, othering, fallacy of scarcity	**Depth Psychology and Family Constellations** Shadow, individuation, transcendent function, transgenerational and inherited trauma
"All lives matter." Passive oppression Phallacy of "reverse racism" and other -isms	**Education** Intersectional feminism, critical race theory, transdisciplinary approach Bully-Victim-Bystander triangle
"Not my experience." "What about my issue?" Stance: single issue, incurious, willful ignorance Stuck as (passive) bystander Unaware of intersectionality	**Systems and Synchronistic Thinking** ecopsychology, ecofeminism, interdependence Stance: open and curious

Returning to the methodology of the Shakti Principle, first introduced in chapter 5, serves this conversation well. Developed by Indian physicist and ecofeminist Vandana Shiva, it measures systemic capacity for vitality. Discerning whether a practice is sustainable/vital might be one of the most effective and creative tools possible, amplifying the value of a plan, action, or intention by the intrinsic aliveness it brings. Shiva develops this theory in *Soil Not Oil* (2007), explaining that pseudosustainability will not serve, and good intentions are not sufficient (133). What matters is if we feel more alive, if we are supporting life in ourselves, each other, and the greater ecosystem. Living systems require energy and attention. Here are her words on how best to tend these systems and how they are linked to us and to Nature: "Life is based on self-organizing energies of the universe, from cells to Gaia, from communities to countries. . . . Reductionist, mechanistic science creates scarcity by blinding itself to the connections that support and maintain the cycle of life, the energy flows that are based on self-organization" (135).

Energy is Shakti—the primordial power of creation, the self-organizing, self-generative, self-renewing creative force of the universe in feminine form. Shakti is power and the personification of the source of all divine and cosmic evolution, the potentialities of nature. The universe is an expression of Shakti and an infinite reservoir of power (136). Reductionism, which focuses only on parts, cannot see or understand the unexpected creativity of natural processes (142).

When uncertain we can evoke Shiva's Shakti Principle, asking:

Is this practice/system yet another form of manipulation, of codependent management or an invitation to a place or state of generative wonder?

Is something new being created, or is this only managerial?

Does this system or practice help us expand or keep us bound, festering?

Scholarship and learning then become a delightful yearning for understanding and connection, supported by discernment. From a feminist post-Jungian perspective, we turn and return into curious quantum mechanics, wondering about how to connect, listen, and move in more-supportive, cocreative, and effective ways. We become synchronistic agents, tending open and curious forums and formats as *embodied* potentiality, free to wonder. The following three regenerative case studies offer examples of these regenerative practices.

REGENERATIVE CASE STUDY: BRINGING NOSTALGIA TO CONSCIOUSNESS

Conscious participation in rituals carries potential for psychic growth. Returning to an examination of nostalgia adds nuanced understanding to the value of the regenerative quality of the bridal recessional. Weddings tend to be nostalgic events—for myriad reasons. Nostalgia, deeply intertwined with memory, might inform an enormous portion of our choices. Unconscious choices can be costly. Threshold moments embody transitional potential; at such opportunities applying conscious awareness, discernment, and intention is invaluable.

Examining nostalgia's function can be phenomenally liberating. From the food we crave, to the entertainment we watch/consume, to the sports we participate in, to the music we make, to the land we call home, our souls are in constant dialogue with memory and meaning making. Very relatedly, the impact of nostalgia, including its shadow side, is a driving force as we track trend cycles—from programming to marketing and social perceptions—and how they relate to the timing of generations newly attaining purchasing power. For example, twenty-year cycles of trends are directly tied to a generational coming of age and gaining access to economic and industry influence. Notice when a whole new crop of screenwriters arrives and takes us—suddenly and pervasively—back to the 1990s.

Bringing our nostalgia to consciousness—and therefore choice—might be one of the most powerful actions we can take as humans. Noticing what our psyches are craving and longing for (and wondering why) can be a vital healing step. Reliving childhood wounds (in a stuck way) can be a painful, nonproductive necrotic festering. Or—when tended consciously, curiously— our wounds can be investigated tenderly, supporting a cathartic, liberating metabolization of previously unconscious material, freeing trapped energy. Similarly, studying our collective nostalgic shadow, via popular culture, systems theory, trauma-informed studies, etc., provides entrée to our vast potentiality for collective and personal healing.

The Diffusion of Innovations, a term coined in 1962 by Everett Rogers in his landmark eponymous book, can be predicted and depicted along a bell curve that begins when a new idea is introduced, used by a creative person or small group known as early adopter. He then identified the formation of subsequent subgroups and their various motivations and levels of engage-ment and adoptions. Understanding the needs and behaviors of each group illuminates the movement and adaptions of ideas over time.

Innovative visionaries tend to be courageous and independent-minded; rather than follow fashions and trends, they create them. Their optimism and risk taking can seem dangerous and idealistic to more pragmatic people. Later, others encounter the innovation and imitate/consume it, jumping on the bandwagon (hello, "influencers"). As the innovation moves toward acceptance and utilization by the mainstream and is no longer full of the vitality of mystery, so the interest from creators usually peters out. Creatives are more interested in the joy of creating and easily move on to something new; they tend to dwell in wonder.

From a depth psychological perspective, Rogers's is a fascinating model of applied archetypal theory. Tracking notions of conservation, fear, and our collective shadow via the diffusion of innovations yields insights into moti-vations. As such, rather than practice rigid identification and its shadowy projection, it's helpful to consider when we might behave more courageously (as innovators) and when more conservatively (as laggards).

Rogers, himself an innovator in the field of communications, identified and followed the progression of trends over four subgroups, arguing that membership might be fixed. Rather than by folks becoming bolder, innova-tive ideas disseminate by becoming more mundane, diluted—meeting the needs of ever-more-conservative segments of the population over time (see Table 6, below). When a trend eventually reaches the palatability required for mass consumption, it has often been drastically watered down, often beyond recognition, losing much of its original integrity and vitality.

Marketers have jumped on this model, noting that having influence does not necessarily mean convincing someone to move toward innovation, but rather d/evolving ideas to serve the differing groups.

Liaising this theory with depth psychology, each group can be understood through their own expression of light and shadow.

- By elevating creatives to superstar status, they also receive proportionate shadowy projections, creating shadowy diva/god/dess complexes. Innovators might be (or be perceived as) ungrounded, flaky, lone wolves, temperamental, or even black sheep. As travelers they are far away from the beaten path, engrossed in their journey.
- Early adopters can be tastemakers, very influential at disseminating an innovation quickly. When fearful, they tend to attempt to bolster their egos, seeking prestige by association, their version of fear-based thinking predicated on social and economic climbing, attention/status seeking. When fearful, they tend to name drop. They can be culture vultures—a necrotic consumptive act. As travelers they might seek glorious chic luxury, then tell you all about it.
- Members of the early majority want simple, safe, streamlined products with guarantees, ideas and things that have been tested and are convenient. They would rather be taking their kids to sports practice than dealing with complexities. Wanting to conserve the good they already possess, their fear of losing what they have can present as fear-based and anti-intellectual. As travelers they might choose a cruise or other all-inclusive package enabling them to relax into feeling safer, perhaps via a commodified sense of luxury.
- Late majority folks, very risk-avoidant, are practical and influenced (regressively) by laggards. Wanting to be perceived as "normal," their own norm might be shame-based communication and avoidance. Traveling might be a group activity, and only to safe places, as they understand them.
- Laggards need to feel their own agency; uncertainty is scary. They can be useful editors and guardians at the gate, as they cannot be easily fooled or persuaded. They can be so focused on critique that they forget to (ever) be positive or open to new ideas; this cuts them off from their own creativity and synchronicity. They stay home.

Table 6. The diffusion of innovations over time

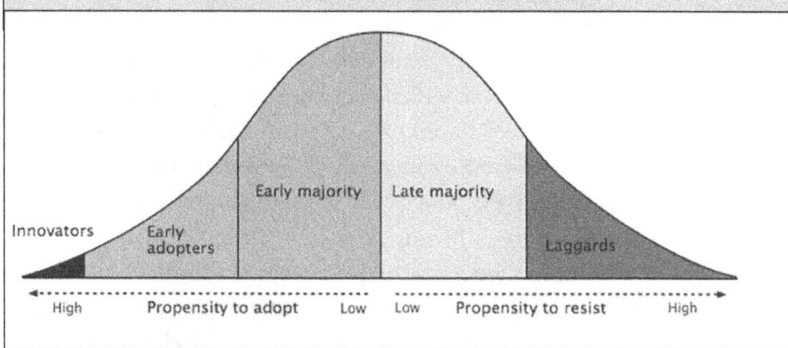

Understanding our membership/s and mobility within and between group/s can inform our capacity to respond with a more flexibility and efficacy.

What happens between groups can be fascinating. This predictability of a trend's interrelation of subgroup functionality (in relation to each other and ideas themselves) can inform our relationships, both with ourselves and with others. Asking what drives us—and whether it comes from a (wonderous) healthy and expansive place or a fear-based reactionary (unconscious) drive—supports the excavation of rich information, psychic content ripe for tending. In this way we effectively apply the Shakti Principle to measure the efficacy of our internal processes. Interconnectedly, bringing nostalgia to consciousness, through embodying a wondering stance, synchronicity supports innovation.

REGENERATIVE CASE STUDY: WRITE A POEM, INVITE SYNCHRONICITY

In *Write a Poem, Save Your Life* (2021) Meredith Heller unfolds her effective tools for writing, growing, and living authentically. Moreover, it's a peek into her deep lifelong relationship with synchronicity. It begins: "At thirteen years old, disenchanted with society and in search of a deeper truth, I leave home and school and raise myself, living in domes I build in the woods, old barns, and abandoned houses along the Potomac River. I do whatever I can for cash: gardening, cleaning, making jewelry from the dead snakes I find on the road. I teach myself to tan the snakeskin, attach it to a tube of beads I've sewn, and make it into bracelets I sell at the store in town for food money" (1). This jolt of a paragraph contains the magnitude of Heller's courage, creativity, and resilience. She survived by cultivating her voice, intuition, and willingness to integrate trauma until it became her ingenuity, her gold.

Likewise, her poetry workshops amplify the potency available through such committed openness to recognizing and healing pain and loss through writing. Teaching techniques for communal word sharing—a cross-fertilization within the group—and other methods for poetic feeding, Heller's leadership is an energized antidote to the patriarchal phallacy of scarcity. Rather than hoarding words, or fearing there's not enough, students blossom. Rather than maintaining silence, participants share in succinct, nurturing containers—both in-person and online—easily supporting each other, building essential empowering connective tissue. In this way Heller nurtures an ever-re/opening to curiosity—Jung and Pauli's vital components for inviting synchronistic experience.

Heller's work is in direct alignment with Slattery's mythic riting practice. By consciously tending our personal myths, writing becomes an embodied, effective personal practice. The unique cross-fertilization can also expand into opportunities for bricolage, exponentially accelerating healing potential.

REGENERATIVE BRIDAL ELIXIR: RE/MAPPING THE WASTELAND

Magdalene returns bearing gifts. For Joseph Campbell, the s/hero returns to their community bringing the boon of their journey—an elixir with the potential to heal the wasteland. It is often knowledge or insight, and frequently unvalued by the community that, unlike the s/hero, has been stuck toiling away and has not gained the (invaluable) perspective attained via completing a quest. For Bower, culmination of the Aletis quest occurs through the creation of her own healthy home, a very personal elixir that then (as healthy grounding) has the potential to radiate out in support of the community. The archetype of the Bride offers such a comprehensive elixir—with the potential for healing psyche, culture, and Nature.

With much attention being paid to the loss of what may have been a Great Mother goddess archetype, it is essential to re/member it was not only our mother who went missing; we also lost the archetype of the maturing, revitalizing Bride, an embodiment of sovereign, erotic, and creative womanhood as equal partner and culture maker. The individuation of the Bride, including the development of her inner masculine, is essential preparation for embodied, sacred marriage. The inner Bridegroom must be prepared for the returning Bride.

Table 7. Symptoms of the phallacy of scarcity		
Symptom Expression/ How It Shows Up	**Description**	**Remedy/Antidote**
Attempts at devouring	Seeking nourishment outside ourselves and our own lives Overconsumption	Bringing nostalgia to consciousness Meditating on cravings: • What are you hungry for? • Where does this come from? • Does it satiate? How/when? • What truly nourishes you?
Overconsumption	Buying/attaining unnecessary material things/services	Meditating and asking: • What do I want? Why? • What feeling am I craving? • What do I truly need? • How might I attain this? Mantra: There is enough for me.
Poor timing	Being out of synch(ronicity) Out of season/rhythm Out of right relationship with others/life	Conversing with life: • Listening • Finding and asking the right questions • Working with time as an ally
Physical symptoms of fear	Examples: • Cold belly? • Jumping at small sounds? • Perception of and/or fear of invasion? • Sense of living in occupied territory?	What am I afraid of? • Not enough love or attention? • Not enough energy, time or money? Who is attempting invasion? Who is occupying my own territory? What do they want? What different boundaries might I need? How can I tend this somatically? • EFT tapping • Meditation • Yoga • Walking and movement

Reclamation of the lost histories and practices of the feminine is occurring. As discussed in chapter 1 via Mary Magdalene's mythology, Magdalenian mythemes found in grail lore, alchemy, Black Madonna mythology, tarot,
and folklore act as threads connecting her with the ancient lineage of Mediterranean Sister-Brides within bounty traditions, rooting her resurgence. By
locating the Bride within the plurality of Magdalenian mythology, including
the canonical and Gnostic Gospels—especially the Gospel of Mary—and the
post–*Da Vinci Code* eruption of scholarship and creativity, a close examination of interdisciplinary scholarship expands the imaginal interplay between
history and mythology in terms of voice, power, and agency.

Exploration of the relationship between Magdalene's history and mythology, beyond her identity as disciple and apostle, toward Bride and equal
partner, informs our world today. Mythology bridges the gap between belief
in an absolute "truth" and the power of imagination, offering instead a process of meaning making.

Tending the reemerging feminine's polyvalent archetypal expressions
broadens our respons/ability, our ability to respond to this phenomenon,
as well as supporting recognition of her various forms and dynamism.
Rather than relying on patriarchal limitations of the feminine familiar in
the distorted and confining Greco-Roman foundation of Western cultures,
as studied by Patricia Reis in *Daughters of Saturn*, the reclamation of the
bridal archetype expands her regeneration beyond prescribed and limited
roles for women.

By also expanding the definition of the wasteland into two interconnected
and reciprocally unhealthy territories, we can better tend their distinct
dis/eases. Not only does the desertified masculine realm abut the swamped
feminine, but their properties also overlap. The constructed dam dividing
the two is the source of necrotic imbalance and requires deconstruction.
What is called for is irrigation of the dry, rational logocentric, masculine
landscape—once devoid of feeling—and the simultaneous relief of feminine
territory carrying disproportionate, flooding, and emotional burden. Such
action requires radical, effective theories and practices.

For example, within mainstream Christian feminist Magdalenian scholarship, the failure to make crucial leaps misses opportunities to connect just
how broadly and deeply the lack of bridal representation in the Christian
myth impoverishes us. By instead identifying the lost centrality of the sacred
marriage at the heart of the Judeo-Christian traditions, its place within the
ancient partnership mythologies, and Magdalene's mythological return as
archetypal Bride, we turn (consciously, curiously) toward livelier, more effectual research, dialogue, and action.

Layered, interconnected, intertextual symbolism between Sumerian, Babylonian, Egyptian, and Judeo-Christian scholarship and literature, as well as the later disciplines of grail lore and alchemy, track how ancient mysticism at the heart of these traditions embodies and culminates in sacred marriage. Alchemy, as exemplified in its ancient Egyptian roots told through the myth of Isis and Osiris, can be traced as a path of individuation as well as a type of bricolaged methodology. The key to alchemical healing in preparation for sacred marriage is that each must continuously work toward his/her own individuation separately, then together.

The loss of Magdalene as half of the Christian story renders Jesus/Jeshua as Fisher King—wounded in his grief at the loss of his Bride—he (and his church) becomes an impotent leader. He is only one half of a greater whole. Outdated masculinist theories and mythological constructs can meet their missing counterpoint in regenerative Magdalenian consciousness. Assumptions made about women's (and men's) individuating journeys can be reimagined.[129] The Fisher King—who has been suffering endlessly and whose wound originates with the loss of the feminine and whose agony radiates out to also ruin the land—can finally be tended. Indeed, no one can thrive when the (divine) masculine is wounded and the (divine) feminine is lost. Under patriarchal blinders even Joseph Campbell, as scholarly grail knight, failed to ask the correct questions or even to recognize the grail herself as she passed him by.

Marion Woodman and Deldon McNeely examine how the wounded masculine reciprocally heals and evolves as the once-abandoned Bride is reclaimed. The return of the Bride is not for her-Self alone but is the movement toward partnership, the sacred marriage at the root of Western traditions, Jung's *coniunctio* embodied in divine union of oppositional energy. By creating and tracking more-inclusive, feminist responses to Jung and Campbell, we more effectively make meaning of the dynamic mythic movement in women's lived experience, investigating and investing in the regenerative movement of the Bride. We learn to ask the right questions.

Jody Bower offers just such a revision with *Jane Eyre's Sisters*. The significance of her findings is remarkable; like Campbell's *Hero with a Thousand*

---

129. Even notorious James Bond has been developing his Magdalenian consciousness. Moving from a type of widowhood, through the underworld—while pausing to cross-dress for International Women's Day—Daniel Craig's twenty-first-century Bond moves toward his own individuation and sacred marriage. In his fourth film, Craig's Bond meets a worthy partner, a wanderer emerging from her own s/hero's journey; together they cross new barriers and tend their erotic, intimate bond. The name of his beloved? Madeleine. See the film *Spectre* and the short subject *James Bond Supports International Women's Day 2011*.

Faces, her landmark study recognizing and amplifying existing, instructive patterned mythemes within women's literature and lives provides vital scholarship on the power and importance of questing. By identifying locating markers and psychic cartography skills, she offers invaluable contributions to our collective individuating potential. When we can find our position and map our trajectories—tracking both where we've been and where we hope to travel toward—we can better integrate the long view, making sense of our steps and agency, coming to consciousness. By cultivating an embodying, committed practice of questing—perhaps life's central regenerative movement—the Aletis/Bride somatically initiates healing potential for psyche, culture, and the realm.

By supporting navigation within literary cartography—recognizing signs, portents, and players we encounter while following female protagonists on their adventures—Bower's mapping offers a psychic GPS (perhaps PPS—a psychic positioning system), allowing us to track the Aletis/Bride as she moves toward what Bower identifies as the healing culmination for women wanderers, the creation of a home of her own—a core theme for Brides—and mature partnership. Individuating women, who intimately know the pain of the dark and choose—or are cast out—to wander, move toward a more embodied, creative, cyclical ecofeminist form of resurrection: regeneration. Venturing outside and beyond (supposedly "safe, secure") patriarchal norms, structures, and spaces, she is willing (and *needs*) to venture into unknown territory. Our ability to wander is inherently predicated upon our ability to wonder. In this way the courageous Aletis/Bride effectively and somatically applies Jung's transcendent function via her wandering ways. Unable to return to an unhealthy home, she leaves (become homeless); venturing forth into the unknown, she holds the tension of these (supposed) opposites. Inherently a Hestian priestess (who knows and deeply values hearth and home as healthy psychic containment), her refusal of intolerable situations pairs with trust in her own process, inviting the (as yet unknown) grace of unknown opportunities.

The exploration of Magdalenian literature—which has developed exponentially within the last several decades—yields tremendous insight when viewed via Susan Rowland's model for feminist post-Jungian critique, exposing deep function of reading and writing fiction; reading can be a radical act of psychic growth and development. Interacting with the written word, we infuse literary landscapes with meaning from our own very personal imaginal realm, allowing the story to become reflexive tonic for psyche. This form of active imagination not only supports identification with the characters and the s/hero's journey but promotes an expansion of our range of feelings, empowerment, and agency. That so many emerging Magdalenian works have been consistently achieving tremendous international popularity further implies significant cultural impact.

Additional literary tools arise via Jane Austen's literary recipe for successful bridal agency. Requiring that her s/heroes strive for partnership with men who are also actively cultivating their inner life, character strength, and their own individuation process, Austen's body of work repeatedly cautions of the dangers inherent in entering into partnership with an unindividuating/ stuck man, primarily the loss of energy necessary for her own individuation process. Positively, in what may be Austen's greatest gift, she illuminates the need for healthy containment as her women move from being trapped in festering options toward the vitality of true partnership. Her work highlights how crucial it is for women to develop their inner masculine, discernment, and critical containment in questing toward healthy inner marriage and mature, worthy partnership.

Along with literary fiction, women's biographies and memoir illuminate the wandering path of the Aletis. Tracking the threads in Elizabeth Gilbert's *Eat, Pray, Love* reveals an individuating Ariadnean mythology, perhaps the most ancient strand of Magdalene's Mediterranean lineage of sacred marriage. Following Austen, Gilbert demonstrates the dangers of encountering the immature/immobilized Theseuses and offers an individuating map toward personal wholeness and eventual partnership with Dionysian divinity. As both Ginette Paris in *Pagan Grace* and Christine Downing in *The Goddess* claim, Ariadne is no victim. Rather, she is an active agent of her own destiny, choosing Theseus and the necessary puzzles, adventure, and subsequent abandonment through which she transforms.

The identification of distinctive, repetitive patterns in four popular European fairy tales, "Cinderella," "Sleeping Beauty," "Snow White," and "Rapunzel," offer retellings of the quest of the wounded masculine as the bachelor prince who seeks the lost, imprisoned, and wounded Bride—his true partner. Through their continual retelling and renewal through literature, the fine and lively arts, and contemporary film, fairy tales capture our imagination as embodied, encoded Magdalenian consciousness, offering layered, regenerative teachings. These stories also amplify patriarchy's vampiric shadow fantasy, where the Bride is at risk of her sisters' and mother's envious projections and the resultant, depotentiating state of confusion. This battle with the feminine shadow is an individuating act for the Bride, who fights for her right to wear her sovereign bridal crown to the altar. Magdalene—like Psyche and Cinderella on their way toward sacred partnership—must first confront traitorous sisters and a wicked usurper queen, while sorting her own psychic seeds, separating projections from her own shadow. The Bride/princess must discern and take healing and regenerative actions through psychic fog in the feminine bog.

Examining the (often unconscious) trauma we all suffer in the twin patriarchal wastelands, along with the tragic calcification of a corrupted Christianity that sent its Bride into exile, leads to understanding sacrifice as an incomplete and necrotic model. Like the middle act of a three-act comedy, the cyclical movement required is regeneration. Here, Magdalene applies her tricky detective skills. Showing up in feminist detective literature, she turns and returns toward life. Close examination of incomplete attempts at renewal supports, like Austen's and Gilbert's literary contributions, an awareness of the patriarchal wound and its need for deeper tending.

Focusing on the potential of Magdalenian consciousness and activism as eco-healing agent, the application of Vandana Shiva's Shakti Principle supports and catalyzes psycho-logical, socio-logical, and eco-logical change in support of green, living, and vibrant interdependent systems, both internally and externally. From both a depth psychological and cosmo/logical perspective, this is the movement from complex wasteland toward a healed, restored Vesica Piscis, the renewed embodiment of the sacred marriage.[130] This homecoming to a world reensouled provides a hopeful prescription for tending the returning Bride within the context of the archetypal sacred marriage as a type of sacred grove, supporting a reenchantment of our interrelated internal and external realms. As above, so below; as She returns, so does the Garden.

Emerging stories of embodied, empowered women sleuths, like Phryne Fisher, offer models of sovereignty, agency, and dynamism. Phryne elevates the art of problem solving to a fine feminine form, expanding into community building, generosity, and exuberant joie de vivre. Successfully embodying the Magdalenian archetypal Bride, she is fully sexual and regal. Consistently evolving, both in her personal individuation and in preparation for relationship with the beloved, her tricky detective skills are always in service to her commitment to supportive sisterhood. Fearlessly dethroning usurper queens, Phryne embodies an empowering model for how regenerative qualities inspire, nurture, and heal the adjacent masculine and feminine wastelands.

A complex roadmap for Magdalene's regenerative power and dynamism resides in the novel *Broken for You*, centered around the individuation of main characters Margaret and Wanda; the relationship between these two women offers a healed version of sisterhood and nurturing motherhood.

---

130. See Keiron Le Grice, *The Archetypal Cosmos*, especially "Epilogue: The Opening of a New Spiritual Era."

By ritualizing the crafting of "fictitious" mythology for surviving Holocaust objects, this evocative act of renewal is amplified through the mosaic art of Wanda/Tink and the greater collective. This remythologizing blurs the gap between history and mythology and is emblematic of Magdalenian consciousness as it reinvigorates storytelling as conscious griefwork. Fully grieving has the power to liberate blocked energy, create psychic space, and renew. Bricolage functions as such a healing, remythologizing methodology. Margaret's very household itself becomes a radical, ecofeminist container for individuation, community, and rebirth.

Mystery invites a quest. Beyond examining the explicit canon of Magdalenian literature deliberately structured around her as a central, transparent figure, I found her appearing in the most unlikely places, repeatedly and convincingly: in films, television series, and novels. She appears as the Bride in various aspects: the outsider, the wanderer, the detective, the lost princess, and the grieving artist. Her movement is consistently toward sovereign coronation and the beloved. She matures from codependent management to healing, fluidly and flexibly. Probing, questioning, questing, the Bride—as daughter, sister, Aletis/wanderer, and *bricoleuse*—is simply committed to becoming her-Self. She is, quite holistically and gracefully, "broken for you." But her breakage is not sacrificial, it is regenerational.

To best tend the soul of the world, tending Magdalene as the lost and returning Bride—the feminine counterpoint of our world's wounded patriarchal soul, returning, re/membered, rising, regenerating from the twin sterile wastelands—is crucial. Magdalene shows us how to heal, to collect our shards, to re/member our way. In each moment we are at choice within a continuum of responses. We can fall back into step-sisterhood, martyrdom, and envy—the corrupt, vampiric evil/usurper queen archetype. Or we can reach forward, toward Magdalenian consciousness, using tricky detective skills, cultivated compassion and curiosity, and our inherent creativity. This level of deep tending of the pernicious residue that is personal and intergenerational trauma regenerates our personal and collective bodies and cultures. Here, applying Dennis Slattery's riting practice transforms depth psychological literary theory into an effective infusion, a direct elixir informing the intertwining creative and healing processes on a deep foundational level.

Magdalene is the archetypal Bride resurfacing for our times. The vast amount of emerging scholarship, literature, and art in which she features overtly and covertly is a testament to how we are, at this potent time of deep unrest and environmental devastation, culturally ripe for this myth and the gifts implicit in reclaiming the sacred Bride. If she is trending, we are mending.

I suggest the feminine's primary movement is bridal, ever evolving toward integration, union, *coniunctio* within that mysterious feminine-masculine continuum. The exile of the Bride has for far too long greatly impeded the individuation of our psyches—both individually and collectively—leaving the Vesica Piscis barren, a compound wasteland, the wounded masculine an incomplete crescent longing for wholeness. The extensive, pervasive, and necessary return of Magdalene signals multiple levels of interdependent regeneration. With her previously disowned shards coming together as therapeutic clues, the regenerating Bride heals her fragmented Self in the psycho/logical realm, her community in the socio-logical realm, and Gaia in the eco/logical realm. Continuing onward from the psychic realm outward toward an exploration of how the returning archetypal Bride also bears gifts for *communitas* and Gaia, these three interconnecting realms together regenerate as a direct result of our comprehensive ecofeminist quest to understand and welcome embodied regeneration of the feminine forms of life.

WORKS CITED AND CONSULTED

"Advancing Women Artists." *Advancing Women Artists*, http://advancingwomenartists.org. Accessed 24 May 2021.

"Adverse Childhood Experiences (ACEs)." *Center for Disease Control and Prevention*, 21 May 2021, https://www.cdc.gov/violenceprevention/aces/index.html.

"Agatha Christie Mysteries Are Still Raking in the Cash a Century On." *Marketplace*, American Public Media, 28 Sept. 2020, https://www.marketplace.org/.

"Agatha Christie's Marple: Nemesis." *Agatha Christie's Marple*, directed by Nicolas Winding Refn, 1 Jan. 2009.

"Agatha Christie's Marple: Sleeping Murder." *Agatha Christie's Marple*, directed by Edward Hall, 5 Feb. 2006.

"AgathaChristie.Com." *AgathaChristie.Com*, https://www.agathachristie.com/. Accessed 2 Oct. 2020.

Aitkenhead, Decca. "Mary and Me." *The Guardian*, 19 Aug. 2006, http://www.theguardian.com/books/2006/aug/19/fiction.features.

Alcott, Louisa May. *Little Women*. Roberts Bros., 1868.

Allums, Larry, and Louise Cowan, editors. *The Epic Cosmos*. Dallas Institute Publications, 2014.

"The Alphabet Versus the Goddess Lecture by Leonard Shlain." *YouTube. Tiffany Shlain & Let It Ripple Studio*, Nov. 1, 2012, https://www.youtube.com/watch?v=2QQuD62RxrU.

Arabi, Shahida. *Becoming the Narcissist's Nightmare: How to Devalue and Discard the Narcissist While Supplying Yourself*. CreateSpace Independent Publishing Platform, 2016.

Arnim, Elizabeth von. *The Enchanted April*. Macmillan, 1923.

"Art | Harmonia Rosales." *Harmonia6.wixsite.com, Website-1*, https://harmonia6.wixsite.com/website-1/collections. Accessed 22 July 2021.

The Ascent of Woman. Directed by Louise Hooper and Hugo Macgregor, Documentary Series, 2015.

Asheville Jung Center: Global Jungian Community. 28 March 2011, http://ashevillejungcenter.org/2011/03/true-grit/.

Austen, Jane, With an introduction by Karen Joy Fowler. *The Complete Novels*. New York: Penguin Classics, 2006.

Austenland. Directed by Jerusha Hess, Fickle Fish Films, Moxie Pictures, 2013.

"Avengers: Endgame's Female Superheroes Are Mistreated and Then United to Take a Bow." *Slate*, April 2019, https://slate.com/culture/2019/04/avengers-endgame-female

-representation-black-widow.html?fbclid=IwAR1Df5nSCfJPMVHxsLNmcLQwUY8T G_5fojnP-uBBwLxLtr5XXfWlaHOj2Jo. Accessed 2 Jan. 2020.

Baigent, Michael, Richard Leigh, and Henry Lincoln. *Holy Blood, Holy Grail*. Delacorte Press, 1982.

Baker, Jennifer. "Review: Broken for You." Book review, *Booklist*, Aug. 2004. Web. Accessed 20 Aug. 2016.

Ballard, Nancer. "The Heroine Journeys Project." *The Heroine Journeys Project*, 29 Jan. 2015, https://heroinejourneys.com/about/.

The Barefoot Artist. Dir. Glen Holsten and Daniel Traub. Itinerant Pictures, 2013.

Baring, Anne, and Jules Cashford. *The Myth of the Goddess: Evolution of an Image*. Viking Arkana, 1991.

Barr, Tricia. "How *Star Wars* Made Me a Feminist—Even When the Franchise Was Not." *POPSUGAR Entertainment*, 18 Dec. 2019, http://www.popsugar.com/node/39361046.

Bartlett, Christy. "A Tearoom View of Mended Ceramics." *Flickwerk—The Aesthetics of Mended Japanese Ceramics*. Cornell UP, Herbert F. Johnson Museum of Art, 2008.

Batalha, Natalie. "Exoplanets and Love: Science That Connects Us to One Another." Interview by Krista Tippett. *onbeing.org*, 14 Feb. 2013, https://onbeing.org/programs/ natalie-batalha-exoplanets-and-love-science-that-connects-us-to-one-another/. Accessed 13 Oct. 2020.

Batalha, Natalie. "A Planetary Sense of Love." Interview by Krista Tippett. *onbeing.org*, 20 May 2019, https://onbeing.org/programs/a-planetary-sense-of-love-natalie-batalha/. Accessed 13 Oct. 2020.

Bateson, Mary Catherine. *Composing a Life*. Atlantic Monthly, 1989.

Bateson, Mary Catherine. "Living as an Improvisational Art." Interview by Krista Tippett. *onbeing.org*, 1 Oct. 2015, https://onbeing.org/programs/mary-catherine-bateson-living -as-an-improvisational-art/. Accessed 19 Oct. 2020.

BBC News. "Demanding Justice for Women and Children Abused by Irish Nuns." *BBC News*, 24 Sept. 2014, http://www.bbc.com/news/magazine-29307705.

BBC Radio 4. "Free Thinking, Dada and the Power of Nonsense." https://www.bbc.co.uk/ programmes/m000k9ws. Accessed 11 Sept. 2020.

Bassil-Morozow, Helena, and Luke Hockley. *Jungian Film Studies*. 1st edition, Routledge, 2016.

Beard, Mary. *Women & Power: A Manifesto*. Routledge, 2016.

Beavis, Mary Ann. "The Cathar Mary Magdalene and the Sacred Feminine: Pop Culture Legend vs. Medieval Doctrine." *Journal of Religion and Popular Culture*, vol. 24, no. 3, Sept. 2012, pp. 419–31, https://doi.org/10.3138/jrpc.24.3.419.

Beavis, Mary Ann. "The Deification of Mary Magdalene." *Feminist Theology*, vol. 21, no. 2, Jan. 2013, pp. 145–54, https://doi.org/10.1177/0966735012462840.

Beavis, Mary Ann. "Mary Magdalene on Film in Twenty-First Century: A Feminist Theological Critique." *Journal of Religion and Film*, vol. 28, no. 1, Apr. 2024, pp. 1–21.

Becoming Jane. Directed by Julian Jarrold et al., Scion Films; distributed by Buena Vista Home Entertainment, 2008.

Begg, Ean C. M. *The Cult of the Black Virgin*. Arkana, 1985.

Belew, Kathleen. *Bring the War Home: The White Power Movement and Paramilitary America*. 1st edition, Harvard UP, 2018.

Bellevie, Lesa. "She Moves in Mysterious Ways: Mary Magdalene in the Internet Age." In *Secrets of Mary Magdalene: The Untold Story of History's Most Misunderstood Woman*, edited by Arne J De Keijzer and Daniel Burstein, CDS Books, 2006.

Beninca, Ariel. *Rabbit Proof Fence Film Review*. https://www.academia.edu/11332542/Rabbit_Proof_Fence_Film_Review. Accessed 17 Sept. 2020.

Berlin, Adele, et al. *The Jewish Study Bible: Jewish Publication Society Tanakh Translation*. Oxford UP, 2004.

Billson, Anne. "Does the 'Female Gaze' Make Sexual Violence on Film Any Less Repugnant?" *The Guardian*, 2 Aug. 2019, http://www.theguardian.com/film/2019/aug/02/the-female-gaze-does-it-make-sexual-violence-on-film-any-less-repugnant.

Billson, Anne. "How the 'Rape-Revenge Movie' Became a Feminist Weapon for the #MeToo Generation." *The Guardian*, 11 May 2018, http://www.theguardian.com/film/2018/may/11/how-the-rape-revenge-movie-became-a-feminist-weapon-for-the-metoo-generation.

Blackie, Sharon. *If Women Rose Rooted: A Life-Changing Journey to Authenticity and Belonging*. September Publishing, 2019.

Blackwood, Sarah. "'Little Women' and the Marmee Problem." *The New Yorker*, https://www.newyorker.com/culture/cultural-comment/little-women-and-the-marmee-problem. 24 December 2019. Accessed 23 Jan. 2020.

Bly, Robert, and Marion Woodman. *The Maiden King: The Reunion of Masculine and Feminine*. Element, 1999.

Boal, Augusto. *Games for Actors and Non-Actors 2nd Edition*. Routledge, 2002.

Bolen, Jean Shinoda. *Goddesses in Everywoman: Powerful Archetypes in Women's Lives*. 13th edition, Harper Paperbacks, 2014.

Bolen, Jean Shinoda. *Gods in Everyman: Archetypes That Shape Men's Lives*. Harper Paperbacks, 2014.

Bolen, Jean Shinoda. *Moving Toward the Millionth Circle Energizing the Global Women's Movement: Advocating a Global Conference on Women*. Conari Press, 2013.

Bolen, Jean Shinoda. *The Myth of Eros and Psyche: Growth Toward Wholeness of the Archetypally Vulnerable Woman: The Tasks to Learn Audio Cassette*. Sounds True Recordings, 1992.

Bolen, Jean Shinoda. *The Tao of Psychology: Synchronicity and Self*. 1st edition, HarperSanFrancisco, 1982.

Bolen, Jean Shinoda. "The Women's Movement in Transition: The Goddess and the Grail." *Magical Blend* 33, Jan. 1992, p. 8.

Bourgeault, Cynthia. *The Meaning of Mary Magdalene: Discovering the Woman at the Heart of Christianity*. Shambhala, 2010.

Bower, Anne, editor. *Reel Food: Essays on Food and Film*. Routledge, 2004.

Bower, Jody Gentian. *Jane Eyre's Sisters: How Women Live and Write the Heroine's Story*. Quest Books, 2015.

Boym, Svetlana. *The Future of Nostalgia*. Illustrated Edition, Basic Books, 2002.

Bradshaw, Peter. "Mary Magdalene Review—Toothless Attempt to Overturn Sunday School Myths." *The Guardian*, 27 Feb. 2018, https://www.theguardian.com/film/2018/feb/27/mary-magdalene-review-rooney-mara-sunday-school-myths.

Brave. Directed by Mark Andrews et al., Walt Disney Pictures, Pixar Animation Studios, 2012.

Breu, Christopher. "Going Blood-Simple in Poisonville: Hard-Boiled Masculinity in Dashiell Hammett's Red Harvest." *Men and Masculinities*, vol. 7, no. 1, July 2004, pp. 52–76. *SAGE Journals*, https://doi.org/10.1177/1097184X03257449.

Brezsny, Rob. *The Televisionary Oracle*. North Atlantic Books, U.S, 2000.

Bride & Prejudice. Directed by Gurinder Chadha, Pathé Pictures International, UK Film Council, Kintop Pictures, 2005.

Bridget Jones: The Edge of Reason. Directed by Beeban Kidron, Miramax, 2004.

Bridget Jones's Diary. Directed by Sharon Maguire, Miramax, 2001.

Brown, Brené. *Daring Greatly: How the Courage to Be Vulnerable Transforms the Way We Live, Love, Parent, and Lead*. Gotham Books, 2012.

Brown, Brené. *The Gifts of Imperfection: 10th Anniversary Edition: Features a New Foreword and Brand-New Tools*. Anniversary edition, Hazelden, 2022.

Brown, Brené. "The Power of Vulnerability." *www.ted.com*, June 2010. http://www.ted.com/talks/brene_brown_on_vulnerability.

Brown, Brené. *Rising Strong*. Random House, 2015.

Brown, Dan. *The Da Vinci Code*. Doubleday, 2003.

Brown, Pamela. *Tales from the Academic Dark Side: Bringing Untold Realities of Academic Positions into the Daylight* AKA: Tales from the Gero-Dark Side: Bringing Untold Realities of Academic Positions into the Daylight*. 2013. *ResearchGate*, https://doi.org/10.13140/2.1.4201.0884.

The Burning Times. Directed by Donna Read, National Film Board of Canada (NFB), Studio D., 1990.

Burstein, Dan, et al., editors. *Secrets of Mary Magdalene: The Untold Story of History's Most Misunderstood Woman*. 1st ed., CDS Books, 2006.

Cagney & Lacey. Directed by Tyne Daly et al., CBS, Filmways Pictures, Orion Television, 1981.

A Call to Spy. Directed by Lydia Dean Pilcher et al., SMT Pictures, 2020.

Calvert, Katherine. "The Idealised Mother and the Socialist Movement in Weimar Germany." *The Institute of Modern Languages Research*, https://modernlanguages.sas.ac.uk/events/event/22835. Accessed 22 Oct. 2020.

Cambray, Joseph. *Synchronicity: Nature and Psyche in an Interconnected Universe*. Texas A&M UP, 2009.

Campbell, Joseph. "The Emergence of the Heroine." *The Feminine in European Myth and Romance*. Theater of the Open Eye, 1985.

Campbell, Joseph. *Goddesses: Mysteries of the Feminine Divine*. Edited by Safron Elsabeth Rossi, illustrated edition, New World Library, 2013.

Campbell, Joseph. *The Hero with a Thousand Faces*. New World Library, 2008.

Campbell, Joseph. "In Search of the Holy Grail: The Parzival Legend." HighBridge, 1990. Audio recording.

Campbell, Joseph. *The Masks of God, Vol 3: Occidental Mythology*. Viking Press, 1964.

Campbell, Joseph. *The Masks of God, Vol 4: Creative Mythology*. 1st edition, Penguin, 1968.

Campbell, Joseph. *The Mythic Dimension: Selected Essays 1959–1987*. Ed. Antony Van Couvering, 2nd edition, New World Library, 2007.

Campbell, Joseph. *Pathways to Bliss: Mythology and Personal Transformation*. Ed. David Kudler, New World Library, 2004.

Campbell, Joseph. *Transformations of Myth Through Time.* Harper Perennial, 1990.

Campbell, Joseph. *The Way of the Animal Powers.* Edited by Robert Walter, 1st edition, Alfred Van Der Marck Editions, 1983.

Campbell, Joseph. *The Way of the Seeded Earth, Part 1: The Sacrifice.* Harper & Row, 1988.

Campbell, Joseph. "The Woman's Journey." *Myths and Mysteries of the Great Goddess.* La Casa de Maria, 1983.

Campbell, Joseph, and Bill Moyers. *The Power of Myth.* New York: Anchor, 1991.

Campbell, Joseph, and Charles Musès. *In All Her Names: Explorations of the Feminine in Divinity.* HarperSanFrancisco, 1991.

Campbell, Joseph, and Safron Rossi. *Goddesses: Mysteries of the Feminine Divine.* New World Library, 2013.

Campbell, Lori M., editor. *A Quest of Her Own: Essays on the Female Hero in Modern Fantasy.* McFarland, 2014.

Canonville, Christine Louis de. "The Narcissistic Mother & the Drama Triangle." https://narcissisticbehavior.net/narcissistic-mother-drama-triangle/. Accessed 22 June 2021.

Canonville, Christine Louis de. *The Three Faces of Evil.* 1st edition, Black Card Books, 2015.

Caputi, Jane. *Goddesses and Monsters: Women, Myth, Power, and Popular Culture.* Popular Press 3, 2004.

Caputi, Jane. "On Psychic Activism: Feminist Mythmaking." In *The Woman's Companion to Mythology*, Pandora Press, 1997.

Carrington, Leonora. *The Hearing Trumpet.* Exact Change, 2008.

Casey, Caroline. *Making the Gods Work for You: The Astrological Language of the Psyche.* Harmony, 2013.

Chapoutot, Johan. *The Law of Blood.* Harvard UP, 2018.

Chemaly, Soraya L. *Rage Becomes Her: The Power of Women's Anger.* Atria, 2019.

Chesler, Phyllis. "New Bio of Sabina Spielrein: Raped by Carl Jung, Then Murdered by the Nazis." *Tablet Magazine*, 7 Nov. 2017, https://www.tabletmag.com/sections/arts-letters/articles/sabina-spielrein-carl-jung.

Chocolat. Directed by Lasse Hallström, Miramax, David Brown Productions, Fat Free, 2001.

Christ, Carol P. "Maiden, Mother, Crone: Ancient Tradition or New Creative Synthesis?" *Feminism and Religion*, 8 Aug. 2016, https://feminismandreligion.com/2016/08/08/maiden-mother-and-crone-ancient-tradition-or-new-creative-synthesis-by-carol-p-christ/.

Chynoweth, Adele. "'The Stain Is Indelible': Rachael Romero's *The Magdalene Diaries*." *N.Paradoxa*, vol. 32, July 2013, pp. 48–58.

Cichon, Joan Marie. "Archaeomythology from Neolithic Malta to Modern Poland: Apprehending the Maternal and Spiritual Realities of Ancient and Present-Day Cultures" In *Myths Shattered and Restored: Proceedings of the Association for the Study of Women and Mythology*, Goddess Ink, 2016.

Cichon, Joan. *Matriarchy in Bronze Age Crete: A Perspective from Archaeomythology and Modern Matriarchal Studies.* Archaeopress, 2022.

Cinderella. Directed by Kenneth Branagh, Allison Shearmur Productions, Beagle Pug Films, Genre Films, 2015.

Cinderella. Directed by Clyde Geronimi et al., Walt Disney Productions, Walt Disney Animation Studios, 1950.

Clark-Stern, Elizabeth. *Out of the Shadows: A Story of Toni Wolff and Emma Jung.* 1st edition, Genoa House, 2015.

Clay, Catrine. *Labyrinths: Emma Jung, Her Marriage to Carl, and the Early Years of Psychoanalysis.* Illustrated edition, Harper, 2016.

Coelho, Paulo. *The Alchemist: 25th Anniversary Edition.* HarperOne, 2014.

Cold Comfort Farm. Directed by David Conroy et al., Acorn Media, 1999.

Cold Comfort Farm. Directed by John Schlesinger, Universal Studios, 1996.

Combs, Allan, and Mark Holland. *Synchronicity: Through the Eyes of Science, Myth and the Trickster.* 3rd edition, Da Capo Press, 2000.

Cori, Jasmin Lee. *The Emotionally Absent Mother.* Experiment, 2010.

Corpse Bride. Directed by Tim Burton and Mike Johnson, Warner Bros., Tim Burton Productions, Laika Entertainment, 2005.

Corrigan, Maureen. "10 Years Later, Mystery Heroine 'Maisie Dobbs' Gains New Life." *NPR,* National Public Radio, 10 June 2014.

Corrigan, Maureen. "'Maisie Dobbs' Book Review." *NPR.org.* National Public Radio, 13 August 2003.

Corson, Roberta Bassett. *Stepping out of the Shadows: Naming and Claiming the Medial Woman.* Mandorla Books, 2022.

Cousineau, Phil. *Soul Moments: Marvelous Stories of Synchronicity—Meaningful Coincidences from a Seemingly Random World.* Conari Press, 1997

Cowan, Louise. *The Epic Cosmos.* Dallas Institute Publications, 2014.

Cowan, Lyn. "Dismantling the Animus." The Jung Page, 1994, https://jungpage.org/learn/articles/analytical-psychology/105-dismantling-the-animus.

Crampton, Caroline. "Is Agatha Christie a Good Writer?" *Shedunnit,* 28 July 2021, https://shedunnitshow.com/.

Crampton, Caroline. "Locked Room." *Shedunnit,* 16 Sept. 2020, https://shedunnitshow.com/.

Crampton, Caroline. "Surplus Women." *Shedunnit,* 31 Oct. 2018, https://shedunnitshow.com/surpluswomen/.

Cruz, Leonard, editor. *A Clear and Present Danger: Narcissism in the Era of President Trump.* Chiron Publications, 2017.

Cunningham, Elizabeth. *Daughter of the Shining Isles.* Barrytown, 2000.

Daly, Mary. *Beyond God the Father: Toward a Philosophy of Women's Liberation.* Revised edition, Beacon Press, 1993.

Daly, Mary. *Gyn/Ecology: The Metaethics of Radical Feminism.* Beacon Press, 1990.

Daly, Mary, and Jane Caputi. *Websters' First New Intergalactic Wickedary of the English Language.* Reprint edition, HarperCollins, 1994.

d'Aulnoy, Baroness Madame. *The Island of Happiness: Tales of Madame d'Aulnoy.* Translated by Jack Zipes, illustrated edition, Princeton UP, 2021.

The Da Vinci Code. Directed by Ron Howard, Columbia Pictures, 2006.

Davis, Essie. "*The Babadook* Actress Essie Davis Opens Up About Hollywood Ambitions and Motherhood," interview by Joel Meares. *Daily Life,* 12 Apr. 2015, http://www.dailylife.com.au/dl-people/interviews/the-babadook-actress-essie-davis-opens-up-about-hollywood-ambitions-and-motherhood-20150411-1mizvq.html.

Death Comes to Pemberley. Directed by Daniel Percival, BBC Drama Productions, Far Moor, Origin Pictures, 2014.

Derkson, Kyle. "Racism and Capitalism in Black Panther." *Journal of Religion & Film*, vol. 2, no. 1 (2018), article 40. *Semantic Scholar*, https://doi.org/10.32873/uno.dc.jrf.22.01.40.

DeSalvo, Louise A. *Virginia Woolf: The Impact of Childhood Sexual Abuse on Her Life and Work*. Reissue edition, Ballantine Books, 1990.

Diaz, Natalie. *Postcolonial Love Poem*. Graywolf Press, 2020.

Dickens, Charles. *Great Expectations*. Chapman and Hall, 1861.

The Dig. Directed by Simon Stone, Netflix, Magnolia Mae Films, Clerkenwell Films, 2021.

A Discovery of Witches. Directed by Juan Carlos Medina, television series, Bad Wolf and Sky Studios, 2018–2022.

Divine Women. British Broadcasting Corporation (BBC), The Open University, 2012.

Downing, Christine. *The Goddess: Mythological Images of the Feminine*. o edition, iUniverse, 2007.

Drayton, Joanne. *The Search for Anne Perry: The Hidden Life of a Bestselling Crime Writer*. Reprint edition, Arcade, 2016.

The Duchess. Directed by Saul Dibb, Paramount Vantage, Pathé, BBC Film, 2008.

Dumont, Marion, and Gayatri Devi, editors. *Myths Shattered and Restored: Proceedings of the Association for the Study of Women and Mythology*. Goddess Ink, 2016.

Eat Pray Love. Directed by Ryan Murphy. Columbia Pictures, 2010.

Edinger, Edward F. *The Mystery of the Coniunctio: Alchemical Image of Individuation*. Inner City Books, 1994.

Edsel, Robert M., and Bret Witter. *The Monuments Men: Allied Heroes, Nazi Thieves, and the Greatest Treasure Hunt in History*. Center Street, 2009.

Edwards, Lee R. *Psyche as Hero: Female Heroism and Fictional Form*. Wesleyan UP, 1987.

Edwards, Selden. *The Little Book*. Plume, 2009.

Edwards, Selden. *The Lost Prince*. Dutton, 2012.

Ehrman, Bart D. *Truth and Fiction in "The Da Vinci Code": A Historian Reveals What We Really Know About Jesus, Mary Magdalene, and Constantine*. Oxford UP, 2004.

Eisenstein, Charles. *Sacred Economics: Money, Gift & Society in the Age of Transition*. Evolver Editions, 2011.

Eisler, Riane Tennenhaus. *The Chalice and the Blade: Our History, Our Future*. Harper & Row, 1987.

Eisler, Riane Tennenhaus, and David Loye. *The Partnership Way: New Tools for Living and Learning*. Harper, 1990.

Elbert, Sarah. *A Hunger for Home: Louisa May Alcott and Little Women*. 1st edition, Temple UP, 1984.

Ella Enchanted. Directed by Tommy O'Haver, Miramax, Jane Startz Productions, Blessington Film Productions, 2004.

Enchanted April. Directed by Mike Newell et al., BBC Films, 1991.

Enloe, Cynthia. *Bananas, Beaches and Bases: Making Feminist Sense of International Politics, 2nd Ed.* University of California Press, 2014.

Enola Holmes. Directed by Harry Bradbeer et al., Netflix, Legendary Entertainment, PCMA Productions, 2020.

Eschenbach, Wolfram von, and Richard Barber. *Parzival and Titurel*. Translated by Cyril Edwards. Oxford UP, 2009.

EverAfter. Directed by Andy Tennant, Twentieth Century Fox, 1998.

Everything Everywhere All at Once. Directed by Daniel Kwan and Daniel Scheinert, A24, IAC Films, AGBO, 2022.

Fagone, Jason. *The Woman Who Smashed Codes: A True Story of Love, Spies, and the Unlikely Heroine Who Outwitted America's Enemies*. 1st edition, Dey Street Books, 2017.

Faithful, George. "Dark of the World, Shine on Us: The Redemption of Blackness in Ryan Coogler's *Black Panther*." *Religions*, vol. 9, no. 10, Oct. 2018, p. 304. https://doi.org/10.3390/rel9100304.

Farrow, Ronan. *Catch and Kill: Lies, Spies and a Conspiracy to Protect Predators*. Fleet, 2020.

Fedele, Anna. *Looking for Mary Magdalene: Alternative Pilgrimage and Ritual Creativity at Catholic Shrines in France*. Oxford UP, 2013.

Ferreday, Debra. "Game of Thrones, Rape Culture and Feminist Fandom." *Australian Feminist Studies*, vol. 30, no. 83, Apr. 2015, pp. 21–36.

Fielding, Helen. *Bridget Jones: Mad about the Boy*. Knopf, 2013.

Fielding, Helen. *Bridget Jones: The Edge of Reason*. Viking, 2000.

Fielding, Helen. *Bridget Jones's Diary: A Novel*. Viking, 1998.

Finding Joe. Directed by Patrick Takaya Solomon, 2011. "Finding Joe." *YouTube*, uploaded by Patrick Solomon, March 19, 2020, https://www.youtube.com/watch?v=s8nFACrLxro.

Fiorenza, Elisabeth. *In Memory of Her: A Feminist Theological Reconstruction of Christian Origins*. 10th edition, Crossroad Publishing, 1995.

Flood, Alison. "'Another Author': Outrage after BBC Elides Bernardine Evaristo's Booker Win," *The Guardian*, 4 Dec. 2019, https://www.theguardian.com/books/2019/dec/04/another-author-outrage-after-bbc-elides-bernardine-evaristo-booker-win. Accessed 14 June 2021.

Fortune, Jane. *Invisible Women: Forgotten Artists of Florence*. Edited by the Florentine Press, 3rd edition, April 2014, Florentine Press, 2009.

Frankie Drake Mysteries. Shaftesbury Films, Canada Media Fund (CMF), Independent Production Fund, 2019.

Fredriksson, Marianne. *According to Mary Magdalene*. Hampton Roads, 1999.

Freke, Timothy, and Peter Gandy. *Jesus and the Lost Goddess: The Secret Teachings of the Original Christians*. Harmony, 2002.

"From 'Where Are You From?' to 'Where Shall We Go Together?' Re-Imagining Home and Belonging in 21st-Century Women's Writing." *Institute of Modern Languages Research*, https://modernlanguages.sas.ac.uk/events/event/22483. Accessed 24 Sept. 2020.

Gadon, Elinor W. *The Once and Future Goddess: A Symbol for Our Time*. 1st edition, Harper & Row, 1989.

Garcia-Navarro, Lulu. "Stephen Miller and White Supremacy." *NPR*. https://www.npr.org/2019/11/17/780231676/stephen-miller-and-white-supremacy. Accessed 2 June 2020.

George, Margaret. *Mary, Called Magdalene*. Viking, 2002.

George, Nina. *The Book of Dreams*. 1st edition, Crown, 2019.

George, Nina. *The Little French Bistro*. Reprint edition, Broadway Books, 2018.

George, Nina. *The Little Paris Bookshop*. Reprint edition, Broadway Books, 2016.

Gibbons, Stella. *Cold Comfort Farm*. Longmans, 1932.

Gibson, Lydialyle. "The Bits the Bible Left Out." *Harvard Magazine*, 16 Oct. 2018, https://harvardmagazine.com/2018/11/karen-king-harvard.

Gilbert, Elizabeth. *Big Magic: Creative Living Beyond Fear*. Riverhead Books, 2015.

Gilbert, Elizabeth. *Committed: A Skeptic Makes Peace with Marriage*. Viking, 2010.

Gilbert, Elizabeth. *Eat Pray Love: One Woman's Search for Everything Across Italy, India and Indonesia*. Riverhead Books, 2006.

Gilbert, Elizabeth. *Elizabeth Gilbert*, https://www.elizabethgilbert.com/bio/. Accessed 3 June 2021.

Gill, Gillian. *Virginia Woolf: And the Women Who Shaped Her World*. Illustrated edition, Mariner Books, 2019.

Gimbutas, Marija. *The Civilization of the Goddess*. HarperSanFrancisco, 1991.

Gimbutas, Marija. *The Language of the Goddess: Unearthing the Hidden Symbols of Western Civilization*. Harper & Row, 1989.

Gollnick, James Timothy, and Canadian Corporation for Studies in Religion. *Love and the Soul: Psychological Interpretations of the Eros and Psyche Myth*. Published for the Canadian Corp. for Studies in Religion/Corporation canadienne des Sciences religieuses by Wilfrid Laurier UP, 1992.

Gordon, Robin L. *Searching for the Soror Mystica: The Lives and Science of Women Alchemists*. UP of America, 2013.

Gramont, Nina de. *The Christie Affair*. St. Martin's Press, 2022.

Grange, Amanda. *Mr. Darcy's Diary*. Sourcebooks, 2007.

Graves, Robert, et al. *The Greek Myths*. Penguin Books, 2012.

Green, Mark. "Golden Age Part of Modernist Literary Movement." *The Bodies from the Library*, https://bodiesfromthelibrary.com/2015/04/27/golden-age-part-of-modernist-literary-movement/. Accessed 14 Sept. 2020.

Greene, Liz. *Jung's Studies in Astrology: Prophecy, Magic, and the Qualities of Time*. Routledge, 2018.

Greenwood, Kerry. *Cocaine Blues*. 1st paperback edition, Poisoned Pen Press, 2011.

Greenwood, Kerry. *Phryne Fisher*, http://phrynefisher.com/Kerrygreenwood.html. Accessed 19 Apr. 2024.

Grimm, Jacob, et al. *The Annotated Brothers Grimm*. Edited by Maria Tatar, 2012.

Grimm, Jacob, and Wilhelm Grimm. *The Complete Grimm's Fairy Tales*. Pantheon Books, 2005.

H.D. [Hilda Dolittle] and Aliki Barnstone. *Trilogy*. New Directions, 1998.

Hagan, Stephanie. "Time, Memory, and Mosaics at the Monastery of Our Lady Mary." *Expedition*, vol. 55, Spring 2013, http://penn.museum/documents/publications/expedition/PDFs/55-1/TOC.pdf.

Hale, Shannon. *Austenland: A Novel*. Bloomsbury, 2007.

Hall, Nor. *The Moon and the Virgin: Reflections on the Archetypal Feminine*. Harper & Row, 1980.

Harding, M. Esther. *Woman's Mysteries: Ancient and Modern*. Longmans, Green and Company, 1937.

Harkness, Deborah E. *The Book of Life: All Souls Trilogy, Book 3*. Viking, 2014.

Harkness, Deborah E. *A Discovery of Witches: All Souls Trilogy, Book 1*. Viking, 2011.

Harkness, Deborah E. *Shadow of Night: All Souls Trilogy, Book 2*. Penguin Books, 2013.

Harkness, Deborah E. *Time's Convert*. Penguin, 2019.

Harlan, Jennifer, et al. "Suffrage at 100: A Visual History." *The New York Times*, 17 Aug. 2020, https://www.nytimes.com/interactive/2020/08/17/us/suffrage-movement-photos -history.html.

Harmon, Katharine. *You Are Here: Personal Geographies and Other Maps of the Imagination*. 1st edition, Princeton Architectural Press, 2003.

Harrison, Jane Ellen. *Prolegomena to the Study of Greek Religion*. Reprint edition, Princeton UP, 1991.

Harrison, Rebecca. "Gender, Race and Representation in the Star Wars Franchise: An Introduction." *Media Education Journal*, vol. 65, no. 2, Sept. 2019, pp. 16–19.

A Haunting in Venice. Directed by Kenneth Branagh, 20th Century Studios, Kinberg Genre, Scott Free Productions, 2023.

Hawke, Ethan. "Give Yourself Permission to Be Creative." TED. https://www.ted.com/talks/ ethan_hawke_give_yourself_permission_to_be_creative. Accessed 13 Oct. 2020.

Healy, Nan Savage. *Toni Wolff & C. G. Jung: A Collaboration*. 1st edition, Tiberius Press, 2017.

Heaslip, April. "Securely Attached: Brazilians and Their Black Madonnas." *Myths Shattered and Restored: Proceedings of the Association for the Study of Women and Mythology*, Goddess Ink, 2016.

Heath, Mary. *Villains and Heroes: An Analysis of Outlander's Portrayal of Sexual Violence*. 2019, Arizona State University, master's thesis, https://www.academia.edu/45079702/ Villains_and_Heroes_An_Analysis_of_Outlanders_Portrayal_of_Sexual_Violence.

Heller, Meredith. *Writing by Heart: A Poetry Path to Healing and Self-Discovery*. New World Library, 2024.

Heller, Meredith, and Susan Goldsmith Wooldridge. *Write a Poem, Save Your Life: A Guide for Teens, Teachers, and Writers of All Ages*. New World Library, 2021.

"Heroine Psyches: Journeys of the Feminine Divine Featuring Will Linn." *YouTube*, Uploaded by All Girls Film Challenge, April 24, 2020, https://www.youtube.com/ watch?v=OguoLdUj1UQ&feature=emb_err_woyt. Accessed 22 Oct. 2020.

Herrera, Hannah. "Shifting Spaces and Constant Patriarchy: The Characterizations of Offred and Claire in *The Handmaid's Tale* and *Outlander*." *Zeitschrift für Anglistik und Amerikanistik*, vol. 67, no. 2, June 2019, pp. 181–96. *www.degruyter.com*, https://doi.org/ 10.1515/zaa-2019-0016.

Hersh, Carie Little. Outl, an Anthropologist's Obsession with Outlander|. My Eclectic Writings Says. "An Anthropologist's Obsession with Outlander." *Relevanth*, 3 May 2018, https://www.relevanth.com/an-anthropologists-obsession-with-outlander/.

Higgins, Lynn A., and Brenda R. Silver. *Rape and Representation*. Columbia UP, 1991.

"Hilary Swank Goes on a Voyage to Mars in Netflix Series 'Away.'" *NPR*, https://www.npr .org/2020/09/06/910194934/hilary-swank-goes-on-a-voyage-to-mars-in-netflix-series -away. Accessed 10 Nov. 2020.

Hill Collins, Patricia, and Sirma Bilge. *Intersectionality*. Polity, 2020.

Hillman, James. *Anima: An Anatomy of a Personified Notion. with 439 Excerpts from the Writings of C. G. Jung*. Trade paper, 2nd print edition, Spring Publications, 1985.

Hillman, James. *Re-Visioning Psychology*. Reissue edition, William Morrow Paperbacks, 1997.

Hillman, James, and Glen Slater. *Senex & Puer*. Spring, 2005.

Hoban, Phoebe. "'We're Finally Infiltrating,'" *ARTnews.com*, 1 Feb. 2007, https://www.artnews .com/art-news/news/were-finally-infiltrating-158/.

Holy See Press Office. *Mary Magdalene, Apostle of the Apostles, 10.06.2016*. Press.Vatican.Va, 10 June 2016, https://press.vatican.va/content/salastampa/en/bollettino/pubblico/2016/ 06/10/160610c.html.

Home Online. www.talkingtransformations.eu, http://www.talkingtransformations.eu/phase -2-touring/online-exhibition/. Accessed 24 Sept. 2020.

Howard, Vickie. "Recognising Narcissistic Abuse and the Implications for Mental Health Nursing Practice." *Issues in Mental Health Nursing*, vol. 40, no. 8, May 2019. *hull-repository.worktribe.com*, https://doi.org/10.1080/01612840.2019.1590485.

Huizinga, Johan. *Homo Ludens: A Study of the Play-Element in Culture*. Random House, 1938.

Humanity Lives Beneath Our Scars. Directed by David Jay, 2017. *www.ted.com*, https://www .ted.com/talks/david_jay_humanity_lives_beneath_our_scars.

The Huntsman: Winter's War. Directed by Cedric Nicolas-Troyan, Universal Pictures, Perfect World Pictures, Roth Films, 2016.

Institoris, Heinrich, and Jakob Sprenger. *The Malleus Maleficarum [of Heinrich Kramer and James Sprenger]*. Translated with introductions, bibliography, and notes by Montague Summers, Blom, 1970.

Into the Woods. Directed by Rob Marshall, BBL Motion Picture Studios, Lucamar Productions, Marc Platt Productions, 2014.

Invisible Women. Forgotten Artists of Florence. WFYI, 2012, PBS, https://www.pbs.org/video/ wfyi-arts-programs-invisible-women/.

"ISIS, ISIL or Islamic State: What's in a Name?" *NPR*, http://www.npr.org/sections/parallels/ 2014/09/12/347711170/isis-isil-or-islamic-state-whats-in-a-name. Accessed 31 July 2016.

Jackson, Kate. "The Literary Crossovers Between Modernist Literature and Golden Age Detective Fiction." *Crossexaminingcrime*, 16 Dec. 2019, https://crossexaminingcrime. wordpress.com/2019/12/16/the-literary-crossovers-between-modernist-literature-and -golden-age-detective-fiction/.

Jacobovici, Simcha, and Barrie A. Wilson. *The Lost Gospel: Decoding the Ancient Text That Reveals Jesus' Marriage to Mary the Magdalene*. Pegasus Books, 2014.

James Bond Supports International Women's Day 2011. WeAreEQUALS, 2011.

James, P. D. *Death Comes to Pemberley: A Novel*. Alfred A. Knopf, 2011.

Jarvis, Chase. *Chase Jarvis LIVE: Brené Brown*. http://blog.chasejarvis.com/blog/live/. Accessed 30 May 2014.

Jessica Jones. Directed by Krysten Ritter et al., 3 Arts Entertainment, ABC Signature, Marvel Television, 2015.

Jesus Christ Superstar. Directed by Norman Jewison, Universal Pictures, 1973.

O Jogo do Herói, http://www.jogodoheroi.com.br/. Accessed 23 June 2021.

"Johnny Flynn Talks About the Joys of Walking and Thinking," *YouTube*, uploaded by Talk the Line, 23 Jan. 2017, https://www.youtube.com/watch?v=rgU_C8CW31Q. Accessed 24 Sept. 2020.

Johnson, Ken, and Marguerite Elsbeth. *The Grail Castle: Male Myths & Mysteries in the Celtic Tradition*. Llewellyn Publications, 1995.

Jones, Michelle, and Lori Record. "Magdalene Laundries: The First Prisons for Women in the United States." *Journal of the Indiana Academy of the Social Sciences*, vol. 17, no. 1, Mar. 2017. *COinS*, https://digitalcommons.butler.edu/jiass/vol17/iss1/12.

Jung, Carl G., et al. *Collected Works of C. G. Jung, Volume 5: Symbols of Transformation*. Princeton University Press, 2014.

Kallos, Stephanie. *Broken for You*. Grove Press, 2004.

Kantor, Jodi, and Megan Twohey. *She Said: Breaking the Sexual Harassment Story That Helped Ignite a Movement*. 1st edition, Penguin Press, 2019.

Karpman, Stephen. "Karpman Drama Triangle." *Karpman Drama Triangle*, https://www .karpmandramatriangle.com/dt_article_only.html. Accessed 22 June 2021.

Keating, Sarah. "The World's Most Accessible Stress Reliever." *BBC Future*, 19 May 2020, https://www.bbc.com/future/article/20200518-why-singing-can-make-you-feel-better -in-lockdown. Accessed 13 July 2021.

Kerényi, Karl. *Dionysos: Archetypal Image of the Indestructible Life*. Princeton UP, 1976.

Kerényi, Karl. *The Gods of the Greeks*. Thames and Hudson, 1951.

Kerényi, Karl. *The Heroes of the Greeks*. Thames and Hudson, 1974.

Kerslake, Patricia. *Science Fiction and Empire*. Liverpool UP, 2010.

Kidd, Sue Monk. *The Book of Longings*. 1st edition, Viking, 2020.

Killing Us Softly 4: Advertising's Image of Women. Directed by Sut Jhally and Jean Kilbourne. Media Education Foundation, 2021.

King, Karen L. "'Jesus Said to Them, 'My Wife . . .': A New Coptic Papyrus Fragment." *Harvard Theological Review*, vol. 107, no. 2, Apr. 2014, pp. 131–59. *Cambridge Journals Online*, https://doi.org/10.1017/S0017816014000133.

Kingsbury, Kate. "How the Polish Black Madonna Became Haitian Vodou Spirit Erzulie Dantor." *Global Catholic Review*. www.academia.edu, https://www.academia.edu/ 38686412/How_the_Polish_Black_Madonna_Became_Haitian_Vodou_Spirit_Erzulie _Dantor. Accessed 11 Feb. 2025.

Kujawa, Joanna. *The Other Goddess: Mary Magdalene and the Goddesses of Eros and Secret Knowledge*. Haniel Press, 2022.

Ladurie, Emmanuel Le Roy. *Montaillou: The Promised Land of Error*. Translated by Barbara Bray, 30th anniversary edition, George Braziller, 2008.

Lahr, Jane, editor. *Searching for Mary Magdalene: A Journey Through Art and Literature*. Welcome Books, 2006.

Łapińska, Magdalena. *The Prevalence of Racial Prejudice and Segregation in Deborah Harkness' All Souls Trilogy. Fantastyka a Realizm/The Fantastic and Realism*. Edited by Weroniki Biegluk-Leś, Sylwii Borowskiej-Szerszun, and Eweliny Feldman-Kołodziejuk, Temida 2, 2019, pp. 79–91.

LaPlante, Eve. *Marmee & Louisa: The Untold Story of Louisa May Alcott and Her Mother*. Reprint edition, Simon & Schuster, 2013.

Larrington, Carolyne. *The Woman's Companion to Mythology*, Pandora Press, 1997.

The Last Temptation of Christ. Directed by Martin Scorsese, Universal Pictures, Cineplex Odeon Films, Ufland Productions, 1988.

Lawhon, Ariel. *Code Name Hélène*. 1st edition, Doubleday, 2020.

Leavy, Patricia, editor. *Handbook of Arts-Based Research*. Reprint edition, Guilford Press, 2019.

Le Grice, Keiron. *The Archetypal Cosmos: Rediscovering the Gods in Myth, Science and Astrology*. Floris Books, 2010.

Le Grice, Keiron. *The Rebirth of the Hero Mythology as a Guide to Spiritual Transformation*. Aeon Books, 2019.

Leloup, Jean-Yves. *The Gospel of Philip: Jesus, Mary Magdalene, and the Gnosis of Sacred Union*. Translated by Joseph Rowe. Inner Traditions, 2004.

Leloup, Jean-Yves. *The Sacred Embrace of Jesus and Mary: The Sexual Mystery at the Heart of the Christian Tradition*. Inner Traditions, 2006.

Leloup, Jean-Yves, and Joseph Rowe. *The Gospel of Mary Magdalene*. Inner Traditions, 2002.

Leonard, Linda Schierse. *Meeting the Madwoman: Empowering the Feminine Spirit*. Random House, 1994.

Lerner, Gerda. *The Creation of Feminist Consciousness: From the Middle Ages to Eighteen-Seventy*. Oxford UP, 1993.

Lesser, Elizabeth. *Cassandra Speaks: When Women Are the Storytellers, the Human Story Changes*. Harper Wave, 2020.

Levin, Janna. "Mathematics, Purpose, and Truth." Interview by Krista Tippett. *onbeing.org*, 10 Jan. 2008, https://onbeing.org/programs/janna-levin-mathematics-purpose-and -truth/. Accessed 13 Oct. 2020.

Levine, Nick. "Benedict Cumberbatch Shares His Views on the Equal Pay Debate." *BBC America*, 5 May 2018, https://www.bbcamerica.com/anglophenia/2018/05/benedict -cumberbatch-shares-his-views-on-the-equal-pay-debate.

The Librarians. Electric Entertainment, 2013.

Lichtman, Susan A. *The Female Hero in Women's Literature and Poetry*. E. Mellen Press, 1996.

Lilla, Jenna. "Symbolism of Zombies: Image of the Shadow." *Deep Sacred*, 15 Dec. 2013, https://deepsacred.com/symbolism/illusion/shadow/symbolism-of-zombies/.

Litinetskaia, Marina, and Julien Daniel Guelfi. "État amoureux normal et pathologique." *Annales Médico-psychologiques, revue psychiatrique*, vol. 179, no. 3, Mar. 2021, pp. 280–85. *ScienceDirect*, https://doi.org/10.1016/j.amp.2021.01.008.

Little Women. Directed by Greta Gerwig, Columbia Pictures, Regency Enterprises, DiNovi Pictures, 2019.

Longfellow, Ki. *The Secret Magdalene: A Novel*. Crown, 2007.

Lorde, Audre. *Sister Outsider: Essays and Speeches*. Crossing Press, 1984.

Lost in Austen. Directed by Dan Zeff, Image Entertainment, 2009.

Lundsgaard, Lene, and Nina Nørgaard. *The Female Hero: An Anthology of Literary Texts on Women's Quest*. Scriptor, 1985.

Lupieri, E., editor. *Mary Magdalene from the New Testament to the New Age and Beyond*. Brill, 2019, https://brill.com/edcollbook/title/55834.

Lupieri, Edmondo F. *Mary Magdalene from the New Testament to the New Age and Beyond*. Brill, 2019.

Lyons, Claire L., and John K. Papadopoulos, editors. *The Archaeology of Colonialism*. 1st edition, Getty Research Institute, 2002.

Lyttle, Allyn D., et al. "Adept Through Adaptation: Third Culture Individuals' Interpersonal Sensitivity." *International Journal of Intercultural Relations*, vol. 35, no. 5, Sept. 2011, pp. 686–94, https://doi.org/10.1016/j.ijintrel.2011.02.015.

Macfarlane, Robert. "Robert Macfarlane: 'Are We Being Good Ancestors? Mostly, No.'" Interview by Kate Kellaway, *The Guardian*, 22 Aug. 2020, http://www.theguardian.com/books/2020/aug/22/robert-macfarlane-are-we-being-good-ancestors-mostly-no.

Macfarlane, Robert. *Underland: A Deep Time Journey*. Illustrated edition, W. W. Norton, 2019.

Magdalene Laundries: Our World. Directed by BBC Films, BBC News Channel, 27 Sept. 2014. https://www.youtube.com/watch?v=ChDRDrb7e-U.

The Magdalene Sisters. Directed by Peter Mullan, Miramax, 2004.

Mahaffey, Patrick J. *Integrative Spirituality: Religious Pluralism, Individuation, and Awakening*. Routledge, 2019.

"'Maisie Dobbs' Book Review." Directed by Maureen Corrigan. *NPR*, http://www.npr.org/templates/story/story.php?storyId=1394563. Accessed 2 June 2015.

Maleficent. Directed by Robert Stromberg, Jolie Pas, Roth Films, Walt Disney Pictures, 2014.

Maleficent: Mistress of Evil. Directed by Joachim Rønning, Walt Disney Pictures, Roth Films, Jolie Pas, 2019.

"Malleus Maleficarum." *Britannica Academic*, https://academic.eb.com/levels/collegiate/article/Malleus-maleficarum/50351.

Malvern, Marjorie M. *Venus in Sackcloth: The Magdalen's Origins and Metamorphoses*. Carbondale: Southern Illinois UP, 1975.

The Man Card: White Male Identity Politics from Nixon to Trump. Created by Jackson Katz, Directed by Peter Hutchinson and Lucas Sabean, Eat the Moon Films, Media Education Foundation, 2020, https://www.themancardmovie.com/?utm_source=mef-blog&utm_medium=blog&utm_campaign=the-man-card-4.

Manne, Kate. *Down Girl: The Logic of Misogyny*. Oxford University Press, 2019.

Manne, Kate. *Entitled: How Male Privilege Hurts Women*. Penguin Books, 2021.

Marie, Leona Volition. *Attaining Sovereignty: Reconciliation, Rupture, Retaliation*. Pacifica Graduate Institute, 2002.

Mary: This Is My Blood. Directed by Abel Ferrara, Wild Bunch, Associated Film, Central Films, 2005.

Mary Magdalene. Directed by Garth Davis, See-Saw Films, Porchlight Films, Universal Pictures International Production (UPIP), 2018.

Massey, Sujata. *The Bombay Prince*. Soho Crime, 2021.

Massey, Sujata. *The Mistress of Bhatia House*. Soho Crime, 2024.

Massey, Sujata. *The Satapur Moonstone*. Soho Crime, 2019.

Massey, Sujata. *The Widows of Malabar Hill*. Soho Crime, 2018.

Mastaler, James S. "The Magdalene of Internet: New Age, Goddess, and Nature Spiritualities." *Mary Magdalene from the New Testament to the New Age and Beyond*, Brill, 2019, pp. 337–63. *Brill*, https://doi.org/10.1163/9789004411067_017.

Master of the Magdalene Legend. *Saint Mary Magdalene Preaching*. c1500–1520. Philadelphia Museum of Art, Philadelphia, Philamuseum.org. Web. 8 February 2016.

McCarthy, Rebecca Lea. *Origins of the Magdalene Laundries: An Analytical History*. McFarland, 2010. *Proquest Ebook Central*, http://site.ebrary.com/id/10373134.

McGowan, Kathleen. *The Boleyn Heresy, Part I: The Time Will Come*. Asherah Press, 2022

McGowan, Kathleen. *The Book of Love*. Simon & Schuster, 2009.

McGowan, Kathleen. *The Expected One*. Simon & Schuster, 2006.

McGowan, Kathleen. "Kathleen McGowan." *Kathleen McGowan*, https://kathleenmcgowan
.com. Accessed 19 Apr. 2024.

McGowan, Kathleen. *The Poet Prince*. Simon & Schuster, 2010.

McNeely, Deldon Anne. *Animus Aeternus: Exploring the Inner Masculine*. King Fisher
Publishing, 2011.

*Medieval Sourcebook: The Golden Legend (Aurea Legenda) Compiled by Jacobus de Voragine,
1275 Englished by William Caxton, 1483*. https://sourcebooks.fordham.edu/basis/
goldenlegend/. Accessed 1 June 2021.

Merisante, Margaret. *Tears and Fragrance for the God's Death and Resurrection: The
Funerary Syncretism of Mary Magdalene with Isis*. 2015, https://www.academia.edu/
12129204/Tears_and_Fragrance_for_the_God_s_Death_and_Resurrection_The_
Funerary_Syncretism_of_Mary_Magdalene_with_Isis.

The Me You Can't See. RadicalMedia, Harpo Productions, 2021.

Miller, B. J. *What Really Matters at the End of Life*. Transcript of TED Talk. https://www.ted
.com/talks/bj_miller_what_really_matters_at_the_end_of_life/transcript.

Mirror Mirror. Directed by Tarsem Singh, Relativity Media, Yucaipa Films, Goldmann
Pictures, 2012.

Miss Fisher and the Crypt of Tears. Directed by Tony Tilse, Every Cloud Productions, 2020.

Miss Fisher's Murder Mysteries. Every Cloud Productions, 24 Feb. 2012.

Moana. Directed by Ron Clements et al., Hurwitz Creative, Walt Disney Animation Studios,
Walt Disney Pictures, 2016.

Molton, Mary Dian, and Lucy Anne Sikes. *Four Eternal Women: Toni Wolff Revisited—A
Study in Opposites*. 1st edition, Fisher King, 2011.

The Monuments Men. Directed by George Clooney, Sony Pictures, 2014.

Morales, Helen. "Fantasising Phryne: The Psychology and Ethics Of." *Cambridge Classical
Journal*, vol. 57, Dec. 2011, pp. 71–104. *Cambridge Core*, https://doi.org/10.1017/
S1750270500001287.

Morgan, Rebekah S. *Rey-Ifying a New Heroine: Interrogating the Curriculum of Femininity
in Star Wars Films*. 2020. Georgia Southern University, dissertation.https://
digitalcommons.georgiasouthern.edu/cgi/viewcontent.cgi?article=3199&context=etd.

Morrison, Toni, and Ta-Nehisi Coates. *The Origin of Others*. 1st edition, Harvard UP, 2017.

Ms. Fisher's Modern Murder Mysteries. Every Cloud Productions, 21 Feb. 2019.

Mundy, Liza. *Code Girls: The Untold Story of the American Women Code Breakers of World
War II*. Illustrated edition, Hachette Books, 2018.

Murdock, Maureen. "Maureen Murdock Interviewed by Mary Davis." *C.G. Jung Society of
Atlanta Quarterly News*, Summer 2005. *maureenmurdock.com*, https://maureenmurdock
.com/maureen-murdock-interviewed-by-mary-davis/.

Murdock, Maureen, and Christine Downing. *The Heroine's Journey: Woman's Quest for
Wholeness*. Reprint edition, Shambhala, 2020.

*The Myth of Eros & Psyche: Growth Toward Wholeness of the Archetypally Vulnerable Woman:
The Tasks to Learn*. Sounds True, 1992.

Nadkarni, Samira. "'I Was Never the Hero That You Wanted Me to Be': Feminism and Resistance to Militarism in *Marvel's Jessica Jones*." *Gender and the Superhero Narrative*, UP of Mississippi, 2018.

Nagendra, Harini. *The Bangalore Detectives Club*. Reprint edition, Pegasus Crime, 2023.

Nagendra, Harini. *Murder Under a Red Moon: A 1920s Bangalore Mystery*. Pegasus Crime, 2023.

"Natalie Portman Responds to Rose McGowan Oscars Cape Criticism." *Deadline*. https://deadline.com/2020/02/natalie-portman-responds-rose-mcgowan-cape-criticism-1202858824/. Accessed 13 July 2021.

Nelson, Elizabeth Eowyn. "Conflict as Creative Act: Psyche's Knife, Separation, and the Feeling Function." *Spring: A Journal of Archetype and Culture*, no. 74, 2006, 297–314.

Nelson, Elizabeth Eowyn. *Psyche's Knife: Archetypal Explorations of Love and Power*. Chiron, 2012.

Neumann, Erich. *The Great Mother*. Translated by Ralph Manheim, Reprint edition, Princeton UP, 1972.

Neville, Katherine. *The Magic Circle*. Ballantine Books, 1998.

New York Stories. Directed by Woody Allen et al., Touchstone, 1989.

Nicholas, Lynn H. *The Rape of Europa: The Fate of Europe's Treasures in the Third Reich and the Second World War*. Knopf, 1994.

North, Ryan. *Gender and the Superhero Narrative*. Edited by Michael Goodrum et al., paper edition, UP of Mississippi, 2018.

Northrup, Christiane. *Dodging Energy Vampires: An Empath's Guide to Evading Relationships That Drain You and Restoring Your Health and Power*. 2nd edition, Hay House, 2019.

O'Connor, Anne Marie. *The Lady in Gold: The Extraordinary Tale of Gustav Klimt's Masterpiece, Portrait of Adele Bloch-Bauer*. Knopf, 2012.

Odajnyk, V. *Archetype and Character: Power, Eros, Spirit, and Matter Personality Types*. 2012 edition, Palgrave Macmillan, 2012.

Oliver, Mary. *New and Selected Poems, Volume One*. Reprint edition, Beacon Press, 2004.

O'Loughlin, Ed. "These Women Survived Ireland's Magdalene Laundries. They're Ready to Talk." *The New York Times*, 6 June 2018. https://www.nytimes.com/2018/06/06/world/europe/magdalene-laundry-reunion-ireland.html.

Once upon a Time. Kitsis/Horowitz, ABC Signature, 2011.

Palmer, Amanda, and Brené Brown. *The Art of Asking: How I Learned to Stop Worrying and Let People Help*. Illustrated edition, Grand Central Publishing, 2015.

Paris, Ginette. *Heartbreak: New Approaches to Healing—Recovering from Lost Love and Mourning*. Mill City Press, Inc., 2011.

Paris, Ginette. *Pagan Grace: Dionysos, Hermes, and Goddess Memory in Daily Life*. Spring Publications, 1990.

Parks, Sheri. *Fierce Angels: The Strong Black Woman in American Life and Culture*. One World/Ballantine Books, 2010.

The Passion of the Christ. Directed by Mel Gibson, Icon Productions, 2004.

Pearson, Carol. *Awakening the Heroes Within: Twelve Archetypes to Help Us Find Ourselves and Transform Our World*. HarperSanFrancisco, 1991.

Pearson, Carol S., and Katherine Pope. *The Female Hero in American and British Literature*. Bowker, 1981.

Perera, Sylvia Brinton. *Descent to the Goddess: A Way of Initiation for Women.* Inner City Books, 1981.

Perrault, Charles. *Tales of Times Past: The Fairy Tales of Charles Perrault.* Translated by Alex Lubertozzi, Top Five Classics, 2020.

Perrault, Charles, and C. J. Betts. *The Complete Fairy Tales.* Oxford UP, 2009.

Perry, Anne. *Bethlehem Road.* Fawcett Books, 1991.

Perry, Anne. *Cardington Crescent.* St. Martin's Press, 1987.

Perry, Anne. *Highgate Rise: A Charlotte and Thomas Pitt Novel.* Random House, 2011.

Philomena. Directed by Stephen Frears, Anchor Bay, 2014.

Pidd, Helen. "Marcus Rashford Sends Message of Support to Tennis Star Emma Raducanu." *The Guardian,* 7 July 2021, http://www.theguardian.com/football/2021/jul/07/marcus -rashford-sends-message-of-support-to-tennis-star-emma-raducanu.

Piovanelli, Pierluigi. "From Galilee to India: There Is Something About Mary (Magdalene)." *Mary Magdalene from the New Testament to the New Age and Beyond,* Brill, 2019, pp. 395–416, https://doi.org/10.1163/9789004411067_019.

Pogrebin, Robin, and Kate Kelly. *The Education of Brett Kavanaugh: An Investigation.* Portfolio, 2019.

Potter, Mary-Anne. "'Everything and Nothing': Liminality in Diana Gabaldon's Outlander." *Interdisciplinary Literary Studies,* vol. 21, no. 3, 2019, pp. 282–96. *JSTOR,* https://doi.org/ 10.5325/intelitestud.21.3.0282.

Press, Joy. *Stealing the Show: How Women Are Revolutionizing Television.* Atria, 2019.

Preston, John. *The Dig.* Penguin UK, 2008.

Psyche & Symbol—Dionysian Unconscious: Destroy and Create New Life. Directed by Joseph Campbell Foundation. https://www.youtube.com/watch?v=XJrtHNI_K2E&t=30s. Accessed 1 Sept. 2021.

Pullman, Philip. *The Amber Spyglass.* Knopf, 2000.

Pullman, Philip. *The Book of Dust: La Belle Sauvage (Book of Dust, Volume 1).* Knopf, 2017.

Pullman, Philip. *The Book of Dust: The Secret Commonwealth (Book of Dust, Volume 2).* Knopf, 2019.

Pullman, Philip. *The Golden Compass (His Dark Materials, Book 1)* Laurel Leaf, 2004.

Pullman, Philip. "Philip Pullman: 'My Daemon Is a Raven, a Bird That Steals Things.'" *The Guardian,* 22 Oct. 2017, https://www.theguardian.com/books/2017/oct/22/philip-pullman -my-daemon-is-a-raven-la-belle-sauvage-interview-questions.

Pullman, Philip. *The Subtle Knife: His Dark Materials.* Knopf, 1997.

Purnell, Sonia. *A Woman of No Importance: The Untold Story of the American Spy Who Helped Win World War II.* Illustrated edition, Viking, 2019.

Putcha, Rumya Sree. *The Dancer's Voice: Performance and Womanhood in Transnational India.* Duke University Press Books, 2022.

Quillan, Jehanne de. *The Gospel of the Beloved Companion: The Complete Gospel of Mary Magdalene.* CreateSpace Independent Publishing Platform, 2010.

Quinn, Helen R., and Yossi Nir. *The Mystery of the Missing Antimatter.* Reprint edition, Princeton UP, 2014.

Quinn, Kate. Book Review: "The Alice Network." *NPR,*https://www.npr.org/2017/06/08/ 530794379/the-alice-network-is-a-crackling-tale-of-spies-and-suspense. 8 June 2017. Accessed 1 July 2021.

Radioactive. Directed by Marjane Satrapi, StudioCanal, Working Title Films, Amazon Studios, 2020.

Raine, Kathleen. *The Pythoness, and Other Poems*. Farrar, Straus and Young, 1952.

Randall, Lisa. "Dark Matter, Dinosaurs, and Extra Dimensions." Interview by Krista Tippett. *onbeing.org*, 12 Nov. 2015, https://onbeing.org/programs/lisa-randall-dark-matter -dinosaurs-and-extra-dimensions-sep2017/. Accessed 13 Oct. 2020.

The Rape of Europa. Directed by Richard Berge et al., Menemsha Films, 2008.

Redniss, Lauren. *Radioactive: Marie & Pierre Curie: A Tale of Love and Fallout*. 1st edition, It Books, 2010.

Reed, Americus. "Why Marvel's 'Black Panther' Is Resonating Globally." *Knowledge@ Wharton*, https://knowledge.wharton.upenn.edu/article/marvels-black-panther/. Accessed 8 June 2021.

Reis, Patricia. *Daughters of Saturn: From Father's Daughter to Creative Woman*. Continuum, 1995.

Ricci, Carla. "Wife, Queen, Goddess: Mary Magdalene and the New Religious-Spiritual Movements (19th–21st Centuries)." *Mary Magdalene from the New Testament to the New Age and Beyond*, Brill, 2019, pp. 364–94, https://doi.org/10.1163/9789004411067_018.

Riordan, Rick. *The Titan's Curse*. Hyperion Books, 2007.

Rioux, Anne Boyd. *Meg, Jo, Beth, Amy: The Story of Little Women and Why It Still Matters*. 1st edition, W. W. Norton, 2019.

Robertson, J. M. *Pagan Christs*. University Books, 1967.

Rogers, Everett M. *Diffusion of Innovations*. 5th edition, Free Press, 2003.

Rosa, Armando Nascimento. *Mary of Magdala: A Gnostic Fable*. Spring Journal, 2009.

Rossi, Safron. *The Kore Goddess: A Mythology & Psychology*. Winter Press, 2021.

"Rosslyn Chapel Was Haven for Bees." *BBC*, 30 Mar. 2010, http://news.bbc.co.uk/2/hi/uk _news/scotland/8594724.stm.

Roth, Tansia L. "Epigenetic Mechanisms in the Development of Behavior: Advances, Challenges, and Future Promises of a New Field." *Development and Psychopathology*, vol. 25, no. 4, pt. 2, Nov. 2013, pp. 1279–91.

Rothwell, Jonathan. "You Are What You Watch? The Social Effects of TV." *The New York Times*, 25 July 2019, https://www.nytimes.com/2019/07/25/upshot/social-effects-television.html.

Rowland, Susan. *C. G. Jung and Literary Theory: The Challenge from Fiction*. Macmillan Press, 1999.

Rowland, Susan. *C.G. Jung in the Humanities: Taking the Soul's Path*. Spring Journal, I nc., 2010.

Rowland, Susan. *Jung: A Feminist Revision*. Polity, 2002.

Rowland, Susan. "Reading Jung for Magic: 'Active Imagination' for/as 'Close Reading.'" In *How and Why We Still Read Jung: Personal and Professional Reflections*, edited by Jean Kirsch and Murray Stein. Routledge, 2013, pp. 86–106.

Rowland, Susan. *The Sleuth and the Goddess: Hestia, Artemis, Athena, and Aphrodite in Women's Detective Fiction*. Spring Journal Books, 2015.

Rowland, Susan. "The Wasteland and the Grail Knight: Myth and Cultural Criticism in Detective Fiction." *Clues* vol. 28, no. 2, 2010, pp. 44–54.

Rowland, Susan. "Writing, Mary Magdalen, and the Fishing Net: Roberts' The Wild Girl and Rosa's Mary of Magdala." *Mary of Magdala: A Gnostic Fable*. Spring Journal Books, 2010. Pp. 141–157.

Rusca, Ruth. *Feminine Mysteries in the Bible: The Soul Teachings of the Daughters of the Goddess*. Bear, 2008.

Sabar, Ariel. "The Unbelievable Tale of Jesus's Wife." *The Atlantic*, 16 June 2016, https://www.theatlantic.com/magazine/archive/2016/07/the-unbelievable-tale-of-jesus-wife/485573/. Accessed 25 May 2021.

Sabar, Ariel. *Veritas: A Harvard Professor, a Con Man and the Gospel of Jesus's Wife*. Illustrated edition, Doubleday, 2020.

Saccucci, Erica-Lyn. "From Disciple to Deviant: The Magdalene in Contemporary Popular Film." *Mary Magdalene from the New Testament to the New Age and Beyond*, Brill, 2019, pp. 318–36, https://doi.org/10.1163/9789004411067_016.

Sanyal, Mithu M. *Rape: From Lucretia to #MeToo*. Verso, 2019.

Savit, Gavriel. *Anna and the Swallow Man*. Knopf, 2016.

Sawelson-Gorse, Naomi, editor. *Women in Dada: Essays on Sex, Gender, and Identity*. MIT Press, 2001.

Sayers, Dorothy L. *Busman's Honeymoon: A Love Story with Detective Interruption*. Camelot Press, 1937.

Schaberg, Jane. *The Resurrection of Mary Magdalene: Legends, Apocrypha, and the Christian Testament*. 1st edition, Continuum, 2004.

Schaberg, Jane, and Melanie Johnson-Debaufre. *Mary Magdalene Understood*. Continuum, 2006.

Schutzman, Mady, and Jan Cohen-Cruz. *Playing Boal: Theatre, Therapy, Activism*. Routledge, 1994.

Sells, Angela. *Sabina Spielrein: The Woman and the Myth*. SUNY, 2017.

"Separate, Then Together: Sacred Marriage Origins in Egyptian Alchemy." *On the Wings of Isis: Reclaiming the Sovereignty of Auset*, Girl God Books, 2020.

Sex in a Cold Climate. Directed by Stephen Humphries et al., Cinema Guild, 2003.

Shiva, Vandana. *Soil Not Oil: Environmental Justice in an Age of Climate Crisis*. South End Press, 2008.

Shlain, Leonard. *The Alphabet Versus the Goddess: The Conflict Between Word and Image*. Penguin Books, 1999.

Shoard, Catherine. "Jane Campion: #MeToo Felt like 'End of Apartheid' for Women." *The Guardian*, 2 Sept. 2021, https://www.theguardian.com/film/2021/sep/02/jane-campion-me-too-power-of-the-dog-benedict-cumberbatch.

Shrek. Directed by Andrew Adamson and Vicky Jenson, DreamWorks Animation, Dreamworks Pictures, Pacific Data Images (PDI), 2001.

Shrek Forever After. Directed by Mike Mitchell, DreamWorks Animation, Pacific Data Images (PDI), 2010.

Shrek the Third. Directed by Chris Miller and Raman Hui, DreamWorks, DreamWorks Animation, Pacific Data Images (PDI), 2007.

Shrek 2. Directed by Andrew Adamson et al., Dreamworks Pictures, Pacific Data Images (PDI), DreamWorks Animation, 2004

Signs Out of Time: The Life of Archaeologist Marija Gimbutas. Directed by Donna Read and Starhawk. Belini Productions, 2004.

Slater, Glen. *Surrendering to Psyche: Depth Psychology, Sacrifice, and Culture*. 1996, doctoral dissertation, Pacifica Graduate Institute1996.

Slattery, Dennis. *Riting Myth, Mythic Writing: Plotting Your Personal Story*. Fisher King Press, 2012.

Slattery, Dennis Patrick, and Phil Cousineau. *The Way of Myth: Stories' Subtle Wisdom*. Mandorla Books, 2021.

Snow White and the Huntsman. Directed by Rupert Sanders, Roth Films, Universal Pictures, 2012.

Snow White and the Seven Dwarfs. Directed by William Cottrell et al., Walt Disney Productions, Walt Disney Animation Studios, 1938.

Soil Not Oil Pledge. MoveOn.org, https://sign.moveon.org/petitions/sign-the-soil-not-oil-1.

Solzhenitsyn, Aleksandr I. *The Gulag Archipelago 1918–1956 I-II*. 1st edition, Harper and Row, 1973.

Spectre. Directed by Sam Mendes, 20th Century Fox Home Entertainment, 2015.

Springer, Odette J. *Changing Woman: Calling the Feminine Home*. 2018. Pacifica Graduate Institute, PhD dissertation.

Starbird, Margaret. *Mary Magdalene: Bride in Exile*. Bear, 2005.

Starbird, Margaret. *The Tarot Trumps and the Holy Grail: Great Secrets of the Middle Ages*. WovenWord Press, 2000.

Starbird, Margaret. *The Woman with the Alabaster Jar: Mary Magdalen and the Holy Grail*. Bear, 1993.

Starhawk. *Truth or Dare: Encounters with Power, Authority, and Mystery*. Reprint edition, HarperOne, 1989.

Strong, Myron T., and K. Sean Chaplin. "Afrofuturism and Black Panther." *Contexts*, vol. 18, no. 2, May 2019, pp. 58–59. *SAGE Journals*, https://doi.org/10.1177/1536504219854725.

Sukhavati–Place of Bliss: A Mythic Journey with Joseph Campbell. Mystic Fire Video, 1998.

The Survivance of the Western Abenaki in Vermont—Middlebury College and the Western Abenaki, https://sites.middlebury.edu/abenaki/the-survivance-of-vermonts-western -abenaki/. Accessed 6 Mar. 2025.

"Survivors Describe Rape, Assaults in Rare Look at U.S. Magdalene Laundries." *PR Newswire*, 10 Dec. 2019, https://www.prnewswire.com/news-releases/survivors-describe -rape-assaults-in-rare-look-at-us-magdalene-laundriesvideo-live-discussion-sponsored -by-janet-janet--suggs-llc-300972545.html.

Sweeney, Megan. *Mendings*. Duke University Press Books, 2023.

Swift, Taylor. "Anti-Hero." *Midnight*. Taylor Swift/Republic Records, 2022.

Tan, Monica. "After 'The Babadook': Jennifer Kent's New Film Tackles Australia's Violent Colonial History." *The Guardian*, 30 May 2016, http://www.theguardian.com/film/2016/ may/30/the-nightingale-not-horror-like-the-babadook-but-a-pretty-horrific-world.

Tangled. Directed by Nathan Greno and Byron Howard, Walt Disney Animation Studios, Walt Disney Pictures, 2010.

Tarter, Jill. "It Takes a Cosmos to Make a Human." Interview by Krista Tippett. *onbeing.org*, 27 Feb. 2020, https://onbeing.org/programs/jill-tarter-it-takes-a-cosmos-to-make-a -human/. Accessed 13 Oct. 2020.

Tatar, Maria, editor. *The Classic Fairy Tales*. Norton, 2017.

Tatar, Maria. *The Fairest of Them All: Snow White and 21 Tales of Mothers and Daughters*. Belknap Press, an imprint of Harvard UP, 2022.

Tatar, Maria. *The Heroine with 1001 Faces*. Liveright, 2021.

Taylor, Joan E. "Mary Magdalene in Film: Response JSHJ." *Journal for the Study of the Historical Jesus*, vol. 20, no. 3, Nov. 2022, pp. 202–8. Brill, https://doi.org/10.1163/17455197-bja10011.

"10 Years Later, Mystery Heroine 'Maisie Dobbs' Gains New Life." *NPR*, directed by Maureen Corrigan, http://www.npr.org/2014/07/10/329568667/10-years-later-mystery-heroine-maisie-dobbs-gains-new-life. Accessed 1 June 2015.

Things We Don't Talk About: Women's Stories from the Red Tent. Directed by Isadora Gabrielle Leidenfrost et al., Soulful Media, 2012, http://www.redtentmovie.com.

Thompson, Nainoa. "Wayfinders: Wayfinding." Interview by Gail Evenari, *PBS*, https://www.pbs.org/wayfinders/wayfinding3.html. Accessed 21 Feb. 2024.

True Grit. Directed by Ethan Coen and Joel Coen, Paramount Pictures, Skydance Media, Scott Rudin Productions, 2010.

True Grit. Directed by Henry Hathaway, Wallis-Hazen, 1969.

Turnbull, Sue, and Marion McCutcheon. "Investigating Miss Fisher: The Value of a Television Crime Drama." *Media International Australia*, vol. 164, no. 1, Aug. 2017, pp. 56–70. SAGE Journals, https://doi.org/10.1177/1329878X17711000.

Turner, K. B., et al. "Ignoring the Past: Coverage of Slavery and Slave Patrols in Criminal Justice Texts." *Journal of Criminal Justice Education*, vol. 17, no. 1, Apr. 2006, pp. 181–95. *Taylor and Francis+NEJM*, https://doi.org/10.1080/10511250500335627.

"Tutu Chooses Gay Marriage over Church." *BBC News*, https://www.bbc.com/news/av/world-africa-36486908. Accessed 7 Mar. 2025.

Tutu, Desmond, and Mpho A. Tutu. *The Book of Forgiving: The Fourfold Path for Healing Ourselves and Our World*. Harper One, 2014.

"UK Honors Jane Austen 200 Years After Death." *Marketplace*, American Public Media, 18 July 2017, https://www.marketplace.org/2017/07/18/uk-honors-jane-austen-200-years-after-death/.

Ulanov, Ann. *Receiving Woman*. Daimon Verlag, 2001.

Ulanov, Ann, and Barry Ulanov. *Cinderella and Her Sisters: The Envied and the Envying*. 4th edition, Daimon Verlag, 2012.

University of Virginia. *Salem Witch Trials Documentary Archive*. http://salem.lib.virginia.edu/home.html. Accessed 4 Jan. 2020 and 15 Apr. 2024.

Vainikka, Vilma. *The Portrayal of Female Characters in the Star Wars Film Saga*. 2018. University of Eastern Finland, master's thesis. *UEF Erepository*, https://epublications.uef.fi/pub/urn_nbn_fi_uef-20180653/urn_nbn_fi_uef-20180653.pdf.

Valenti, Jessica. *The Purity Myth: How America's Obsession with Virginity Is Hurting Young Women*. Seal Press, 2009.

Van der Meer, Annine. *Unveiling Mary Magdalene: Hidden Sources Restore Her Disfigured Image*. PanSophia, 2021.

Veaux, Alexis De. *Warrior Poet: A Biography of Audre Lorde*. 1st edition, W. W. Norton, 2006.

von Franz, Marie-Louise. *Alchemy: An Introduction to the Symbolism and the Psychology*. Inner City Books, 1980.

von Franz, Marie-Louise. *The Interpretation of Fairy Tales*. Shambhala, 1996.

von Franz, Marie-Louise. *Shadow and Evil in Fairy Tales*. Shambhala, 1995.

Wade, Francesca. *Square Haunting: Five Writers in London Between the Wars*. Illustrated edition, Tim Duggan Books, 2020.

Warner, Marina. *Alone of All Her Sex: The Myth and The Cult of the Virgin Mary*. Knopf, 1976.

Warner, Marina. *Fairy Tale: A Very Short Introduction*. Illustrated edition, Oxford UP, 2018.

Warner, Marina. *Once Upon a Time: A Short History of Fairy Tale*. Reprint edition, Oxford UP, 2016.

Watkins, Mary, and Helene Shulman. *Toward Psychologies of Liberation*. Palgrave Macmillan, 2008.

Waxman, Sharon. *Loot: The Battle over the Stolen Treasures of the Ancient World*. 1st edition, Times Books, 2009.

Webby Awards. https://www.webbyawards.com/about/. Accessed 23 Jan. 2020.

Weldon, Glen, et al. "'Enola Holmes': Sherlock's Little Sister Gets on His Case." *Pop Culture Happy Hour, NPR*, https://www.npr.org/2020/09/17/914139731/enola-holmes-sherlock-s-little-sister-gets-on-his-case. Accessed 6 Oct. 2020.

Wertheim, Margaret. "The Grandeur and Limits of Science." Interview by Krista Tippett. *onbeing.org*, 23 Apr. 2015, https://onbeing.org/programs/margaret-wertheim-the-grandeur-and-limits-of-science-feb2017/. Accessed 13 Oct. 2020.

"What About the 'Lost Children' (and Mothers) of America?" *The Marshall Project*, 3 Nov. 2017, https://www.themarshallproject.org/2017/11/03/what-about-the-lost-children-and-mothers-of-america.

Whyte, David. *Consolations: The Solace, Nourishment, and Underlying Meaning of Everyday Words*. Many Rivers Press, 2015.

Wiking, Meik. "The Dark Side of Happiness." TEDx Copenhagen, 10 May 2016, https://www.youtube.com/watch?v=PbtzY-8IFTQ&t=895s.

Wilson, Sarah J., et al. "Finding Your Voice: A Singing Lesson from Functional Imaging." *Human Brain Mapping*, vol. 32, no. 12, Dec. 2011, pp. 2115–30. *PubMed*, https://doi.org/10.1002/hbm.21173.

Wiltshire, John. "Mrs. Bennet's Least Favorite Daughter." *Persuasions: The Jane Austen Journal*, vol. 23, 2001, pp. 179–87.

Winspear, Jacqueline. *The American Agent: A Maisie Dobbs Novel*. Harper, 2019.

Winspear, Jacqueline. *The Consequences of Fear: A Maisie Dobbs Novel*. Harper, 2021.

Winspear, Jacqueline. *A Dangerous Place: A Maisie Dobbs Novel*. Harper Perennial, 2016.

Winspear, Jacqueline. *In This Grave Hour: A Maisie Dobbs Novel*. Harper, 2017.

Winspear, Jacqueline. *Journey to Munich*. Harper, 2016.

Winspear, Jacqueline. *Leaving Everything Most Loved*. New York: Harper, 2013.

Winspear, Jacqueline. *Maisie Dobbs*. New York: Soho Press, 2003.

Winspear, Jacqueline. *Pardonable Lies*. New York: Henry Holt, 2005.

Winspear, Jacqueline. *This Time Next Year We'll Be Laughing*. Soho Press, 2020.

Winspear, Jacqueline. *What Would Maisie Do? Inspiration from the Pages of Maisie Dobbs*. Harper, 2019.

The Wisdom of Trauma. Directed by Maurizio Benazzo and Zaya Benazzo, Science and Nonduality, 2021.

Witcombe, Christopher. "Mary Magdalene: Early Legends." *Art History Resources*, http://arthistoryresources.net/investigating-mary-magdalen/mm-early-legends.html.

Wolkstein, Diane, and Samuel Noah Kramer. *Inanna, Queen of Heaven and Earth: Her Stories and Hymns from Sumer*. 1st edition, Harper Perennial, 1983.

Woman in Gold. Directed by Simon Curtis, Anchor Bay, 2015.

Wonser, Robert, and David Boyns. "Between the Living and Undead: How Zombie Cinema Reflects the Social Construction of Risk, the Anxious Self, and Disease Pandemic." *Sociological Quarterly*, vol. 57, no. 4, Sept. 2016, pp. 628–53. *Taylor and Francis+NEJM*, https://doi.org/10.1111/tsq.12150.

Woodman, Marion. *The Ravaged Bridegroom: Masculinity in Women*. First Thus edition, Inner City Books, 1990.

Woodroof, Martha. *"Chocolat" Author Returns with a Dark Confection*. NPR, https://www.npr.org/templates/story/story.php?storyId=89881757. Accessed 2 June 2020.

Woolf, Virginia. *The Waves*. Harvest Books, 1978.

Woolever, Megan Rose. "Mary Magdalene: Dark Madonna, Female Christ." Tales and Totems: Myth and Lineage in Goddess Scholarship, Association for the Study of Women and Mythology Symposium. Portland, Oregon: 11 April 2015. Conference Paper.

Woolover, Megan Rose. "Mary Magdalen: Priestess of Sacred Sexuality." *Mary Magdalene Studies Association Journal*, 2023.

Workman, Sarah. "Female Valor Without Renown: Memory, Mourning, and Loss at the Center of Middle-Earth." *A Quest of Her Own: Essays on the Female Hero in Modern Fantasy*, McFarland, 2014.

Worsley, Lucy. *Agatha Christie: An Elusive Woman*. Pegasus Crime, 2022.

Yeh, Lily. "From Broken to Whole." TEDxCornellU. https://www.youtube.com/watch?v=fVCXF6PN0g4. Accessed 10 June 2015.

Yeh, Lily. "How Art Can Heal Broken Places." *Moonrise: The Power of Women Leading from the Heart*, edited by Nina Simons and Anneke Campbell, Park Street Press, 2010, pp. 46–56.

Yehuda, Rachel. "How Trauma and Resilience Cross Generations." Interview by Krista Tippett. *onBeing.org*, 30 July 2015, https://onbeing.org/programs/rachel-yehuda-how-trauma-and-resilience-cross-generations-nov2017/. Accessed 13 Oct. 2020.

Yemanja Wisdom from the African Heart of Brazil. Directed by Donna Roberts and Donna Read, Project Zulu, 2015.

Zagar, Isaiah. "Artist Talk," Philadelphia's Magic Gardens, 17 Nov. 2015.

Zerach, Gadi et al. "The Role of Fathers' Psychopathology in the Intergenerational Transmission of Captivity Trauma: A Twenty Three-Year Longitudinal Study." *Journal of Affective Disorders*, vol. 190, Oct. 2015, pp. 84–92.

Zinn, Howard. *A People's History of the United States*. Reissue edition, Harper Perennial Modern Classics, 2015.

Zweig, Connie, and Jeremiah Abrams, editors. *Meeting the Shadow: Hidden Power of the Dark Side of Human Nature*. Tarcher/Putnam, 1991.

INDEX

ABOUT THE AUTHOR

Photo courtesy of the author

APRIL C. HEASLIP, PhD, is a mythologist, educator, and artist who earned her doctorate in Mythological Studies with emphasis in depth psychology at Pacifica Graduate Institute. She holds a master's in Social Ecology from Goddard College and a bachelor's in Psychology and Women's Studies from West Chester University after studying at the Universidade Federal de Uberlândia, Brazil. Uniting interconnected levels of inquiry via women's studies, literary and film studies, post-Jungian psychology, and sustainability, her work focuses on applied ecofeminist mythology and the curative powers of creativity and synchronicity.

www.ingramcontent.com/pod-product-compliance
Lightning Source LLC
Chambersburg PA
CBHW030346270326
41926CB00009B/985